Dore Burleigh Reundon
312-223-6240 House

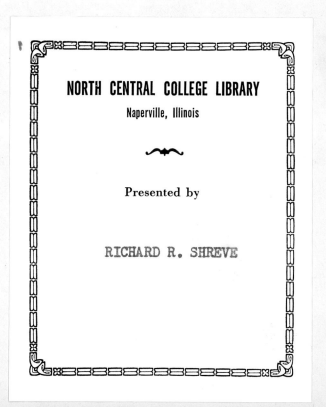

the social dynamics of marketing

the social dynamics of marketing

CONRAD BERENSON and HENRY EILBIRT

Bernard M. Baruch College of The City University of New York

RANDOM HOUSE
New York

First Edition

987654321

Copyright © 1973 by Random House, Inc.

Library of Congress Cataloging in Publication Data

Berenson, Conrad, comp.
    The social dynamics of marketing.

    Includes bibliographies.
      1. Marketing—Social aspects—United States.
I. Eilbirt, Henry F., 1914–   joint comp.
II. Title.
HF5415.1.B47   380   72–7387
ISBN 0–394–31456–5

Manufactured in the United States of America

Designed by James McGuire

Cover photo by John Murello

Cover design by Jeannie Friedman

Preface

At present there are two philosophies by which the basic course in market-ing is organized. The traditional approach to marketing is one in which the various *functions* of marketing (such as buying, selling, planning, credit) are covered in great detail. Here the student is given a good deal of infor-mation on the number of retailers in the country and what they do, the number of wholesalers in the country and what they do, and so forth. This method of viewing marketing has survived about 45 years of business and social change. At present, however, it lacks a good deal of relevance to the objectives of the students who take the course, as well as to the faculty who teach it.

The second primary perspective through which marketing is taught is the "managerial" approach. In this method the student is presumed to be a marketing manager and is taught a perspective that integrates a number of marketing inputs, such as pricing, advertising, market research, product planning, and customer service. Thus a framework is constructed that re-quires that the student consider marketing problems as a manager would and that he solve these problems through the manipulation of these market-ing inputs.

There is still a large degree of support for the traditional approach to marketing, although in the past eight or nine years the managerial approach has taken a large share of the text market. However, a trend is developing that, if extended (and there is every reason to believe that it will continue), will add a third major perspective to the two approaches described. This trend suggests that students who take marketing courses are really not in-terested in being either *functional specialists*, such as retailers, wholesalers, buyers or sellers, or *marketing managers*, who must manipulate numerous marketing inputs daily in order to make managerial decisions. Instead, the great majority of the students of marketing take only the basic course and want to know only how marketing relates to life around them—to society— and how it can help them be more educated and thoughtful participants in society. Instead of being bored with statistics on retail and wholesale trading areas, they want to know whether prices really are higher in the ghetto; they want to know whether advertising is a worthwhile effort for society as a whole or whether it does indeed raise prices; they want to know something about truth in packaging; and other issues that they talk about in the real world. Unless the basic course in marketing relates to this real world and provides them with ample food for thought and discussion, they will be pas-sive rather than active participants in their education.

As a result of the above considerations marketing educators today are becoming more and more aware of the shortcomings of the traditional and managerial approaches to marketing. In lectures, in articles, at professional meetings, and in curriculum revisions, a good deal of thought is being devoted to examining marketing from a "societal" point of view. This book brings together a number of significant articles that bear upon the latter view, and it ties them together in a framework that provides the reader with the background and importance of the various issues.

September 1972

Conrad Berenson
Henry Eilbirt

Bibliography for Key

Buzzell, Robert D., *et al. Marketing: A Contemporary Analysis.* New York: Mc-Graw-Hill, 1972.

Cundiff, Edward W., and Still, Richard R. *Basic Marketing: Concepts, Decisions, and Strategies.* 2nd ed. Englewood Cliffs, New Jersey: Prentice-Hall, Inc., 1971.

Davis, Kenneth R. *Marketing Management.* 3rd ed. New York: The Ronald Press, 1972.

Gist, Ronald R. *Marketing and Society: A Conceptual Introduction.* New York: Holt, Rinehart & Winston, 1971.

Kerby, Joe K. *Essentials of Marketing Management.* Cincinnati, Ohio: South-Western Publishing Co., 1970.

Kotler, Phillip. *Marketing Management: Analysis, Planning, and Control.* 2nd ed. Englewood Cliffs, New Jersey: Prentice-Hall, Inc., 1972.

Lazer, William. *Marketing Management: A Systems Perspective.* New York: John Wiley, 1971.

McCarthy, Edmund J. *Basic Marketing: A Managerial Approach.* 4th ed. Homewood, Illinois: Richard D. Irwin, 1971.

Narver, John C., and Savitt, R. *Conceptual Readings in the Marketing Economy.* New York: Holt, Rinehart & Winston, 1971.

Staudt, Thomas A., and Taylor, Donald A. *A Managerial Introduction to Marketing.* 2nd ed. Englewood Cliffs, New Jersey: Prentice-Hall, Inc., 1971.

Stanton, William J. *Fundamentals of Marketing.* 3rd ed. New York: McGraw-Hill, 1971.

Sturdivant, F. D., *et al. Managerial Analysis in Marketing.* Chicago: Scott Foresman, 1970.

Wentz, Walter B., and Eyrich, Gerald I. *Marketing: Theory and Applications.* New York: Harcourt Brace Jovanovich, 1970.

SELECTION KEY COORDINATING READINGS WITH CHAPTERS OF OTHER TEXTBOOKS

	Buzzell, et al.	Cundiff and Still	Davis	Gist	Kerby	Kotler	Lazer	McCarthy	Narver and Savitt	Staudt and Taylor	Stanton	Sturdivant et al.	Wentz and Eyrich
Part I: The Marketing Process Examined													
Section 1: The Overall Marketing System in the United States	1, 2	1	1	1, 2		1, 2	1, 21	1	1, 2, 3, 4, 5	2	1	1, 2	1, 2
Section 2: Marketing Subsystems	10, 11, 12, 23	2, ③, 4	2			3, 9, 10, 11	4	2, 28, 29	5, 6, 10, 11	3, 31	2	6, 11	1, 2
Part II: Marketing Practice and the Public Interest													
Section 3: The Social Responsibilities of Business and Marketing	27	23, 24	1	3, 4, 5	1, 24	22	22	30	14, 16	32	29	1, 2	27, 28, 29
Section 4: The Consumer Faces Marketing	14			3		24	16, 17, 18, 19, 20	3	16		29		27, 28, 29
Part III: The Social Implications of Specific Marketing Practices													
Section 5: Advertising: Critics and Defenders	22	18	14	18	17, 18, 19, 20	17, 18	14	22	12	24, 25	24	8	19
Section 6: The Changing Perspective in Product Liability	14	8, 9, 10, 11	11	20	10, 11	12, 13, 22	10	10, 11, 14	11	12, 13, 14	9, 10, 11	7	14, 15, 16

viii

	Buzzell, et al.	Cundiff and Still	Davis	Gist	Kerby	Kotler	Lazer	McCarthy	Narver and Savitt	Staudt and Taylor	Stanton	Sturdivant et al.	Wentz and Eyrich
Section 7: The Social Consequences of Product Innovation	14, 15	8, 9, 10, 11	11	20	10, 11	12, 13, 22	10	10, 11, 14	11	12, 13, 14	9, 10, 11	7	14, 15, 16
Section 8: The Social Implications of Company Pricing Policies	16, 17	19, 20, 21	16	21, 22, 23	21, 22, 23	14	11	23, 24, 25, 26, 27	13	27, 28, 29	18, 19, 20, 21	9	8, 9, 10, 11, 12, 13
Section 9: Marketing to the Poor	3, 4, 5	5, 6, 7		3	6, 7, 8		17, 18, 19, 20	6	14, 16	5	4, 5, 6, 7	4, 5	
Section 10: Salesmanship: The Social and Ethical Perspective	21	16, 17	13	18	17, 18, 19, 20	19	15	20, 21	12	26	23	8	20
Section 11: Antitrust Legislation Affecting Marketing	27	23		5, 6	24	3	23	27	14	29	30	3	27
Section 12: Marketing and the Issue of Privacy	25, 27	22	8	4, 11	9	10	7, 22	4	14	6, 7, 31	3, 29	14	21, 22, 23, 24, 25, 26
Part IV: The Future of Marketing						24	28			32	30		

ix

Contents

Part Three   The Social Implications of Specific Marketing Practices

Section 5   Advertising: Critics and Defenders   122

15. Morality in Advertising—A Public Imperative   William
    G. Capitman   123
16. Is Advertising Wasteful?   Jules Backman   132
17. Americans and Advertising: Thirty Years of Public Opin-
    ion   Stephen A. Greyser and Raymond A. Bauer   143
18. What's Ethical? Admen Cast Votes   *Advertising Age*   153

Section 6   The Changing Perspective in Product Liability   166

19. The Lengthening Reach of Liability   167
20. Product Liability Requires Strict Quality Control
    Richard G. Moser   172
21. Seals of Approval   Bess Myerson Grant   177
22. Court Opens the Door for Suit Against Issuer of Product
    Seal   *Product Engineering*   185

Section 7   The Social Consequences of Product Innovation   189

23. Planned Obsolescence: Rx for Tired Markets?   Martin
    Mayer   190
24. Competitive Aspects of Planned Obsolescence   Edward
    M. Barnet   199
25. Why the U.S. Is in Danger of Being Engulfed by Its Trash
    U.S. News & World Report   202

Section 8   The Social Implications of Company Pricing Policies   208

26. Why Corporations Find It Necessary to "Administer"
    Prices   Robert F. Lanzillotti   209
27. The Psychology of Pricing   Benson P. Shapiro   214
28. When Is the Price Too High?   Alfred R. Oxenfeldt   222
29. Break for Drivers: Gas-Price Wars   *U.S. News & World
    Report*   224

Section 9   Marketing to the Poor   228

30. Consumer Practices of the Poor   Louise G. Richards   229
31. Comparing the Cost of Food to Blacks and to Whites—
    A Survey   Donald E. Sexton, Jr.   245
32. Some Consumption Pattern Differences Between Urban
    Whites and Negroes   James E. Stafford, Keith K. Cox,
    and James B. Higginbotham   257

the marketing process part one examined

Eight or ten thousand years ago Stone Age villages were ". . . largely self-supporting, growing their own food and using local materials for its tools, weapons and houses. Because the people . . . had only limited contacts with outsiders, each village tended to develop a localized culture. This condition of relative isolation permitted two settlements . . . to exist side by side for hundreds of years with little inter-change of culture and . . . few modifications in [their] pattern of living."*

Such a mode of life is virtually incomprehensible to us today, although many of our grandparents might not have found it so. Think of a contemporary breakfast. The oranges on our tables may have come from California or perhaps from some Mediterranean country. The toast originated on wheat farms 1000 miles distant. The cheeses may have been imported from Europe. The coffee we drink probably originated in Latin America; the cocoa likely came from Africa.

All of these products, which we assemble and use so easily and thoughtlessly, appear in our kitchens as end products of a series of related transactions involving many people and institutions. The network, or system, "knows" none of us. It is highly impersonal. No one can tell, up to the last transaction, precisely where any unit will end up. Yet this highly impersonal system is so organized that it can meet extraordinarily varied demands whenever and wherever the consumer chooses to exercise that demand. A 15-minute walk through any shopping center will illustrate this point. However, it gives us no insight into the huge apparatus that lies between the shopping center and the origin of a product.

Clearly, then, some kind of general marketing system governs the physical movements of goods to places when and where they are likely to be purchased. This movement itself results from transactions in which people repeatedly buy goods that they expect to resell—until the goods finally reach their destination, the ultimate consumer. In this sense marketing can be understood as commerce with a well-defined direction.

In another sense marketing has been defined as "the delivery of a standard of living."* Large and small units that we see as business firms or enterprises seek to discover what their customers need and want (marketing research); seek to direct consumers to buy their own brands (sales promotion); and, if successful, need to deliver goods (the distribution system).

These two basic concepts of marketing will be seen from a number of different angles throughout this book.

---

* T. W. Wallbank and A. M. Taylor, *Civilization Past and Present* (Chicago: Scott, Foresman and Co., 1960), pp. 29–30.

* Paul Mazur, "Does Distribution Cost Enough?", *Fortune* (November, 1947), Vol. 30, p. 138.

section I
the overall
marketing
system
in the
united
states

The marketing process can be viewed from a number of different angles. Here we begin with a look at the American marketing system, viewed as a large unit. What we want to grasp is the total reach and scope of a marketing system in a country that generates the huge gross national product of nearly $1 trillion.

How does this vast system work? What is behind the retail institutions with which we are all familiar? What tasks must the marketing system accomplish? And how do these tasks get done? Questions of this sort are what concern us here. Note that apart from the inclusion of imports and exports, the description that follows omits the huge portions of the world market system comprising Western Europe, Japan, and the rest of the world—all of which are linked together by trade. As vast as the system that you will see is, it nevertheless understates the size of the actual total marketing system.

John B. Matthews
Robert D. Buzzell
1 The Marketing System
Theodore Levitt
Ronald E. Frank

This first article is a chapter in a textbook on marketing. It is a clear and vivid description of how marketing works in the United States (and generally in all industrial countries today). The authors tie the business firms and the final consumer into the total pattern. This network also includes the large and less well-known intermediary structure that operates to move goods from producers to consumers of goods.

. . . the individual firm is only one small part of a large and complex marketing system consisting of the many business institutions engaged in the performance of marketing functions, as well as the various kinds of customers served by them. The marketing system, in turn, is but one aspect of the even more complex economic and social system of a nation and of the community of nations.

The problems faced by a marketing executive are largely determined by the functioning of the total marketing system. Equally important, the actions of the numerous decision-makers in the system, taken collectively, determine how well the system performs. This two-way relationship between individual business firms and the total marketing system imposes a dual responsibility on the marketing executive. He must first understand his job within a company so that he recognizes its problems and deals with them effectively. But in order to do this, he must also know enough about the marketing system and its functioning to see how it shapes and limits his task.

As background for the subsequent treatment of marketing management problems, a brief overview of the marketing system is presented. The discussion is confined primarily to the contemporary marketing system of the United States. But it should be emphasized that marketing institutions and

activities are not just American idiosyncrasies. Every nation—advanced
or underdeveloped, democratic or totalitarian, large or small—has a marketing system. . . .

.   .   .

Elements of the   Just what is the marketing system? Like many other commonly
Marketing   used words, *system* is hard to define precisely.
System

The term *marketing system*, as used here, involves:

1. All the business institutions engaged in the performance of marketing
   functions
2. The legal, historical, and customary relationships among these institutions
3. The customers served by business institutions, including both household
   consumers and business firms
4. The marketing tasks performed by the system.

All these things constitute a system in the sense that they are interrelated
and combine to achieve a common set of goals. . . .

Business   The major types of institutions involved in the marketing sys-
Institutions and   tem are depicted in Figure 1. The arrows in the diagram repre-
Relationships   sent the flow of goods and services to final users. There is, of
                        course, a corresponding flow of money and credit instruments
in the opposite direction.

The major categories of institutions, as shown in Figure 1, are producers of raw materials, including farms, mines, fisheries, forestries, etc.;
manufacturers and processors of finished or semifinished goods; service industries, such as banks, insurance companies, etc.; retail and wholesale
intermediaries or middlemen; household consumers; and institutional users
including government. This whole complicated apparatus has evolved from
progressively greater *specialization* in the economy. Each type of institution
specializes in different kinds of activities.

To illustrate how all these types of businesses enter into the marketing
process, consider the steps in the sequence of production-distribution-con-
sumption for bread. The principal raw material, wheat, is grown by farmers and sold by them, perhaps through a cooperative marketing association, to a miller. The miller processes the wheat into flour and sells it to
baking companies. The latter, in turn, use the flour and other raw and
processed materials—yeast, packaging materials, etc.—to produce bread
and other baked goods, which they sell to retail stores. Finally, housewives
purchase the bread for their families' consumption. Because bread is a
perishable product, it is not feasible to utilize wholesale middlemen in distributing the finished product to retailers. But wholesale intermediaries may
participate in the sale of wheat to millers and in the sale of flour to bakers.

The businesses involved in the marketing of a product, up to the point at

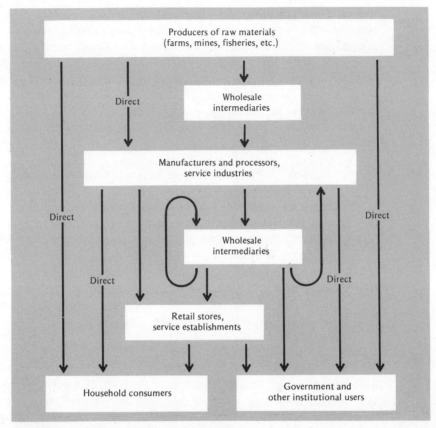

FIGURE 1.   The marketing system.

which its form is changed by manufacturing or processing activities or at which it is finally consumed, constitute a marketing channel. A more formal definition is as follows:

The *marketing channel* for a product or service is the course through which title to, and control over, the product or service passes from original producer to end users. It comprises all the business institutions and individuals who participate in the purchase and/or sale of the product or service, up to the point at which its form is changed or the point at which it is finally consumed.

Terms sometimes used synonymously are *channel of distribution*, *distribution channel*, and *trade channel*. The marketing channel for a processed food product might include the manufacturer, a wholesale intermediary, a retail intermediary, and the household consumer who finally uses the product.

To some extent, the marketing channel for a product or service constitutes a subsystem of the overall marketing system. An executive in a firm is much more affected by and concerned with the institutions in his own channel(s) than with others outside of it. For example, a marketing executive in a manufacturing firm must select wholesale and retail outlets to handle his firm's products and work with them to develop effective marketing policies. He is also directly concerned with other manufacturers in his channel(s), since they are more or less directly in competition with him. Similarly, an executive in a wholesale or retail firm is affected more by the manufacturers whose products he handles, by wholesale and retail firms handling similar product lines, and by the customers who finally use these products than he is by businesses or customers not included in his marketing channel(s).

Middlemen   Most of the terms used in Figure 1 to describe institutions are self-explanatory. Some, however, call for explicit definition.

The term *intermediary* or *middleman* designates an institution that buys and/or sells products and services, but does not process, manufacture, or otherwise change the *form* of products except as an incidental activity.

For instance, a drugstore buys and resells drugs, proprietary medicines, etc. A distinctly secondary activity (and one of declining importance in the post-World War II years) is that of compounding prescription drugs for customers. In contrast, a tire manufacturer may own and operate warehouses and retail stores, but this activity is subsidiary to the main business of manufacturing.

Note that the definitions of marketing channel and middleman stress the flow of title and control over goods and services rather than physical distribution. Although transportation agencies such as trucking firms play a vital role in marketing, they are not included in marketing channels or classified as marketing institutions because in most instances such agencies play a passive role in the marketing process. The institutions involved in exchange, on the other hand, have much greater and more direct control over the process.

Middlemen are further classified as wholesale and retail. *Retail* middlemen are those that sell goods to household customers; thus, drugstores, food stores, and automobile dealers are all retail middlemen. Service establishments selling directly to household customers, such as barbershops, can also be regarded as essentially retail institutions. *Wholesale* middlemen are those that sell to business firms and to institutional customers such as the government. The distinguishing feature of a wholesale transaction is that the goods or services are used by the buyer in the production of *other* goods and services or are *re*sold.

Customers   The marketing channel for a product or service may be long, *and Markets*   including many distinct levels or steps; or it may be short, including only one or a few. In either case, the end result is that goods and services are sold to *customers* who consume or use them.

As shown in Figure 1, customers may be classified into two basic groups: ultimate or household consumers and business and institutional users. This distinction is of such basic importance that formal definitions of each customer type are useful.

Ultimate or *household consumers* are those who use (consume) products and services in order to enjoy the satisfactions embodied in them.

Business and *institutional users* are those that utilize goods and services in the conduct of their operations in order to produce goods or render services to ultimate consumers and/or to other businesses and institutions.

For example, when a housewife purchases toothpaste for her family's use, the various members of the family are ultimate consumers. They use the toothpaste to derive certain satisfactions arising from cleanliness, pleasant taste, etc. In contrast, when a bank purchases a bookkeeping machine, it is a business user and employs the machine in the performance of financial services for depositors and borrowers, including household consumers and business firms.

Both goods and services may be classified as (ultimate) consumer or business.

Consumer goods and *services* are those purchased and used by household consumers.

Business goods are those used by business firms either as materials or components of other goods or in the operation of the business itself.

Thus, toothpaste is classified as a consumer good because it is purchased almost altogether by ultimate or household consumers. Virtually all bookkeeping machines, on the other hand, are purchased by business and institutional customers.

The distinction between consumer and industrial goods and services is not, however, a hard and fast one. Many products and services are sold in *both* markets. For example, an automobile sold to a household is a consumer product, while the same automobile sold to a taxicab operator is a business product. Similarly, life insurance on John Doe, husband and father, is a consumer service while keyman life insurance on John Doe, business executive, is a business service.[1]

.   .   .

The various types of customers who purchase a product or service constitute the *markets* for that product or service. Markets may be categorized in several ways on the basis of customer characteristics. For example, manufacturers of electronic components (transistors, tubes, etc. make a distinction between the "OEM" market (original equipment manufacturers who buy their products for assembly into such finished products as television sets) and the "replacement" market, consisting of household consumers and business users who purchase the products to replace worn-out parts.

A market is simply a group of customers with certain characteristics. Customers may be grouped in terms of how they use a product or service (OEM versus replacement); location (the United States market versus the Canadian market); type of business (banks versus insurance companies for bookkeeping machines); and in any other ways that seem useful for analysis and decision-making.

Tasks of the
Marketing
System

The economic justification for the existence of the marketing system, and of individual institutions in it, lies in the performance of certain essential tasks or functions. There are many variations in these tasks, depending on the type of products, services, and customers involved as well as on the specific circumstances, but the same basic functions must be performed in all cases.

Perhaps the best way to explain the tasks performed by the system is through a specific (hypothetical) example. The Creswell Corporation is a manufacturer of toys. What must be done to market these toys? In the first place, the manufacturer must somehow determine what kinds of toys to produce, when to produce them, and what quantities to produce. The company's survival depends on how effectively these decisions are made since its products must be sold to customers in relatively free and open competition with those of other producers.

All raw material producers, manufacturers, and processors must make similar decisions. In this way, the system as a whole performs the function of *adjusting the production of goods and services to the needs of customers.* As Adam Smith noted long ago, "consumption is the sole end and purpose of all production." A basic task of the marketing system is to permit production to be directed to its purpose, i.e., to adjust to demand.

Marketing executives of the Creswell Corporation and other manufacturing concerns must also make decisions about prices, terms of sale, advertising. . . . The policies adopted by the manufacturer constitute the marketing mix by means of which he hopes to attain survival and some degree of success in the marketplace.

The Creswell Corporation cannot, in all likelihood, sell its products directly to ultimate or household consumers. Some raw material producers and manufacturers do sell "direct" by mail, through door-to-door salesmen or through their own retail stores, but usually large-scale direct selling is not feasible. Consequently, appropriate retail outlets—toy stores, department stores, variety stores, etc.—must be identified and induced to handle the products. If a large number of outlets is desired, it may also be necessary to use one or more kinds of wholesale outlets. If so, then the Creswell Corporation may employ salesmen to solicit business both from larger retailers and from wholesale outlets who, in turn, sell to retailers. The wholesale and the retail outlets, as well as the consumers who purchase the toys, must *buy* the products. This involves selection of specific items from those available, negotiation, determination of purchase quantities and timing, and so forth. These basic tasks of selling and buying (or exchange) are present in the marketing of any product or service.

Besides exchanging title to products, the marketing system must perform tasks necessary for their physical distribution. The Creswell Corporation's toys must be transported from factories to consumers' homes with intermediate stops at warehouses and retail stores. Similarly, since the timing of production and of demand do not coincide exactly, especially in the light of the heavy demand at Christmas, the toys must be stored until needed. In connection with physical distribution, the toys must also be packaged to prevent damage and to facilitate efficient handling.

As the toys are stored, transported, and exchanged, provision must be made for *financing* the investment in inventories, as well as other working capital required for marketing activities. At the same time, certain *risks* are inherent in the marketing process, such as the risk of physical deterioration or damage, loss in value due to changing toy styles, and so forth. The system must also provide for bearing these risks.

Still another important task of the marketing system is that of transmitting *information*. The manufacturer must inform retailers and wholesalers of the products available, their prices, and terms of sale perhaps through catalogues and trade shows in addition to the solicitation of salesmen. Consumers must also be informed, through advertising, display, and personal selling in retail stores. Finally, information must flow in the other direction: there must be "feedback" so that manufacturers, wholesalers, and retailers can learn what to produce, buy, and display.

Thus, we come full circle in this illustration of the tasks performed by the marketing system. Even this simple illustration should make it clear that the job of the marketing system—covering, as it does, thousands of different kinds of products and services, and serving a widely dispersed and heterogeneous market—is truly an immense undertaking. It is hardly surprising, therefore, that the total cost of performing the task is very great.

．　　．　　．

NOTES

1. Keyman insurance is life insurance carried by business firms on key executives, to compensate firms for losses associated with the death of such executives.

QUESTIONS FOR DISCUSSION

1. Using a typical day, indicate how the general marketing system affects and influences your daily life.
2. How does information about marketing come into existence? Where can it be found?
3. What is a channel of distribution? How does it differ from a transportation mode?
4. How can one describe the size of the American marketing system?
5. How can one measure the cost of marketing?
6. "For every dollar's worth of final sales of final buyers the distributive mechanism has to arrange and carry out almost two dollars of intermediate purchases and sales."
   a. What are "final buyers"?
   b. What is meant by the "distributive system"?
   c. What are "intermediate purchases and sales"?
   d. What accounts for the 2 to 1 ratio?

7. "The marketing channel for a processed food product might include the manufacturer, a wholesale intermediary, a retail intermediary. . . ." Select a "processed food product," and trace its progress from the manufacturer to your purchase of it at the store.
8. How do you account for the fact that so small a proportion of total sales are made to "final buyers"?

SUGGESTED READINGS

Bell, Martin, L., *Marketing Concepts and Strategy* (Boston: Houghton-Mifflin Co., 1966), Chaps. 2–5.

Cox, Reavis, *et al., Distribution in a High Level Economy* (Englewood Cliffs, New Jersey: Prentice-Hall, Inc., 1965), pp. 36–43.

McCarthy, E. Jerome, *Basic Marketing: A Managerial Approach* (4th ed.; Homewood, Illinois: Richard D. Irwin, Inc., 1971).

Stanton, William J., *Fundamentals of Marketing* (3rd ed.; New York: McGraw-Hill Book Co., Inc., 1971), Chaps. 1–2.

Warner, David S., *Marketing and Distribution: An Overview* (New York: McGraw-Hill Book Co., Inc., 1969), Part I.

section 2
marketing subsystems: the business enterprise and the household

Thus far we have been speaking about the idea of the marketing system as one vast mechanism. It is also possible, however, to sort out this large system into smaller pieces, or subsystems. A number of such subsystems might be identified.

Two are most significant for the student of marketing: (1) the firm, business unit, or enterprise and (2) the household.

As we have already seen, business firms are the most important mechanisms for getting goods to consumers. Much of the business done by companies is with each other, which is in part the result of specialization in manufacturing. A bushel of wheat must go through many changes to become a cake, and it must pass through a number of phases: farmer, local elevator transportation, grain elevator, commodity exchange firms, flour mill, baker, and perhaps baked-goods jobber and retailer. In the end, however, all of this intricate, complete "motion" exists because these are consumer households that have known or expected demands for cake.

Clearly, we are dealing with institutional forms that are at the center of modern economic life.

2 Marketing Functions, Interactions, and Plans*

Conrad Berenson
Henry Eilbirt

Most marketing texts have sections dealing with the individual marketing functions such as advertising, sales, and marketing research. But how does one unit of the marketing department relate to other such units? Who coordinates the various marketing activities, and what criteria are used for the task? What does the marketing organization look like? The answers to these questions, together with some perspectives on how marketing plans are constructed, are given in this article.

Marketing Functions   The activities that occur in the marketing departments of large enterprises are quite diverse and often complex. Figure 1, an organization chart, will assist the reader in understanding the relationship of each marketing job to the other jobs within the marketing area as well as within the organization as a whole. The chart used is fairly typical for large manufacturing enterprises.

Technical Service Department   This part of the marketing organization has the responsibility for all phases of the service function of the enterprise, for example, establishing (together with the marketing vice-president) service policy, tactics, objectives, and standards; developing and implementing warranty programs; handling customer complaints; providing spare parts; having technical specialists do work in the customers' plants; and providing telephone and mail advice to users and prospective users.

Sales Department   This department has the responsibility for establishing, together with the marketing vice-president, the sales objectives of the enterprise and for their attainment. This includes the hiring, training, and direction of the firm's sales force; the measurement of its performance; the establishment of criteria for measuring that performance and

---

* This article was written by the authors for this text.

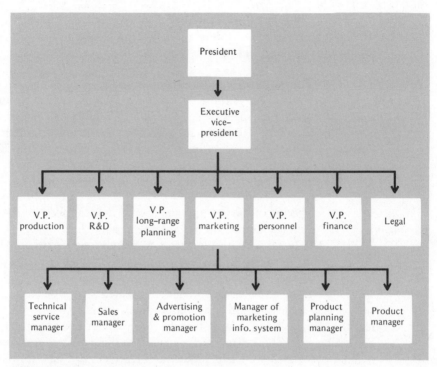

FIGURE 1.   Marketing's role in the firm.

for creating meaningful channels of communication among prospective users, customers, and the corporation.

Advertising and Promotion Department   This department, in cooperation with the vice-president for marketing, has the responsibility of determining what the media mix shall be, that is, the combination of media that will most economically attain the firm's advertising and promotional objectives. This responsibility extends to all media and at all levels, that is, to wholesalers, retailers, ultimate consumers of the firm's products, suppliers, and so forth.

Marketing Information Systems Department   This department has the responsibility for the creation of an information flow that is capable of providing an acceptable base for management decisions in marketing. The market-research function is only one part of the work, which is the responsibility of the marketing-information unit. The latter's work also includes close cooperation with such organizational units as economic research, operations research, long-range planning, the controller, the computer center, marketing planning, and sales management. In general, the mission of the marketing-information department is to provide a continuous study of marketing factors that are important to an enterprise. In so doing, it utilizes both internal and external data sources; receives, analyzes, and distills a great volume of information; and provides outputs in a meaningful form for management decision purposes.

Product
Planning
Department

The work of this department consists of analyzing the product line for the purpose of making additions, deletions, and other product changes. The latter includes the establishment of quality standards and the modification of products to conform to the financial, technical, and marketing resources of the enterprise. In short, this department's function is to provide a product line that is consistent with a long-term profitable growth and the survival of the enterprise.

Product
Managers

The job of the product manager is to take full responsibility for managing a portion of the firm's product line. In some cases this responsibility might extend to merely one or two products; in others to 100 or more. In any event, the product manager is responsible for coordinating the various marketing elements, such as technical service, sales, advertising and promotion, market research, and product planning, in such a way as to optimize his product line's profit. At the same time he has the responsibility to see that he is not interfering with the profit-optimizing goals of other product managers or that he is not creating discord in other departments, such as production, research, and finance. In essence, the job of the product manager is a microcosm of the job of the vice-president for marketing.

The Marketing
Manager

The marketing manager, or vice-president for marketing, is the chief marketing executive. All the individuals who head other marketing functions report to the marketing manager. His job is to function as a master chef, taking from the various functions those bits and pieces of their output that are necessary for him to optimize the entire marketing program of the corporation. He brings together the resources of such branches as technical service, sales, marketing research, and the like, while at the same time coordinating his activities with those of other departments, such as production, long-range planning, and finance.

Interaction
of Marketing
with Other
Departments

In the preceding section the functions of the various marketing elements are briefly delineated. It is obvious, however, that the various marketing functions cannot operate in isolation. They not only interact with one another, but also have a responsibility to all other areas of the firm's organization, such as production, personnel, and R&D.

Just as the vice-president for marketing can be viewed as a master chef who coordinates the various marketing functions to optimize the overall marketing objectives of the firm, so must the president of the corporation be considered a master chef. He coordinates the various functions that *he* directly supervises but that are on a still higher level; that is, he brings together such activities as production, long-range planning, marketing, finance, and legal. Each of these major divisions of the enterprise has objectives that at times conflict with the objectives of the other elements of the enterprise. What is important is that the objectives of the marketing area, for example, are not maximized at the expense of some other department, such as finance or production. At the same time it is important that the objectives of the other departments are, in turn, not maximized at the expense of marketing.

It would be very easy, for example, for marketing to increase sales and customer satisfaction tremendously, by reducing profits to a point that would drive the vice-president for finance into a frenzy. It is also possible to establish such superior quality standards that the vice-president for production would be hard put to attain them. At the same time it would be simple for the vice-president for production to have his work force grind out a good deal of product of a substandard, or at best marginal, quality, in order to reduce production cost. This, however, would make it quite difficult for the firm's marketing personnel to sell profitably in the long run. Hence the production people must recognize that they have a responsibility toward marketing; the marketing people must recognize they have a responsibility toward production; and so on, throughout every department of the firm's organization. In short, rather than each unit of the enterprise maximizing its own benefits to the exclusion of all others, each unit must coordinate and interact with every other one to benefit the *entire firm*, and not just one part of the firm.

A carefully drawn, overall business plan for the enterprise is necessary to ensure that each of the major units of the enterprise, as well as all of the minor units of the enterprise, operate cooperatively and toward a common end. Such a plan specifies the role and responsibility, the tactics, policy, and strategy of each element of the organization. In addition to such a plan, a control system that is designed to monitor implementation of the plan has been found to be essential. The proper approach to be used in constructing plans for the individual functions of the enterprise is to see to it that each departmental plan is derived from a master plan for the firm. In the section following, the characteristics of a typical marketing plan will be briefly reviewed.

The Marketing Plan   The plan itself is a written document that specifies a systematic and integrated program for achieving certain marketing objectives within a prescribed span of time. Briefly, it should state what is to be done and how, by whom, and by when it is to be done. Each marketing plan is different. Each must reflect the special needs and interests of the firm. However, all marketing plans do contain certain common elements. The principal areas that must be carefully described in all marketing plans are a statement of objectives; a detailed time schedule; a statement of assumptions; a description of the environment in which the plan operates; a review of the competitive situation, the market history, and the position of the corporation's products; a study of customer needs; a financial analysis; and, finally, a control system.

In constructing the marketing plan, it is important to recognize that for most medium- and large-size companies there is no such thing as *a* market; instead the company sells to a series of target markets, each with its own requirements in terms of products, sales, strategies, customer service, financing, and the like. It is the job of marketing management to analyze its potential customers carefully and to divide the entire array of customers into market segments that are capable of being successfully and profitably attacked by specific marketing strategies.

For each market segment the marketing planner must consider such items as:

The size, scope, and share of the market for that segment
Who uses the product
How, why, and when they use it
What the product strategy for penetrating that market segment is
How effective this strategy has been in the past
What marketing channels are available to the firm
How good these channels are
What pricing issues are relevant
What the proper relationship between cost and price is

In analyzing each market segment, it is extremely important to investigate not only those needs that are at present filled by the firm, but also those customer needs that are as yet unfilled.

In constructing the marketing plan, it is also important to bear in mind the concept of the *marketing mix*. According to this concept every marketing action can be undertaken in a variety of ways, and for each action there are a number of marketing elements that can be selected in varying proportions in order to achieve a specific objective. Thus a certain sales goal can be achieved by increasing advertising, reducing price, increasing the number of salesmen, changing quality, or changing style, and so forth. The job of the marketing manager is to select the proper mix of appropriate elements to achieve a particular goal at a particular time. Furthermore, the fact that a specific marketing mix was successful last year or this year is no assurance that it will be successful next year. Prudence would dictate a searching evaluation of all possible alternatives whenever a marketing plan is constructed.

The marketing plan obviously takes into account factors that have quite a large range. As such, the task of market planning is not one that can be delegated to a low-level assistant; rather it is a job for the top-level marketing executive, since it requires careful coordination and understanding of all of the marketing activities that the enterprise must undertake. At the same time it requires that these activities in turn be coordinated with those undertaken by other departments of the firm.

3 The GE Puzzle
Alvin A. Butkus

One might think that success in marketing some products will automatically bring further success with others. This supposition is unfortunately not so. A list of today's largest and most profitable enterprises will show rather extensive changes from a similar list of a decade ago, and the latter list will be quite different from that compiled ten years prior to its creation. Effective product planning and product management are not easy tasks in a highly competitive marketing environment. As the following article demonstrates, General Electric has found this out the hard way. In computers, color television, nuclear power plants, and jet engines it has experienced product and marketing difficulty. Products, strategies, life cycle planning, and so forth have not paid off in a way that would cause either management or stockholders to exult.

Long past dusk, the lights are still burning in the high, old-fashioned corner office over Manhattan's scruffy Lexington Avenue. The building itself is so dated, its entrance so unpretentious, that it is hard to picture it as the headquarters of the nation's fourth-largest industrial power. And up on the 45th floor, in the loneliness of the now nearly empty building, sits Fred J. Borch . . ., looking like a man who is trying to fit together the pieces of a massive puzzle.

The puzzle, of course, is the $8.4-billion (total sales) General Electric Co., a company that has long proved its ability in such old-fashioned industries as light bulbs and electric motors, but which seems to run into nothing but trouble when it comes to the high-technology industries in which the big profits of the 1970s will be made.

Case in point: GE has finally admitted that it cannot compete in computers, bailing out in May from a business that has bled, conservatively, $400 million from profits (equal to $4.44 a share before taxes) over the past fourteen years. What's more, the record has been far from sizzling in Fred Borch's other major diversification moves of the 1960s: nuclear power and commercial jet engines. In fact, GE executives do not expect the company to make any profits from either jet engines or nuclear power until 1972.

Reprinted from Alvin A. Butkus, *Dun's Review* (July, 1970), Vol. 92, No. 1, pp. 34–38, 69–70.

On the surface it looks pretty bad for GE. Plagued by losses in its technological ventures, plus the fourteen-week strike that affected almost all its product lines, the company's profits dipped 22% last year to $278 million, or $3.07 a share. Then, as bitter icing on the cake, GE began 1970 with the strike still on and hit a loss of $43 million in the first quarter, its first red ink since the war adjustment year of 1946.

Even worse for Fred Borch is the inevitable comparison with GE's traditional rival Westinghouse. While the Pittsburgh company has had many of the same problems as GE, its management during the past few years has been able to keep earnings steadily rising.

Indeed, in an age when the financial performance of chief executives comes under quick fire, and even a Stuart Saunders can lose the top spot at a Penn Central, it would appear that Fred Borch is nearing one of the most momentous years in his career. On everybody's books, 1971 must be GE's year to either put up or shut up. Many analysts believe the company has run out of reasonable excuses, and that by next year it must show profits on the order of $5 a share (well over its record high of $4.01 in 1967) if it is to retain its prestige in the financial and business community.

How do they figure it? For one thing, they point out that GE will no longer have the losses of its computer division, which last year cost it an estimated 44 cents a share. In addition, the company expects to almost break even in nuclear power and commercial jet engines next year, which in 1969 cut another estimated 33 cents and 44 cents respectively from earnings.

There is, of course, more to it than that. Eliminating these losses will not do the trick entirely. Borch also needs to keep pumping up sales and profits in GE's traditional lines as well. And this may take some more long nights of work, considering that consumer spending has fallen off this year and is expected to have a slow recovery in 1971.

To be sure, the diversity of a company like GE is supposed to iron out the good and bad performances of its individual components. On the other hand, most of GE's sales are tied to mature, slow-growing "production" industries, in which its dominant position over many products gives it little room to profitably increase its share of the market.

As of the beginning of this year, GE's sales mix was broken down into these components: light industrial products (electric motors, process computers, microwave telecommunications equipment, capacitors, batteries and semiconductors), 32%; consumer products (light bulbs to television sets, toasters and small air-conditioners), 25%; heavy industrial equipment (locomotives, ship turbines and steam turbine generators), 24%; and space and military sales (radar, space systems, jet engines and marine power plants), 19%.

It was, of course, with a more dramatic growth curve in mind that Fred Borch bought his way into commercial jet engines, nuclear power and computers. He is still paying handsomely. During the past three years, the attempt to lift GE onto a steeper curve has run to slightly more than $500 million a year in capital expenditures—nearly five times the budget in 1963, the year Borch became chief executive. With a cash flow that has yet to top $700 million a year, Borch has been forced to abandon GE's tradition of financing its growth internally. In fact, its long-term debt at present stands at slightly less than $700 million.

Now the cash-hungry computer operation has been sold and GE executives say that the other problem lines are on the verge of paying off. To understand why it has taken them so long, it is necessary to go back and take a look at what went wrong.

Playing Catch-up Ball   The trouble in commercial jet engines started right at the beginning, and GE has been playing catch-up ball ever since. The company, which had been supplying engines for military planes since 1942, got into commercial aircraft with contracts to make the engines for General Dynamics' Convair 880 and 990. The result: an eventual loss of $90 million.

At the same time, United Aircraft's Pratt & Whitney division walked off with orders for both Boeing's and Douglas' first jet airliners. This gave P&W an iron grip on the commercial jet-engine business throughout the 1960s, and GE was left out in the cold. And not just because it bet on the wrong horse. Top management also neglected to develop a successor to its postwar jet, the J-47, used to power the B-47 bomber and the F-86 Saber fighters used in Korea.

German-born Gerhard Neumann, who joined GE as an engineer in 1948 after a colorful career in China as a mechanic with Claire Chennault's Flying Tigers and as a technical intelligence agent under General "Wild Bill" Donovan, was given the job of getting GE back into the commercial jet engine business. Pouring millions into developing three engines, Neumann came up with a contract to build the engines for the SST, billed as the commercial jet of the next century. By now, some air-industry experts feel certain the plane will never get off the ground.

Neumann planned to get another commercial jet engine contract via the backdoor—winning the contract for the engines on the Air Force's super cargo plane, the Lockheed C-5A, an aircraft he surely felt would be converted into a commercial airliner. He got the contract all right, but now Lockheed cannot afford to build a commercial version.

The real irony of the C-5A debacle is that GE's financial muscle was strained to the point where it had to bow out of the bidding for the engines on Boeing's 747, of which 197 are already either delivered or on order. Again P&W got the upper hand. "We made the choice ourselves," snaps Neumann. "Look, we were fighting for the SST and developing the engines for the C-5A. We just couldn't take on any more business. It was that simple."

On the plus side, Neumann did get the contract to supply engines for the McDonnell Douglas version of the airbus, the DC-10. This is his first strong grip on the commercial jet-engine business, and Neumann believes it is big enough to make the venture profitable for GE. Though McDonnell Douglas holds orders for only 184 GE-powered aircraft, Neumann believes that figure will climb to 800 eventually. To get even more commercial business, Neumann is eyeing the possibility that Boeing might still come up with its version of the airbus, a modified 727. Or the strong possibility that Rolls-Royce will not have the financial backbone to develop and produce the engines for the Lockheed airbus, the L1011, could open another door for GE. Despite a $48-million British government loan to Rolls, some GE men feel Rolls may be overextended.

But when can Fred Borch expect to get some profits from the commercial jet-engine venture, into which he has poured an estimated $200 million? There is no relief this year. "We really expected to begin contributing to corporate profits by 1970," Neumann explains. "But when Lockheed and its engine supplier, Rolls-Royce, announced its long-range engine, we had to develop one also, two years ahead of schedule. That meant delaying profits until around 1972. But in 1971, we'll be damn close to breaking even. Then profits will grow at an accelerated rate."

That B-1 contract, provided Congress votes the funds for the plane, could help immeasurably. On the seven prototypes alone, GE stands to make a cool $30 million. And if the Defense Department decides to take the plane into service, the Air Force estimates it will need 200 to 250 planes. To GE, that could mean $1 billion in profits.

The Nuclear-Power Stew   The company's nuclear-power business has been in somewhat the same stew, though the waters are cooling rapidly. So far, GE holds orders for 52 nuclear-power plants, giving it a firm grip on roughly 45% of the market. The rest is split between Westinghouse Electric, Babcock & Wilcox and Combustion Engineering. But to get that much business, GE had to invest anywhere from $150 million to $250 million. Dr. A. Eugene Schubert, vice president of GE's Nuclear Energy division, believes the venture will break into the black in the early 1970s. Losses are clearly narrowing, and analysts believe the venture will contribute to profits in 1972 when the company's last turnkey contract is completed. But it is still questionable whether GE will make any big money in nuclear generation before 1980.

With Combustion Engineering—which did not get into the nuclear field until 1966—piling up the nuclear profits already, what is taking GE so long? When the big push for nuclear orders got under way in the early 1960s, the technology of light water reactors was not proved. GE, along with others, went ahead anyway and took on a lot of business. In addition, to establish its position in the market, GE took on eleven turnkey plants. Normally, in generating plants, GE is only a supplier.

"First we ran into production problems with Babcock & Wilcox pressure vessels," explains George J. Stathakis, the division's deputy general manager. "Then, in some cases, we had problems finding the right skilled labor." And the problem that Stathakis obviously sidesteps is that a concerted opposition by conservationists slowed building even more. All things added up, it now takes as long as seven years to install a nuclear-power plant. Originally, GE thought it would take just two years.

The production and labor problems of nuclear power, it must be admitted, were ably solved by Schubert and his team. Still persisting is the concern over air and water pollution. Just how this problem will be solved no one is willing to guess. But considering the money already invested in the business, it is fair to assume that GE and other companies in nuclear power will come up with enough technological improvements to pacify the public.

But there is a bigger question that hangs over the head of GE's nuclear-power business. Some utilities are pushing hard for another type of nuclear reactor, called the fast-breeder reactor. "The current plants are uneconomical," Chairman Charles Luce of Consolidated Edison commented recently. "They use only 2% of the uranium placed in them. On the other hand, the fast-breeder reactor uses up to 60%."

Retorts George Stathakis: "We don't doubt that the fast-breeder reactor should come into commercial operation around 1980, or slightly beyond. But we are putting a great deal of time and money into our current reactor and we think it will be marketable for many decades."

Regardless, GE is hedging its bets. Along with the federal government and other reactor builders, it is investing several million dollars in an experimental fast-breeder reactor in Fayetteville, Arkansas. While GE plans to spread research over several years, Gulf Oil's General Atomic division and North American Rockwell's Atomics International are pushing ahead with fast-breeder research. And they are getting a helping hand from the AEC, as well as from the utilities. If the schedule is accelerated, GE might well be left sitting with a huge investment in a power plant that is obsolete before it returns any sizable profits. Says Stathakis: "We're trying to build a sound business, one in which there is some standardization allowing you to repeat what you've done several times. But another part of that business base is new ideas. It's a matter of balancing these things to get the most profitable venture."

More profitable, one hopes, than computers. In Borch's spectacular sale of GE's entire computer business and its European time-sharing operation to Honeywell, the total price paid for GE's most adventurous venture was in the neighborhood of $500 million. GE's investment in computers: some $260 million in direct investment, $400 in losses, countless executive hours and an incalculable amount in terms of lost opportunities.

Ironically, GE is getting out of computers just when its foreign operation —66% ownership of France's Companie des Machines Bull, 100% of

Italy's Olivetti computer subsidiary and 75% ownership of Britain's G.F.I.S., Ltd., plus sales of exported machines—was beginning to make ends meet. Bull cleared nearly $800,000 last year after losing at least $100 million. Olivetti-GE got into the black in 1968. With some 15% of the total market, GE ranked second only to IBM in Europe.

But the fact remains that in the U.S., where it really counted, GE just could not make it. After pouring gobs of money into computers, Borch got only red ink and a piddling 4% of the U.S. computer market, ranking GE a weak fifth among the Big Eight companies in 1969 computer shipments (behind IBM, Univac, Honeywell and Burroughs). The only remaining tie overseas is an experimental time-sharing link, via satellite, between London and GE's computer center in Cleveland.

And the prospect of the operation becoming profitable before the mid-1970s was remote. Says Lawrence L. Dengler, GE's Information Systems marketing manager: "In computers you have to keep investing huge amounts of money to develop new equipment. That alone is enough to stop me when someone asks if we would have been profitable by 1972."

Certainly the spending would have continued had GE decided to stay with computers. Its small/medium and medium-sized units are all but obsolete, and with other members of the industry already reaching beyond the third generation, GE would have had to spend right across the board to remain competitive. It is for this reason that many observers believe Borch had no choice in selling out. Says Dr. Louis T. Rader, vice-president of GE's process control division from 1964 to 1969 and now a professor at the University of Virginia: "I think the board of directors forced him [Borch] to make the decision. The drain on earnings just couldn't continue."

"GE just didn't understand what the business was all about," says M. James Arachtingi, a vice-president of Auerbach, Pollak & Richardson, who is Wall Street's top computer analyst.

While it also may be sold ultimately, GE's U.S. time-sharing business was not a part of the Honeywell deal. Perhaps in order to avert the kind of beating he took in the computer sale, Borch has brought in Arthur E. Peltosalo, who is widely regarded around GE as "Dr. Fixit." Peltosalo's job is to straighten out an operation that lost $20 million in 1969.

"The problem is simple," explains Peltosalo, who ran the foreign computer operation almost until the day it was put on the trading block. "Expenses outran revenues. You solve that problem just by bringing in the right people. I told Fred the operation will be profitable by the end of the year, and it will be."

One of the "right people" is Paul R. Leadley, who headed up the profitable European time-sharing operation. And Peltosalo also has made some other moves. He has consolidated nineteen time-sharing centers into three, eliminating 400 employees, raised his prices and zeroed in on certain industries such as banking, petrochemicals and manufacturing.

The Hard Sell   But even as GE attempts to learn the XYZs of its high-tech-
nology businesses, it is showing some new aggressiveness in the
ABC's of appliances. Consumers may be putting record high amounts of
disposable income in the bank, but GE is coming up with its own brand of
consumerism to try to snag some of that money. "We're going after a
bigger share of the television business and we're going to get it," says
Stanley C. Gault, vice-president of GE's Appliance and Television group.

How? His voice cracking with the fervor of a car salesman's, Gault
replies: "We're offering the customer a deal no other television manufacturer had the guts to follow. We're telling the consumer we'll take the set
back if he isn't satisfied. And we think our sets are so good he won't bring
it back."

What Gault is now combating is GE's messy entrance into color television. In the mid-1960s, a latecomer to the color-TV market, GE tried to
hurry the process. Inevitably, the company failed to work all the bugs out
of its product, the industry's first portable color-TV set. On top of that,
GE was in the wrong place at the wrong time: people just did not want a
portable. Then, as GE switched its marketing emphasis to the bigger models, the portable idea caught on. As a result of its waffling, GE was left
with no more than 5% of the color-TV market, far behind RCA, Zenith,
Motorola, Admiral and Magnavox. Now GE has pumped up its production
and sales force for a run at the bigger share.

GE also missed an opportunity in high-priced major appliances. Industry figures are closely guarded, but it is known that the market for the top-
of-the-line appliances (such as refrigerators, stoves and freezers) grew more
rapidly than GE had planned. "In a company this size you can bet on only
so many horses," says Gault. "We just didn't have any spare production
facilities to remedy the situation."

4 Kodak and Polaroid: An End to Peaceful Coexistence

Philip Siekman

"Friendly" competition among marketers is a strategy that can be found throughout the world. Now and then, such a strategy must be changed into a more aggressive approach to further the attainment of a firm's goals. The following article tells how Kodak and Polaroid, giants of the amateur photography business, are embarking upon such a strategic evolution. At the same time, it provides fascinating insights into how these two highly effective marketers of consumer and industrial goods formulate and carry out their product planning and development, and product management activities.

Confronting each other in the title of this article are the only still cameras manufactured in any quantity in the U.S. On the one hand is the latest version of Eastman Kodak's easy-loading Instamatic, a product line so successful that one must look back to Singer's foot-powered sewing machine or Hoover's vacuum cleaner for a comparable example. On the other is the Colorpack II Polaroid Land camera. Some 70% of the still cameras bought in the U.S. are either Instamatics or Polaroids, ample measure of the domination their makers hold over the $2-billion amateur-photography business.

Up to this point the relationship between Kodak and Polaroid has been an impressive demonstration of peaceful coexistence. Almost as though they were in different industries, the two companies have commanded separate monopolies; neither has intruded to any great extent on the other's terrain. Polaroid has waxed strong doing its thing, one-step or instant photography, without sign of a serious competitor. Kodak has prospered doing practically everything else in photography; it towers so impressively over the core of its business, conventional amateur cameras and film, that it is difficult to understand why anybody else bothers.

This pacific duopoly was, in large part, dictated by necessity. Kodak

Philip Siekman, "Kodak and Polaroid: An End to Peaceful Coexistence", *Fortune* (November, 1970), Vol. 82, No. 5, pp. 82–87, 118, 122, 124.

could not find a way around Polaroid's high, broad patent wall. Polaroid could not make a camera that was foolproof enough, portable enough, or cheap enough to compete on even terms with Kodak's easy-loading Insta-matics. Nor did either company have much cause to take on the other in battle. During the Sixties both grew rapidly, mutually benefiting from the increase in disposable income, in leisure time, in travel, and, above all, in that favorite photographic subject, babies. Polaroid had about all the growth it could handle, yet its business still looked too small to Kodak, which is physically and psychologically committed to volume production.

Now, however, the Kodak-Polaroid arrangement verges on dissolution. These two powerful, skillful companies are turning—slowly and reluctantly to be sure—to face each other across the broad expanse of the business. Polaroid has reached such size that continued substantial growth probably can be obtained only by penetrating deep into the mass, "Get the baby in the bathtub, Harry," market that is Kodak's prime territory. Polaroid has made forays in Kodak's heartland, the market for simple cameras selling for $20 or less. And in three new factories within an hour's drive of its headquarters in Cambridge, Massachusetts, it is moving with a sense of urgency and in an atmosphere of secrecy toward production of a totally new camera and film that it describes in terms Kodak has to consider ominous.

Meanwhile, back in Rochester, Kodak is gathering its forces for defense and counterinvasion. It has finally—belatedly, some would say—decided that in-camera processing not only is here to stay, but promises to be a big enough market to warrant serious attention. For about a year Kodak has been making confident promises to develop and market an alternative to the Polaroid system at some unannounced point in the near future.

A Contest of Equals   Kodak's size and reputation are so great that many investors apparently assume the tide of battle must eventually swing against its smaller rival. Although Kodak had neither product nor timetable, its announcement last December of an interest in instant photography helped drive Polaroid's stock-market price sharply down. But the contenders are more equal than they seem. While Kodak's sales ($2.7 billion worldwide in 1969) are five times those of Polaroid ($465,600,000 domestic plus $70 million unconsolidated foreign), they are spread across thousands of products in the fields of professional, industrial, and scientific photography, as well as plastics, fibers, and chemicals. Its direct sales of cameras and film to U.S. amateurs—and the segment of its research and promotion budgets allocated to this part of its business—are probably about the same as Polaroid's.

In an "all or nothing" encounter—if it came to that—Polaroid would, of course, be risking its corporate life. While the company still makes its original product, synthetic polarizing material sold mostly for use in sunglasses, amateur photography accounts for over 80% of its sales. Even for Kodak the risk is considerable. High-margin amateur supplies contribute a disproportionate share of its profits. Security analysts believe Kodak's pretax margin on photographic film runs as high as 70%. Moreover, a major shift to in-camera processing would jeopardize not only sales of conventional equipment and film, but also the $200 million or so Kodak gets annually through its direct share of the film-processing business and its sales of supplies to independent processors.

Like belligerent nations trying to postpone a confrontation until the reserves are called and the armament factories tuned, Kodak and Polaroid insist that they really do not have evil designs on each other. This attitude partly reflects nostalgia for happier days when competition was what took place in other industries. Partly, it is rooted in a long, close association that is physically evidenced by the fact that Kodak sells $50 million worth of materials annually to Polaroid.

Edwin H. Land, Polaroid's sixty-one-year-old founder, principal shareholder, guiding genius, president, board chairman, and head of research, is the most emphatic in his professions of amity. Land's admiration of Kodak ("It's a great company") knows but one bound. He doubts that it can close Polaroid's twenty-two-year lead in the technology of instant photography—"They don't know what they're getting into." Even if Kodak could catch up, it would, in Land's opinion, be pointlessly wasting its share of the nation's pool of scientific and technical talent in the effort; everybody, including the public, would be better off if Kodak didn't try to duplicate what Land has already accomplished.

Kodak's executive team, headed by Dr. Louis K. Eilers, who became chairman of the board last May, and Gerald B. Zornow, who succeeded him as president, is slightly more belligerent. Although Polaroid has made its way mostly by expanding the market rather than by taking sales away from Kodak, the giant's pride has been pinked. The front end of the Land camera—shutter, lens, exposure meter—is as marked by an inventive thumb as the back or instant-photography part, and Polaroid's reputation as the industry innovator makes Kodak executives waspish. Eilers, for example, occasionally refers to Dr. Land as "*Mister* Polaroid." Kodak's determination to get into Polaroid's business is not to be doubted. Yet underneath there is an admiration for Land and Polaroid, an unspoken wish that the opponent were somebody else.

Kodak has long played the role of paternalistic industry leader, earning what Land calls " a reputation for creative dignity" by forewarning competitors when it was about to introduce standard-setting products, by supplying film base to others, and by giving technical advice and encouragement to practically all comers. Kodak did this not so much out of benevolence as out of the caution that comes to a company with overwhelming market dominance. At least nine out of ten rolls or cartridges of film sold in the U.S. are packed in its bright yellow boxes, and the specter of antitrust must walk the streets of Rochester nightly.

Kodak's pacesetting role extends back to the nineteenth century and the days of George Eastman. Yet to recall its pioneering roots is to run the danger of underestimating its present achievements. Kodak sustains its rule over the industry less by historical impetus than by a brilliant contemporary performance in marketing, production, and product design. The curtain rose on this performance in 1963, the year the company introduced the cartridge-loading Instamatic and, almost as significant, the year Eilers became executive vice president and Zornow was named vice president of marketing.

Few, if any, consumer products have been more successful than the Instamatic. Although the U.S.-made line extends upward in price and sophistication to $144.50, most Instamatics sell for around $20 or less and are little more than innovative box cameras. But they are easy to use and even in the hands of the "aim and shoot" amateur produce satisfactory, sometimes remarkable photographs. Just as important, they can be turned out with consistent quality in highly mechanized factories. In the first twenty-six months, Kodak sold ten million Instamatics. Last year over nine million were bought throughout the world, bringing the seven-year total to nearly 50 million.

Getting Them to Buy More Film   With a success of this scale on its hands, Kodak has abandoned the market for low-volume, sophisticated still cameras, which have a high labor content, and has concentrated exclusively on the Instamatic line. It imports a top-of-the-line Instamatic Reflex from its German subsidiary, but with this exception even the most expensive models are simply the standard body with trimmings, aimed more at the amateur with a penchant for conspicuous consumption than at the hobbyist or professional.

At Kodak, however, the Instamatic's triumph is measured less in numbers sold, and more in the tremendous boost the camera has given to film sales. Executives at Kodak, as well as Polaroid, tire of explaining, again and again, that the photography business is not a case of giving away razors in order to encourage blade sales. Both companies insist that they make a profit on cameras. Yet the bread and butter of the industry is repeat sales of film, a product with a heartwarming profit margin that increases dramatically as production expands.

Any buyer of a new camera tends to use more film during the first year than he does at any other time. For this reason alone the Instamatic would have greatly stimulated Kodak film sales. But Instamatic buyers, encouraged not only by the easy-to-use features of the camera, but by the introduction of flash cubes and good-quality color prints, continue shooting pictures at a far faster rate than amateurs did in the past. Instamatic owners buy an average of about eight cartridges of film a year as compared to a little over three rolls for owners of earlier simple cameras. As a result, over half of all the film manufactured by Kodak is now packed in the drop-in Instamatic cartridge. More than 70% of that is higher-priced, higher-margin color film.

Against this background, Kodak's marketing strategy has been a straightforward, well-executed effort to expand distribution and encourage still greater film use by making picture taking even more foolproof. Last year, when Instamatic sales showed signs of softening, Kodak introduced the blister-packed $9.95 Instamatic 44, essentially the same camera as the previous bottom of the line, the Instamatic 124, which sells at discount for about $14. Trading on the Instamatic reputation and the 44's bargain price, Kodak was able to get into supermarkets, the most important retail outlet it had yet to exploit. That brought the Instamatic within the physical and financial reach of a new group of camera owners—children, who have become the principal users of the 44.

This year, before the price leader could seriously damage the market for more expensive models, Kodak brought out a remodeled Instamatic line, the X series, which uses a Sylvania-developed flash cube that does not require batteries, a prime cause of trouble for amateurs. The Instamatic X re-establishes a difference between the regular line and the supermarket camera, which is unchanged. Its new features give dealers something to promote. Owners of older cameras have a good reason to buy a replacement—and to buy more film than last year. And while the X line probably costs no more to manufacture than the older line, it has provided a vehicle for price increases of $2 or $3 on new versions of its most popular models.

That Famous First Customer   With attention sharply focused on high-volume, low-priced cameras, Kodak long considered the relatively low-volume, high-priced Polaroid as little more than an interesting invention by an old friend. Kodak was Land's first customer in the Thirties for synthetic polarizing material—a sale he keeps tacked up in his memory as a restaurant owner keeps his framed "first dollar" hanging over the cash register. In the Forties, as Land began experimenting with one-step photography, Kodak supplied him with special materials and was publicly thanked for its "sympathetic interest." And from 1957 to 1963 the two companies worked together, marrying Polaroid's concepts and Kodak's film-production experience to bring instant color film from the laboratory to the market. Since the introduction of Polacolor in 1963, Kodak has been sole supplier of the negative material that Polaroid combines with positive paper and pods of chemicals in its color-film packs.

Kodak, which is also one of the suppliers of Land camera lenses, was well served by its friendly supplier relationship with Polaroid. While Polaroid did the pioneering and missionary marketing, Kodak got a tail-end ride at little risk. In retrospect, Kodak might have been better off if it had invested heavily during the Sixties in research on instant photography, preparing for a time when the market would mature. But many Kodak executives thought in-camera processing would never amount to very much.

In Kodak's view, the Land camera was—and still is—everything that a camera for the mass market should *not* be. It is too big, too expensive, and too difficult to use. A quick sequence of photographs is impossible. A Land camera user leaves behind a trail of refuse. Additional prints and enlargements are inconvenient to obtain. The film seems expensive. And despite elegant innovations that are a delight to the technically minded, it forgives few errors. Not only does conventional film have greater latitude, but many mistakes by Instamatic users can be corrected during processing. With the Land camera, as even a Polaroid sales executive admits, "you've got to pay attention."

"Sales Are a Better Barometer"   Only recently have the men in Rochester been able to turn the Polaroid issue around and view it from a more intriguing angle.

If there is so much wrong with the camera why does it sell at all? As Eilers has admitted, "No matter what you think, sales are a better barometer than my opinion." The point is that pictures available in a minute (or ten seconds for black and white) are so appealing that Polaroid's customers willingly put up with the system. If all or most of its liabilities could be eliminated, instant photography might be a devastating competitor to the conventional system.

Kodak caught a hint of this in 1965 when Polaroid began a tentative invasion of Kodak's back yard, the low-priced camera market. At that time the least expensive Land camera sold for about $50, and at that price new customers were becoming harder to find. Polaroid had also discovered that its film sales had a "high decay rate." As the novelty wore off, Polaroid owners put the cameras on the shelf and forgot them. Polaroid needed a way to expand the number of Land cameras sold each year and thus enlarge its film market.

The first answer was the Swinger, which produces only relatively small (2½ by 3¼ inches) black-and-white photographs, but which was made to sell at discount for about $14. Although Polaroid encountered serious quality-control problems (since overcome) with the Swinger's roll film, some seven million were sold in the first three years.

Nevertheless, Polaroid almost inadvertently backed out of that first foray into the bottom of the market. In 1968 it brought out the Big Swinger, which uses the same larger film pack as the rest of the Polaroid line and which was priced to sell for about $5 more than the smaller camera. Although Polaroid expected to sell both versions, the Big Swinger and its 3¼-by-4¼-inch print demolished the little Swinger's market and U.S. production of the latter was stopped.

Last year Polaroid repeated that performance. It spent over $2 million in ten days to introduce the Colorpack II, a camera similar to the Big Swinger except that it uses color as well as black-and-white film and is again priced $5 higher than its predecessor—$29.95 list or about $24 in discount stores. Once more Polaroid expected to keep both cameras in the line and, once more, the more expensive newcomer wiped out the cheaper model. Polaroid emptied its warehouse of Big Swingers only by selling them, probably at a loss, to A & P and Sears, which marketed the cameras at less than $10.

None of this was nearly as disastrous as it might seem. A lot of film was and still is sold to Swinger owners. Polaroid was able to dip into the bottom of the market and bring back customers by persuading Swinger owners to trade up. An estimated 40% of the Colorpacks are being sold to Swinger owners, pushing Polaroid color-film sales ahead of less profitable black and white for the first time. And the Colorpack II has been, the company says, "the most successful in our history." Half of the nearly four million Polaroid cameras sold in the last twelve months were Colorpacks. (The upper half of the line ranges in list price from $59.95 to $199.95.)

Not So Veiled Threats   Land now wonders whether or not it was a tactical error to poke sticks at Kodak with the Swinger venture and awaken it to the potential of instant photography. "The longer they waited," he says, "the better for us." It has been Land himself, however, who has done the most to arouse Kodak. Once a year, in a transformation that has onlookers believing in fairy godmothers who can convert pumpkins into carriages, Land turns from shy scientist to spellbinding showman in order to tell his shareholders about the wonders his laboratories have in store. As far as Kodak is concerned, the last couple of performances have been spine tinglers.

At last April's annual meeting, Land showed off an instant version of color-reversal film, the material that is used both for still color transparencies and for amateur movies. During the session, Land took colored 16-mm. motion pictures with a conventional movie camera, removed the film, processed it briefly in a black box, and projected his instant color movie onto a screen.

The present market for color-reversal film is relatively small and stagnant. Sales of home movie equipment never manage to match the enthusiastic sales projections that are recast each time the equipment is improved. Movies are expensive, as well as difficult to take and edit for projection. Even those amateurs who buy movie equipment tend to get discouraged and put it on the shelf. Color transparencies are only slightly more popular. A favorite of the advanced amateur and the professional, transparencies have much less appeal to the snapshooter who likes to pass around pictures of the kids or the vacation cottage.

Nevertheless, an estimated $380 million is spent annually to purchase and to process color-reversal film. If Polaroid's new material were to be usable in present and future Land cameras *and* in ordinary still and movie cameras (as the April demonstration indicates), Polaroid would not only expand the versatility of its own equipment, but would wedge into the conventional film market. In fact, instant color-reversal film probably will not be commercially feasible unless Polaroid is able to combine the two markets, its own and a portion of the conventional business. This has to disturb Kodak. In addition to selling most of the color-reversal film marketed in the U.S., it processes 40% of it for its customers. In any case, anxiety-prone Kodak executives don't have to wait long to find out. In a new Polaroid plant, a tribe of white-coated technicians is lovingly tending a four-story machine that is already turning out the film. Market introduction cannot be far off.

"More Than Anybody Ever Dreamed Of" From Kodak's standpoint, however, the most distressing news out of Cambridge is Land's promise to market a completely new generation of Polaroid cameras and film. Land is being far more secretive about this new system than he has been about any development in the past. (He described Polacolor in late 1957, demonstrated it in 1960, and finally marketed it in 1963.) But it has been a difficult exercise in self-restraint. He is openly delighted with what he and his co-workers have wrought.

Land claims that the new system is extraordinarily compact (prototype cameras are said to be "as thick as a cigar case"). He also says it is extraordinarily easy to use, produces a picture of unprecedented brilliance and depth of color, and "is more than anybody ever dreamed of having in the mass market." It thus seems a large step toward Land's personal goal—"To make photography an everyday thing for everybody." Convinced that "artistic ability and need for artistic expression are almost universal," his aim is to eliminate the barrier of mechanics and techniques between talent and execution. "All that should be necessary to get a good picture is to *take* a good picture, and our task is to make that possible."

Laying the demands of that task against the laws of optics indicates that Land's new system will be so sophisticated in design and so complex in manufacture that it will be priced well above what Kodak would regard as a mass-market camera. Outsiders who have peeked at Polaroid patent applications guess that it will contain a tilting mirror, a motor-driven ultra-refinement of the focal-plane shutter (which exposes the negative segment by segment), and a good many small gears and other parts. The price of such a camera could easily be in the $150 range, substantially above the price most Americans psychologically estimate to be the "right" price for a camera. Land seems to be gambling that the system will be so different that the public will look on it as a totally new product. There is no reason why the general public absolutely would not pay as much for a camera as a television set. But it will take a major shift in attitude toward photography—which, of course, is what Land has in mind.

Land has strongly implied that the new camera and film will be marketed sometime in 1971. However, Kodak seemed to be discounting his promises when it signed a licensing and royalty agreement with Polaroid last December. The agreement gives Kodak the right to begin making and marketing the present Polaroid color film, Type 108, under its own label in 1976, or in 1975 if the color negative is improved by Kodak. In return, Kodak has agreed to continue supplying the color negative it has always sold to Polaroid.

Both companies are close-mouthed about their affairs, and both have been especially reticent about the new contract. However, it is plausible to assume that Kodak opened the negotiations because it thought Polaroid was on the verge of manufacturing its own negatives. As Polacolor's sales had expanded in the Sixties, production volume had become more and more interesting to Kodak. Sometime last year, Kodak presumably concluded that it was about to lose the leverage it would have in licensing negotiations as the sole supplier of the Polaroid negative.

In fact, there is an intriguing possibility that Kodak was mousetrapped. Polaroid has indeed made pilot runs of its own Type 108 negative material. But with Kodak now locked into a contract to supply the color negative for at least another five years, it would not be surprising if Polaroid forgot all about making its own Type 108 negative and concentrated on developing and manufacturing the new system for which it definitely will make the whole film pack, including the negative. It is not easy to see what Kodak gets out of its contract with Polaroid. Although there should be some 20 million of the present type of Polaroid cameras around by the mid-Seventies, Kodak may nevertheless have obtained the right to make an obsolete product with dwindling sales. Kodak's strategy makes sense, however, if Land's new system is not as imminent (or as good) as he says it is. Recently Eilers offered this comment, with an air of understatement, "He has made announcements before which have taken a bit of time to produce."

Eilers might not be quite so sanguine if he were to drive past three completely new Polaroid facilities. One, in New Bedford, Massachusetts, is the biggest building the company has ever constructed. Polaroid says it will be used to make the new color-film negative. A second plant, in Waltham, Massachusetts, will be used to assemble the film pack. In the third plant, part of a complex of new buildings in Norwood, Massachusetts, Polaroid will manufacture the new camera—a major shift in policy since the company has always farmed out the bulk of its camera manufacture and assembly operations, chiefly to Bell & Howell and U.S. Time. (Polaroid will buy lenses for the new camera from an outside source that it has not identified except to say the supplier will not be Kodak.) The company is spending more than $150 million on the three facilities, construction work is about finished, and production machinery is being installed.

Search for Alternatives   Kodak is nowhere near that close to marketing its own version of instant photography. Although Zornow says, "We do have target dates in mind," the company faces a tough job for it must, in effect, re-invent the process. While the basic Land patents on one-step photography have run out, Polaroid's patents on the present cameras and the color-film pack do not begin to expire until 1984. As recently as last April, Kodak executives admitted that the company had yet to choose a method of its own that would lead it around Polaroid's patent barrier, that further development work would be needed after the choice was made, and that it would then have to decide whether its in-camera system was commercially feasible.

Kodak investors who find that list of chores depressing should be reminded that developing an alternative to the Polaroid system is not the company's only option. Kodak could, for instance, go its own route with a camera that lacks the instant-processing feature but is in other respects dramatically superior to anything in the past. In fact, as Land has suggested, Kodak might be far better off if it didn't try to duplicate his work, but instead focused its development efforts on something totally new.

Whatever Kodak's motivation in last year's negotiations, it at least tacitly exploited its role as a monopoly supplier of negative for Polacolor. While this sort of hard bargaining is fair enough, it is but one sign out of many that Eastman Kodak is no longer the accommodating competitor it once was. Zornow frankly admits, "We're not in business to serve other manufacturers. . . . You don't hold their hand forever." That's not the way Kodak executives used to talk. But, says Zornow, "We're not in the same position as we were a number of years ago. . . . People are biting away at business we would like to have."

In the Eastman quarter of Kodak's business—fibers, chemicals, plastics— it has as much competition as anybody. In photography, however, Kodak is still dominant and the threats are more potential than real: inroads by Bell & Howell into the slide-projector market, a rising flow of still and movie cameras from Japan (which exported over $100 million worth of photographic equipment to the U.S. last year), and, most worrisome of all, a renewed drive by outsiders against that stoutest of Kodak citadels, color film.

Moving Target The attack on Kodak's share of the color-film market was not
No More   kicked off because Kodak has been making mistakes. Rather,
                  Eilers points out, "We ran out of things we were doing right."
In the past Kodak was somehow able to introduce a still better color film every time a competitor got even near to Kodak quality.

Always one step behind, other film manufacturers—Minnesota Mining, GAF, Britain's Ilford (now a CIBA subsidiary), and the Belgo-German combine, Agfa-Gevaert—were left with crumbs of the market, e.g., manufacturing private-brand film for mail-order houses. Now, color film has been so improved that future advances will be small and hard to achieve. "We're no longer a moving target," says Eilers. "We're moving, but not quite so fast." Within the last year several film manufacturers have begun selling color-reversal and color-print film of what even Eilers concedes is "pretty good quality."

Among these, Japan's Fuji Photo Film, a complete newcomer to the U.S. film market, seems the most determined. The Kodak of Japan (it has 70% of the Japanese film business), Fuji is already test-marketing its color film, mostly in Georgia and the Carolinas, and is rolling out across the U.S. Fuji has solved one problem always faced by Kodak competitors— standardization by independent photo processors on the chemicals and techniques needed to process Kodak film. Fujichrome and Fujicolor, which are on sale in an Instamatic-type cartridge, can be processed in the same manner as Kodachrome and Kodacolor.

Whether Fuji can break Kodak's firm hold on distribution channels is another question. Its U.S. distributor, Ehrenreich Photo-Optical, a small Long Island company, will give dealers a better discount, but will make no effort to compete on retail price. No reasonable company would. Kodak's volume and margins are so high that it probably could price its film below most competitors' costs and still turn a profit. Four years ago, for example, the British Government's Monopolies Commission forced Kodak to cut its color-film prices in the U.K. by 20%. That finished off an already weak Ilford, which subsequently dropped out of the color-film business in Britain, and raised Kodak's market share from 70 to 85%. British officials knew what they were doing: they believe that a monopoly can be "advantageous to public interest if it results in economies of scale which are passed on to the consumer."

The Salesman and the Scientist   A social historian who believes that great institutions throw up the kind of men needed to guide them in times of change would find much evidence to support his theory in Rochester. Seven

years ago the average age of Kodak's board was sixty-five, and seven of the sixteen members were in their seventies. As Eilers, who is sixty-three, says, "When you get older, you're after security." Kodak was slow, careful, and self-satisfied. No longer. The average age of board members has dropped to fifty-nine. And Kodak has recognized what Eilers calls "the necessity for an aggressive leadership." Having spent a number of years in the sharply competitive Eastman side of the business, Eilers is one answer to that need. The other is Gerry Zornow, who was appointed president after only six months in the job of executive vice president.

Zornow is in sharp contrast to his predecessors, most of whom were technically oriented. Starting as a trainee and rising through the ranks, he has spent his full career in marketing and is the first salesman to reach Kodak's top rank, an achievement that is as intertwined with the success of the Instamatic as Iacocca's career at Ford has been with the Mustang. Zestfully at home in the camaraderie of the golf course or the sales convention, Zornow describes himself as "a rather competitive person," a man with gusto for what he calls "belly-to-belly" selling. Well tailored, quietly self-confident in the executive suite, he retains a preference for the folksy phrase that he came by naturally or by self-training on the road. Talking about the need for further change in men and their attitudes at Kodak, he notes that he doesn't plan "just to shake the bag in order to get dust all over the particles."

Few men could differ more from Zornow than Edwin Land, Polaroid's leader scientist. Withdrawn, reflective, dog-restless away from a laboratory where he can patiently, joyously unravel some piece of the skein of knowledge, Land will at times dismiss marketing as what you need "when you don't have an idea." Intently in search of innovation and invention, he professes to believe that the right product will sell itself or, as he says with a smile that acknowledges and thus averts an approach to pretension: "Virtue and a good product are invincible."

"Different Cultures" This contrast in the personalities and attitudes of the two leaders reinforces a myth—shared by the companies as well as the public—that Kodak and Polaroid are, in Land's words, "quite different cultures," one a giant marketing organization, the other a small, imaginative gadfly. In part, the image that the two rivals have of themselves is self-perpetuating. Because Polaroid views itself as a successful innovator, it is willing to gamble heavily on still more invention. Because Kodak views itself as a giant marketeer with many products and many responsibilities, it leashes its technical confidence with caution and prudence. In fact, Kodak possesses and exercises superb technical skill. And the promotional and sales abilities Polaroid has displayed in building a market where none existed before are a matter of wonder and admiration to everybody but itself.

Like great protagonists who gradually take on first superficial and then more profound characteristics of each other, Polaroid and Kodak grow closer and closer in style and manner. In each case, management has always tended toward the paternalistic—neither is unionized. Kodak is clearly steeling itself for a major, Polaroid type of gamble on invention. And while Polaroid thinks of itself as merely an extraordinarily successful Route 128 company, it has become a major corporation with the same commitment to volume production, the same dependence on mass marketing, the same requirements for a structured industrial bureaucracy as Kodak. To put only four or five new Land cameras on each retail counter means manufacturing and distributing more cameras than Polaroid sold in total in 1955.

Even the flaws are similar. When the top Kodak men stayed on and on into old age, giving the impression that they would finally be interred in a desk drawer, they stifled the ambition of men beneath them, and by longevity or inclination blocked the opportunity for potential replacements to gain experience and maturity. Training a new president never seemed a pressing matter. While the attitude at the top has changed, it could take years to alter the tone and temper of so large and venerable a company.

In a different fashion with the same effect, Land rules Polaroid. There is no No. 2 man in Cambridge, only a group of "No. 3's" with their aspirations submerged by Land's brilliance or by his financial control or, if necessary, by his ability to alter gently the balance of authority beneath him when one subordinate appears to have become a shade more equal than the rest. When he was recently asked what qualities his successor should have, Land launched into a description of such a paragon of talent, intelligence, and virtue that even he paused, laughed, and said, "We're making him down in the laboratory."

The Testing Ground   One still more important similarity remains: Neither Kodak nor Polaroid has ever encountered serious competition, or come in second best in any matter of great importance. Although they choose different words to say so, both Kodak and Polaroid believe that they have served themselves and the public as well without competition as they would have with it. "We don't need competition," says Land, "because of the perfectionist drive at the heart of the company." Yet there are few men so inner directed, so heated in their pursuit of an ideal that they can exert themselves to the limit when the necessity to do so is not visible, external, and pressing. There are even fewer companies, which are but gatherings of mostly ordinary men, that can do so even for a short time. And there are probably no corporations of any size that can manage it year after year. In time, the inspired leader flags, or his example is diminished by scale, or he simply exhausts lesser mortals.

The beneficial stimulus of mutual competition is already visible at Kodak and Polaroid. Kodak is being pressed into a search for alternative systems it might never have embarked on but for Land. And while Polaroid would have someday devised its new camera and film, Kodak or no, the speed with which the system is being developed and brought to market has accelerated before the threat of Kodak's entry into instant photography.

In all this lies ground for suspecting that the Kodak-Polaroid encounter will not prove to be a confrontation between two markedly different rivals from which one victor and one vanquished will emerge. Far more likely is a testing of two great increasingly similar companies that have never before been fully tested, out of which each will emerge stronger than before. Pushed by competition to produce a better product at a better price, to respond more quickly, to move more lithely, to plan more effectively, Polaroid and Kodak are likely to discover that markets expand to accommodate the energy of the companies within them. Almost inadvertently, they could find themselves sharing a market far larger than possibly even the imaginative Dr. Land foresees. In that case, it will, indeed, be a lovely war.

QUESTIONS FOR DISCUSSION

1. What differences, if any, exist between technical service departments in large industrial manufacturing enterprises and customer service departments in large consumer goods firms?
2. What do you think the role of the product manager should be in writing and implementing the marketing plan for the area of responsibility?
3. To what extent should product managers get involved with his work of the product planning department?
4. How do you account for the fact that firms that are successful in marketing one line of products are not always successful with their other lines?
5. What steps could a company take to see to it that the experiences obtained from one marketing program are effectively transferred to other programs?
6. How do you think a firm's "image" is affected by its divestiture of products or product lines?
7. The Kodak-Polaroid case shows how competitors manage to cooperate with profit to both. Is this situation unique? Cite any additional cases where such cooperation exists. What market and technological conditions permit such business behavior?
8. The Polaroid Land camera is cited in a previous article as ". . . too big, too expensive, and too difficult to use." This is certainly true, yet the camera's success has been phenomenal. Why? What lesson is there to be learned for the marketing of other products that may be too big or awkward?
9. Both Kodak and Polaroid have successfully innovated a series of photographic products. How long can they keep this up? What can they do to assure themselves of a stream of profitable new products?

SUGGESTED READINGS

Harper W. Boyd, Jr., and Robert T. Davis, *Readings in Sales Management* (Homewood, Illinois: Richard D. Irwin, Inc., 1969).

D. Maynard Phelps and J. Howard Westing, *Marketing Management* (Homewood, Illinois: Richard D. Irwin, Inc., 1968).

Richard R. Still and Edward W. Cundiff, *Sales Management: Decisions, Policies and Cases* (Englewood Cliffs, New Jersey: Prentice-Hall, Inc., 1969).

Frederick D. Sturdivant *et al., Managerial Analysis in Marketing* (Glenview, Illinois: Scott, Foresman and Company Inc., 1970).

Donald L. Thompson and Douglas J. Dalrymple, *Retail Management Cases* (New York: The Free Press, 1969).

marketing practice and the public interest part two

No reader needs to be reminded that we live in a time of sharply focused issues that are of great concern to American society. It is probable that almost all of these are or can be related directly to business. Some of these issues are in fact the consequences of marketing activities, such as charges of deceptive advertising, unfair pricing, and so on. In other issues, such as the questions of poverty or the notion of privacy, business has an important role.

In short, we hold that marketing systems and marketing practice are not merely technical matters that concern the marketing specialist or the businessman. They are matters of deep concern to and embedded in the public interest. The student of business must understand the ramifications of what business does and what questions are raised by what it does. He must also note and comprehend the reactions of public and private agencies to business action.

Indeed, every student and every citizen should understand matters of such paramount importance, for the activities of business touch each of us so continually and affect everyone so profoundly that some knowledge—at least of the system and the issues it raises—is increasingly required.

In this part of the book we shall seek to identify the major issues of this kind to show their relation to present marketing practice and to offer, insofar as is possible, the various points of view in the current discussions of these questions.

section 3
the social responsibilities of business and marketing

Traditionally, corporate executives have felt responsible to their stockholders but not to the public. Today social responsibility increasingly is an accepted role of the businessman. Debate about this obligation to society centers less on *whether* such an obligation exists than on *how* it should be carried out.

The following selections deal with the businessman's role vis-à-vis society. They define "social responsibility," describe the various forms such an obligation takes, examine the ethical aspects of the businessman's behavior, and reveal how businessmen feel about these matters.

Our major concern here is marketing and the social problems with which it has become involved. First, it will be interesting to review the challenges that have been offered to the entire field of marketing as a part of the business structure. The issues raised in connection with marketing practice can be usefully separated from other facets of business activity, and we believe that a strong case has been made concerning the marketing operation specifically. We also believe that these operations can be regulated and altered without immediate reference to other business functions.

Accordingly, in our view, general and marketing executives as well as students of marketing are under an intellectual obligation to understand and to assess the validity of both general and specific complaints regarding marketing practice.

5 Understanding the Social Responsibility Puzzle: What Does the Businessman Owe to Society?

Keith Davis

Emerson once observed that commercial prosperity is the fuel of outstanding cultures. In fact, business and the general culture of a society influence each other and interact constantly. Thus, for example, nonprofit organizations such as schools, hospitals, or churches frequently adopt business practices just as changes in the general culture powerfully affect business fashions.

The expectations of some segments of society, such as labor and intellectuals, particularly, have had profound effects on management's self-image. One result has been their raising as a serious question the issue of social responsibility in what has become the powerful institutional system called "modern business." To what extent are the men who substantially direct this system—collectively called "management"—responsible for the social results of what their businesses are doing?

Other than giving an occasional brief look at marketing ethics, most marketing texts neglect the problem of social responsibility. It is important to raise this question in all business textbooks.

Professor Davis looks at this "puzzle" in an attempt to sort out the effect of business actions, the challenge to contemporary management, and the issues raised by various approaches to this problem.

How does a modern business manager know what to do in the area of social responsibility? One observer says, "A businessman has no responsibility to the public except to sell at as low a price as he can." Another says, "The job of business is to make a profit, and as long as it stays within the limits of the law, it has no other responsibility." At another extreme a local activist charges, "Business materialism and unemployment are the main

Reprinted from Keith Davis, "Understanding the Social Responsibility Puzzle", *Business Horizons* (Winter, 1967), Vol. 10, pp. 45–50, by permission of the author and the publisher.

causes of juvenile delinquency, and business must give a job to every teen-ager in order to prevent delinquency." And a local humanist thinks that business should pay for a new hospital because, "Business can get the money, but we can't afford to raise our taxes anymore."

In the face of all these claims, what guides does a manager have to assist him in making judgments concerning social responsibility? Should he avoid involvement in his community? Should he pay attention only to the loudest claimant, or to each squeaky wheel? Should he support only those activities in which he has a personal interest? Certainly he knows that, regardless of the claims made upon him, he cannot solve all of society's problems. If he tried to do so, he would preempt the work of those institutions that deal specifically with social problems. Furthermore, his resources are limited; he must husband them wisely and put them to the best long-run use. But how should he respond to these different claims on his organization?

Discussions about social responsibility have reached a high pitch in re-cent years, and I predict that interest will continue at a high level because the social system is undergoing changes that require new modes of conduct. Both fad and fetish have developed around this interest in social responsi-bility. The public press abounds with pious statements of its existence, but there seems to be considerable confusion about why it exists, how it arises, and how important it is for business and other organizations in our society. The following comments will consider these issues and, hopefully, shed some light on them. I will examine social responsibility in terms of a fun-damental model that fits together many of the loose pieces in the social re-sponsibility puzzle. Although my basic model substantially applies to any organization, including unions, government, cooperatives, and newspapers, this discussion is within the context of a business organization.

What Is Social Responsibility?   The substance of social responsibility arises from concern for the ethical consequences of one's acts as they might affect the interests of others. This idea exists in most religions and philos-ophies of the world. Quite frequently, however, a tendency exists to limit its application to person-to-person contacts. Social responsibility moves one large step further by emphasizing institutional actions and their effect on the whole social system. Without this additional step, personal and institu-tional acts tend to be divorced. A businessman can lead a model personal life, but continue to justify his organization's pollution of a river because no direct personal consequence is involved. He can consider river pollution a "public problem" to be solved by public action. The idea of social re-sponsibility, however, requires him to consider his acts in terms of a whole social system and holds him responsible for the effects of his acts anywhere in that system.

Social responsibility, therefore, broadens a person's view to the total social system. When a man's primary frame of reference is himself, he may be counted upon for antisocial behavior whenever his values conflict with those of society. If his values are limited primarily to a certain group or organization, he tends to become a partisan acting for that group. But, if he thinks in terms of a whole system, he begins to build societal values into his actions, even when they are for a certain organization. This is the essence of social responsibility. For the manager it means realizing that the business system does not exist alone and that a healthy business system cannot exist within a sick society.

The Growing Emphasis

Pluralism

Actions for the benefit of a private organization may also be socially responsible; to require that all acts be *only* in the public interest, compared with *both* public and private interests, is to deny the pluralism of society. Centers of initiative are many in a free society, and in order to maintain these centers, their goals must be served, as well as the general welfare. But the price that society exacts for this pluralism is that private organizational acts be made with concern for their public effects. A pluralistic society, therefore, is a social system in which diverse groups maintain autonomous participation and influence in the social system; it connotes a concurrent private freedom and public responsibility. Pluralism—and the private freedom from which it arises— is a basic cause of our growing interest in social responsibility.

Pluralism is a basic reality in modern business culture. Business is influenced by all other groups in the system, and it, in turn, influences them. Eells and Walton have observed, "Pluralism always implies multiplicity, frequently diversity, and sometimes conflict. It is as much the generator as the result of freedom. . . . It is . . . as much opposed to the ambitious pretences of a James Stuart (the king can do no wrong), as it is to the Rousseauian version of democracy (the collectivity can do no wrong)." [1]

The fact that pluralism diffuses power suggests that progress is made through responsible negotiation and compromise among power centers. There is neither monolithic decision making by one organization nor pure democracy of the masses operating free of organizational constraints. Many power centers exist in pluralism—none completely independent, but each with some autonomy.

Pluralism also implies that business is a joint venture of responsible citizens and groups of citizens, such as investors, managers, workers, communities, scientists, and others. Together these groups offer diverse inputs and expect diverse outputs. Viewed as a whole, the outputs are more than economic; social, psychological, political, and other outputs are also expected. This joint venture involving many groups is not necessarily a conflict or struggle for absolute power. Rather, it represents the efforts of people to reconcile their needs through a variety of organizational interests.

In pluralism, the business institution, therefore, becomes responsible to a variety of claimant groups in a variety of ways, rather than being responsible only to stockholders, and these claimants in turn have responsibilities to business because of their power to affect it.

We can thus conclude that pluralism in modern society is increasing our interest in social responsibility because it multiplies the centers of social power, all of which need to be concerned with social responsibility as they relate to each other in the social system. Pluralism is a major consideration in solving the social responsibility dilemma.

Other Reasons   However, several other reasons exist for the recent emphasis on social responsibility. The *first* reason is that modern society is more complex, with each of its parts more dependent on other parts. A new social dependency is evident. A century ago the acts of a businessman in India were of little significance to the United States; today with the world tied together in technology, communication, and politics, and with U.S. firms operating in India, business developments in that country are significant to a U.S. firm.

A *second* reason is that society has more wealth and culture that it wishes to conserve. Therefore, it is less willing to risk the disruptions that might occur from irresponsible acts in our society, such as sale of dangerous drugs, nationwide transportation strikes, or stream pollution. The climate of public opinion increasingly insists that actions by all institutions and persons must be responsible. Too much is at stake to risk irresponsibility, so responsible business action becomes necessary in order to maintain a favorable public image.

A *third* reason for interest in social responsibility is that the social sciences are giving us new knowledge about how business affects the social system beyond the company gates. Though we have always known that business affects the social system, we were not sure how, so we were not able to offer many proposals for improving its social function. We had to wait for more knowledge of the business mission in society. Even when we did have an idea for improved responsibility, we tended to accept Adam Smith's model of pure competition in which business was bound by the fetters of competition and really could not take any actions for the public good except to sell at the lowest possible price. Today, however, we recognize that business has more flexibility for responsible action because it no longer lives in pure competition, and the rules of pure competition do not apply.

Fourth, the growing power of government looms on the sidelines waiting to add restrictive controls the moment business becomes lax in any area of responsibility. Businessmen have learned that once a government control is established, it is seldom removed even though conditions change. When freedom and initiative are lost to government, they are lost for the long run. If these are the facts, then the prudent course for business is to understand fully the limits of its power and to use that power responsibly giving government no cause to intervene.

A *fifth* reason for our increasing emphasis on social responsibility is that current ethical concepts are programming people to favor more responsible action. The businessman shares the attitudes and values of society just as he did a century ago and reflects today's attitudes of more responsible conduct in his actions.

Finally, and perhaps most important, ownership and control are more and more separated in modern business. The career manager takes the longer view over time and the broader view among claimants on the organization. The separation of owner and manager has not been required by law but has developed *de facto* by delegation because this arrangement worked best. Unfortunately, this arrangement also obscures the location of responsibility. When the owner managed, the acts of the firm proceeded from his initiative, and the identity and power of the firm resided in him. In this situation, both the law and the people of the community could directly fix responsibility without confusion. But with the separation of ownership and management, normal legal channels of responsibility have eroded. No one is sure how much public responsibility managers have or through what channels it is controlled. One concept, however, makes managerial responsibility clear: the power-responsibility equation.

How Much Responsibility?

The Power-Responsibility Equation

Most persons agree that businessmen today have considerable social power. Their counsel is sought by government, and what they say and do influences their community. Social power comes to businessmen because they are leaders, are intelligent men of affairs, and command vast economic resources. The assets of the Bell Telephone System, for example, were about $30 billion in 1963, making it the largest business in the world. Among manufacturers, General Motors and Standard Oil of New Jersey had both assets and sales of over $10 billion in 1963. The annual sales of General Motors Corporation were greater than the gross national product of the Netherlands! [2]

In many ways businessmen speak for the important institution we call "business." They speak for or against legislation, economic policy, labor relations policy, and so on in their roles as businessmen. To the extent that businessmen—or any other group—have social power, the lessons of history suggest that social responsibility of an equal amount arises therefrom. Stated in the form of a general relationship, *social responsibilities of businessmen arise from the amount of social power they have.*

The idea that responsibility and power go hand in hand appears to be as old as civilization itself. Wherever one looks in ancient and medieval history—Palestine, Rome, Britain—men were concerned with balancing power and responsibility. Men have often failed to achieve this balance, but they have generally sought it as a necessary antecedent to justice. This idea has its origins in reason and logic. It is essentially a matter of balancing the two sides of an equation. As stated by one philosopher, "The demand of the law in a well-ordered society is that responsibility shall lie where the power of decision lies. Where that demand is met, men have a legal order; where it is not, they have only the illusion of one." [3]

The idea of equal power and responsibility is not a stranger to business either. For example, one of the rules of scientific management is that authority and responsibility should be balanced in such a way that each employee and manager is made responsible to the extent of his authority, and vice versa. Although this rule refers only to relationships within the firm, it should apply as well to the larger society outside the firm. As a matter of fact, businessmen have been strong proponents of balanced social power and responsibility in external society, particularly in their views on responsibilities of labor leaders.

The logic of reasonably balanced power and responsibility is often overlooked by those who discuss social responsibility. Some argue that business is business and anything that smacks of social responsibility is out-of-bounds. Milton Friedman contends that "few trends could so thoroughly undermine the very foundations of our free society as the acceptance by corporate officials of a social responsibility other than to make as much money for their stockholders as possible." [4] Another author speaks of the "frightening spectacle" of a powerful business group that in the name of social responsibility "imposes its narrow ideas about a broad spectrum of unrelated noneconomic subjects on the mass of man and society." [5] He advocates a powerful democratic state to look after general welfare, leaving business to pursue its main objective of material gains within limits of everyday civility.

The objections to social responsibility are meaningful. Indeed, many dangers await as business moves into untrodden areas of social responsibility. The fallacy of these objections is that they are usually based on an economic model of pure competition in which market forces leave business theoretically without any social power and, hence, no responsibility (a balanced zero equation). This zero equation of no power and no responsibility is a proper theoretical model for pure competition, but it is theory only and is inconsistent with the power realities of modern organizations. They possess such great initiative, economic assets, and power that their actions do have social effects. In reality, therefore, the "no responsibility" doctrine assumes that business will keep some of its social power but will not worry about social responsibility.

At the other extreme, some persons would have business assume responsibilities as a sort of social godfather, looking after widows, orphans, public health, juvenile delinquency, or any other social need, simply because business has large economic resources. This position overlooks the fact that business operates in a pluralistic society, which has other institutions available to serve people in these areas. Business is one of many centers of initiative in the social system; hence, no need exists to make it a monolithic dispenser of welfare, overshadowing the state as it cares for everyone's problems. The "total responsibility" doctrine also confuses business's function of *service* to society with *servitude* to society. Workers, investors, and others participate in a business as free men—not as slaves of society. They have their own lives to live, and business is their cooperative venture for fulfilling their own needs (private needs) while serving others (public needs).

The "no responsibility" and the "total responsibility" doctrines are equally false. According to the first doctrine, business keeps its power but accepts no responsibility, thereby unbalancing the power-responsibility equation. According to the second doctrine, responsibility far exceeds power, again unbalancing the equation.

The Iron Law of Responsibility   If business social responsibilities could be avoided or reduced to insignificance, business would be released from a heavy burden. Social responsibilities are difficult to determine and apply. Their relationships are complex. If the complexities of social responsibility could be avoided, business decisions would certainly be easier to make. But what are the consequences of responsibility avoidance? If responsibility arises from power, then the two conditions tend to stay in balance over the long run, and the avoidance of social responsibility leads to gradual erosion of social power. This is the Iron Law of Responsibility: *Those who do not take responsibility for their power, ultimately shall lose it.*[6] Its long-run application to man's institutions certainly stands confirmed by history, though the "long run" may require decades or even centuries in some instances.

As it applies to business, the Iron Law of Responsibility insists that to the extent businessmen do not accept social-responsibility obligations as they arise, other groups eventually will step in to assume those responsibilities. This prediction of diluted social power is not a normative statement of what I think *should* happen. Rather, it is a prediction of what *will tend to* happen whenever businessmen do not keep their social responsibilities approximately equal to their social power. An early study of business social responsibilities presented this idea as follows, "And it is becoming increasingly obvious that a freedom of choice and delegation of power such as businessmen exercise would hardly be permitted to continue without some assumption of social responsibility." [7]

History supports the mutuality of power and responsibility in business. Take safe working conditions as an example. Under the protection to common law, employers during the nineteenth century gave minor attention to worker safety. Early in the twentieth century, in the face of pressure from safety and workmen's compensation laws, employers changed their attitudes to accept responsibility for job safety. Since then, very few restrictions have been imposed on business power in this area because business in general has been acting responsibly. Accident rates have been reduced dramatically until the workplace is safer than most areas away from work.

For an opposite example, consider unemployment. Business in the first quarter of this century remained callous about technological and market layoff. As a result, business lost some of its power to government, which administers unemployment compensation, and to unions, which restrict business by means of tight seniority clauses, supplemental unemployment benefits, and other means. Now business finds itself in the position of paying unemployment costs it originally denied responsibility for, but having less control than when it did not pay! Business power has drained away to bring the power-responsibility equation back into balance.

Consider also the equation in terms of a current problem—gainful employment of older workers. The plight of workers in the over-45 age bracket is well-known. Despite public pronouncements of interest in them and despite their general employability, many of them find job opportunities limited or even nonexistent. At this time the power of initiative is still substantially with business, but it is being gradually eroded by fair employment practice laws. Will management stop this erosion by taking more responsibility? I do not know, but in any case the power-responsibility equation gradually, but surely, finds its balance.

I believe that the logic of balanced power and responsibility is a useful model for understanding the social-responsibility dilemma in which business managers exist today. And the Iron Law of Responsibility offers the historical imperative that social responsibility must be balanced with power in the long course of business history. More specifically, in the operating areas where social power exists, social responsibility exists also—and in approximately the same amount.

Social responsibility is expressed in law, custom, and institutional agreements that define conditions for responsible use of power, but, more important for our purposes, it is expressed in responsible self-regulation by informed, mature managers who understand the social system in which they operate. Managers are the long-run key to effective social responsibility by business institutions. With socially competent managers, we can have a socially competent business system and the productivity and human fulfillment that successful business can bring.

NOTES

1. Richard Eells and Clarence C. Walton, *Conceptual Foundations of Business* (Homewood, Ill.: Richard D. Irwin, Inc., 1961), pp. 360 and 363.

2. "The 500 Largest U.S. Industrial Corporations," *Fortune* (July 1964), pp. 179–198.

3. John F. A. Taylor, "Is the Corporation Above the Law?" *Harvard Business Review* (March–April, 1965), p. 126.

4. Milton Friedman, *Capitalism and Freedom* (Chicago, Ill.: University of Chicago Press, 1962), p. 133.

5. Theodore Levitt, "The Dangers of Social Responsibility," *Harvard Business Review* (September–October, 1958), p. 44.

6. Keith Davis and Robert L. Blomstrom, *Business and Its Environment* (New York: McGraw-Hill Book Company, 1966), p. 174.

7. Howard R. Bowen, *Social Responsibilities of the Businessman* (New York: Harper & Row, Publishers, 1953), p. 4.

6 Would You Want Your Daughter to Marry a Marketing Man?

Richard N. Farmer

One important approach to looking at marketing is to think of it as the way in which business operates to "produce" and to "maintain" customers. This means that marketing can be seen as a set of operations or practices. In general, the study of marketing has concerned itself with using various methods and techniques as effectively as possible.

Richard Farmer's article digs underneath this structure to examine the questions related to marketing ethics.

Despite the title of the article, Farmer is deadly serious in questioning the significance of much of modern marketing. He believes that many aspects of the field of marketing are both irrelevant and unethical. Each reader must judge for himself whether the author is right or wrong.

．　．　．

. . . The whole world, including the United States, appears to be moving in a direction in which marketing is decidedly *not* prepared to go. Unless this trend is recognized for what it is, and unless marketing scholars finally face up to the essential and basic questions in marketing, the entire field of marketing is in for considerable difficulty.

．　．　．

If the marketing people manage to do so, the field of marketing will prosper. If not, it will be regarded as an interesting cultural quirk of the mid-twentieth century, which temporarily attracted the attention of some very intelligent people.

The two basic issues which have to be faced are that *marketing is unethical*, and that *marketing is irrelevant*.

Reprinted from Richard N. Farmer, "Would You Want Your Daughter to Marry a Marketing Man?", *Journal of Marketing* (January, 1967), Vol. 31, pp. 1–3. Reprinted from *Journal of Marketing*, published by the American Marketing Association.

Marketing Is
Unethical

For the past 6,000 years the field of marketing has been thought of as made up of fast-buck artists, con-men, wheeler-dealers, and shoddy-goods distributors. Too many of us have been "taken" by the tout or con-man; and all of us at times have been prodded into buying all sorts of "things" we really did not need, and which we found later on we did not even want.

In itself, this can be looked on as a problem of personal gullibility. Yet marketing men who conduct serious studies of how to persuade more people to buy more products and services will continue to be in ethical difficulties.

When one examines physical distribution, channel theory, or similar kinds of distribution problems, this point does not hold. After all, the production-oriented side of marketing does offer a great deal to a human race which has never been efficient enough to give all persons their material due.

But when we turn to advertising, sales-promotion, and other techniques and studies calculated to "push" goods on uninterested individuals, that is another question. . . .

One can point to many refutations of the above point, most of which are believed by marketing men and persons involved in sales work.[1] Any group of intelligent and able people working in an exciting and technically demanding field can convince themselves of the value of their work. But the real question is: *Does anybody else believe it?*

Unfortunately, too few of the intellectually important people do. It is true that some surveys have indicated a certain satisfaction with advertising;[2] but the 80% or so who feel satisfied may be typically those whose opinions will not count in the future. The scholars, opinion-makers, intellectuals, clergymen, and others whose words will count continue to remain skeptical, or simply bored about the present state of sales promotion.[3]

Elaborate surveys are not needed to verify this point. Merely follow some student discussions in the coffee shop or in other uninhibited surroundings. Observe the concern of so many businessmen over the fact that so many college graduates are going into nonbusiness fields. Read some of the nonadvertising publications that do not give a sop to advertisers.

What is "visible" about marketing is not the intriguing, truly exciting research work in a variety of behavioral and technical areas. Instead, it is the picture of some pitchman selling hair spray on television!

Marketing Is
Irrelevant

The United States is the only nation both wealthy enough and inept enough to operate consistently below potential output-capacity most of the time.

Except for the war-years, this country has not operated up to economic potential since 1910. Only in 1917–1918, 1927, 1942–46, 1953, and 1956–57 has unemployment been below 3%.[4] In 1964, a year of extremely good economic performance, some $27 billions of output was lost through the full-employment gap.[5] The American economy could have produced this much more if all resources (land, labor, and capital) had been fully employed. Not only were many men unemployed, but factories and fields also were not used to capacity, largely because the demand for such goods and services did not exist.

While the reasons for this failure to obtain full utilization of productive potential are exceedingly complex, the output of our economy rarely exceeds 90% of potential capacity, and more often operates around the 80 to 85% level.

The sales-promotion aspects of marketing have reached full flower in this country. In most other countries sales-promotion activities do not flourish because everything produced is almost immediately consumed. Production, not marketing, is the key factor around which the economy turns.

For this reason the American concept of organizing the firm around marketing possibilities is almost incomprehensible to many foreign managers. Such orientation implies that the firm can always produce more than the market can absorb, which can happen generally only in an economy operating below potential capacity.

To operate at less than capacity implies that there is always more than the consumers can afford. In this situation competition, even "cut-throat" competition, becomes very real indeed.

Two Ethical Questions
Two kinds of ethical questions arise here.
First, is it right to prevent people from consuming when you obviously can produce the goods, but when the consumers do not have the necessary income?
Second, if you can produce more, and if someone somewhere is in want, is it ethical to allow any factories and farms to produce at less than full capacity?
With some two-thirds of the world in perpetual poverty, is it right to try to move up the American average propensity to consume from its present 92% of disposable income to 93%? Intensive marketing promotion may be able to induce more consumption out of available income, but it might prove more desirable to utilize savings for more socially useful ends.

Calvinism and Tradition
The feeling that marketing is largely irrelevant is by no means restricted to people in other countries. In one sense, a great many Americans are Calvinists; and our country was built on a doctrine of self-denial, plus concern for hard labor and good works. In the older American tradition, consumption meant survival but not necessarily enjoyment. A lot has been done in marketing to make people forget their

guilt feelings about consumption, as they drive along in anodized chariots or sit beside their swimming pools.

But curiously, the trend today is back to the old ethic. There are problems of economic development, of urban renewal, of poverty, and of racial conflict; but for the most part marketing people have avoided such issues.

Even though they enjoy the fruits of marketing, most of the rest of the world, and certainly many Americans, see the basic irrelevance of marketing quite clearly.

. . . For a group that has been so brilliant in selling and distribution as have American marketers, this is sad.

Perhaps marketing men have sold everybody everything, except themselves and the significance of marketing.

The Other Side of the Coin   Marketing *can* be both ethical and relevant, although unfortunately the image presented by American practitioners does not suggest that this could be the case. In a world largely preoccupied with production problems, questions of distribution and product-mix can prove intractable without proper utilization of marketing techniques; and many Communist and Socialist countries have learned this to their dismay.[6]

The growing complexity of the world's economies leads inevitably to the need for more efficient marketing methods and tools. As soon as the questions of the supply of basic food, shelter, and clothing have been solved for the majority of the world population, questions of what to do next will require the services of marketing experts of the highest caliber. Moreover, in spite of the annoying amount of "noise" produced by some promotional activities, advertising and sales promotion do produce some quite tangible benefits.[7]

But too many marketers in the United States create an image of vulgar hucksters, unable to share in the most important part of the world's work. The tragic part of this preoccupation with the less important parts of marketing is that relatively few of the long-run distribution problems ever get the attention they deserve.[8]

•   •   •

NOTES

1. Examples are in Steuart Henderson Britt's *The Spenders* (New York: McGraw-Hill Book Co., 1961).
2. Raymond A. Bauer, "Some Insights Into the Support and Criticism of Advertising," paper delivered at the 1965 Annual Meeting, American Association of Advertising Agencies, pp. 2–4.
3. Same reference as footnote 2. Also, see Colston E. Warne, "Advertising— A Critic's View," *Journal of Marketing,* Vol. 26 (October, 1962), pp. 10–14.

4. Lance E. Davis, Jonathan R. T. Hughes, Duncan M. McDougall, *American Economic History* (Homewood, Illinois: Richard D. Irwin, Inc., 1961), p. 95.

5. Council of Economic Advisers, *Economic Report of the President, 1965* (Washington, D.C.: U.S. Government Printing Office, 1965), pp. 82–83.

6. Barry M. Richman, *Soviet Management: With Significant American Comparisons* (Englewood Cliffs, New Jersey: Prentice-Hall, Inc., 1965), pp. 108–131.

7. Martin Mayer, *Madison Avenue, USA* (New York: Pocket Books Inc., 1959), pp. 312–328.

8. Reavis Cox, *Distribution in a High-Level Economy* (Englewood Cliffs, New Jersey: Prentice-Hall, 1965), pp. 230–231.

7 The Social Values of Marketing

C. W. Cook

In the previous article Farmer has described one point of view. But in response one may ask, "How do marketing practitioners view the charges and complaints by critics?" Naturally outright fraud and deception are regrettable and should be curbed by law enforcement. As to the more intricate question concerning the utility or value of marketing, this extract shows how a marketing executive perceives the subject.

The contributions marketing makes in our society are social as well as economic. This is a point that we in marketing need to stress strongly now, when the climate in which the marketing function must be carried on is the most socially conscious in the entire history of our country. For it is in the name of social progress that critics of business—some public figures and their political and philosophical allies—are training their fire power these days on some long-established, time-tested marketing aims and methods.

It is inevitable, in a country where freedom of thought and speech is encouraged, that there will be differences of viewpoint about so complicated a subject as marketing. And there are differences, even about such obvious contributions as the economic values of marketing. But what should concern us particularly is the current tendency to question the *social* worthiness of the function which is our responsibility. For as policy-setting top executives and senior marketing people, it is our mission to create and serve the consumer market which supports all the activities of production, from raw material sources to finished products, and to do this as efficiently and acceptably as possible.

It seems clear that we need to develop a more effective way of presenting the role of marketing in the light of today's heightened social consciousness. We must not let the values that marketing contributes to the well-being of our society get lost. So it is about these values that I would like to share some thoughts with you.

Reprinted from C. W. Cook, "The Social Values of Marketing", *The Conference Board Record* (February, 1967), Vol. 4, pp. 32–37, by permission of the publisher.

There are, as I see it, three social responsibilities of marketing which contribute to its social value: First, to offer a *social product*; second, to make it available at a *social price*; and third, to make a *social profit* in the process.

I would like to examine each briefly in relation to the public welfare and the realities of human nature.

A Social Product   How might a social product be defined? (And it will simplify this discussion if you will permit me to use the term "product" to include "services" also.) What are its characteristics? What are its social values?

To the social theorist there seem to be four conventional or rational measurements of value which apply to any product:

- Its quantitative value
- Its intrinsic or qualitative value
- Its functional or utilitarian value
- Its serviceability or durability

All four of these values are, of course, valid. Their relative importance depends on the nature of the product, or the use to which it is to be put by the consumer. But I hardly need to remind you who are in the thick of the competitive battle of the marketplace that this by no means exhausts the list of reasons consumers buy a product, or buy one product in preference to another—or to all others. Indeed, it leaves out one of the values most important to the great mass of consumers.

Before naming this important value let me enumerate just a few of the very human reasons people buy many of the products they do buy, quite often paying a premium price for them.

Because a product provides sheer gratification in ownership.
Because it possesses exclusiveness of form, shape, design, materials, workmanship, finish.
Because it produces a sense of pride in the ability to afford, or the taste to appreciate.
Because of the anticipated admiration of friends.
Because of the attractiveness of the package.
Because it promises to produce a quiet sense of well-being.
Because the product reflects the purchaser's personality.
Because it would make a gift of special charm or appropriateness.
Because it offers an outlet for the purchaser's energy, skill or creativity.
Because it indulges some suppressed desire.

It will not have escaped you, I am sure, that there is little relationship between any of these reasons for buying and the four conventional measurements of value mentioned earlier. But, irrational, extravagant, even frivolous, as some of them seem, they lump themselves under the single important value I have postponed naming until now. This is their *satisfaction-value.*

There are two forms of satisfaction-value. One is *satisfaction-in-use*; the other is *satisfaction-of-ownership*. Both, I submit, have definite social value, because they serve a need or craving in the life of the purchaser. Usually they make him or her quite willing to pay whatever their price, within reason. This seems to nettle the school of sociologists who focus on the four rational values—quantitative, intrinsic or qualitative, functional or utilitarian, serviceability or durability. But it is a sober reality of the marketplace. While the four rational values are important, accepting them as the sole criteria of product-value would involve abandoning the free-choice principle on which our American social system is based.

There is no question that all of us *could* live much more economically—or more sensibly, if you prefer—than we do.

We do not actually *need* agreeably flavored toothpaste, in a convenient tube, to keep our teeth clean. We could brush them with baking soda or plain table salt.

We do not actually *need* clothing in the latest fashion and the newest fabrics and colors. Garments of coarse cotton, wool or linen, without form or style, would effectively cover and protect our bodies.

We do not actually *need* the smart and comfortable motorcars we drive. A jeep would take our families any place we might want to go.

We cannot honestly argue that we actually *need* our present broad assortment of appetizing and convenient foods and beverages. We could exist indefinitely on water, coarse bread, milk, and a few fruits and vegetables. Furthermore, we could prepare meals starting from scratch, with low-cost bulk raw materials, as our grandmothers did.

But who of us would be willing to live in such a strictly functional or utilitarian fashion? Or how ready would any of us be to give up all the *satisfaction-values*?

Our penchant for buying-for-satisfaction has been summed up succinctly by Lee A. Iacocca, vice president of the Ford Motor Company:

> People buy cars for all kinds of reasons. Some people buy because a color or a grille or a roof line makes them feel good. Some people buy because of miles per gallon and cents per mile. The point is that people buy for a reason that makes sense to them.

While he was speaking of motorcars, the reason for purchasing any product that makes sense to any man or woman constitutes its *satisfaction-value* to that person.

A basic-necessities economy might be built on a narrow and strictly utilitarian marketing philosophy. But life would be terribly drab. And the economy would suffer—swiftly. Jobs would become scarce. Growth opportunities would be so lacking that the incentive on which our private enterprise system is based would all but cease to exist. The United States of America as we know it could not survive under so narrow a social philosophy.

The aim of marketing under our system, which has brought us a steadily rising economy, is to supply the whole range of products and services to serve consumers' very human cravings of the mind and spirit, as well as of the body. I submit that this is a *social right*. For it is not society as a whole, but the *social individual* who establishes the social value of any product—by his or her purchases.

These purchases may encompass a whole category of products which Dr. Ernest Dichter, the well-known philosopher of human motivation, has whimsically characterized as "sinful products." These he defines as products that come into conflict with Puritanical moral standards. Included would be, for example, liquor, candy, cigarettes, fattening foods, cola drinks, coffee, cosmetics, and many others.

None of these products is absolutely essential. But we would fight to keep them. They do something for our spirits, our ego, our sense of good living. They, and the right to possess them, are the driving force which motivates us to work and to seek advancement, in order to enjoy more and more of the products and services which "make sense to us." In other words, they help to make us productive servants of our modern society, as well as consumers. Thus they contribute *social* as well as *economic* values to our American life.

A Social Price   Assuming a social product to market, one with values transcending intrinsic or strictly utilitarian qualities, the second consideration of those of us responsible for marketing policy is the *price* at which the product is to be offered.

Specifically, can it be sold at a *social price?* The very term seems contradictory. How can the price of any product be *social*, when price is an essentially *commercial* element in the sales transaction?

It seems to me that much of the misunderstanding about the nature and function of the marketing process is revealed by this simple question. The assumption is that social and commercial considerations are uncongenial, if not definitely antipathetic. But are they?

Suppose we ask this simple question: What *is* a "social price"—for *any* product? The quick answer is likely to be, "The lowest price at which it can be offered."

Reasonable as it seems, this answer is *one-sidedly social* in that it focuses too sharply on the consumer. Establishing a social price involves striking a balance between the well-being of *five* disparate groups, each of which has a natural—and legitimate—interest in the price at which a given product is offered. These groups are:

1. The people with the enterprise to embark in the business of developing, producing and marketing the product, and those who manage and staff the business.

2. The people who provide the capital to finance the business.
3. The people who produce and distribute the product, including production, clerical, sales and administrative personnel, and the transportation and delivery workers who make it physically available to consumers in their communities.
4. The people who purchase and use or consume the product. (The only group which benefits directly from the quick answer: "The lowest price at which it can be offered.")
5. Finally, and of great social importance, the federal, state and local governments which are so heavily dependent for their support on the taxes collected from successful business enterprises.

Thus it becomes evident that the social price must provide earnings that will make it worthwhile for people with capital to invest their funds in the enterprise, and to provide a margin for the management to reinvest in continually improving the product, and re-tooling from time to time to produce it still more economically.

The social price must enable the enterprise to pay prevailing wages to those who make and market the product, and to employ competent people to manage it. Those who transport and distribute must also be compensated.

In this way profitable employment is maintained and the whole economy is supported.

And if it is to be a true social price it must be sufficient to provide a margin of profit to contribute to federal, state and local taxes, as already mentioned. For if a business enterprise earns no profits, it is a drag on the nation's economy.

At this point the basic function of marketing—the building and maintaining of a consumer market for any product—injects itself, and it must be faced.

The quick definition of a social price for a product—"The lowest price at which it can be offered"—assumes that the lower the price, the more people can and will buy it. This assumption would be sound if the makers of the product had an absolute monopoly in the marketplace. But under our free-choice, private enterprise system we insist—quite properly, I am sure we will all agree—that monopoly be outlawed. The result is a competition between products so intense that only those which are promoted by effective advertising will be given shelf space in retail outlets.

If there were a more economical way of reaching the consumer, we may be very sure that some enterprising company in every industry would be using it. The bald fact is, that a social price must of necessity include a margin for introduction and continuous promotion.

A Question of Value . . .   Yet some social theorists argue that the advertising and promotional activities used to create and maintain the market for a product are a sheer waste of money: that consumers should be offered lower prices by eliminating, or at least drastically limiting, these marketing expenditures.

This might be true in a world peopled with utterly unemotional consumers, dedicated to strictly functional living, and satisfied with purely utilitarian products; but not in our modern world of very human men, women, and children, who insist on satisfactions of the mind and spirit as well as of the body.

Recently an eminent English economist and writer, Walter Taplin, divided consumer expenditures into two categories: "The things we need to keep us alive and the things we need to make life worth living."

As men with marketing responsibility, it is our obligation to provide *both*. But it is our obligation, also, to provide value for the price asked—social value, if you please.

Part of this value is in the product itself, in ingredients and production costs. Part is often added in the packaging and promotion functions of the marketing process.

Because I know the food business best, I naturally start with this category of products to validate my point. By picturing on the package and in the advertising of a dessert, for instance, the delectable dishes it will provide, and describing in mouth-watering words their flavor, texture, and nutritional characteristics, the consumer is led to *anticipate* enjoyable eating, as well as to identify the product's special virtues while eating it. Without this mental picture, many people would consume the dessert with much less relish. The consumer might receive a scant money's worth, no matter how low the price.

Or suppose we take an example from the field of kitchen appliances. The advertising of an electric can opener, or one of the new Teflon-lined cooking utensils, can create a mental picture of a minor miracle of convenience in meal preparation that will send a woman to the kitchen to get dinner for her family with a sense of having magic servants at her elbow.

In the field of services, the cruises offered by steamship lines are made far more enjoyable by the anticipation of gay shipboard parties and the romance of their ports of call, as pictured in TV and print advertisements and illustrated folders. People get far more pleasure for their money than if their travel appetite had not been whetted in advance by this picturesque promotion.

Or consider today's miracle antibiotics. Above and beyond their scientific merit, may not their efficacy be at least partially dependent on the psychological benefit of the patient's *anticipation* of relief or a cure?

Modern cosmetics can—and often do—make a woman prettier (if not pretty) because, when using them, the promise of the advertising makes her *feel* prettier. So she *is* prettier. She gets her money's worth in satisfaction-in-use.

. . . and of
Value Added
All of these satisfactions are human—and therefore *social* rather than *economic*—aspects of price-value. The point is that advertising can and does add a considerable measure of value to perhaps a majority of products. And it is a social value that makes the price socially reasonable.

Let me register right here that we who bear marketing responsibility cannot afford to forget that the irrationality and ever-so-human foibles of the public, who comprise the huge market for goods and services in this country of ours, neither argue for nor condone *over*-promising a product's satisfactions or benefits. Neither do they excuse overcharging for it in relation to the value of its ingredients and the costs involved in its creation, production, promotion, and distribution. Nor do the foibles of human nature offer any excuse for dishonesty in claims, in advertising or on the package. Not only is this true with respect to benefits, but also to quantity, quality, utility, serviceability, and other values, claimed or implied.

A Social Profit   In the competitive Donnybrook of today's marketplace, little thought is likely to be given to such a seemingly idealistic consideration as a "social profit." But in view of the critical attitude that is cropping out in political circles toward some aspects of marketing, I believe it timely to ask ourselves what might reasonably be considered a *social* profit.

Many otherwise intelligent people seem to think of the word "profits" as a synonym for "greed." In reality, profits are synonymous with economic and social health, for we could not have a healthy economy or a healthy society without the profits earned by business.

True, there are always a few businessmen who are greedy for more profits than they are entitled to; just as there are a few men and women in every line of human endeavor who are greedy for more glory or fame, or a greater financial reward, than their contribution merits. But in both instances they are the exception rather than the rule.

Another common misassumption is that businesses make profits automatically.

All of us know that this is not so. Yet I believe most people would be surprised at these figures from a government publication, *Profits and the American Economy*, issued by the Department of Commerce:

> In 1961–62 some 1,190,286 active corporations filed Income Tax returns with the U.S. Internal Revenue Service. Of these, 474,697 reported a net loss. This is 39.8 per cent of all corporations which filed Income Tax returns. . . . This indicates the seriousness of the risk-taking involved in entrepreneurship.

The same government publication also makes this point:

> It is evident that entrepreneurship, guided as it is by the profit incentive, serves as a bridge between productive resources and consumers, and by so doing provides a vital service to all of us. Additionally, in its constant endeavor to lower its cost to meet competition, entrepreneurship, guided by the profit incentive, helps to get goods which consumers want most, produced at the lowest possible cost.

These two brief excerpts sum up the contributions of competition as both an economic and a social factor in profit-making. For of necessity profits earned in today's competitive marketplace serve social as well as economic purposes.

In short, only the theorists question the need or value to society of profits. The realists have always recognized this value. Back in the early days of the labor movement, Samuel Gompers wrote: "Companies without profits mean workers without jobs. Remember, when the boss is in financial trouble, the worker's job isn't safe."

In modern times, George Meany stated in a *Fortune* magazine article: "We believe in the American profit system. We believe in free competition. The American private enterprise system, despite some defects, has achieved far greater results for wage earners than any other social system in history."

The social contribution of profits to the support of our government is too well recognized to need argument. But I find that many people are surprised at the size of the tax contribution made by a single corporation in the course of a year. As an example, in fiscal 1966 my own company paid some $82 million in federal, state and local taxes. This compares with less than $53 million paid to General Foods' stockholders in dividends, and a little over $41 million retained in the business for reinvestment in its future growth and security.

On a business-wide scale, in calendar 1965 the income tax bill for all U.S. corporations from the federal government alone was more than $31 billion, which went to the support of our society. And this figure does not include substantial state and local taxes, nor the enormous amounts paid in personal income taxes by stockholders to federal, state and local governments.

There is a school of business thought which criticizes the accounting phrase, "profits before taxes." This phrase, they argue, is a misstatement, since the portion of earnings earmarked for taxes is not available to the management for any other use. The argument advanced by some that these taxes are part of the "cost of doing business" only confirms that they are not "profits" in the proper sense of the term.

From an accounting standpoint it makes little difference how taxes are designated; the harm comes when critical writers and speakers quote the total figure to show what "huge profits" corporations made. They fail to mention the really significant contribution more than half of corporate profits is making to the social welfare of the nation, of the various states, and of local communities.

A Practical   We who administer business enterprises have a very practical
Responsibility   responsibility for the wise social use of the part of the profits re-
                    tained in our businesses. Except as private citizens with a vote,
we have no control over the expenditure of that portion of profits paid in federal, state and local taxes. And our responsibility for the portion distributed as dividends ends when the dividend checks are mailed. But when we

plan the use of profits retained in the business, we exercise a most important social responsibility.

In this respect, it seems to me that there is a definite difference between managements' *economic* responsibility to *earn* profits, and its *social* responsibility to *administer* the retained portion of profits so intelligently that the enterprise will continue to grow, provide employment, and pay taxes, to the end of serving our society. This it commonly does, as we in management realize but the general public seems not to appreciate, by supporting scientific research, pioneering in the development of new products, steadily improving present products, and in general keeping up with the changing needs and wants of the consuming home and family.

Sooner or later—and usually sooner!—in any consideration of profit, the question of what is a *fair* profit is inevitably raised. Of all the attempts made to define a fair profit, I like best the one given by Bert S. Cross, chairman of the 3M Company: "A profit is a fair profit," he said, "as long as we have sold a man a product he can use and is willing to buy." Certainly that concept serves our society better than the innumerable theoretical proposals for limiting profits by mathematical formula, or by any other artificial method that does not take the competitive factor into account.

Under our competitive system, the body-social has a most effective way of governing profits. If the consuming public stops buying a product, it frequently means that profits *are* too high. When that happens, prices come down, either because the industry fears the loss of its market and reduces prices, or because individual producers reduce their prices and their competitors are forced to follow.

Our System
Works
This free-choice, private enterprise, profit-motivated system of ours, which is highly competitive, may seem irrational, wasteful in some respects and at times a bit silly and "sinful." But it has the saving grace that it *works*. And economic truth is established by practical experience, not by theoretical arguments.

No other economic system in the history of the world, no matter how rational or how socially idealistic, has ever approached it in the prosperity ours has produced. What is more, it has provided our country with a substantial margin which we have been able to share with older peoples whose highly touted socialistic economies continue to fail to meet even the basic needs of their people.

Yet theorists insist on tampering with our machinery. Frequently I find myself wishing that I could still be around 50 or 100 years from now, to witness the puzzlement that is bound to prevail among historians who try to make head or tail out of our times.

How will they reconcile, for instance, the fact that after our country has contributed billions of dollars for two decades to advance the freedom of mankind all over the world, there are now under serious consideration a number of regulatory proposals to reduce marketing freedoms within our own borders? "Why," they are bound to ask, "was there such a zeal in the mid-1960's to standardize, to limit, and to legislate in a way that would undermine free choice?"

But perhaps the most confusing paradox historians will uncover is that, at the very time that more and more controls were being urged by the theorists to hobble our economy, in Soviet Russia, where a strictly controlled economy had prevailed for half a century, the trend was clearly turning toward greater freedom of action. A recent issue of *Fortune*[1] magazine stated:

> Soviet authorities have been making increased use of price cuts, installment buying, advertising and product differentiation . . . Consumer goods producers are beginning to promote their plant names or "production marks." The government is encouraging the practice because an enterprise that is proud enough of its mark to call attention to it inevitably tends both to make a better product and to keep on improving it.

This article should baffle future historians, especially when, in preserved copies of our nation's mass communication media of the same period, they read about the all-out efforts being made in the U.S. on behalf of package standardization, grade labeling, limitation of advertising, and various other proposals for depriving American business of the marketing tools and techniques which made our economy so great; and even worse, for depriving American consumers of their traditional right of free choice. And it is worth noting that, in the light of its vociferous insistence upon "the right to be an individual," the upcoming generation promises to be even more jealous of its freedom to choose than the present generation.

We in marketing have it in our power to change the course of economic history during the final third of this eventful century. In fact, we are challenged to do just that: to demonstrate that our system, given freedom to function without crippling laws and regulations, will continue to be the best suited to provide a social product, at a social price, and with a social profit —a profit made, not at the expense of the public, but as a result of acceptable service to the public.

I would add a further challenge: we must find ways to bring to the public a clear and helpful understanding of the *social* as well as the *economic* aspects of the entire production-promotion-distribution process which is the area of special interest and competence of this group of management and marketing executives.

I have saved until the end the golden text of my paper: Nearly two thousand years ago Seneca, the Roman philosopher, made this thoroughly modern observation: *"It is every man's duty to make himself profitable to mankind."* I wonder if that doesn't say it all.

NOTE

1. August, 1966.

8 Where Do Corporate Responsibilities Really Lie?

Arthur N. Lorig

We have seen, in the two preceding articles, contrasting views about social responsibility on the part of business. The obvious question is: To what extent are these also the views of business executives? Is "social responsibility" a myth with respect to business executives? Has the publicity given to the many books and articles exhorting managers to accept greater social responsibility overshadowed the reality of their actions? Few studies have been made to see how managers really do feel about their social roles; this paper presents one of those that have been recorded.

To whom do top corporate executives feel most responsible? To society, as some claim? Or to a lesser group such as employees, stockholders, creditors, or customers? Some writers and university students—influenced, no doubt, by professors—insist that a corporation's chief responsibility is to society and that business decisions are made in accordance with that understanding. This is so contrary to my own belief and observations that I have undertaken to find the answer by going directly to those who administer corporations with a survey questioning where their chief loyalties do, indeed, lie.

The results of the survey were much as I expected: corporate executives do *not* feel their greatest responsibility is to society. Overwhelmingly, they reported that their chief responsibility was to stockholders as the owners of business. No other group was even a close second. Responsibility to society ranked at the very bottom, far below the closest group.

Furthermore, no real difference was found between the views of top exectives (presidents and chairmen of boards of directors) and the controllers and financial executives. And, perhaps surprisingly, no discernible difference resulted from variation in size of corporations. The executives of corporations with annual sales of over $1 billion felt almost exactly as those of corporations with sales under $50 million. (Corporations with annual sales

Reprinted from Arthur N. Lorig, "Where Do Corporate Responsibilities Really Lie?" *Business Horizons* (Spring, 1967), Vol. 10, pp. 51–54, by permission of the author and the publisher.

under $1 million were not included in the survey, for their executives are not likely to regard responsibility to society as an important consideration in their operations.)

The Survey   Questionnaires were sent to 300 companies in the United States. (The companies selected were the odd-numbered ones in the list of 600 used by the American Institute of Certified Public Accountants in compiling its 1965 edition of *Accounting Trends and Techniques*.) The questionnaire listed groups interested in corporations (creditors, employees, society as a whole, stockholders, and others to be written in) and requested that responsibilities to them be ranked 1, 2, 3, and so forth. Groups of similar importance were to be given the same rank.

One-half of the questionnaires were sent to the corporation presidents, who sometimes were also the chairmen of the boards of directors. In a few instances, answering the questionnaire was delegated by the president to another executive such as a vice president or director of public relations. The remaining questionnaires were mailed to the controller or, if none was listed in *Poor's Register of Corporations,* to the treasurer or other chief financial officer. Two groups were used because it was thought that the officers dealing with finances might regard corporate responsibilities differently than do presidents. As mentioned previously, this was not the case.

To be certain that answers would be given freely and frankly, no identifying names or symbols were used on the questionnaires or return envelopes. Executives were invited to write out their views in letter form; some chose to do this, usually to explain their views at length or to state why they elected not to participate in the survey. The other respondents are unknown.

One hundred and fifty-two usable responses were received. An additional nine indicated the executives could not, or chose not to, rank their group responsibilities. Seven more ranked all groups equally and hence were omitted when the tabulation was completed. It is significant that a total of 173 replies was received, constituting a 58 per cent response. Considering the work pressures, the response was gratifying.

Results   The figures tell the story clearly. Table 1 presents the assignments of rank 1. The tally of rank 1 assignments in Table 1 is slightly greater than the number of responses used because some executives assigned rank 1 to more than one group. Some gave no ranking whatsoever to certain groups; hence, only one group, the stockholders, has a full 152 rankings. Customers as an important group were not included in the questionnaire list, but thirty-four executives added that group as a write-in. Other write-ins, such as suppliers and government, were very few and were ranked quite far down, none being ranked first.

With 84.2 per cent of the respondents ranking the stockholders as the

TABLE 1   Summary of Rank 1 Designations

	Times Group was Ranked	Times Group was Given Rank 1	Percentage of Responses Given Rank 1
Chief Executives			
Stockholders	72	59	81.9
Employees	66	8	12.1
Customers	23	6	26.1
Creditors	51	6	11.8
Society	55	3	5.5
Controllers and Finance Executives			
Stockholders	80	69	86.2
Employees	76	8	10.5
Customers	11	0	0.0
Creditors	73	8	11.0
Society	70	0	0.0
Total			
Stockholders	152	128	84.2
Employees	142	16	11.3
Customers	34	6	17.6
Creditors	124	14	11.3
Society	125	3	2.4

group to which they owe greatest responsibility and only 2.4 per cent placing society as a whole in that rank, the evidence is conclusive that corporations are considered by the responding executives to be instruments of the stockholders, not society. However, several pointed out that providing a profitable operation for the stockholders served to benefit society as a whole. The reasoning usually was not given, but some hints appeared occasionally. For example, one executive stated that "no business can long expect to maximize profits [for the stockholders] unless it also consistently makes available to its customers products and services of competitive quality at competitive prices . . . and serves the basic interests of the society in which it is organized." Several mentioned that if the stockholders, employees, and customers were treated properly, society as a whole would be served. On the other hand, a couple of warnings were given that management does not have the right to utilize the assets and power of the corporation to carry out personal, political, or social viewpoints that are not demonstrably in the best interests of the shareholders.

Much the same information and conclusions are obtained by comparing the average ranks assigned to the various groups. Table 2 presents this comparison. The average group rankings for different sizes of corporations were also determined; sizes were measured by the annual sales reported on the questionnaires. Table 3 compares these rankings and discloses no appreciable difference in rank assignments because of corporate size.

TABLE 2   Average Ranks Assigned to Groups

	Times Group Was Ranked	Average Rank
Chief Executives		
Stockholders	72	1.28
Employees	66	2.20
Customers	23	2.22
Creditors	51	2.92
Society	55	3.78
Controllers and Finance Executives		
Stockholders	80	1.20
Employees	76	2.16
Customers	11	2.55
Creditors	73	2.75
Society	70	3.91
Total		
Stockholders	152	1.24
Employees	142	2.18
Customers	34	2.32
Creditors	124	2.82
Society	125	3.86

TABLE 3   Average Ranks by Size of Corporation as Determined by Sales

Sales ($ millions)	Stockholders	Employees	Customers	Creditors	Society
$5–50	1.25	2.05	2.00	2.85	3.79
50–500	1.23	2.18	2.56	2.80	3.95
500–1,000	1.33	2.29	2.60	2.68	3.70
Over 1,000	1.10	2.24	1.80	3.14	3.81
All corporations	1.24	2.18	2.32	2.82	3.86

Reasoning Behind the Rankings   The questionnaires invited the executives to give the reasons behind their selections for first rank; in most cases they complied. The reasons offered for ranking the stockholder group first were that (1) stockholders are the corporate owners; (2) stockholders, through their representatives the boards of directors, hire the executives to run the business; (3) stockholders created the corporations to make a profit for them and they take the greatest risk; and (4) the executives hold a trust or stewardship relationship toward the stockholders' properties and are accountable for those properties. Several replies were to the effect that if the stockholders' interests were safeguarded properly, those of the other groups would automatically be taken care of.

Some interesting single reasons were given also: the corporation is an economic, not a social, institution—a pooling of resources for profit; stockholders have a responsibility to society, but the corporation does not; stockholders are the primary source of new funds; and, first responsibility to the stockholders is necessary in building the company image. Several vigorous declarations were received—it is inconceivable to rank stockholders other than first; it is the American way of life.

The reasons given by those ranking other groups first (such as creditors, customers, and employees) dwelt upon the importance of the group to the operation of the corporation. The few executives insisting that all groups should be ranked equally also used this line of thought—the essential nature of each group to the corporation's existence and successful operation. As one executive stated, "Which of your children do you love the most? It is like riding a bicycle—you must keep your balance."

Probably no better summarization could be found of the prevailing attitude of top executives toward groups of principal concern to corporations than the letter received from a vice-president of a corporation with multi-billion dollar annual sales. It accompanied the return of the questionnaire and is quoted with his permission.

In the . . . Company, the stockholder is regarded as the owner of the business. Dividends are viewed as distribution of profits. While acknowledging our considerable responsibilities to all other groups our prime responsibility is still to the owners as it is in all other forms of business organization. Although the interests of the various groups occasionally conflict and the short-term resolution may appear to be inconsistent with stockholder interest, each decision is made with the long-term interest of the stockholder in mind.

Every business enterprise is formed with one basic objective—to make a profit. The fundamental economics of capitalism is the formation of capital with the objective of producing a profit for the owners. This is undoubtedly more obvious in smaller corporations where owner and manager are the same. In our opinion, it becomes even more important that this fundamental be recognized as a company becomes larger. Profits benefit all other groups through the creation of jobs, payment of taxes, etc., but the stockholder is the prime beneficiary and is most directly interested in increasing the wealth position of the company. Other groups have their own interests and responsibilities which are naturally oriented toward self-interest. Creditors are interested in company well-being primarily from the standpoint of solvency. Employees are vital to the success of a business and their loyalty is coveted by management, but the majority of them are primarily interested in the preservation and security of their own jobs rather than in the creation of new ones. Society as a whole is a little remote from the individual company and, of course, has many interests of which business is only one. Customers want high quality at the lowest possible cost and will go elsewhere, as they should, if the company cannot meet their requirements. Communities are interested in local purchases, job stability, and tax revenues and are fearful of volatile-type businesses. There is an interrelationship of all these interests and the corporation must be responsive and responsible to all of them within its own objectives and limitations. These responsibilities cannot be met without profits, and profits will not result unless corporate obligations are met.

The stewardship function of management has tended to become somewhat blurred in the emphasis on the income statement, earnings per share, and "growth," but the preservation of capital is still a basic responsibility to the stockholder and almost all spending proposals consider return on investment and risk as major criteria. Motivations vary among individual managers, but our officers and directors recognize there are limitations to the risks that can be taken with company assets.

A principal criterion of success of a company is its ability to raise substantial amounts of long-term capital at favorable cost. The stockholder is the basic source of this capital. Unless his long-term objectives are met, there will be no funds and, hence, no fulfillment of other responsibilities and obligations of the corporation. In this particular area, the management and stockholders are particularly well attuned. Both are interested in long-term 'growth.' Individual manager motivation may be prestige, personal reward, sense of accomplishment, or other things, but the basic objective is the same for both groups.

Last, but far from least, is that the stockholder has a recourse other than selling his stock to register dissatisfaction—the vote. This is not legal fiction. Even in the largest corporation, the proxy fight is not impossible. It happens just enough to sober any manager who may tend to identify the company as something separate from the stockholders. Stockholder relations activities are increasing throughout the country. More and more information about company activities is disbursed to stockholders.

This is partly because the stockholder has a right to know as an owner and partly because he can be a source of capital, may be a customer, and can be an ambassador of the company in the community, all of which contributes to the mutual objectives of the company and its owners and also to the special interests of other groups.

QUESTIONS FOR DISCUSSION

1. Select one public issue and explain what the "social responsibility" of business is with respect to it.
2. Is it fair to stockholders for a corporation to consider social objectives in addition to making a profit?
3. What do you think of the argument "There is no such thing as social responsibility. What goes under the guise of that phrase are really actions taken to pursue the long-run interests of the corporation."
4. What do *you* think the social and ethical responsibilities of *marketing* executives should be?
5. Should customers, the public, or the government have a seat on a firm's board of directors to help guide that corporation into socially responsible actions?
6. Do you think that there is a fundamental conflict among morality, law, and sound business objectives?
7. What checks and balances should firms establish if they want to act in a "socially responsible" way?

8. If the enterprise has responsibilities to the consumer, the consumer has responsibilities to the firm. What should these be? How can they be enforced? Are they reliable?
9. What role should the government play—if any—in establishing the extent and kind of social responsibility of the private enterprise?

SUGGESTED READINGS

Boorstin, Daniel J., "Welcome to the Consumption Community", *Fortune* (September, 1967), Vol. 76, pp. 118–138.

Bowen, Howard R., *Social Responsibilities of the Businessman* (New York: Harper & Row, 1953).

Clasen, Earl A., "Marketing Ethics and the Consumer", *Harvard Business Review* (January–February, 1967), Vol. 45, pp. 79–86.

Davis, Keith, and Robert L. Blomstrom, *Business and Its Environment* (New York: McGraw-Hill Book Co., Inc., 1966).

Eells, Richard, and Clarence C. Walton, *Conceptual Foundations of Business* (Homewood, Illinois: Richard D. Irwin, Inc., 1961).

Farmer, Richard N., "The Revolutionary American Businessman", *California Management Review* (Summer, 1967), Vol. 9, No. 4, pp. 79–84.

Finley, Grace J., "Business Defines Its Social Responsibilities", *Conference Board Record* (November, 1967), Vol. 4, pp. 9–12.

Hollander, Stanley C., "Social Pressures and Retail Competition", *Business Topics* (Winter, 1965), Vol. 13, pp. 7–14.

Kelley, Eugene J., "Marketing and Moral Values in an Acquisitive Society", *Marketing: A Maturing Discipline* (Proceedings of the Winter Conference Chicago: American Marketing Association, December, 1960), pp. 195–203.

Levitt, Theodore, "The Dangers of Social Responsibility", *Harvard Business Review* (September–October, 1958), Vol. 36, p. 44.

Patterson, James M., "What Are the Social and Ethical Responsibilities of Marketing Executives?" *Journal of Marketing* (July, 1966), Vol. 30, pp. 12–15.

Taylor, John F. A., "Is the Corporation Above the Law?" *Harvard Business Review* (March–April, 1965), Vol. 43, No. 2, p. 126.

Weiss, E. B., "Marketers Fiddle While Consumers Burn", *Harvard Business Review* (July–August, 1968), Vol. 46, No. 4, pp. 45–53.

section 4 the consumer faces marketing

The cutting edge of criticism concerning businessmen and their "lack of social responsibility" has, in general, been created by intellectual critics — social philosophers, economists, journalists. Such criticism calls attention to problems, creates a rationale for analysis, and proposes solutions.

To the extent, however, that these problems represent real difficulties or inequities or evils, they must be perceived by the public, that is to say, by the American consumer. A consumer movement, as a reaction to business and marketing practices versus consumer interest, is over a hundred years old. However, only within the last decade has this movement become so prominent as to be accorded the label "consumerism."

Consumerism essentially takes three forms. In the first place, it often has a direct impact on the business via the old rule that "the squeaking axle gets the grease." In other words, if the complaints are audible enough, they are likely to get attention.

Secondly, consumer feelings tend, by and large, to remain dormant under the caption "You can't fight City Hall." Nevertheless, a combination of exposé and intermittent public anger together with the educational efforts of the critics, generates periods from time to time when strong pressure is brought upon legislators for corrective action. Currently, we appear to be in the middle of such a period. Perhaps more education for larger segments of the public may also be changing permanently the shape of consumers-to-be.

Finally, some Americans are seeking consumer information and thus are becoming more sophisticated buyers. The growth of consumer testing organizations is testimony to this fact.

In this section we shall examine the rise and meaning of consumerism, legislative reactions to it, and some managerial perceptions of its meaning and importance.

9 The Consumer Movement in Historical Perspective

Robert O. Herrmann

"Consumerism" is sure to be one of the key words of the 1970s. It affects marketing at two points. First, it is obviously related to the entire scope of questions about marketing ethics. Much of that dilemma centers on the question: Is what marketing men are doing fair and just to their customers?

Second, it furnishes a new dimension to the question of consumer behavior. It seems clear that the consumer movement itself, if and as it broadens and deepens, will have powerful effects on consumer motives, attitudes, and actions.

Nevertheless, today's interest in consumerism should not be viewed as a space-age development. Since the early 1900s recurrent periods of consumer activity have had many characteristics in common with the present consumer movement. This article presents a brief history of the consumer movement as well as some predictions about its future.

· · ·

The situation of consumers and economic life of the country changed rapidly in the last four decades of the 19th century. Industrial output and employment increased five-fold. The population doubled, and the proportion living in urban areas rose from 20 to 40 per cent. During the period, a national network of railroads was completed, creating the possibility of nationwide markets. A few manufacturers of consumer goods recognized the opportunity and began to trademark their wares and to advertise them in the new mass-circulation magazines.

The rapid growth of the cities and industrialization produced a new and unfamiliar set of problems—urban poverty, tenement housing, immigrant ghettos, municipal corruption, hazardous working conditions, sweat shops, child labor and a variety of consumer problems. . . .

A variety of local reform organizations concerned with local social problems and political reform appeared between 1890 and 1900. . . . The first Consumers' League, formed in New York City in 1891, began its work by

Robert O. Herrmann, *The Consumer Movement in Historical Perspective* (University Park, Pennsylvania: February, 1970), pp. 2–31. Reprinted with the permission of the author and the Department of Agricultural Economics and Rural Sociology. The Pennsylvania State University.

preparing a "white list" of shops which paid minimum fair wages, had reasonable hours and decent sanitary conditions. In 1898, the local groups joined in a national federation, the National Consumers' League, the first national consumers organization. By 1903, the national organization had grown to 64 branches in 20 states.

· · ·

The nationwide rail network and the development of refrigerated cars opened a national market to the food processors and meat packers. The packers' and canners' understanding of the principles of food preservation and bacteriology were, however, still rudimentary. Preservatives were used liberally to ensure freshness, or, at least, its appearance. Formaldehyde was added to canned meats, and canned peas were dosed with copper sulphate to produce the proper green shade of freshness. . . .

. . . The first general pure food measure was not introduced until the early 1890's. This bill seems to have elicited some substantial public support. Its sponsor, Senator Paddock, reported that 10,000 petitions supporting it had come to Congress. After amendments to meet Southern objections, the bill passed the Senate in 1892. The House, however, failed to take action and the bill died.

A second attempt to obtain a Pure Food law was begun in 1902. The bill made little headway, but support for new legislation was gathering. The General Federation of Women's Clubs, the National Consumers' League, and state food and dairy chemists joined together. The muckraker press publicized the dangers of adulterated and dyed food and the hazards of unlabeled patent medicines containing opiates and large quantities of alcohol. Although Pure Food bills twice passed the House, Republican opposition kept the bills from ever coming to a vote in the Senate.

After Theodore Roosevelt was elected in his own right in 1904, an attempt was made to enlist his support for pure food legislation. In his annual message to Congress the following year, Roosevelt urged the enactment of a pure food and drug law. Opposition to the bill in the Senate faded when the American Medical Association threatened a full-scale fight in its behalf. The bill was passed by the Senate on February 21, 1906, and disappeared into committee in the House. That same month, Upton Sinclair's *The Jungle*, an exposé of the working conditions in the Chicago packing houses, appeared. The public was nauseated by the graphic descriptions of adulteration techniques and the unsanitary conditions:

> These rats were nuisances, and the packers would put poisoned bread out for them and they would die, and then rats, bread and meat would go into the hoppers together. . . . Men, who worked in the tank rooms full of steam . . . fell into the vats; and when they were fished out, there was never enough of them to be worth exhibiting—sometimes they would be overlooked for days, till all but the bones of them had gone out to the world as Durham's Pure Leaf Lard!

The President's reaction was similar to the public's. He was, moreover, concerned about the deficiencies in federal inspection detailed in the book.

When two independent investigations bore out Sinclair's charges, Roosevelt put all his bulk behind the passage of meat inspection legislation. A rider to the agricultural appropriation bill providing for the expansion of the federal inspection bill was prepared and introduced in the Senate. It passed three days later without debate and without a dissenting vote. .

. . .

Sales of meat and meat products had dropped by half and it appeared that important European markets might be lost. Fearful that these losses might be permanent, the packers began to realize that a strengthened system of federal inspection was the only way to save their reputations. A substitute bill passed the House after a brief debate and without a roll call on June 19th. It was signed by the President on June 30th and went into effect the next day. The momentum created by the meat inspection issue had also carried the Pure Food Bill to the floor of the House where it was passed on June 23rd. It also was signed into law on June 30th.

[In 1906] the fight for the pure food law finally [was] won, but only after years of effort, the help of a full-scale scandal and strong pressure from a powerful president.

. . .

The Second Era: Consumer incomes rose gradually in the 1920's, while prices re-
The 1930's   mained relatively stable. . . . Sales of autos, refrigerators, vac-
                      uum cleaners, radios and phonographs were brisk. Consumers
were flooded with advertising from billboards, electric signs, newspapers, magazines and the new medium of radio. . . .

Although consumer problems aroused little interest among the general public, educators began to recognize the need for more and better consumer education. Consumer problems had been a major concern of Home Economists from the formative years of their association at the turn of the century. In the mid-Twenties, spurred by concern about the "scanty amount of economics in our home economics," they began new research into consumer problems to provide the information needed to improve teaching in the area. . . .

As the decade passed, vague discontent grew among consumers who were deeply involved in purchasing new and unfamiliar consumer durables and a growing array of other new products with little information to go on except that gleaned from the deluge of advertising to which they were subjected. This discontent found expression in 1927 in *Your Money's Worth*, a book by Stuart Chase and F. J. Schlink. The book, subtitled "A Study in the Waste of the Consumer's Dollar," vehemently attacked advertising and high-pressure salesmanship and called for scientific testing and product standards to provide consumers with the technical information they needed to make purchase decisions. The book gave expression to a widely felt concern. . . .

At the close of their book, Chase and Schlink proposed the formation of a consumer-sponsored organization to do product testing and described the testing activities of a local "Consumers' Club" at White Plains, New York. The stream of inquiries from the readers of *Your Money's Worth* soon convinced Schlink that the local Consumers' Club he had organized should be expanded. In 1929, Consumers' Research, Inc. was formed to perform this testing work on a larger scale.

The new organization was only one of a number of new product testing laboratories which appeared in the late 1920's. The potential of scientific testing of consumer goods was accepted widely; several major department stores and trade associations also began testing laboratories about this time.

. . .

The depression gave new immediacy to consumer education. Emphasis was given to identifying the best buys at the lowest cost and to frugal management. Consumers were urged: "Wear it out, use it up, make it do." Inexpensive substitutes for heavily advertised products were suggested and students practiced making their own toothpaste and face creams. Budgeting was taught as a device for cutting down on expenditures.

. . .

Weakened by court decisions and out-dated by new technology, the Pure Food and Drug Act of 1906 was, by the 1930's, badly in need of revision. Early in the 1930's, the New Deal administration did offer a new bill, inspired, as legend has it, by FDR's own reading of Kallet's and Schlink's *100,000,000 Guinea Pigs*. The bill, written in the Food and Drug Administration but often attributed to its administration sponsor, brain-truster Rexford Tugwell, would have extended FDA powers to include not only labeling but newspaper and magazine advertising as well. Cosmetics were to be placed under FDA control along with food and drugs. In addition, definite label information and the grade labeling of food were called for.

The FDA dramatized the need for new legislation with an exhibit of useless and dangerous patent medicines, unsafe cosmetics and unadulterated foods. The exhibit, dubbed "The Chamber of Horrors" by the press, showed quack cures for cancer and tuberculosis and included tragic before and after pictures such as the ones of a once pretty matron blinded by Lashlure, an eyelash dye. When hearings began on the bill in 1933, the American Home Economics Association and the National Congress of Parents and Teachers were the only groups actively supporting it. The opposition damned the bill as an interference with consumer choice and "the right of self-medication." The newspapers, cowed by fear of lost advertising revenue, or for other reasons, gave little attention to the bill.

In 1935, FDR sent a message to Congress urging the new legislation but never gave the measure full support, apparently because of a feeling that he should reserve his political clout for more important measures. Nor did the bill get much support from Henry Wallace, in whose department the FDA was housed, since Wallace viewed the proposed legislation as a city-dweller's bill. The battle continued and in 1936, Ruth De F. Lamb's *The American Chamber of Horrors* documented the FDA's case in print and carried it to a wider audience. Gradually opposition to the bill by special interests drew more concerned groups into the fight. By the end of the five year fight, 16 national women's organizations had become involved.

A shocking new tragedy seems to have provided the final impetus for Congressional action. In 1937, a liquid form of one of the new sulfa wonder drugs was placed on the market. Although the drug was safe enough in capsule form, its liquid form, *Elixir Sulfanilamide,* proved lethal and nearly 100 died. A new section quickly was added to the proposed bill requiring that manufacturers prove the safety of new drugs to the satisfaction of the FDA before placing them on the market. Substantial changes had occurred in the rest of the bill in the course of five years of hearings and controversy, the grade-labeling provisions had been dropped and the responsibility for control of advertising had been given to the Federal Trade Commission. Business opposition had softened, the newer versions of the bill were much more acceptable than the early ones, and the damage which continuing opposition to the bill could do to public relations was coming to be recognized. Finally in June 1938, a much modified version of the bill, too weak to suit either Tugwell or the militants in the consumer testing organizations, was passed.

By the late 1930's, the impact of the consumer movement had become a subject of increasing concern to the business community. In order to gauge the impact of the movement on public opinion, the Advertising Research Foundation commissioned a national survey by Dr. George Gallup. In 1940 Gallup reported that about a quarter of those questioned in his study had read one of the "Guinea Pig" books and about half of this group said they had changed their buying habits as a result of what they had read. About one-fifth had read research reports of one of the product rating services. While about half favored the idea of compulsory grade labeling, about three-quarters admitted that they were willing to pay more for nationally known brands. About half favored stricter regulation of advertising content. Slightly less than half favored the idea of a new cabinet department to represent the interests of consumers. Gallup found that the movement had developed its greatest strength among teachers, the higher incomes and the more intelligent and among the young. He concluded that the movement had made considerable headway and was likely to continue to grow because of its strength among influential groups.

**The Third Era:
The 1960's**   The tempo of activity in the consumer movement and its impact had increased throughout the Thirties. Consumerism undoubtedly would have gained even greater influence in the next few years if the coming of World War II had not diverted all attention to the problem of national survival. . . .

With the end of the war, [Consumers Union's] circulation began a remarkable upward climb as consumers sought product information to guide them in spending their wartime savings. Circulation grew from 50,000 in

1944 to almost a half million in 1950. There was, however, little activity among grass-roots consumer organizations. . . .

.   .   .

Despite the relative quiet of the Fifties, flare-ups of consumer concern did occur. One such incident came after the publication of Vance Packard's *The Hidden Persuaders* in 1957. Packard, accepting the ad agencies' and market researchers' claims about their powers at face value, argued that the public was being manipulated without realizing it. The resulting round of charges and counter-charges received extensive press coverage and showed that, given the right issues, there still was public interest in consumer problems.

The beginning of the third era of the consumer movement often is dated from John F. Kennedy's Consumer Message to the Congress in Spring 1962. In fact, Kennedy's influence may have begun even earlier. Arthur Schlesinger, Jr. has pointed out that, in his 1960 campaign, Kennedy "communicated, first of all, a deeply critical attitude toward the ideas and institutions which American society had come in the Fifties to regard with such enormous self-satisfaction." . . .

In the preamble to his Consumer Message to Congress in March 1962, President Kennedy enunciated the now famous Consumer Bill of Rights: (1) the right to safety, (2) the right to be informed, (3) the right to choose and (4) the right to be heard. The main body of the message outlined needed improvements in existing programs and needed new programs. The regulation of food and drugs was one of the areas singled out for special attention. The weaknesses of the existing laws in ensuring that drugs on the market were both effective and safe had become clear in the course of the Senator Kefauver's hearings on the regulation of the drug industry. The new legislation was passed only after a new tragedy, as appalling as those which produced legislation in 1906 and 1938, forced action upon the Congress. Word of the thalidomide case reached the public in June; by August, legislation expanding the powers of the FDA had been passed and signed into law.

.   .   .

About this same time, a new surge of interest in consumer education occurred. Educators and the public both came to recognize that consumer education was an important and useful subject for all students, college-bound and vocational, and boys and girls alike. Consumer education, with its real-life problems, was found to be a useful method of arousing student interest in topics in English, math, social studies and science. The new curricula continued to stress both buymanship techniques and money management, and gave new emphasis to the problems and uses of installment credit. New emphasis also was given to the idea that one's spending should reflect personal goals, rather than someone else's idea of a good budget.

.   .   .

CU continued to grow rapidly during the Fifties. By its 25th anniversary in 1961, it was publishing nearly a million copies per issue of *Consumer*

Reports with an estimated readership of 4 million. CU increasingly came to view itself as an organization to promote consumer education, rather than simply as a product testing agency. It concerned itself with educating consumers about all phases of their relationship with the consumer market: interest rates, guarantees and warranties, life insurance, product safety, and choosing a doctor.

In addition, CU has devoted a significant portion of its budget to the educational and organizational aspects of the consumer movement. It has inspired and financed much of the consumer movement, providing it with a stable organizational base as well as leadership. It has sponsored conferences on consumer problems throughout the country, supplied expert testimony at government hearings and worked with a variety of adult education groups in developing consumer education programs.

. . . CU has attracted chiefly those with higher incomes and better educations. In 1969, the median income of its members was about $14,000.

· · ·

In January 1964, President Johnson created the new White House post, Special Assistant for Consumer Affairs, and appointed Esther Peterson to fill it. In Esther Peterson the President had found an experienced publicist and organizer. A strong personality, and outspoken in expressing her views, Mrs. Peterson made the consumer and his problems front-page news. . . .

· · ·

After the liberal landslide in the election of 1964, the possibilities for new consumer legislation brightened. In the spring and summer of 1965, hearings were held on tire and auto safety. The hearings revealed to shocked senators the lack of any deep concern over safety problems in either industry. The auto safety hearings, however, ended on an inconclusive note after attention was diverted from the manufacturer's responsibilities for auto safety by arguments which placed the responsibility for auto safety on the driver.

This view was challenged a few months later when Ralph Nader's *Unsafe at Any Speed* presented evidence of the role of faulty engineering, construction and design in auto accidents and injuries. Public concern mounted and, in his State of the Union message in January 1966, President Johnson promised new legislation. In March, hearings began on the administration's Highway Safety Act of 1966. When the news of General Motors' investigation of Nader's background and activities broke, Congressional opinion was thoroughly alienated. The safety legislation passed later that year was significantly stronger than the bill originally proposed by the White House.

The time also was propitious for another important piece of consumer legislation. Senator Philip Hart's "Truth in Packaging" Bill was passed and signed into law in late 1966 after 5 years of Congressional inaction.

Consumer prices continued to rise gradually up to the middle Sixties. Food prices and the all items index each increased about 1 per cent a year between 1960 and 1965. After this relative stability, the 5 per cent increase in food prices in 1966 came as a major jolt to consumers. . . . The buy-

ing power of many groups in the population had increased gradually or just
kept pace with price increases after the recessions of the early Sixties. Suddenly these groups were faced with an actual decline in purchasing power.
Consumer discontent found open expression in October in a wave of consumer boycotts of food stores which began in Denver. Store contests and
games, which had been used widely in the previous year received most of
the housewives' blame and were the target of their attack, although the real
problem was short supplies of meat and produce.

. . . In his State of the Union Message and his Consumer Affairs message in February [1968], the President called for passage of a long list of
consumer bills. During the course of the year, a "Truth-in-Lending" Bill
finally was passed, 8 years after the original bill was introduced by Senator
Paul Douglas. Other new legislation on poultry inspection, pipeline safety,
fraudulent land sales and hazardous appliance radiation also were passed.

**The Past
as Prologue**   It seems clear that the consumer movement is destined to be a
recurring if not a permanent feature of the American scene. The
movement has arisen as a reaction to three persisting problem
areas (1) ill-considered applications of new technology which result in dangerous or unreliable products, (2) changing conceptions of the social responsibilities of business and (3) the operations of a dishonest fringe and
the occasional lapses of others in the business community. There is little
reason to believe that any of these problem areas ever will disappear completely. Historically, consumers have been most sensitive to these problems
in periods when consumer purchasing power is under pressure from rising
prices.

The history of the consumer movement demonstrates that new technology
frequently has been applied without full understanding of or concern for
its potential dangers. The automobile had been around for seventy years
before Ralph Nader got general recognition of the fact that autos included
unsafe design features and sometimes were ill-engineered. Although the dangers of incompletely understood new technology have been most dramatic
in the area of food and drugs, new legislation to control these dangers has
come only after some dramatic revelation has focused public opinion on the
problem. This legislation often has come long after the problem was first
recognized.

The consumer no longer judges business on its products alone, but also
on the social costs involved in producing them. The public's ideas of what
constitutes a social cost have evolved rapidly in the past 70 years. The
passage of the Pure Food and Drug Act and the Meat Inspection amendment in 1906 recognized the social costs of injurious drugs and adulterated

and contaminated food. The work of the Consumers' Leagues brought public recognition that unsafe working conditions, long hours and the exploitation of child and female labor also had social costs. Gradually the public view expanded again to include air pollution and water pollution as social costs. Now a new group of factors, which may seem even less tangible, is coming to be regarded as social costs. These include discriminatory hiring practices, unnecessarily rigid job qualifications, locational decisions which ignore areas of high unemployment, neglect of the needs of the low-income consumer, failure to provide retail competition in ghetto areas and the use of legal tactics and biased laws against poorly educated and powerless installment debtors.

Step by step, the concept of the social responsibility of business has been broadened to include not only its relations with its shareholders, but also with its competitors, its customers, its employees, its neighbors and now is coming to include those who are neither its customers or employees but perhaps could and should be.

A narrow definition of the consumer interest might deal solely with safe, reasonably priced and accurately labeled products. To its credit, the consumer movement has never defined the consumer interest so narrowly, but has come to include more and more aspects of the social cost of business in its considerations.

The business community can and should expect continuing challenge from the consumer movement since there is little reason to believe that the same problems which have perpetuated the movement in [the] past will not continue in the future. The application of new technology will continue to produce problems. The public's concept of responsible business behavior will continue to evolve. And until the millennium arrives, fraud and dishonesty seem likely to persist. Consumer concern with these problems is likely to continue to be especially acute as long as the current period of inflation persists.

In the past, business has fought the consumer movement bitterly, resisting its charges and responding with its own accusations. If Ralph Nader's observation is correct and the consumer movement is moving from ideology to ethics as a basis for action, business' old pattern of response will become less and less appropriate. If the consumer movement is moving from the role of an implacable, ideologically motivated foe to that of a reasonable advocate of a documented case, it, more than ever, deserves a fair hearing. In the future, the business community may be better advised to regard the consumer movement as an early warning system for impending trouble rather than as the unappeasable enemy of the past.

10 A Guide to Consumerism

George S. Day
David A. Aaker

In the previous article we were able to learn something about the development of a consumer movement in this country. Today, the movement is widely identified as "consumerism." The rapid growth of this movement is by now an obvious fact. In this article, the authors seek to interpret the underlying causes for the consumerist upsurge and to give some indication of where it is taking us.

Consumerism has played an expanding role in the environment of business decision makers. Despite wishful thinking by some, the following analysis of consumerism is as relevant today as it was in 1964 when it was writtten:

1. As evidenced by consumer agitation at the local-state-federal levels, business has failed to meet the total needs and desires of today's consumers.
2. Into this business-created vacuum, government forces have quickly moved to answer this consumer need.
3. The areas of consumer interest are so diverse that they offer government agencies and legislators almost limitless reasons for additional regulation of business and commerce.
4. If business managers want to avoid such new government regulations (with the attendant possibilities of excessive and punitive legislation), they will have to take positive action to demonstrate that the business interest is in more general accord with the consumer's needs and wants.[1]

The ensuing six years has seen the passage of considerable consumerism legislation and a substantial broadening of the concept's scope. During this period one constant factor has been a lack of agreement on the extent of the influence of consumerism or its long-range implications. Businessmen have suffered from a myopia that comes from perceiving consumerism primarily in terms of markets with which they are very familiar. Their emphasis on the peculiarities of these few markets often leads them to overlook similar problems in other contexts and, thus, to discount the seriousness of the overall problem they face. Legislators and members of the consumer movement are more responsive to the broad problems facing consumers, but their lack of understanding of specific market situations too often leads to inappropriate diagnoses and solutions. Fortunately the two basic perspec-

Reprinted from George S. Day and David A. Aaker, "A Guide to Consumerism", *Journal of Marketing* (July, 1970), Vol. 34, pp. 12–19; by permission of the authors and the American Marketing Association.

tives are demonstrating a healthy convergence. The goal of this paper is to encourage this convergence by putting consumerism into a perspective that will facilitate understanding.

The Scope of Consumerism   The term *consumerism* appears to be uniquely associated with the past decade. Even in this short period it has undergone a number of changes in meaning. Vance Packard, one of the earliest adopters of the term, linked consumerism with strategies for persuading consumers to quickly expand their needs and wants by making them "voracious, compulsive (and wasteful)." [2] His usage clearly reflected the concerns of the fifties with planned obsolescence, declining quality, and poor service in saturated consumer goods markets. The term was not put to wider use until 1963 or 1964, when a variety of commentators identified it with the very visible concerns triggered indirectly by Rachel Carson, and directly by Ralph Nader's auto safety investigations and President Kennedy's efforts to establish the rights of consumers: to safety, to be informed, to choose, and to be heard. [3]

The most common understanding of consumerism is in reference to the *widening* range of activities of government, business, and independent organizations that are designed to protect individuals from practices (of both business and government) that infringe upon their rights as consumers. This view of consumerism emphasizes the direct relationship between the individual consumer and the business firm. Because it is an evolving concept, there is no accepted list of the various facets of this relationship. The following is representative:

1. *Protection against clear-cut abuses.* This encompasses outright fraud and deceit that are a part of the "dark side of the marketplace," [4] as well as dangers to health and safety from *voluntary use of a product.* There is substantial agreement in principle between business and consumer spokesmen that such abuses must be prevented, but there is often a wide divergence of opinion on the extent of the problem. As a result the government has taken the initiative in this area, usually after the divulgence of a sensational abuse. This has been the case with much of the legislation dealing with drug, tire, auto, and pipeline safety, and meat and fish inspection. Even so, this is the least controversial and oldest aspect of consumerism.

2. *Provision of adequate information.* The concern here is with the economic interests of the consumer. The question is whether the right to information goes beyond the right not to be deceived, to include the provision of performance information that will ensure a wise purchase. Much of the controversy and confusion over consumerism revolves around this basic issue. [5] The two polar positions identified by Bauer and Greyser are the business view that the buyer should be guided by his judgment of the manufacturer's reputation and the quality of the brand, versus the view of the consumer spokesmen that information should be provided by impartial sources and reveal performance characteristics. [6]

3. *The protection of consumers against themselves and other consumers.* Some

of the thrust behind consumerism comes from the growing acceptance of the position that paternalism is a legitimate policy. Thus, the National Traffic and Motor Vehicle Safety Act of 1966 is not concerned with the possibility that the buyer has an expressed but unsatisfied need for safety, and emphasizes instead that carelessness may have undesirable consequences for innocent participants.[7] There is a sound basis in economic theory for such intervention whenever the action of a buyer serves only his own best interest and fails to take into account the effects on others. However, this principle is being extended to situations of "implied consumer interest" where the individual is deemed unable to even identify his own best interest (e.g., the mandatory installation of seat belts and the provision for a "cooling-off" period after a door-to-door sale). This is a strong justification for the protection of inexperienced, poorly educated, and generally disadvantaged consumers. More controversial by far is the extension of this notion to all consumers on the grounds that manipulated preferences may be disregarded when the consumer is not acting in his best interest.[8]

The above three facets of consumerism suggest the current thrust of the movement. Yet, it would be naïve to portray consumerism as a static entity. It has had a dynamic past and continues to evolve and change at an increasingly rapid rate. For example, the emphasis of the consumer movement of the thirties and later was on dangerous and unhealthy products and "dishonest or questionable practices which are believed to hamper the consumer in making wise decisions . . . and obtaining useful information." [9] The emphasis today is clearly much broader.

There is a high probability that the scope of consumerism will eventually subsume, or be subsumed by two other areas of social concern: distortions and inequities in the economic environment and the declining quality of the physical environment. The forecast of a greater identity between these social problems and consumerism rests on the fact that they are associated with many of the same basic causes, have common spokesmen, and seem to be moving in the same direction in many respects. Yohalem has indicated that the ultimate challenge of consumerism to industry is "toward ending hunger and malnutrition . . . toward alleviating pollution of the air, water and soil . . . toward educating and training the disadvantaged . . . toward solving these and other problems of a society rather than strictly of an industrial nature." [10]

Concern over the *economic environment* dates back to the end of the last century. The long-run manifestation of this concern has been antitrust law and enforcement, which has swung back and forth between protecting competition and protecting competitors. Despite various ambiguities in antitrust interpretation, this has been a major effort to ensure consumers' "right to choose" by increasing the number of competitors. Some regard it as "the fundamental consumer edifice on which all other measures are bottomed." [11] Judging from the recent intensification of concern over the economic role of advertising and promotion (insofar as they increase price and raise barriers to entry to new markets), reciprocity, restrictive distributive arrangements, conglomerate mergers, and related topics, it appears that antitrust issues will be a continuing impetus to consumerism. In a period of rapid inflation it is not surprising that advertising and promotion costs have come under additional scrutiny for their role in contributing to high prices, particularly food prices. This promises to be a durable issue, considering a task force of the White House conference on food, nutrition, and health has recommended lower food prices, by reducing promotion not related to nutritional or other food values, as a major item in a national nutrition policy.[12]

More recently, consumerism has become identified with the widespread concern with the quality of the *physical environment*. The problems of air, water, and noise pollution have become increasingly salient as the tolerance of the public for these abuses has decreased. In effect a "critical mass" of explosive concern has suddenly been created. The consumer movement has rapidly rearranged its priorities to become a part of this critical mass. This shift is not surprising in view of the desire to broaden consumerism to include problems arising from indirect influences on the consumer interest. It also follows naturally from the long standing concern with built-in obsolescence and poor quality and repairability, for these problems contribute to pollution in a "disposable" society.

As the consumer movement joins with conservationists and interested legislators there is a growing likelihood of government action. The argument for such intervention has been well stated by Andrew Shonfield:

> Increasingly the realization is forced upon us that the market, which purports to be the reflection of the way in which people spontaneously value their individual wants and efforts, is a poor guide to the best means of satisfying the real wishes of consumers. That is because market prices generally fail to measure either social costs or social benefits. In our civilization these grow constantly more important. Simply because some amenity—let it be a pleasant view or an uncongested road or a reasonably quiet environment—is not paid for directly by those who enjoy it, there is no measure of the cost of the disinvestment which occurs when a profitable economic activity destroys what already exists. Unless the State actively intervenes, and on an increasing scale, to compel private enterprise to adapt its investment decisions to considerations such as these, the process of economic growth may positively impede the attainment of things that people most deeply want.[13]

The result may well be increased controls on producer-controlled emittants and, perhaps, "quality standards . . . or other regulatory devices in the interest of upgrading product quality and repairability." [14]

The Underlying Causes of Consumerism   Additional insights come from a consideration of the factors underlying the recent upsurge of interest in consumerism. It appears that increasingly discontented and aroused consumers have combined with a growing number of formal and informal institutions capable of focusing discontent, to create enough pressure to overcome the advantage of the traditionally more effective lobbies representing the producer's interests. Since a particular government action means much more to the individual producer (who will be totally affected), than to the individual consumer (who divides his concern among many items), this clearly involved a significant effort.

The Discontented   The discontented consumer is not part of a homogeneous group
Consumer   with easily described complaints. The fact is great variation ex-
             ists among consumers in the extent of their discontent and there
is a wide variety of underlying causes. Nonetheless, it is possible to distinguish specific sources of discontent that are traceable to the marketing environment from other more pervasive concerns with the nature of society.

PROBLEMS IN THE MARKETPLACE: To some observers the leading problem is imperfections in the state of information in consumer markets.[15] They believe consumers would be adequately cared for by competition *if* they could learn quickly about available brands and their prices and characteristics. However, as products and ingredients proliferate, each consumer is less and less able to make useful price and quality comparisons. This inability leads to "increasing shopper confusion, consequent irritation and consequent resentment." [16] The problem is most severe for products which are purchased infrequently, exhibit a rapid rate of technological change, and whose performance characteristics are not readily apparent. Hence, increasing pressure is applied for tire standards, unit prices, truth-in-lending, truth-in-funds, information about the designlife of durable goods, and so on. The truth-in-packaging bill is another manifestation of this problem, for it aims to help the consumer cope with the volume of information available relative to grocery and drug products. Since advertising has not been notable as a source of adequate, or even accurate information that could alleviate the problem, it has been under continuing attack.[17] To the extent that retailing is becoming more and more impersonal, the whole situation may become worse. Thus,

> . . . as a result of the character of contemporary retail establishments, the vastly increased number of consumer products, and the misleading, deceptive and generally uninformative aspects of advertising and packaging, the consumer simply lacks the information necessary to enable him to buy wisely.[18]

This is not an unusually intemperate charge; nor is it denied by the finding that 53% of a sample of adults disagreed with the statement that, "In general, advertisements present a true picture of the product advertised." This response measures both a concern over genuine deception and differences in people's tolerance for fantasy.[19] Nonetheless the potential for dissatisfaction is large.

The proliferation and improvement of products, resulting from attempts to better satisfy specific needs and/or reduce direct competition, has also had other consequences. As one appliance executive noted, ". . . the public is staging a revolt of rising expectancy. Customers today expect products to perform satisfactorily, to provide dependable functional performance and to be safe. This threshold of acceptable performance is steadily rising. . . ." [20] Unfortunately the complexity and malfunction potential of many products has also been rising.[21] The result is an uncomfortable level of dissatisfaction with quality, compounded by inadequate service facilities.[22] This situation is not confined to hard goods, for one result of rapidly rising sales is overburdened retail and manufacturing facilities, which leads to deteriorating quality and service for almost all mass-merchandised goods.[23]

These problems are occurring at a time when consumers are generally less willing to give industry the benefit of the doubt—an understandable reaction to the well-publicized shortcomings of the drug, auto, and appliance manufacturers. Even without these problems, more skepticism is to be expected from consumers who have found that their assumptions about the adequacy of laws covering reasonable aspects of health, safety, and truthfulness are wrong. Recent disclosures involving such vital issues as meat inspection and auto and drug safety have hurt both government and industry by contributing to an atmosphere of distrust. According to Stanley Cohen, the meat inspection battle was particularly important here, "because for the first time the public had a clear cut demonstration of the jurisdictional gap (between state and federal governments) that limits the effectiveness of virtually all consumer protection legislation." [24]

PROBLEMS IN THE SOCIAL FABRIC: The present imperfections in the marketplace would probably not have generated nearly the same depth of concern in earlier periods. The difference is several changes deep in society that have served as catalysts to magnify the seriousness of these imperfections.

The first catalyst has been the new visibility of the low-income consumer. These consumers suffer the most from fraud, excessive prices, exorbitant credit charges, or poor quality merchandise and service. Unfortunately, solutions oriented toward improving the amount and quality of product information have little relevance to low-income buyers who lack most of the characteristics of the prototype middle-income consumer.[25]

Low income consumers are often unaware of the benefits of comparative shopping.
They lack the education and knowledge necessary to choose the best buy, even if it were available. Because of their low income they have fewer opportunities to learn through experience.
They often lack the freedom to go outside their local community to engage in comparative shopping.
They lack even a superficial appreciation of their rights and liabilities in post-sale legal conflicts.
Nothing in their experience has reinforced the benefits of seeking better value

for their money; consequently, the low-income buyer lacks the motivation to make improvements in his situation.

Thus, the low-income consumer environment is a perfect breeding ground for exploitation and fraud. The extent of the distortion in the ghetto marketplace has only recently been widely comprehended and related to the overall failure of society to help the disadvantaged.[26]

The second catalyst is best described as a basic dissatisfaction with the impersonalization of society in general, and the market system in particular. Evidence for this point of view is not difficult to find, particularly among young people. A survey of college student opinion found 65% of the sample in strong or partial agreement with the statement that "American society is characterized by injustice, insensitivity, lack of candor, and inhumanity." [27] Similar levels of disenchantment were reported among parents and nonstudents of the same age. The need seems to be felt for social organizations that are responsive—and perhaps the impression of responsiveness is as important as the specific responses that are made.

There is little doubt that large American corporations are not regarded as responsive by their customers. According to Weiss, both manufacturers and retailers are "turning a deaf ear," while increasingly sophisticated consumers are demanding more personal relationships and security in their purchases.[28] This situation stems from a series of changes in the marketing environment—the rise of self-service and discounting (in part because of the difficulty of obtaining good sales employees), the high cost of trained service personnel, and the intervention of the computer into the relationship with consequent rigidifying of customer policies and practices. The prospects for improvement are dim, because the benefits of good service and prompt personal attention to complaints are difficult to quantify and consequently are given low priority when investment decisions are made. As more consumers are seeing the government as being more sympathetic, if not more helpful, the prospect for arbitration procedures to settle complaints is increased.

The most disturbing feature of the catalyzing effects of the recently visible low-income consumer, the growing dissatisfaction with the impersonalization of society, and concern over the quality of the physical environment is their intractability. These problems are almost impervious to piecemeal attempts at correction. In view of the small likelihood of large-scale changes in social priorities or social structures, these problems will be a part of the environment, for the foreseeable future.

The final and most enduring catalyst is the consequence of an increasingly better educated consumer. The Chamber of Commerce recently noted that the consumer of the present and future "expects more information about the products and services he buys. He places greater emphasis on product performance, quality and safety. He is more aware of his 'rights' as a consumer and is more responsive than ever before to political initiatives to protect these rights." [29]

The Activist
Consumer
The discontented consumer found many more effective ways to express feelings and press for change during the 1960s than ever before. The development of means of translating discontent into effective pressure distinguishes recent consumer efforts from those of the 1910 and 1935 eras.

The consumer has been more ably represented by advocates such as Ralph Nader, Senator Warren Magnuson, and a number of journalists who pursue similar interests. These men are able to identify and publicize problems, and to follow up with workable programs for improvement. In a real sense, they are self-elected legal counsels to a typically unrepresented constituency. Many consumer problems would have remained smoldering but unfocused discontents without their attention. New product researchers have frequently found consumers do not seem to know what is bothering them or realize that others are similarly troubled until the extent of the problem is publicized or an alternative is provided.

The institutional framework has also been expanded and strengthened in recent years. Traditional bodies, such as Consumers Union and Consumers Research, Inc., have now received support from permanent bodies in the government such as the Consumer Advisory Council and the Office of the Special Assistant to the President for Consumer Affairs. These agencies have been specifically developed to avoid the problems of excessive identification with regulated industries which plague some of the older regulated bodies.

This decade has also seen greater willingness on the part of consumers to take direct action. Consider the protest of housewives in Denver over the costs of trading stamps and games. While this was probably due to general dissatisfaction over the effects of inflation on food prices, it did represent an important precedent. More sobering is the extreme form of protest documented by the National Commission on Civil Disorders. "Much of the violence in recent civil disorders has been directed at stores and other commercial establishments in disadvantaged Negro areas. In some cases, rioters focused on stores operated by white merchants who, they apparently believed, had been charging exorbitant prices or selling inferior goods. Not all the violence against these stores can be attributed to 'revenge' for such practices. Yet, it is clear that many residents of disadvantaged Negro neighborhoods believe they suffer constant abuses by local merchants." [30]

The Changing
Legal and
Political Scene
Pressures for change have been directed at a legal and political structure that is much more willing to take action than before:

1. Overall, there is more acceptance of government involvement in issues of consumer protection. Also, the federal government has been more prepared to take action because the state and local governments have generally defaulted their early legal responsibility in this area.[31]

2. A combination of factors has contributed to the expanded role of the

federal government. Congress is no longer so dominated by the rural constituencies who appear less interested in these matters; consumer legislation is relatively cheap and appears to generate goodwill among voters; and various tests of the influence of business lobbyists have shown that their power is not as great as originally feared.[32] In fact, many observers feel that industry may have been its own worst enemy by often opposing all consumer legislation without admitting any room for improvement or providing constructive alternatives.[33] Worse, they may have demonstrated that industry self-regulation is not workable.[34]

3. The consequence is a Congress that is responsive to the economic interests of consumers. A significant proportion of the enacted or pending legislation is a result of Congressional initiative and is directed toward ensuring that consumers have adequate and accurate shopping information. This is very different from earlier legislation which was enacted because a tragedy dramatized the need to protect health and safety.[35]

4. A large number of legal reforms have been slowly instituted which attempt to correct the imbalance of power held by the manufacturers; e.g., the expansion of the implied warranty, and the elimination of privity of contract.[36] Of special interest are current efforts to give the individual consumer more leverage by making the practice of consumer law profitable for attorneys. The mechanism being promoted is the consumer class action which permits suits by one or a few consumers on behalf of all consumers similarly abused.[37] This will make fraud cases, where individual claims are smaller than legal costs, much more attractive to investigate and litigate.

The Future of Consumerism   One of the main conclusions from past efforts to forecast social phenomena is that naïve extrapolations are likely to be wrong.

A better approach in this situation is to utilize the interpretation that consumerism is, at least partially, a reflection of many social problems that are certain to persist, and perhaps be magnified in the future. This diagnosis rules out the possibility that consumerism activity will decline significantly in the future; the unanswered questions concern the rate of increase in this activity and the areas of greatest sensitivity.

One index of activity, the amount of federal consumer legislation pending, should slow its rate of increase. Only a limited number of consumer bills can be considered at a time; over 400 such bills were pending in Congressional committees at the end of 1969.[38] Also more attention will have to be given to implementing and improving existing legislation, rather than writing new legislation. For example, there is evidence that the truth-in-lending bill will not achieve its original goals; partly because of lack of understanding of the problem and partly because of inadequacies and confusion in the enacted legislation.[39] Similarly, it is dismaying that after two years of experience with the truth-in-packaging bill it is being referred to as "one of the best non-laws in the book."[40] In this particular situation the problem seems to lie with the interest and ability of the various regulatory agencies to implement the law. This is not an isolated example of enforcement failures. The Food and Drug Administration (FDA) recently estimated that fewer than two-thirds of all food processors have complied with standards to prevent some forms of food contamination. One result has been an increased pressure for a powerful central consumer agency[41] to implement, modify and coordinate the 269 consumer programs that are presently administered by 33 different federal agencies.[42]

The very nature of the contemporary marketplace will probably continue to inhibit basic changes in business operations. Weiss points out some manufacturers and retailers will always equate responsible with legal behavior.[43] These tendencies are reinforced by the competitive structure of many markets where success depends on an ability to appeal directly to the "marginal float." One view of this group is that they constitute a minority who are "fickle . . . particularly susceptible to innovation that may not be relevant, and to attention getters such as sexy TV jokes or giveaway games."[44] While research support is lacking, this widely held view helps explain some of the behavior consumerists complain about.

There are signs that concerned parties are making efforts to rise above emotion to rationally identify and realistically attack the problems. Two major, if embryonic, research efforts are under way which aim at providing decision makers in business and government with empirically based knowledge to supplement the intuition on which they now too often solely rely. The first is the Consumer Research Institute sponsored by the Grocery Manufacturers Association, and the second is an effort by the Marketing Science Institute.[45] Although both research organizations have close ties with business, neither was established to justify or defend vested interests. Their objectives are to promote basic, academic research that will be respected by all parties. The MSI group specifically proposes to obtain participation at the research-design phase of each project of those who would potentially disagree about policy. Although the government now has no comparable effort, it is reasonable to expect movement in this direction. Cohen has suggested that the FTC should establish a Bureau of Behavioral Studies "whose function would be to gather and analyze data on consumer buying behavior relevant to the regulations of advertising in the consumer interest."[46]

An early study, which might be regarded as a prototype to the CRI and MSI efforts, experimentally examined the relationship between deceptive packaging (with respect to content weight) and brand preference.[47] It demonstrated that experimentation can provide useful information to policy makers.

These research approaches and the forces behind them should not only generate influential information, but should also help stimulate some basic changes in orientation. We can expect to see, for example, the simplistic "economic man" model of consumer behavior enriched.[48] The last decade has seen great progress made in the study of consumer behavior. This progress should contribute directly to a deeper analysis of consumerism issues. Hopefully, the dissemination of relevant knowledge will help eliminate present semantic problems.[49] Such a development must accompany rational discourse.

Business managers, whether progressive or defensive, can be expected to develop new, flexible approaches toward insuring that the rights of the consumer will be protected. Even though the motives may be mixed, there is no reason why effective programs cannot be developed.

NOTES

1. Tom M. Hopkins, "New Battleground—Consumer Interest," *Harvard Business Review,* Vol. 42 (September–October, 1964), pp. 97–104.
2. Vance Packard, *The Waste Makers* (New York: David McKay, 1960), p. 23.
3. Rachel Carson, *Silent Spring* (Boston, Mass.: Houghton Mifflin Company, 1962); Ralph Nader, *Unsafe At Any Speed* (New York: Pocket Books, 1966); and "Consumer Advisory Council, First Report," Executive Office of the President (Washington, D.C.: U.S. Government Printing Office, October, 1963).
4. Senator Warren Magnuson and Jean Carper, *The Dark Side of the Marketplace* (Englewood Cliffs: Prentice-Hall, 1968).
5. *Freedom of Information in the Market Place* (Columbus, Mo.: F.O.I. Center, 1967).
6. Raymond A. Bauer and Stephen A. Greyser, "The Dialogue That Never Happens," *Harvard Business Review,* Vol. 45 (November – December, 1967), p. 2.
7. Robert L. Birmingham, "The Consumer As King: The Economics of Precarious Sovereignty," *Case Western Reserve Law Journal,* Vol. 20 (May, 1969).
8. Same reference as footnote 7, p. 374.
9. Fred E. Clark and Carrie P. Clark, *Principles of Marketing* (New York: The Macmillan Company, 1942), p. 406.
10. Aaron S. Yohalem, "Consumerism's Ultimate Challenge: Is Business Equal to the Task?" address before the American Management Association, New York, November 10, 1969.
11. Statement of Leslie Dix (on behalf of the Special Committee on Consumer Interests), Federal Trade Commission, *National Consumer Protection Hearings* (Washington: U.S. Government Printing Office, November, 1968), p. 16.
12. "Food Ads to Get Wide Ranging Scrutiny at White House Session," *Advertising Age,* Vol. 41 (December 1, 1969), p. 1.
13. Andrew Shonfield, *Modern Capitalism: The Changing Balance of Public and Private Power* (New York: Oxford University Press, 1965), p. 227.
14. Stanley E. Cohen, "Pollution Threat May Do More for Consumers Than Laws, Regulations," *Advertising Age,* Vol. 41 (March 2, 1970), p. 72.
15. Richard H. Holton, "Government-Consumer Interest: The University Point of View," in *Changing Marketing Systems,* Reed Moyer, ed. (Chicago, Ill.: American Marketing Association, Winter, 1967), pp. 15–17.
16. E. B. Weiss, "Line Profusion in Consumerism," *Advertising Age,* Vol. 39 (April 1, 1968), p. 72.
17. Louis L. Stern, "Consumer Information Via Increased Information," *Journal of Marketing,* Vol. 31 (April, 1967), pp. 48–52.
18. Richard J. Barber, "Government and the Consumer," *Michigan Law Review,* Vol. 64 (May, 1966), p. 1226.

19. Raymond A. Bauer and Stephen A. Greyser, *Advertising in America: The Consumer View* (Boston: Graduate School of Business Administration, Harvard, 1968), p. 345.

20. Robert C. Wells, quoted in James Bishop and Henry W. Hubbard, *Let The Seller Beware* (Washington: The National Press, 1969), p. 14.

21. "Rattles, Pings, Dents, Leaks, Creaks —and Costs," *Newsweek,* Vol. 45 (November 25, 1968), p. 93.

22. See, Federal Trade Commission, "Staff Report on Automobile Warranties" (Washington: no date), and "Report of the Task Force on Appliance Warranties and Service" (Washington: January, 1969).

23. "Consumers Upset Experts," *New York Times* (April 13, 1969), F. 17.

24. Stanley E. Cohen, "Business Should Prepare for Wider Probe of Consumer Protection Laws," *Advertising Age,* Vol. 39 (January 8, 1968), p. 59.

25. Lewis Schnapper, "Consumer Legislation and the Poor," *The Yale Law Journal,* Vol. 76 (1967).

26. David Caplovitz, *The Poor Pay More* (New York: The Free Press, 1963).

27. Jeremy Main, "A Special Report on Youth," *Fortune,* Vol. 79 (June, 1969), pp. 73–74.

28. E. B. Weiss, "The Corporate Deaf Ear," *Business Horizons,* Vol. XI (December, 1968), pp. 5–15.

29. Report of Council on Trends and Perspective on, "Business and the Consumer — A Program for the Seventies" (Washington, D.C.: Chamber of Commerce of the United States, 1969).

30. "Exploitation of Disadvantaged Consumers by Retail Merchants," *Report of the National Commission on Civil Disorders* (New York: Bantam Books, 1968), pp. 274–277.

31. Ralph Nader, "The Great American Gyp," *New York Review of Books,* Vol. 9 (November 21, 1968), p. 28.

32. Stanley E. Cohen, "Giant Killers' Upset Notions That Business 'Clout' Runs Government," *Advertising Age,* Vol. 40 (July 14, 1969), p. 73.

33. Jeremy Main, "Industry Still has Something to Learn About Congress," *Fortune,* Vol. 77 (February, 1967), pp. 128–130.

34. Harper W. Boyd, Jr., and Henry J. Claycamp, "Industrial Self-Regulation and the Consumer Interest," *Michigan Law Review,* Vol. 64 (May, 1966), pp. 1239–1254.

35. Philip A. Hart, "Can Federal Legislation Affecting Consumers' Economic Interests Be Enacted?" *Michigan Law Review,* Vol. 64 (May, 1966), pp. 1255–1268.

36. David L. Rados, "Product Liability: Tougher Ground Rules," *Harvard Business Review,* Vol. 47 (July–August, 1969), pp. 144–152.

37. David Sanford, "Giving the Consumer Class," *The New Republic,* Vol. 40 (July 26, 1969), p. 15. Partial support for this concept was given by President Nixon in his "Buyer's Bill of Rights" proposal of October 30, 1969.

38. See, "Nixon shops for consumer protection," *Business Week* (November 1, 1969), p. 32.

39. "A Foggy First Week for the Lending Law," *Business Week* (July 5, 1969), p. 13. This result was accurately forecasted by Homer Kripke, "Gesture and Reality in Consumer Credit Reform," *New York University Law Review,* Vol. 44 (March, 1969), pp. 1–52.

40. Stanley E. Cohen, "Packaging Law Is on Books, But Ills It Aimed to Cure Are Still Troublesome," *Advertising Age,* Vol. 40 (September 1, 1969), p. 10.

41. Same reference as footnote 18, and Louis M. Kohlmeier Jr., "The Regulatory Agencies: What Should Be Done?" *Washington Monthly,* Vol. 1 (August, 1969), pp. 42–59.

42. "Wide Gaps Exist in Consumer Food Safety," *Congressional Quarterly* (November, 1969).

43. E. B. Weiss, "Marketeers Fiddle While Consumers Burn," *Harvard Business Review,* Vol. 46 (July–August, 1968), pp. 45–53.

94   The Consumer Faces Marketing

44. See Stanley E. Cohen, "Consumer Interests Drift in Vacuum as Business Pursues Marginal Float," *Advertising Age,* Vol. 40 (March 24, 1969), p. 112.

45. "Business Responds to Consumerism," *Business Week* (September 6, 1969), p. 98, and Robert Moran, "Consumerism and Marketing," *Marketing Science Institute Preliminary Statement* (May, 1969).

46. Dorothy Cohen, "The Federal Trade Commission and the Regulation of Advertising in the Consumer Interest," *Journal of Marketing,* Vol. 33 (January, 1969), pp. 40–44.

47. James C. Naylor, "Deceptive Packaging: Are Deceivers Being Deceived?" *Journal of Applied Psychology*, Vol. 6 (December, 1962), pp. 393–398.

48. David M. Gardner, "The Package, Legislation, and the Shopper," *Business Horizons,* Vol. 2 (October, 1968), pp. 53–58.

49. Same reference as footnote 6.

11 Business Responds to Consumerism

This article, originally published in September 1969 but still pertinent and realistic, presents clear documentation of consumer displeasure and unrest. Consumers have often felt that it is impossible to get satisfaction from businessmen following purchase of a product. Yet complaints about business practices, largely in the marketing area, sooner or later result in some action, generally legislative, such as federal or state acts to regulate business. Studied in conjunction with textbook discussions of governmental interaction with marketing, product development, and the marketing concept, the following selection shows how consumers' expressions and the legislative threat have spurred industry toward greater attention to the consumer.

First Banana: "Hey, did you hear about the man who crossed a parrot with a tiger?"

Second Banana: "No! What did he get?"

First Banana: "I don't know. But when it talks, you better listen!"

Whatever else consumerism is, it's beginning to look like a tigerish sort of parrot, and business, it seems, would do well to listen.

Some businesses are not only listening, they are doing something. Appliance makers are starting to print their warranties in clear English. Auto makers are trying to get new cars to customers with all the screws tightened and all the weatherstripping in place. Textile manufacturers are looking more closely at the clothes their products end up in, to make sure the fiber is really suited to the suit.

Every class of manufacturer whose product ends up sold at retail—from foods and finance service to toys and tires—is thinking, more or less intensively, about what to do when Ralph Nader, or Consumers Union's Walker Sandbach, or Senator Warren Magnuson (D-Wash.), or Representative Benjamin Rosenthal (D-N.Y.), or another of the growing corps of influential consumer protectors comes knocking at the door.

Reprinted from "Business Responds to Consumerism", *Business Week* (September 6, 1969), pp. 94–108, by special permission of the publisher. Copyright © 1969 by McGraw-Hill, Inc.

Impetus   Few businessmen make any secret of it: Fear is the spur. Banks and finance companies have had a taste of consumer credit regulation and worry that they may some day be held responsible for the reliability of products financed through notes they have bought. No one has to teach Detroit the power of safety crusades; performance, pricing, and warranty revision may come next. Overnight, the delicate credibility of the toy and baby-food industries could be destroyed all over the country. Cosmetic and drug manufacturers, regulated for years, are uncomfortably aware that what they have swallowed so far may be only the beginning.

Read, for example, a recent press release issued by the Democratic Study Group, an informal alliance of liberal congressmen. After warming up with an indictment of the Nixon Administration in the field of consumer protection, the group lists no fewer than 30 separate desired pieces of legislation to regulate business in its relations with the public: 10 laws dealing with product safety (including drugs, toys, tires, fish, eggs, and medical devices); five on consumer information (package labeling and pricing, product testing); six on deception and fraud; three on consumer credit; and six others that range from electric power reliability standards to the guarantee of reasonable access to liability insurance.

New Weapons   A laundry list compiled by the Chamber of Commerce of the U.S. is even longer: 86 major bills before the Congress, and more dumped into the hopper every day.

The Nixon Administration itself, despite the Democrats' criticism, is readying a package of consumer-oriented legislation. In a recent speech, Mrs. Virginia Knauer, the President's consumer adviser (who has turned out to be just as tart-tongued as her Democratic predecessors), outlined the first bill in the program: an act that enables consumers economically injured by fraudulent or deceptive marketing practices to pool their small claims and bring "class actions" in the Federal courts. The proposed law is similar to several already introduced in Congress. Nader says such a bill is potentially the most powerful weapon that could be put in the hands of consumers.

If anyone, at this late date, thinks that all this is just so much political wind, he should glance at the major legislation of the past few years:

The National Traffic & Motor Vehicle Safety Act, which took on the whole automobile industry.

The Fair Packaging & Labeling Act, which was passed over the strenuous objection of the mammoth food industry.

The Consumer Credit Protection Act, which vitally touches the banking and finance industries as well as every retail organization that grants credit.

If one thing can be said for the lawmakers, it is that they are not afraid to tackle the biggest. Consumerism is powerful politics. Senator Magnuson used consumerism as a key issue in his successful drive for re-election last year. His theme: "Let's keep the big boys honest."

Senator Frank E. Moss (D-Utah), who recently won a signal victory over the cigarette makers, is considered by Republican strategists to be vulnerable next year in his bid for re-election. He recently scheduled a public hearing in connection with his campaign to tighten the Truth-in-Packaging Law. Where did he hold the hearing? Salt Lake City, of course.

Bandwagon   Among politicians, consumer protection is becoming institutionalized, just as defense, taxation, space, oil, and banking. Staff assistants to senators are making careers of consumer protection; they spend much of their time keeping up their bosses' interest with a stream of clippings, reports, studies, gossip, draft bills, draft speeches.

Some legislators need no encouragement. For each session of Congress through the years, Representative Leonor K. Sullivan, a serene and comfortable lady who represents a Democratic district in St. Louis, has introduced an omnibus package of amendments to the Federal Food, Drug & Cosmetic Act (this year's version, all 120 pages of it, is designated H.R. 1235). She watches with equanimity as her bill dies in the Interstate & Foreign & Commerce Committee. But every so often, bits and pieces of it turn up in other bills that do get passed, and she is perfectly prepared to continue submitting variations of her bill to the end of her Congressional career.

Futhermore, anyone in the business community who expects the Republicans to capture the Senate next year and overturn the consumerist establishment should reconsider. The consensus in Washington is that consumer protection is no longer the exclusive concern (if it ever was) of the liberal Democrats. Conservatives of the stripe of Senator John Tower (R-Tex.) are becoming interested. Votes, it seems, are votes, and everyone is a consumer.

Boiling Point   There's an explanation why consumer issues have become good politics. In the very broadest sense, consumerism can be defined as the bankruptcy of what the business schools have been calling the marketing concept.

For all the millions of words written on the subject in the last 20 years, the marketing concept is a fairly simple idea: The proper way to run a business, and especially a consumer-goods business, is to find out the customer's wants and needs, felt and unfelt. The next step is to work back through the chain from customer to manufacturer, and design and produce a product that fills those needs and wants better than anything else on the market. With proper attention to efficient production, good distribution, attractive packaging, and effective promotion, the manufacturer should have few troubles.

But the whole system, which has worked brilliantly since the mid-1950s, is precariously balanced on one assumption: that the consumer is capable of exercising intelligent choice, and inclined to exercise it. The consumer, it is said, "votes with her pocketbook."

More and more people are beginning to believe that the assumption is not at all self-evident. Dr. Peter F. Drucker, the management consultant, lectured the marketing conference of National Association of Manufacturers last April in these terms: "Consumerism means that the consumer looks upon the manufacturer as somebody who is interested, but who really doesn't know what the consumer's realities are. He regards the manufacturer as somebody who has not made the effort to find out, who does not understand the world in which the consumer lives, and who expects the consumer to be able to make distinctions which the consumer is neither able nor willing to make."

In atomic physics, there is the concept of critical mass—a point at which enough fissionable material is present to support a violent reaction. The U.S. consumer economy is at the point of critical mass, and consumerism is the explosion. A great many things have come together at once:

PRODUCT COMPLEXITY. "The product," complains John J. Nevin, the head of Ford Motor Co.'s central marketing staff, "is getting more complex as we are building it better. We've kept pace with complexity, but we haven't licked it." Few consumers can peer under the hood of an eight-cylinder, air-conditioned, power-assisted automobile and understand what is there.

THE BUSINESS BOOM. The country's productive capacity is beginning to gape at the seams under the pressure to get the goods out on the market at any cost. Last fall, *The New York Times* reported that 5% of certain classes of women's wear needed some repair by retailers before they could be placed on sale. Says one Detroit executive: "Things have moved so fast —from 6-million cars to 9-million in less than a decade. How do you increase repair stalls fast enough?"

THE MARKETING BOOMERANG. In a sense, consumer marketing and advertising have been too successful. Convinced that quality and convenience are forever on the rise, that the technical genius of industry can work miracles, that the new is always better, that the computer can solve anything, the customer expects a lot that cannot be delivered. "We are suffering," says Herbert M. Cleaves, senior vice-president of General Foods, "from a revolution of customers' rising expectations. The consumer never had it so good, but he wants to know 'what have you done for me lately?' " Marketing overkill is even harming products that do perform well. "They've been screaming about how good their products are for so many years, people no longer believe them," says Morris Kaplan, technical director of Consumers Union.

FULL EMPLOYMENT. It's a truism that no one wants to be an auto mechanic or repairman anymore. There are better and easier jobs in the factories. And present repairmen are so beset by customers that they can't take the trouble they used to. Says John C. Bates, director of General Motors' service section. "It's not that they don't do the work, but that they don't cater to the consumer anymore. If you get respect, you don't complain. Ten years ago, management in a dealer's repair shop had pretty good control over his people. As labor shortages developed, there's been an abrogation of control."

Anomie, or the feeling of disorder and isolation; the sense, in short, that a bad situation has no bottom. The white, suburban, middle class, which constitutes the principal market for goods and services, believes that government is cold and unresponsive, that taxes are too high, that Negroes are too aggressive, that the Vietnam war will never end. The middle class is at its collective wit's end. And now the last refuge, the goods and services the suburbanite buys with his devalued dollars to support the good life, seems to have let him down.

Together, the discontents have produced the broadest consumer protection movement in U.S. history, a movement that is not only concerned with protecting consumers against physical harm and outright fraud, but that also attempts to guarantee performance, efficacy, and to regulate the total relationship between buyer and seller. In legal terms, emphasis has moved from torts to contracts.

"There is a lack of balance in the consumer's capacity to deal equally with the guy who's got an item to sell," says Senator Gaylord Nelson (D-Wis.) one of the most active consumerists in Congress. The aim is to redress that balance.

One appliance executive ticks off on his fingers the big issues that are coming up: safety, of course, and the problems of product recall; some machinery for the resolution of customer grievances; improvement and standardizations of product warranties; provision of a lot more information to the consumer on what he is buying and how well it will perform.

Facing Up to Reality   "The most encouraging thing," says General Electric Co.'s associate counsel, Winston H. Pickett, "is that businessmen are taking consumerism seriously and addressing themselves to it on a systematic and continuous basis." Adds a key man in a powerful Senate committee: "People are changing; or at least everyone is willing to play the game and make the right pronouncements."

Both men were addressing themselves to the No. 1 problem: How should business respond to the consumer challenge? The question—and its various answers—are likely to occupy a lot of high-priced time for a good many years to come. And that in itself is a problem. "We're not a huge company."

says E. G. Higdon, president of Maytag Co., "and we don't have a lot of loose management with nothing to do. The consumerism boom is putting the time pressure on some of our top people. You don't go out and employ someone to go to Washington and sit down and listen. You have to send someone who knows this business, who is capable of representing us adequately, and who can come back with the proper information to let us form our own opinions."

Actually, the business response to government regulation has been fairly predictable over the years, and falls into several stages.

Deny everything. Nearly everyone goes through a phase of shock when hallowed business practices are questioned, and this is the automatic response.

Blame wrongdoing on the small, marginal companies. In any industry where fragmentation and ease of entry are the rule, the argument is popular that the major companies are blameless, but that the small outfits must cut corners to survive.

Discredit the critics. "Hell," says one Congressional staff man, "I've had publishers worried about circulation sales investigations down here peddling stuff on the Communist nature of consumerism based on 1942 documents."

Hire a public relations man. A big campaign to modify public opinion is alluring. But, as one PR man says, "there's no sense in a PR campaign if you have nothing to say."

Defang the legislation. Trade associations and Washington law firms are specialists in this, and it is often effective, at least for a while. It worked for the tobacco industry in 1965. It also worked in respect to the Truth-in-Packaging Law.

Launch a fact-finding committee to find out whether anything really needs to be improved in the way the company does business. The food industry is deeply involved in this now.

Actually do something, whether you think you are guilty or innocent. Carl Levin, a PR man who runs the Washington office of Burson-Marsteller, cites the case of his client, Reserve Mining Co., the big taconite processor in Minnesota. Reserve has been criticized for dumping ore tailings into Lake Superior. "Reserve thinks it's right," says Levin. "But if everyone's wearing a mini-skirt, you wear one too. Whether it's a real public interest or merely what the public thinks is its interest, it must be taken into account. They're trying to do something short of closing down the plant."

More and more businessmen are convinced that the rewards—or the avoidance of penalties—will come only in the later stages of this cycle. Says GE's Pickett: "You're going to do something voluntarily or involuntarily. These aren't fancied grievances. The dimensions are a matter of dispute, but not the existence of them."

How does industry answer these complaints? Consider the case of the food industry. Regulation is certainly nothing new, and the processors have been living with minimum standards of health and cleanliness for decades. But in the early 1960s, the proposals to regulate labeling on consumer packages cropped up. By the time the Fair Packaging & Labeling Act was passed in 1966, the grocery industry had earned a reputation for primitive intransigence that would have shamed a 19th Century railroad baron.

But packaging was only the beginning. Some of the labeling regulations are just being promulgated, and the industry is under attack on additives and plant inspection.

Introspection   In 1967, the Grocery Manufacturers Association commissioned a study by McKinsey Co. to try to get some new ideas. A number of alternatives were discarded, including a massive public relations campaign and an expensive continuing opinion survey to find out what is bugging the consumer. What finally came out of it all was the Consumer Research Institute, run by James Carman, a business administration professor from the University of California.

CRI is a foundation sponsored by major manufacturers that sell through supermarkets, by the National Association of Food Chains, the National Association of Wholesale Grocers of America, by several large ad agencies, and a group of magazines with a healthy interest in food advertising.

The studies themselves—planned or actual—vary in stature. Some of them merely put out brush fires, such as a study now in the works on cents-off deals in supermarkets.

A project in the planning stage is so-called "unit-pricing." Several bills now in Congress would require retailers to stamp the price per ounce, or pound, or foot on packages. "We want to do some decent research," says Carman. "How much would it cost? Would it change the way goods are priced physically; that is, would the actual price-stamping have to change? Would it promote more or fewer pricing mistakes?"

Carman's biggest expenditure area is in consumer information studies. For example, one scholar is looking at the state of consumer testing and grading programs in Europe in an effort to determine whether a similar program would make sense in an American environment. Another project will study what product information consumers actually use.

Feedback   Carman's sponsors very much want to know what's bugging consumers. So far he has no answer.

The U.S. Chamber of Commerce thinks it has a method that might work. The Chamber has designed a program that it is trying to sell to its local affiliates. The proposition: a series of local meetings between business and consumers designed to get some kind of feedback on dissatisfaction—and get some action on injustices.

There are other schemes. One of the original alternatives to Carman's institute was a national market research study proposed by A. Edward Miller, at the time (1967) president of Alfred Politz Research, and now president of World Publishing Co. Miller's scheme involved a $100,000 study, jointly paid for by government and industry to isolate the areas of consumer discontent.

Miller also proposed a continuing study, called the Consumer Index of Buying Satisfaction, to provide both the regulators and the regulated with something better than letters of complaint as a clue to consumer dissatisfaction.

CRI is the packaged-goods producers' principal effort at the moment. Individual companies, of course, are doing more. General Foods, for example, early this year set up the Center for Applied Nutrition, which is charged with research into the problems of nutrition and hunger. It is no secret that one of the issues of increasing interest to the consumerists is whether convenience foods are more or less nourishing than food the housewife prepares herself, and whether consumers think they are getting more sustenance than they really are.

Likely New Targets   The major dialogue in the business community is taking place not in the food industry but among the durable goods makers, which are less accustomed to severe regulation. They are, to put it bluntly, in a sweat. The areas that are bugging them are warranties, repair, reliability, consumer grievance mechanisms, and product safety. And the principal argument is how fast to move to head off unwelcome regulation.

The battleground is over industry-wide product standards and product certification. Are they desirable? Are they prudent? Are they anti-competitive? The National Commission on Product Safety, appointed by the President, distrusts self-regulation and is pushing for federal standards and surveillance. The commission has gone so far as to enlist the Antitrust Div. of the Justice Dept. In May, Arnold B. Elkind, chairman of the commission, asked Assistant Attorney General Richard W. McLaren for an advisory letter on the antitrust implications of self-regulation. In June, McLaren replied, and his very cautious response has provided ammunition for the warring points of view.

In July, for example, the commission announced that Justice does not think voluntary safety standards necessarily violate the laws, but that setting such standards "would appear to be a task more appropriately entrusted to a governmental body than private groups of manufacturers."

True, McLaren said that, but the statement was taken out of a context that bore on quite a different point. Donald L. Peyton, managing director of the United States of America Standards Institute (USASI), a private organization supported by trade associations to promulgate voluntary standards, has photocopies of McLaren's letter and the safety commission's press release. He implies that Elkind distorted McLaren's views to frighten industry away from self-regulation.

But a careful reading of McLaren's statement reveals that Elkind need distort nothing: The general tenor of McLaren's opinion is that self-regulation could be extremely dangerous.

Dilemma   There's nothing surprising in that. The anti-competitive aspects of voluntary codes have been recognized for years. A product standard rigged to favor one or two producers, or a certification program too costly for small manufacturers, is very likely in violation of the antitrust statutes.

Juel Ranum, board chairman of the Association of Home Appliance Manufacturers, an organization that is doing more than most in the area of performance standards and consumer grievance, puts the fears of industry very explicitly indeed: "The one thing I haven't heard in Washington is what a politician would do if a company in his particular area were threatened by standards that it was unwilling or unable to meet. This is a real dilemma, because if the standards are to mean anything, they will have to raise the level, not lower it. At the present time, if we as an industry attempted to write a standard that every single manufacturer could not meet now, it would be absolutely construed as a violation of antitrust laws, as an attempt to drive some companies out of business."

The danger is no illusion. USASI's Peyton admits: "I can get GE and Westinghouse to reduce current leakage. But the standard would put 50 manufacturers out of business."

Nevertheless, USASI (the name [was] changed [in October 1969] to American National Standards Institute because the Federal Trade Commission thinks the present name sounds deceptively like an arm of the U.S. government) believes that voluntary certification is both safe and feasible, despite the opposition or lethargy of some of its members. Says one of Peyton's associates: "We have a consumer council loaded with consumer-oriented manufacturers, some of whom are sitting on it to make sure that no standards are written on his industry."

Yardsticks   USASI recently launched a national certification program that will offer something of a breakthrough in self-certification for performance.

Peyton would like to see graded standards, which would get an industry off the antitrust hook by finding room for manufacturers of every degree of efficiency and size. "There's nothing illegal, immoral, or fattening about component performance levels for a whole industry," he says. "Why not have performance points as well as price points and market the product accordingly?"

One reason, says a testing engineer, is that it is harder to do than most people in or out of Washington think. "Take tires. Quality grade labeling is an almost impossible situation. Everyone's been working on it, but the chore is beyond man's knowledge and they're a year past the deadline for Commerce Department regulations."

There are other reasons why people in industry doubt USASI's success.

Companies joining the certification program must satisfy USASI that product liability insurance covered USASI. Testing costs are also higher under the program because the testing laboratory that actually administered the certification standard would have to post a bond with USASI for the life of the program plus 10 years. To be legal, the certification must be open to any company. Says one observer: "Suppose a company that's not an association member came along and asked for the USASI seal. He hasn't contributed a nickel to the association's certification program, which includes expensive advertising to acquaint the public with its value. The first time a Hong Kong air-conditioner importer comes along, USASI is down the drain."

Debate   USASI is not the only institution pushing reluctant manufacturers to adopt some form of self-certification. Hoffman Beagle, president of Electrical Testing Laboratories, one of the oldest independent testing labs in the business, thinks that self-certification sponsored by an industry association can work.

He has made it work in a few cases. For example, the aluminum window manufacturers administered their own program for years, but found that the inspection system left something to be desired. In 1963, Beagle's laboratory took over policing of the standards, including random sampling of production. "We have in all our programs sole authority without recourse to determine the facts of compliance. If we gig someone, it costs them money."

Beagle is puzzled by the consumerist issue. "You'd think the woods would be full of new clients these days," he says. "But it's not so." He doesn't think cost is the reason. "I have yet to find an industry where a viable certification program could not be instituted at a cost per unit that leaves the pricing structure unaffected," Beagle says.

Others disagree. Baron Whitaker, president of Underwriters' Laboratories, which certifies electrical safety, puts his finger on a fundamental paradox in trying to graft consumer protection measures onto a sophisticated market economy. "If you put in extra safety features or extend product life, the cost has to come out of somewhere. There's no Santa Claus."

Delicate Balance   To understand exactly what all this means in terms of competing in a cutthroat market, maintaining dealer margins, and maintaining pricing points in the volume segments of a business, listen to John W. Craig, senior vice-president of the appliance division of Admiral Corp.: "Does attention to the consumer cost money? Certainly it does. You get nothing free any more. The only solution is cost-improvement programs. Our engineering, purchasing, and manufacturing departments have annual requirements set up calling for taking a certain amount off manufacturing costs without interfering with performance, features, or reliability."

In the face of that kind of optimism, a lot of marketing men can only grin wryly. In most hardgoods industries—including the automobile business, where it has been raised to a high art—cost control and engineering adjust-

Tire Makers' Bumpy Recall Campaign

What happens when an unprepared industry runs into the consumer buzz-saw is clearly illustrated by the recent woes of the tire manufacturers.

The question of tire safety has been around a long time. But the 1966 National Traffic & Motor Vehicle Safety Act for the first time required auto manufacturers to recall cars and parts —including the original equipment tires—when safety-related defects are discovered.

Through a Congressional oversight, replacement tires were not mentioned in the law.

Late in 1968, the National Highway Safety Bureau found that one of every 11 tires it tested failed to meet Federal safety standards. Ralph Nader got hold of the report and spread it all over the newspapers. The Safety Bureau began pressuring Akron to institute voluntary recall programs, and the industry was in trouble.

RECALLS: Finally, in January, 1969, Mohawk Rubber Co. announced that it was recalling 10,000 of its 7.35 x 14 Airflo tires—about half the company's 1968 production of that model—and would replace them with its costlier Bonanza tires. Since then, there have been at least eight more recalls, and Akron has found that rubber doesn't always bounce back:

Mohawk retrieved 3,356 of the 10,000 tires, but 2,776 of these were from inventory. Only 580 came from customers.

General Tire & Rubber Co. went searching for 42,000 General Jet tires, but can account for only 8,259.

Goodyear Tire & Rubber Co. got a great deal of publicity when an upside down "6" in a tire mold caused a figure in the load rating to look like a "9." But only eight of the 2,000 tires involved have been found.

Obviously, hunting down tires is a lot harder than recalling autos. While there are 29,000 car dealerships in the country, there are at least 250,000 places to buy tires. Besides, car dealers know who buys their cars; tire dealers know only in the case of credit purchases.

COMPLIANT: To launch a recall campaign, a rubber company sends a registered letter to the dealers involved and covers media with news releases. The company will call in all tires of a particular serial number and destroy them, even though only a handful might prove defective.

Because of the dismal performance of the recall campaigns, Senator Gayord Nelson (D-Wis.) introduced an Administration-backed bill last April that would require tire makers to notify owners by letter of any suspected defects in their tires, and to replace the tires with new ones. To comply, manufacturers would have to keep track of who owned all tires.

To everyone's surprise, the Rubber Manufacturers Assn. backed the bill, although the industry had resisted two earlier versions. But by this time, the handwriting was on the wall, and RMA admitted that the companies had been designing a voluntary recall system for more than a year.

By the time the Nelson bill gets through Congress—perhaps as early as January—all manufacturers will have onstream an alphanumeric code that tells the week the tire was made, who made it and in which plant, and the size and style.

SNAGS: The code, which replaces the individual manufacturer's serial numbers with more detailed and standardized information, is merely an identification system. More important—and more difficult—is to get customers to fill out registration cards with their names and addresses and the code numbers of the tires they buy—and then return the cards.

Mohawk found in its experiments earlier this year that the return of its postage-paid registration cards was high when the dealers cooperated fully. Firestone Tire & Rubber Co. found, in its own series of tests, that purchasers seldom returned the registration cards when left to their own devices. Returns from company-owned stores were best, but still poor.

Goodyear already has prepared a registration card in anticipation of the law. The customer has to pay the postage, but Goodyear hopes the strong wording will induce him to spend the 6¢: "Important! Your tire identification number must be registered now for your protection under Federal motor vehicle law."

CRITICISM: Tire men complain that the law puts no pressure on dealers to see that the registration cards are returned. Nor are tire executives enthralled at the prospect of keeping records on the 200-million tires they make every year. "The logistics are staggering," moans one. Manufacturers swallow hard when they think of the cost. Independent studies put the cost at between $2 and $2.50 per tire (about half what Nader claims auto makers pay for original equipment). Uniroyal, Inc., has estimated it will cost 75¢ just to register a tire, while Cooper Tire & Rubber Co. figures the program will add 2% a year to its manufacturing cost, even if not a single tire is recalled.

Saddest of all, claim tire men privately, the whole recall program is unnecessary. "The defects we're talking about simply don't cause accidents," says one. "As far as we can tell, tires are involved in less than 1% of all car accidents, and in those cases it's almost always because the tire was bald, not because it was defective. If anybody thinks he's going to save any lives with all this, he's kidding himself."

ments are matters of a fraction of a cent. The whole point: to bring in the product somehow at a competitive price level in the face of rising costs. The trick is to do it without losing much of the quality or durability. A major program of improvement in response to consumerist demands plays havoc with such a delicately balanced system. It is the lucky company that can raise its prices enough to cover the costs and still meet competition.

Herd Instinct   These competitive pressures are precisely why whole industries try to act together on new standards, as Senator Magnuson points out in his book, *The Dark Side of the Marketplace*: "When asked why they had not incorporated the $2 instinctive release on their wringer washing machine, one company admitted that even such a small expenditure that would require some alterations in production would require a higher price, giving competitors an edge in a low-income market, where every dollar-off counts. . . . Recently, an automotive engineer told me that many in the auto industry were secretly glad that a law was passed, mandating the use of the safety features by all companies, for competition had long prevented their adoption by one company alone."

The problem of how to satisfy everyone in the system at once pops up everywhere you look.

The problem of repair, for example, is both knotty and expensive. GE has erected a huge edifice to solve it: factory service branches which now account for 80% of its major appliance service calls.

Detroit Revs Up   The auto industry naturally is in the biggest bind. Ford is gearing up its HEVAC (heating, ventilation, air conditioning) laboratory, which will experiment with modular design for car climate control systems, among other things. The reason: air-conditioning is the company's biggest warranty headache, and it shows up early enough to be covered by even the shortest warranty period.

For the first time, too, Ford is asking its engineers to consider ease and accessibility of repair when they design a car, especially at the lower-priced end. The luxury models, whose owners presumably don't care one way or the other, will still emphasize style over fast—and cheap—repair. "Lee Iacocca (executive vice-president of Ford) can't stand exposed screw heads," says one man, " so there are none in the Continental." When you want to fix a car, it's nice to be able quickly to find the screws that hold it together.

The experiment with Maverick, which is billed as a repair-it-yourself car, is another indication of Ford's direction. The owner's manual is not all that easy to follow, but the company claims the last Ford with such a manual was the 1931 Model A Ford car.

GM is experimenting with a program, still in the pilot stage, in which an inspector selects a new car at random from a dealer's lot and drives it. GM calls it the "Would-I-buy-this-car-test."

Sharper Focus   The auto companies are paying a lot of attention to the "short-term" quality problems, the ones that show up in the first 10 days of a car's life: vent leaks, faulty door handles, and the like. Building quality through basic engineering and design is more difficult and more time-consuming. But Ford's Nevin points out that even the little repairable items may represent basic design failure. "Take a vacuum or electrical system where there is routinely a 5% defect rate. Maybe the plant simply can't build the part to that design."

Finally, there is the problem of customer relations. GM's Bates believes that the attitude of people dealing with consumers has a lot to do with customer satisfaction. So early this year the company began a series of meetings for dealer employees on owner relations that eventually clocked 37,000 employees. GM is also setting up incentive programs for mechanics. It makes contributions to a fund for mechanics with the best repair records, based on how often or seldom a customer who has just had his car fixed has to return for another go-around.

Satisfying the consumerists isn't all headache by any means. Celanese figured out a set of end-use licensing standards for its Fortrel and Arnel fibers that is widely known in consumerist circles. Celanese got into the program because it was a late starter in an industry dominated by DuPont's brand names, and it felt it had to invest real money in building confidence in its merchandise. The lure: the ad budget Celanese spends to support the products of everyone from the mill to the cutter that makes the clothing. To get Celanese's money, everyone has to conform to the standards the company has established.

A Hazy Outlook   In the struggle over the new consumerism, businessmen are often angry, and even more often bewildered. But by and large, they don't appear to be cynical.

If they were, the record shows that probably the safest course would be to let Congress pass any sort of regulatory bill it pleased, then sit back and watch the regulators fail to enforce it.

Consider, for example, the Fair Packaging & Labeling Act—"Truth-in-Packaging"—enacted in 1966. It will come as a surprise to many people who remember the publicity generated by the bill's passage that, despite the redesign of a host of supermarket packages to conform with the act's provisions, some parts of the law are still not officially in effect. The effective date for drug and cosmetics packages is now Dec. 31. Food packaging regulation went into effect only two months ago.

In some instances, even the official dates may prove unrealistic. One section of the act, for example, charges FDA with promulgating regulations governing "cents-off" deal labels on packages. FDA has yet to issue such regulations. Exactly why is in some dispute. A Senate Commerce Committee staffer believes that FDA, with all its other problems, simply assigned a low priority to the intricacies of promotional labeling. But other observers maintain that the agency simply found the task beyond its capabilities, that it just doesn't know enough about high-powered packaged goods marketing to draw up meaningful rules.

Trials and Errors   To do it justice, FDA has made a number of efforts to stretch its limited resources.

Two years ago, the agency launched an experiment in self-inspection with General Foods to see whether food manufacturers could manage the surveillance of food processing on their own. The experiment was conducted in GF's modern plant in Dover, Del., and covered two products—a gelatin dessert (a "low risk" product) and a custard ("high risk").

The program has undergone a series of modifications, and will be terminated this month. The result: "It worked not as well as we both had hoped," according to GF's Herbert Cleaves. The problem was the endless paperwork involved in reporting to Washington—a chore to produce, and certainly a chore to read. Cleaves thinks that "with refinements" self-certification can be made feasible in the food industry. If the biggest and most modern food processors could take some of the strain off FDA, it would have more resources to police smaller operators.

Despite imaginative ideas like these, however, an internal study group set up by FDA recently declared that the agency "had been unable to develop the kind of concerted and coordinated efforts needed to deal adequately and simultaneously with problems of pesticide residues, food sanitation, chemical additives, microbiological contamination, drug and device safety and efficacy, hazardous household products, medicated animal feeds, and myriad other problems." In short, said the study group, "we are currently not equipped to cope with the challenge."

Frustrations   The Federal Trade Commission is not in much better shape. It
                is an agency, as Louis M. Kohlmeier, Jr., points out in his new
book, *The Regulators,* that was designed by Congress to be the national expert on monopoly and economic concentration and has ended up as the national authority on phoney chinchilla-farming schemes. As a matter of fact, to any business reporter who regularly sees FTC's fat packets of new releases cross his desk, it sometimes seems that the commission's major activity is enjoining infractions of the fur-labeling act in Bent Spoon, North Dakota.

What has happened, of course, is that FTC has over the years been saddled with responsibility for a variety of consumer protection measures—mainly involving deception and fraud—which it is not really equipped to handle.

The load on FTC is so great, and the administrative machinery so cumbersome, that it is the despair of the commissioners. Mary Gardiner Jones, a liberal Republican commissioner, asserts that the commissioners, no matter how well intentioned, have no time to get out into the business world to see what's going on, and certainly no time to think about a rational and imaginative regulatory policy regarding the marketing of consumer goods.

The result is a very real frustration, even for businesses facing the threat of regulation. Both the home appliance manufacturers and the auto people have been waiting a year for the final draft of FTC's promised report on warranty practices.

What makes them impatient, of course, is the pending warranty legislation in Congress. Early drafts of both the House and Senate bills are tough, and, in the opinion of many in industry, almost impossible to live with. They include not only the requirement for a full parts-and-labor express warranty if any guarantee of product performance is offered at all, but a section requiring compulsory arbitration of warranty grievances. The specter of compulsory arbitration over the repair of a $10 toaster makes the appliance men's hair curl. So they are counting on the FTC report to put matters in somewhat better perspective.

Similarly, the synthetic fiber and textile industry is discouraged over the delay in reporting on the amendment to the Flammable Fabrics Act. The amendment, ramrodded by Senator Magnuson, was passed 18 months ago. The Secretary of Commerce was supposed to define the extent and nature of the textile fire hazard by end-use of the fabric and report recommendations to the industry. Only two small sections of the report have been issued, and the industry is still waiting for the rest. "They just haven't done their homework," says an executive of one big fiber producer.

Uncertainties   More than one businessman has said in exasperation—though never on the record—that thoroughgoing enforcement of existing laws would in some ways be preferable to the arbitrary system of random prosecution. Business sits around waiting for lightning to strike. "It's an awful way to try to build an intelligent policy of response to legislation," one man complains.

Then, too, Kohlmeier argues in his book that the regulatory agencies are more concerned with protecting the interests of the regulated industries than with the needs of the consuming public. His argument is persuasive, particularly in regard to the Interstate Commerce Commission, which has consistently maintained a floor under freight rates, and the Federal Communications Commission, which is generally regarded to have botched the allocation of television frequencies.

Businessmen faced with specific new regulation, however, don't always believe they have a friend at the regulatory agency. They may not be afraid of the regulators now but they are genuinely scared about the potential for regulation in the age of consumerism. Ralph Nader predicted recently that within the next decade some businessmen will end up in jail if their products injure a consumer.

12 What You Should Know About the New Truth in Lending Act

The utility of credit as an economic device has permeated every level of economic activity. Its use is so widespread—whether in the form of bank loans, commercial paper, government borrowing, the "open book," or other numerous forms and instruments—that it is generally conceded to be a foundation of modern economic life.

As far as marketing practice is concerned, the extension of credit is a method by which buying is made possible, and it is also useful as a sales stimulant and as a weapon in the competition among firms. Although few people buy goods only because of easy credit terms, such terms do act as a temptation to those who have the buying motivation.

In this perspective, credit has come under criticism for two reasons. First, it has been argued that too many buyers can resist everything but temptation. In other words, installment terms or other easy credit notions are dangerous to those who use them. Secondly, the credit terms can be and often are deceptive. The buyer becomes involved in highly complex arithmetic when seeking to discover the true cost of credit.

The following article reviews these assertions and their implications.

On July 1, 1969, a new law often called "Truth in Lending," became effective. This law is important to anyone who is now borrowing money, or who may borrow money in the future—and that includes just about everyone. This new law requires lenders to state clearly all borrowing costs on loans for such things as home mortgages, vacations, automobiles, education, certain loans to farmers, and loans to meet other personal needs. Lenders, and others who must make disclosure include banks, personal finance companies, insurance companies, credit unions, even doctors or dentists who regularly permit extended payments of their bills.

The purpose of the Truth in Lending Act is to enable you, the individual borrower, to shop around for the best deal when borrowing money in much

Reprinted from *What You Should Know About the New Truth in Lending Act* (June, 1969), courtesy of Manufacturers Hanover Trust Company, New York.

the same fashion as you shop around for the best buy in a new car, or say, a color television set. So that you can do this, the law requires all lenders to state the total costs of borrowing in exactly the same language. Specifically, the costs of money must be stated in dollars and cents and also as an annual percentage rate. Thus you will be able to make comparisons, and, if you choose, borrow where it costs you the least.

Here are some questions and answers which highlight important aspects of the law. They are intended only as a guide.

Q. What types of credit are covered under the new regulation?

A. Credit extended to you for personal, family or household use that does not exceed $25,000. Real estate credit transactions (any credit involving a mortgage on real estate) are covered regardless of the amount of loan.

Q. What is the finance charge?

A. It's the total costs to you of credit (with a few exceptions) whether you are charged directly or indirectly. Included are interest, fees, discounts, and service or carrying charges as well as the cost of insurance, provided the lender insists that you buy it from him.

Q. Does every cost go into the finance charge?

A. No. Some are excluded such as taxes, licenses, registration fees, and some real estate closing fees.

Q. How do I know what the finance charge is?

A. The lender must show it to you in writing (or typed or printed) and the finance charge must stand bold and clear on the page. The lender also is required to show the finance charge computed as an annual percentage rate, sharp and clear. The annual percentage rate must be accurate to the nearest one quarter of one per cent.

Q. What should I look for in advertising?

A. In general, a lender may not advertise any one credit term, such as down payment or the carrying charge or the time permitted for payment, unless he clearly states *all the credit terms*. Study these terms—pay particular attention to the total dollar costs of borrowing and to the annual percentage rate.

Q. What are my rights under the Truth in Lending Act?

A. As a general rule, you may cancel a credit transaction within three business days when a lender acquires a lien on any real property which you use as your residence. (You have no such cancellation right, however, where the lender acquires a first mortgage on your residence and the purpose of the loan is to enable you to acquire that property.) Also, a creditor may be liable for twice the amount of the finance charge—minimum $100, maximum $1,000—plus court costs and attorney's fees, if he fails to make disclosures as required. (If a creditor willfully or knowingly disobeys the law or new regulation, and is convicted, he could be fined up to $5,000 or be imprisoned for one year, or both.)

Q. Does this new regulation fix interest charges?

A. No. It does not suggest maximum or minimum rates. These generally are set by state law. How much you will be charged is up to the lender. The regulation requires that you be told how much you are to be charged.

• • •

13 Consumer Protection Laws Now in Effect

Year Passed	Law	Major Provisions
1962	Kefauver-Harris Drug Amendments	Requires drug manufacturers to file all new drugs with the FDA and to label all drugs by generic name. All drugs must be pretested for safety and efficacy.
89th Congress 1966	Fair Packaging & Labeling Act	Regulates the packaging and labeling of consumer goods. Provides that voluntary uniform packaging standards be established by industry.
1966	National Traffic & Motor Vehicle Safety Act	Authorizes the Department of Transportation to establish compulsory safety standards for new and used tires and automobiles.
1966	Child Protection Act	Strengthens Hazardous Substances Act of 1960 and prevents the marketing of potentially harmful toys. Permits FDA to remove inherently dangerous products from the market.
1966	Drug Abuse Amendments	Regulates the sale of amphetamines, barbiturates.
1966	Cigarette Labeling Act	Requires cigarette manufacturers to label cigarettes: "Caution: Cigarette smoking may be hazardous to your health."
90th Congress 1967	Wholesome Meat Act	Requires states to upgrade their meat inspection systems to stringent Federal standards and clean up unsanitary meat plants.

Reprinted from: *Consumerism: A New and Growing Force in the Marketplace* (New York: Burson-Marsteller, 1970), pp. 34–36, by permission of Burson-Marsteller.

Year Passed	Law	Major Provisions
1967	National Commission on Product Safety	Establishes a seven-member commission to review household products that represent hazards to public health and safety and file recommendations for necessary legislation.
1967	Flammable Fabrics Act Amendments	Extends scope of 1953 Flammable Fabrics Act to allow the Secretary of Commerce to establish regulatory standards for clothing, bedding, draperies and other interior furnishings.
1967	Clinical Laboratories Act	Requires all clinical laboratories operating in interstate commerce to be licensed by the Federal government.
90th Congress 1968	Fire Research & Safety Act	Provides funds to collect, analyze and disseminate information on fire safety, to conduct fire prevention education programs and conduct projects to improve efficiency of fire-fighting techniques.
1968	Truth-in-Lending	Requires full disclosure of annual interest rates and other finance charges on consumer loans and credit buying including revolving charge accounts.
1968	Automobile Insurance Study	A two-year comprehensive study and investigation by the Department of Transportation to focus on the adequacy of state regulation of auto insurance and to evaluate industry rates, compensation, sales and policy discrimination practices.
1968	Natural Gas Pipeline Safety	Authorizes the Secretary of Transportation to develop minimum safety standards for the design, installation, operation and maintenance of gas pipeline transmission facilities.
1968	Poultry Inspection	Requires states to develop inspection systems which meet Federal standards for poultry and poultry products.
1968	Fraudulent Land Sales	To require Federal registration of all land offered for sale through the mail to protect consumers against sharp and unscrupulous practices.

Year Passed	Law	Major Provisions
1968	Radiation Control for Health & Safety	Directs Secretary of HEW to set and enforce standards to control hazardous radiation from television sets, X-ray equipment and other electronic devices. Establishes a committee to advise him on performance standards for electronic products capable of emitting radiation.
91st Congress 1969	Child Protection and Toy Safety Act of 1969	Amends the Federal Hazardous Substances Act to protect children from toys and other articles which contain thermal, electrical or mechanical hazards.
1969	National Commission on Product Safety	Extends the life of the National Commission on Product Safety until June 1970.
1970	Public Health Smoking Act	Bans cigarette commercials on radio and television effective Jan. 2, 1971. Requires all cigarette packages to be labeled: "Warning: The Surgeon General has determined that cigarette smoking is dangerous to your health."

14 Major Federal Government Agencies with Consumer-Related Responsibilities

Name	Year Founded	Function
President's Committee on Consumer Interests	Established by executive order, 1964	Composed of representatives of ten government agencies with the Special Assistant to the President for Consumer Affairs as chairman. The committee coordinates activities of Federal agencies, facilitates communications on consumer affairs between government, business and the consumer and provides consumer education.
Consumer and Marketing Service/United States Department of Agriculture (USDA)	Established by the Secretary of USDA, 1965	Protects consumers by assuring that farm products are safe, wholesome and efficiently marketed through food inspection and grading; advises consumers of available, plentiful foods and best buys.
Environmental Health Service	Established by HEW Secretary's reorganization order, 1970	Provides leadership and direction to programs and activities designed to assure effective protection for every American against hazards to health in his environment and in the products and services which enter his life.
National Highway Safety Bureau / Department of Transportation	Established by law, 1966	Administers a national highway safety program to make roads and highways safer for motorists and pedestrians. Sets national standards of tests and regulations for drivers and manufacturers.

Reprinted from: *Consumerism: A New and Growing Force in the Marketplace* (New York: Burson-Marsteller, 1970), pp. 45–46, by permission of Burson-Marsteller.

Name	Year Founded	Function
Department of Transportation	Established by law, 1966	Responsible for transportation promotion, safety and policy. Enforces gas pipeline safety and public safety regulations involving transportation.
Department of Justice	Established by law, 1870	Provides means for the enforcement of Federal laws, furnishes legal counsel in Federal cases, and interprets laws under which other departments act. Enforces Federal laws for consumer protection through cases referred to it by other government agencies.
Federal Power Commission	Established by law, 1920	Independent agency regulating interstate aspects of the electric power and natural gas industries, including the issuance of licenses for construction and operation of non-Federal hydroelectric power projects on government lands or on navigable waters of the U.S., the regulation of rate and other aspects of interstate wholesale transactions in electric power and natural gas, and the issuance of certificates for state pipelines and construction and operation of pipeline facilities.
Federal Trade Commission	Established by law, 1915	An independent agency with five commissioners which regulates commerce between states; prevents false and deceptive advertising; controls unfair business practices, policies, product labeling and prevents sale of dangerous flammable fabrics.
Food and Drug Administration	Established by law, 1906	Regulatory division of HEW which controls the marketing of drugs, food, cosmetics, medical devices and potentially hazardous consumer products.

QUESTIONS FOR DISCUSSION

1. Consumerism has, in the past, been a cyclical movement. Is there any reason to believe that it will change from its cyclical pattern and become permanently entrenched in our society?
2. Which factors have been most significant in promoting the growth of the present era of consumerism?
3. To what areas of marketing do you think the proponents of consumerism will turn?
4. If you were manager of a marketing department in a consumer products firm, what actions would you recommend in view of the present emphasis on consumerism?
5. In what ways is the present trend toward franchising of retail stores related to the consumer movement?
6. What role, if any, should the federal government play in responding to the calls for action uttered by the proponents of consumerism?
7. Can trade and industrial associations play an effective role with respect to the pressures generated by the consumer movement? What should this role be? What is it now?
8. What role should the federal government play in providing product information to consumers? Should the costs of any government activity in this area be borne by the government or by the producer of the product in question?
9. How effective do you think the reports of the independent testing laboratories are in satisfying the customer's need to know about the products that are on the market?
10. Do you think that consumers should have representation on the Board of Directors of those enterprises that deal primarily with the consumer?

SELECTED READINGS

Bishop, James, Jr., and Henry W. Hubbard, *Let the Seller Beware* (Washington, D.C.: National Press, 1969).

————, "Consumers Union Puts on Muscle", *Business Week* (December 23, 1967), No. 1999, pp. 84–86.

Campbell, Persia, *The Consumer Interest: A Study in Consumer Economics* (New York: Harper & Row, 1949).

Curran, Barbara, and David I. Fand, "An Analysis of the Uniform Consumer Credit Code", *Nebraska Law Review* (1970), Vol. 49, No. 4, pp. 727–744.

Day, George S., and David A. Aaker, "A Guide to Consumerism", *Journal of Marketing* (July, 1970), Vol. 34, No. 3, pp. 12–19.

Hofstadter, Richard, *The Age of Reform* (New York: Random House Inc., 1955).

Sorenson, Helen, *The Consumer Movement: What It Is and What It Means* (New York: Harper & Row, 1941).

Stern, Louis L., "Consumer Protection Via Increased Information", *Journal of Marketing* (April, 1967), Vol. 31, pp. 48–52.

U.S., Congress, Senate, Hearing Before the Consumer Committee on Commerce, *National Commission on Product Safety*, 90th Cong., 1st sess., Serial No. 90–1, March 1, 1967.

U.S., Congress, House, Hearing Before Subcommittee, Government Operations Committee, *Consumer Information Responsibilities of the Federal Government*, 90th Cong., 2nd sess., June 27–July 25, 1967.

the social implications of specific marketing practices
part three

The student of marketing and the citizen in general are vitally affected by marketing practice, which includes, as we saw in Part I, such functions as advertising, personal selling, product (or brand) management, marketing research, credit extension, and pricing policy. It is important, therefore, that everyone understand the issues raised by these practices.

In this part of the book, accordingly, the complaints are reviewed in detail; the defenses are placed in evidence; and other material that appears relevant is introduced so that the reader can judge the merits of charge and response. It is our hope that this will help students to form secure and valid judgments concerning the various marketing practices.

section 5
advertising:
critics
and defenders

One of the areas of marketing practice best known to the public at large is advertising. To the television viewer, bus or train rider, newspaper or magazine reader, ads are as common and familiar as sleep and food.

In this section we shall examine the social issues raised by advertising. A serious consideration of this subject must include a review of the complaints against advertising and the responses to these complaints by business, government, academic students, and consumers in the marketplace. These should enable the reader to formulate an individual point of view regarding the social usefulness of this multi-billion dollar sector of marketing practice.

15 Morality in Advertising— A Public Imperative

William G. Capitman

Most textbook treatments of advertising deal primarily with its functions, techniques, and characteristics. However, advertising also plays an important social role, for which it has both its critics and its defenders. Article 16 reflects a defense of advertising as socially beneficial. Article 15, on the other hand, presents a balanced critical view.

The Clearwater River, fifty miles upstream from Potlatch Forests Incorporated pulp and paper mill, is, as *Newsweek* put it, "a scene of breathtaking natural beauty." [1] The Potlatch people apparently agreed; they photographed it, added the caption *It costs us a bundle, but the Clearwater River still runs clear,* and ran an ad. But at the plant site, and downstream from the picture location, Potlatch pumps fresh water in from the stream and pumps out forty tons of suspended organic wastes. Simultaneously, Potlatch exudes some 2.5 million tons of sulfur gasses and 1.8 million tons of particulates into the air. The implication that the river, as shown in the ad, was the creation of Potlatch is belied by the subsequent photos, never shown in the ads, taken of the situation at the plant and below it. Says *Newsweek*: "When an enterprising local college newspaper editor pointed out the discrepancy between ad copy and reality, the company responded by cancelling all corporate advertising." Other such incidents and the growing concern throughout the country with questions relating to the social responsibility of corporations all point to the need for a new view of the morality of advertising.

What do we mean by morals in advertising and how can we approach the question? Is all advertising and are all parts of a given ad to be subject to the same rules and standards of morality? There is a need for discussion and assessment of the moral state of advertising now, as well as the establishment of guidelines and rules for the future.

Theodore Levitt, in his article "The morality (?) of advertising," has performed a valuable service in raising the discussion of the role of advertising

Reprinted from William G. Capitman, *MSU Business Topics* (Spring, 1971), Vol. 19, pp. 21–26.

in our society to a new level of abstraction.[2] The article provides a framework for considering the question of advertising morals in particular, and business morality in general. Despite his thoughtful consideration and the development of a rationale for a conception of advertising morality, the argument in its totality is likely to lead down some blind, and even unprofitable, alleys. Levitt conceives of the roles of advertising and packaging as being much the same as those of art and poetry, in that they all help create the symbolic and anticipated world rather than simply reflect reality. "I shall argue that embellishment and distortion are among advertising's legitimate and socially desirable purposes, and that illegitimacy in advertising consists only of falsification with larcenous intent," Levitt says.[3] He believes the common purpose of art and advertising is to "persuade."

Levitt's distinction is a nominal one: "Commerce, it can be said without apology, takes essentially the same liberties with reality and literality as the artist, except that commerce calls its creations advertising, or industrial design, or packaging. As with art, the purpose is to influence the audience by creating illusions, symbols, and implications that promise more than pure functionality." [4]

Art and Advertising   This argument presents serious problems. Although one can generalize similarities by using the word *persuade*, it seems to me that such a formulation evades and justifies rather than clarifies the issues. There is a sharp distinction between what the artist and the company are being persuasive about. The artist, broadly speaking, is concerned with convincing people that his conception of reality is worth considering. He does not regard what he is doing as reality, or even as the only way to perceive reality. His purpose is to bring new insights by trying new forms, and his work becomes art when it communicates some level of his differentiation to others, even though objective interpretation may arrive at conclusions different from his intentions. One cannot question the facts that there are fads and fashions in art; that internal artistic politics and mores often have more to do with an artist's success than the quality of his work; or that the artists, if they are to be fully devoted to their life's work, must live by selling their accumulated product. Still, it is only in terms of the need to market and sell his product that the artist can be seen as trying to persuade in anything like the sense *persuasion* is used in advertising.

What advertising does is use the tools of art, both visual and verbal, for a totally different purpose. Its object is to convince someone to act in a specified way and in a specified area. Business clearly has revealed its understanding of this intention through various efforts, such as persuading people to act by engaging their unconscious. A few years ago James Vicary experimented abortively with subliminal advertising. This process communicates messages the recipient is not conscious of receiving, and operates by evading the individual's censors in order to reach and affect basic and perhaps instinctual elements in the human make-up. By so doing, the person affected presumably would feel an uncontrollable impulse to buy the product without ever having been conscious of being exposed to the persuasion.

This key difference in function between art and advertising cannot be disregarded lightly. It results in the development of a different set of standards and criteria by which we judge the merit of a painting or a poem on the one hand, and a package or an advertisement on the other. If we are to talk of advertising morality we must take this into account.

There are other distinctions that must be made between advertising and art: the former is institutionalized, the latter is not. Advertising, for the most part, is a corporate effort, while art is a highly personalized, individual effort. Advertising, regardless of its artistic merit, is terminated if it is not successful in persuading people to act, a criterion which can be measured by sales. Art is not so terminated or measured and, in fact, the work of an artist may never have an influence in his own time. Art and art forms are more or less effective techniques of selling regardless of the artistic merits of the persuading construct. Advertising's function is to operate immediately. Its artistic aspects usually are buried in volumes of the "100 Best Advertisements" of one year or another; there is no necessary relationship between advertising persuasiveness and artistic merit.

Advertising: Symbols and Symbolism

If advertising is seen as using the techniques of art for affecting a different sort of persuasion than does art, what then can we say about advertising morality? One point of departure is to begin to discuss the broader effect of advertising on the polity, and whether or not such effects are legitimate, or "good." It seems important to me to discuss the world of symbolism which advertising creates and which the public uses. Cigarette advertising is a case in point. From the inception of the use of tobacco, certain elements in the society have regarded use of the product as immoral. The consequences of smoking were seen as destructive, morally speaking, and diverting from propriety. Cigarette smoking soon became a mass activity nonetheless. Since the U.S. Surgeon-General's report, there has been an accumulation of evidence that cigarette smoking has a direct and negative effect upon the physical well-being of an individual. One of the first successful attacks was made upon cigarette symbolism when government and public pressure forced cigarette advertising on television to be removed from time in which children might view it. Cigarette manufacturers also were pushed to remove from their advertising any implications and suggestions that there are *social* and *sexual* advantages to be gained from smoking which might appeal to the immature. The restrictions were based on the impropriety or immorality of the advertising, rather than any "fraudulent claim" made with "larcenous intent."

**Moralizing
Seems Fruitless**

Moralizing about the very existence of advertising seems to me fruitless. One might just as well moralize about the existence of evil, pornography, automobiles, detergents, or telephones. Morality is concerned with what is "good" or "bad" in human behavior, not with the existence of artifacts. In C. P. Snow's *The New Men*, his protagonists argue about the morality of developing atomic energy, in which was implicit the danger of human destruction. The question of morality had to do with the obligations of the human beings and human institutions that would employ this new force. If there was a moral conclusion to be arrived at, it was that human beings had the obligation to use the artifacts which they created for "good" rather than "evil" purposes, and that it is not moral to divorce oneself from the consequences of one's behavior.

The moral questions raised about advertising, then, are not related to its existence—it is a humanly developed artifact—but, rather, to its consequences. Whether embellishment is good or bad depends upon the consequences of that embellishment, both in commercial and non-commercial terms, and making that determination is not so simple as it sounds.

In the first instance, it is a simple-minded economistic error to assume that a product is only a physical thing. Levitt properly points out that "symbolic" satisfactions are provided by products and that these are a vital part of the role that a product plays in our society. But symbols really are shorthand statements about reality, and they too can lie about reality and about a product. The fact that they are symbols does not make them any less subject to moral objection. Just as they can lie, however, they can be truthful, and perhaps even more truthful about the essence of a product than a simple informative statement. So the fact that advertising is symbolic is not the essential problem of advertising morality.

Several years ago, in expression of the role of advertising as a symbol system, I described advertising as having a reality of its own and having a special effect upon the realities of the consumer's life. However, I did not exclude the possibility that advertising was *more* than simply a symbol system. It is, in fact, in toto, a *communication* system which, like other such systems, operates on a variety of levels. One level is the communication of factual information about the product. It requires considerable effort to regard price, as stated in an advertisement or on a package, as having only a symbolic meaning. *All* advertisements have this factual or informational element in their matrix.

**Implication and
Embellishment**

One of the great temptations to an advertiser and his agency is to turn these facts into symbols, or to at least manipulate the factual elements so that they do not mean quite what they say. There is extensive usage of this process of implication in advertising, ranging from suggestions that products are more effective than they actually are to implications in a photograph (as in the Potlatch-Clearwater River incident) that the corporation is engaged in activities that enhance the beauty of the environment when, in fact, it is not. This sort of implication always deals with apparent facts about the product or the producers and usually arises from the corporate conception of what the consumer wants to believe about a purchase. The implication usually concerns the desirable consequences of purchase in a factual or performance sense.

This manipulation is of a different order from the symbolic aspects of an ad or package which imply that what might be called social and environmental benefits will accrue to the user, and about which one might expect a choice. Thus, for example, the factual elements relating to deodorants have to do with their ingredients, their performance, and their price. The environmental elements have to do with sociality, status, insecurity, and so forth. Sometimes environmental elements are closely allied to performance. The performance of a deodorant can be perceived as the process of providing security in social situations. In this instance the symbolic meanings of the product become more important to the consumer than do the factual elements. However, this does not provide a basis for dodging moral consequences. Factual statements in an advertisement, those relating to ingredients, physical performance, and price, never can be embellished without becoming lies.

Misleading Advertising   This is not to say that a fact cannot be presented forcefully and dramatically, which often is done by using symbolism. For example, for some years proprietary drug products of various forms presented performers as physicians in their ads. The purpose of this was to present dramatically the qualities of the product in an environment that symbolized authority and, specifically, medical authority. But the practice was stopped by the FTC because it was misleading; it implied that doctors were, in fact, recommending the products being advertised.

The process of producing an advertisement is of interest when we talk about morality, for in most corporations, and in most decisions, the extent to which one will embellish a fact in an advertisement or a package is a legal question rather than a moral one. The question is whether the various institutions which act as censors of the corporation—the FTC; the television stations, which are themselves under the eye of one agency or another; the legal system—will let the corporation have its way. The question of consequences in the marketplace is seldom considered, other than some broad conception of public acceptance, but the parameters of that acceptance almost always are seen as broader than the legal limitations. Some corporations tend to believe that they can sell sows' ears as silk purses insofar as their ability to move the public is concerned. It is not moral considerations that prevent them from doing so, but anticipated legal consequences.

People object to misleading advertising only because they expect to believe it. If advertising really were being approached as cynically as studies suggest, there would be no concern with misleading ads but a sense of wonder at honest ads. The dismay over advertising is related to its factual distortion rather than the fact that it is not symbolically true. There is no clear evidence that symbolism offends, although there is considerable latitude in taste and fantasy. It would appear that the public is ready to distinguish between facts and symbols, and feels free to have opinions about the latter. However, facts presented according to conventions as being true are a different matter. It is only by testing or by prior knowledge that the consumer can determine whether the facts are untrue or misleading.

Specific problems of morality regarding facts arise over time. A manufacturer may produce and advertise a product which in all respects and by all known standards contains safe ingredients and does what it promises to do. Subsequent investigation may reveal that one of the ingredients could be dangerous, or that the product has unexpected side effects either on the user or on the environment although the producer had no way of knowing this beforehand. Further, it might be posited that new facts are slow in disseminating among the public. Disregarding for a moment that there may be agencies that will force the company to do something about the products, what steps can be taken and what moral questions arise concerning the continued advertising of the product after it has been exposed as harmful or misleading? There are several possibilities: The company can stop advertising and withdraw the product; the company can use its advertising to disseminate the new information and continue to market the product; it can disregard the new facts and continue to advertise as before.

The moral question is whether one action or another is right or wrong, good or bad in terms of its consequences as they affect the various parties. A moral decision would be one in which self-interest is secondary, but in which one acts on the basis of a principle, and one examines the consequences of so acting. Another aspect of a moral decision will involve the fact that what is good for one group may be bad for another. For example, the decision to stop advertising and withdraw a product has consequences for the employees, the distributors, and the consuming public. The problem for moralists then becomes one of balancing the greater good against the lesser evils. It was much easier to make these decisions when the clearcut rule existed that the actions of a purchaser in the marketplace were totally his own responsibility. However, caveat emptor has been much revised. It only had meaning if one could assume the perfection of the competitive system and equality of power and knowledge on the part of both buyer and seller. In a situation in which we know that competition is notably imperfect and where, for the most part, knowledge and power are clearly out of balance between buyer and seller, new versions of old moral principles once again come into play.

Reality and Fantasy

If we turn to what I have termed the environmental or social aspects of advertising—what Levitt sees as the symbol world of advertising—some of the subtler difficulties of moral issues are revealed. In the first instance there is clearly a range of symbolic devices and meanings used in advertising. One might broadly distinguish between symbols of reality and fantasy. Conceive of the two as on a continuum, at some point of which the two merge or overlap. Symbols of reality involve clear portrayals of more or less real situations in which social consequences accrue as a result of the use of a product or service. The social consequences are identifiable with the real life position of the viewer, either in terms of his own experience or other social experiences. Fantasy, on the other hand, is a clear portrayal of unreality—like the man from Glad appearing on the scene, magically, to solve a sandwich-packaging problem—but it may be symbolic of a real situation at one level or another.

Many critics of advertising tend to regard symbolism as one of its greatest faults. Ralph Nader, for example, asserts that much of advertising is designed to "evoke and provoke the emotions and weaker instincts humans are often prey to" and, in effect, it "strips" the consumer of his "sovereignty" in the marketplace.[5] Such an opinion reflects a conclusion about the effectiveness of symbolism in advertising and about the ability of the consumer to deal with this symbolism. In addition, it also means we have decided that consumers have neither the intelligence nor discriminatory power to differentiate between fact and symbol given a fair opportunity to do so; that symbolic values are not real values; and that the satisfactions involved in product choice and purchases are confined to the physical parameters.

If this view of the human condition in the United States is accepted, we must then conclude that anything other than the starkest reality and functionality is immoral in advertising, or packaging, or product design. At its best, such a decision means that beauty or decorativeness have no place in marketing, and this is inevitably contrary to the ethos of a better quality of life. Such a conclusion might please those who wish to retail the essentials of the Puritan ethic in American life, but it will not correspond to the aspirations and desires of a rather sophisticated populace.

Good Taste or Morality

One must distinguish between taste and morality in considering these elements of environment. Good taste is not a moral issue. Rather, it seems to be related to social class, education, values, and other societal and personal factors. The question of the taste level of advertising is an issue that needs consideration, but it is, in most respects, separate from the issue of morality. Again, the moral question regarding the use of symbols or surrounds in advertising is related to the good or bad consequences of the symbolizing or the truth or falsehood of the symbol as used in this context. These moral questions about symbolism are, at one level, at least closely tied to the levels of morality and hypocrisy in the system as a whole. The issue, for example, of whether or not to use nudity in advertising is confused by the equivocal nature of public moral standards on nudity.

Advertising, however, tends to treat this matter not as a moral but as a sales issue. One goes as far as one can in using nudity, where it is regarded as appropriate, but the consideration is whether or not it will cause a negative or positive response among one's market. If one can go a little beyond conventional standards and thereby offend only a few, but titillate many, the morality of nudity is only a sales, and perhaps a taste, issue rather than a moral one. The moral aspects, in the last analysis, will depend upon one's personal or institutional conception of the moral nature of nudity. If one's personal morality says that nudity is bad in this context, but one nevertheless uses nudity *because* it is morally bad, because it is titillating, because it attracts attention, then one clearly and consequentially has committed a moral breach. Therefore, when dealing with symbolism in advertising and the morality of the use of specific symbols, motive is indeed an issue as is objective effect.

This is not merely a question of counting angels on the head of a pin. Moral questions can have broad social consequences. For example, for years advertising has developed a set of conventions regarding social stereotypes. Working-class people and old people are funny; to be middle class is a virtue, middle-class people are beautiful, and they live in suburban houses surrounded by things; ordinary poor people do not exist; Negroes are invisible and are menials, and so forth. In effect, an image of the society and its inhabitants has been created which is untrue and perhaps dangerous; in my conception it is immoral. There is an obvious need to change this for moral reasons, not simply in response to public pressure.

The basis of all morality is the concept that adherence to a commonly held moral code is good for everyone, in the short as well as the long run. There are two difficulties here. First, we are not clear about our moral code, and it is changing. Second, we have established a different set of strictures for the operation of business. A faulty set of theories has separated business and other institutions from normal human activity, and a legal structure has been created that treats business as incapable of morality. Instead of morality, there is the rather flimsy and incomplete web of the law. *Ad hoc* regulations must be made to keep business within bounds because the human beings who run business institutions are creatively seeking new ways to get around these strictures. At the end of World War II we discovered in the Nuremberg trials a new concept of a soldier's morality. A human being no longer could claim immunity on the grounds that he was obeying an order from a superior; the act that he was commanded to do had to be moral and proper. This issue has been raised again in regard to My Lai and Vietnam.

If we can change so ancient a code as that of military obedience, we also can look upon the role of business, and individuals involved in it, in a new way. We can evolve new moral standards for behavior which, in the long run, may be more effective and meaningful than the imperfect legal structure.

NOTES

1. *Newsweek* (December 28, 1970), p. 49.
2. *Harvard Business Review* (July–August, 1970), pp. 84–92.
3. Ibid, p. 85.
4. Ibid.
5. *Christian Science Monitor* (December 15, 1970), p. 13.

16 Is Advertising Wasteful?

Jules Backman

Advertising has been criticized by many economists as being wasteful. This is in sharp contrast to the generally held view of marketers that advertising makes a definite contribution to the economy. The following selection, written by an economist whose research was supported by a grant from the Association of National Advertisers, concludes that advertising is *not* wasteful and that it is an efficient marketing tool. In reaching this conclusion, Professor Backman reviews advertising's informational role as well as its place in the marketing mix and in engendering competition and mass markets.

With some exceptions, economists generally have criticized advertising as economically wasteful. All the criticisms are not so extreme as one widely used economics text which states:

> Overall, it is difficult for anyone to gain more than temporarily from large advertising outlays in an economy in which counteradvertising is general. The overall effect of advertising, on which we spent $14 billion [actually $15 billion—JB] in 1965, is to devote these productive resources (men, ink, billboards, and so forth) to producing advertising rather than to producing other goods and services.[1]

Most critics do not go this far in condemning advertising. However, they do emphasize that advertising may be wasteful in several ways: by adding unnecessarily to costs, by an inefficient use of resources, by promoting excessive competition, and by causing consumers to buy items they do not need. This article brings together the scattered criticisms of advertising and answers to them and thus presents an overview of the debate in this area. The nature of these criticisms and the significance of waste in a competitive economy are first reviewed. Attention is then given to the vital informational role played by advertising, particularly in an expanding economy. Advertising is only one alternative in the marketing mix, and hence its contribution must be considered among alternatives rather than in absolute terms.

Reprinted from Jules Backman, "Is Advertising Wasteful?" *Journal of Marketing* (January, 1968), Vol. 32, pp. 2–8. Reprinted from *Journal of Marketing*, published by the American Marketing Association.

Variations on a Theme   The criticism that advertising involves economic waste takes several forms.

Competition in Advertising   The attack usually is centered on competition in advertising which some critics state flatly is wasteful.[2] Others have been concerned about the relative cost of advertising as a percentage of sales. Sometimes an arbitrary percentage, such as 5%, is selected as the dividing line between "high" and more "reasonable" levels of expenditure.[3]

Such cutoff points are meaningless, since the proper relative expenditures for advertising are a function of the product's characteristics. It is not an accident that relative advertising costs are highest for low-priced items which are available from many retail outlets and subject to frequent repeat purchases (for example, cosmetics, soaps, soft drinks, gum and candies, drugs, cigarettes, beer, etc.).

Particularly criticized are emotional appeals, persuasion, and "tug of war" advertising where it is claimed the main effect is to shift sales among firms rather than to increase total volume of the industry. For example, Richard Caves states: "At the point where advertising departs from its function of informing and seeks to persuade or deceive us, it tends to become a waste of resources." [4]

In a competitive economy competitors must seek to persuade customers to buy their wares. We do not live in a world where a company stocks its warehouse and waits until customers beat a path to its doors to buy its products. If this is all that a business firm did, we would have economic waste in terms of products produced but not bought as well as in the failure to produce many items for which a market can be created. In the latter case, the waste would take the form of idle labor and unused resources.

Inefficient Use of Resources   Economists have criticized advertising most vigorously as involving an inefficient use of resources. This criticism has been directed particularly against advertising where the main effect allegedly is a "shuffling of existing total demand" among the companies in an industry. Under these conditions, it is stated, advertising merely adds to total costs and in time results in higher prices. There undoubtedly is a shifting of demand among firms due to many factors including advertising. But this is what we should expect in a competitive economy. Moreover, there are many products for which total demand is increased (for example, television sets, radio sets, cars, toilet articles) for multiple use in the same home. In the sharply expanding economy of the past quarter of a century there are relatively few industries in which total demand has remained unchanged.

It must also be kept in mind that the resources devoted to competitive advertising usually are considered to be wasteful "in a full-employment economy" because they may be utilized more efficiently in other ways. Thus the extent of "waste" involved also appears to depend upon whether the economy is operating below capacity. This point is considered in a later section.

Adds to Costs   Sometimes, it is stated that if advertising succeeds in expanding total demand for a product, the result is a shift of demand from other products, the producers of which will be forced to advertise to attempt to recover their position. The net result of such "counter-advertising" is to add to costs and to prices.

But all increases in demand do not necessarily represent a diversion from other products. Thus, an expanded demand for new products is accompanied by an increase in income and in purchasing power flowing from their production. Moreover, during a period of expanding economic activity, as is noted later, the successful advertising may affect the rate of increase for different products rather than result in an absolute diversion of volume.

Creates   Another variation is the claim that advertising is wasteful be-
Undesirable   cause it ". . . creates useless or undesirable wants at the ex-
Wants   pense of things for which there is greater social need. When
                  advertising makes consumers want and buy automobiles with tail fins, tobacco, and movie-star swimming pools, there is less money (fewer resources) available to improve public hospitals, build better schools, or combat juvenile delinquency." [5] It is claimed that many of these types of products are useless and anti-social. Criticism of advertising is nothing new. In the late 1920s Stuart Chase claimed: "Advertising creates no new dollars. In fact, by removing workers from productive employment, it tends to depress output, and thus lessen the number of real dollars." [6]

These are value judgments reached by the critics on the basis of subjective "standards" which they set up. "What is one man's meat is another man's poison," as the old saying goes. The real question is who is to decide what is good for the consumer and what should he purchase?

In a free economy, there is a wide diversity of opinion as to what combinations of goods and services should be made available and be consumed. Obviously, tastes vary widely and most persons do not want to be told what is best for them. In any cross section of the population of the country there will be a wide disagreement as to what constitutes the ideal components of a desirable level of living. Each one of us must decide what purchases will yield the greatest satisfactions. We may be misled on occasion by popular fads, advertising, or even advice of our friends. But these decisions in the final analysis are made by the buyers and not by the advertisers, as the latter have found out so often to their regret.

Competition   The critics of advertising are really attacking the competitive
and "Waste"   process. Competition involves considerable duplication and
                   "waste." The illustrations range from the several gasoline stations at an important intersection to the multiplication of research facilities, the excess industrial capacity which develops during periods of expansion, and the accumulations of excessive inventories.

There is widespread recognition that inefficiencies may develop in advertising as in other phases of business.[7] Mistakes are made in determining how much should be spent for advertising—but these mistakes can result in spending too little as well as too much.

We cannot judge the efficiency of our competitive society—including the various instrumentalities, such as advertising—by looking at the negative aspects alone. It is true that competition involves waste. But it also yields a flood of new products, improved quality, better service, and pressures on prices. In the United States, it has facilitated enormous economic growth with the accompanying high standards of living. The advantages of competition have been so overwhelmingly greater than the wastes inherent in it that we have established as one of our prime national goals, through the antitrust laws, the continuance of a viable competitive economy.

Informational Role of Advertising Advertising plays a major informational role in our economy because (1) products are available in such wide varieties, (2) new products are offered in such great numbers, and (3) existing products must be called to the attention of new consumers who are added to the market as a result of expansion in incomes, the population explosion, and changes in tastes.

The most heavily advertised products are widely used items that are consumed by major segments of the population. This does not mean that everyone buys every product or buys them to the extent that he can. Some of these products are substitutes for other products. For example, it will be readily recognized that cereals provide only one of many alternatives among breakfast foods. In some instances, heavily advertised products compete with each other like, for example, soft drinks and beer. In other instances, additional consumers can use the products so that the size of the total market can be increased (for example, toilet preparations).

Potential markets also expand as incomes rise and as consumers are able to purchase products they previously could not afford. As the population increases, large numbers of new potential customers are added each year. Continuous large-scale advertising provides reminders to old customers and provides information to obtain some part of the patronage of new customers. The potential market is so huge that large scale advertising is an economical way to obtain good results.

In addition, the identity of buyers changes under some circumstances and new potential buyers must be given information concerning the available alternatives. It has also been pointed out that some of these products are ". . . subject to fads and style changes" and that ". . . consumers become restive with existing brands and are prepared to try new varieties." Illustrations include cereals, soaps, clothing, and motion pictures.[8]

The consumer has a wide variety of brands from which to choose. Product improvements usually breed competitive product improvements; the advertising of these improvements may result in an increase in total advertising for the class of products.

When any company in an industry embarks on an intensified advertising campaign, its competitors must step up their advertising or other sales efforts to avoid the possible loss of market position. This is a key characteristic of competition.

On the other hand, if any company decides to economize on its advertising budget, its exposure is reduced and its share of market may decline if its competitors fail to follow the same policy. Thus, for some grocery products it has been reported that ". . . competition within a sector may have established a certain pattern with regard to the extent of advertising, and any company dropping below this level faces possible substantial loss of market share." [9]

These results flow particularly if the industry is oligopolistic, that is, has relatively few producers who are sensitive to and responsive to actions of competitors. However, as the dramatic changes in market shares during the past decade so amply demonstrate, this does not mean that the companies in such oligopolistic industries will retain relatively constant shares of the market.[10]

The informational role of advertising has been succinctly summarized by Professor George J. Stigler:

> . . . Under competition, the main tasks of a seller are to inform potential buyers of his existence, his line of goods, and his prices. Since both sellers and buyers change over time (due to birth, death, migration), since people forget information once acquired, and since new products appear, the existence of sellers must be continually advertised. . . .
>
> This informational function of advertising must be emphasized because of a popular and erroneous belief that advertising consists chiefly of nonrational (emotional and repetitive) appeals.[11]

Elsewhere, Professor Stigler has pointed out that ". . . information is a valuable resource," that advertising is "the obvious method of identifying buyers and sellers" which "reduces drastically the cost of search," and that "It is clearly an immensely powerful instrument for the elimination of ignorance. . . ." [12]

Often this information is required to create interest in and demand for a product. Thus, it has been reported:

> . . . to a significant degree General Foods and the U.S. food market created each other. Before a new product appears, customers are rarely conscious of wanting it. There was no spontaneous demand for ready-to-eat cereals; frozen foods required a sustained marketing effort stretching over many years; instant coffee had been around for decades, supplying a market that did not amount to a tenth of its present level. General Foods' corporate skill consists largely in knowing enough about American tastes to foresee what products will be accepted.[13]

Similarly, J. K. Galbraith, who has been very critical of advertising, has recognized that:

> A new consumer product must be introduced with a suitable advertising campaign to arouse an interest in it. The path for an expansion of output must be paved by a suitable expansion in the advertising budget. Outlays for the manufacturing of a product are not more important in the strategy of modern business enterprise than outlays for the manufacturing of demand for the product.[14]

We live in an economy that has little resemblance to the ideal of perfect competition postulated by economists. However, one of the postulates of this ideal economy is perfect knowledge. Advertising contributes to such knowledge. Thus, in such an idealized economy, even though advertising may be wasteful it would still have a role to play. But in the world of reality, with all its imperfections, advertising is much more important. Advertising is an integral and vital part of our growing economy and contributes to the launching of the new products so essential to economic growth.

How Much Is　　In 1966, total expenditures for media advertising aggregated
Informational?　$13.3 billion.[15] It is impossible to determine exactly how much
　　　　　　　　　of this amount was strictly informational. However, the following facts are of interest.

Classified advertising was $1.3 billion
Other local newspaper advertising, largely retail, was $2.6 billion
Business paper advertising was $712 million
Local radio and TV advertising was $1.1 billion
Spot radio and spot TV advertising was $1.2 billion
National advertising on network TV, network radio, magazines and newspapers was $3.7 billion
Direct mail was $2.5 billion

Classified advertising and local advertising are overwhemingly informational in nature. Certainly some part of national advertising also performs this function. These figures suggest that substantially less than half of total advertising is of the type that the critics are attacking as wasteful;[16] the exact amount cannot be pinpointed. Moreover, it must be kept in mind that a significant part of national advertising is for the promotion of new products for which the informational role is vital.

From another point of view, even if there is waste, the social cost is considerably less than suggested by these data. Thus, in 1966 about $10 billion was spent on advertising in newspapers, magazines, radio, and television; another $746 million was spent on farm and business publications. Without these expenditures, these sources of news and entertainment would have had to obtain substantial sums from other sources. It has been estimated that ". . . advertising paid for over 60% of the cost of periodicals, for over 70% of the cost of newspapers, and for 100% of the cost of commercial radio and TV broadcasting." [17] Thus, advertising results in a form of subsidization for all media of communication. Without it, these media would have to charge higher subscription rates or be subsidized by the government or some combination of both.

Advertising and Expanding Markets   Economic growth has become a major objective of national economic policy in recent years. Rising productivity, increasing population, improving education, rates of saving, and decisions concerning new investments are the ingredients of economic growth. In addition, there must be a favorable political climate including tax policies and monetary policies designed to release the forces conducive to growth.

Advertising contributes to economic growth and in turn levels of living by complementing the efforts to create new and improved products through expenditures for research and development. One observer has described the process as follows:

. . . advertising, by acquainting the consumer with the values of new products, widens the market for these products, pushes forward their acceptance by the consumer, and encourages the investment and entrepreneurship necessary for innovation. Advertising, in short, holds out the promise of a greater and speedier return than would occur without such methods, thus stimulating investment, growth, and diversity.[18]

Among the most intensive advertisers have been toilet preparations (14.7% of sales), cleaning and polishing preparations (12.6%), and drugs (9.4%). The markets for these products have been expanding at a faster rate than all consumer spending.

Between 1947 and 1966, personal consumption expenditures for these products increased as follows: [19]

	1947	1955	1966
		(millions of dollars)	
Toilet articles & preparations	1,217	1,915	4,690
Cleaning, polishing & household supplies	1,523	2,480	4,487
Drug preparations and sundries	1,313	2,362	5,062

As a share of total personal consumption expenditures, the increases from 1947 to 1966 were as follows:

Toilet articles and preparations from 0.76% to 1.01%
Cleaning, polishing and household supplies from 0.94% to 0.97%
Drug preparations and sundries from 0.82% to 1.09%

These increases in relative importance are based upon dollar totals. However, the retail prices of these products rose less than the consumer price index during the postwar years.

Between 1947 and 1966, the price increases were as follows:

Total consumer price index	45.4%
Toilet preparations	14.6
Soaps and detergents	2.6
Drugs and prescriptions	22.8

Thus, the increase in relative importance of these highly advertised products has been even greater in real terms than in dollars.

Between 1947 and 1966, the increase in *real* personal consumption expenditures has been:

Toilet articles and preparations from 0.68% to 1.12%
Cleaning, polishing and household supplies from 0.87% to 1.05%
Drug preparations and sundries from 0.82% to 1.24%

Clearly, advertising appears to have contributed to an expansion in the demand for these products and to the growth of our economy with the accompanying expansion in job opportunities and in economic well-being. There may have been some waste in this process—although all of such expenditures cannot be characterized as wasteful—but it appears to have been offset in full or in part by these other benefits.

The charge of large-scale waste in advertising appears to reflect in part a yearning for an economy with standardized, homogeneous products which are primarily functional in nature. An illustration would be a refrigerator that is designed solely to be technically efficient for the storage of food. However, customers are also interested in the decor of their kitchens, in convenience and speed in the manufacture of ice cubes, in shelves that rotate, and in special storage for butter. These are additions to functional usefulness which "an affluent society" can afford but which a subsistence economy cannot.

Advertising in a High Level Economy The concept of waste must be related to the level achieved by an economy. Professor John W. Lowe has observed that "Perhaps a good deal of the 'wastefulness' assigned to advertising springs from the fact that a large part of the world's population cannot consider satisfying *psychological wants* when most of their efforts must be devoted to *needs*." [20] (Italics added.)

In a subsistence economy, scarcity is so significant that advertising might be wasteful, particularly where it diverts resources from meeting the basic necessities of life. Such an economy usually is a "full employment economy" in the sense that everyone is working. But the total yield of a full employment subsistence economy is very low, as is evident throughout Asia, Africa, and South America.

Professor Galbraith has noted that "The opportunity for product differentiation . . . is almost uniquely the result of opulence . . . the tendency for commercial rivalries . . . to be channeled into advertising and salesmanship would disappear in a poor community." [21]

In the high level American economy, there usually are surpluses rather than scarcity. The use of resources for advertising to differentiate products, therefore, is not necessarily a diversion from other uses. Rather, it frequently represents the use of resources that might otherwise be idle both in the short run and the long run and thus may obviate the waste that such idleness represents.

The Marketing Mix   The concept of waste cannot ignore the question—waste as compared with what alternative? Advertising cannot be considered in a vacuum. It must be considered as one of the marketing alternatives available. Generally it is not a question of advertising or nothing, but rather of advertising or some other type of sales effort.

It is a mistake to evaluate the relative cost of advertising apart from other marketing costs. It is only one tool in the marketing arsenal which also includes direct selling, packaging, servicing, product planning, pricing, etc. Expenditures for advertising often are substituted for other types of selling effort. This substitution has been readily apparent in the history of the discount house. These houses have featured well-advertised brands which were presold and, hence, virtually eliminated the need for floor stocks and reduced the need for space and many salesmen.

Advertising is undertaken where it is the most effective and most economical way to appeal to customers. It is a relatively low cost method of communicating with all potential customers and this explains its widespread adoption by many companies. To the extent that less efficient marketing methods must be substituted for advertising, we would really have economic waste.

Summary and Conclusions   There is wide agreement that the informational role of advertising makes a significant contribution to the effective operation of our economy. There is also agreement that inefficiency in the use of advertising is wasteful, as are other types of inefficiencies that are part and parcel of a market-determined economy. The gray area is so-called competitive advertising, largely national, which is the main target of those who insist advertising is wasteful. Although precise data are not available, the estimates cited earlier indicate that the charge of competitive waste applies to substantially less than half of all advertising expenditures.

Competition unavoidably involves considerable duplication and waste. If the accent is placed on the negative, a distorted picture is obtained. On balance, the advantages of competition have been much greater than the wastes.

Advertising has contributed to an expanding market for new and better products. Many of these new products would not have been brought to market unless firms were free to develop mass markets through large-scale advertising. There may be some waste in this process, but it has been more than offset by other benefits.

Where burgeoning advertising expenditures are accompanied by expanding industry sales, there will tend to be a decline in total unit costs instead of increase, and prices may remain unchanged or decline. In such situations, it seems clear that advertising, while adding to total costs, will result in lower total *unit* costs, the more significant figure. This gain will be offset to some extent if the increase in volume represents a diversion from other companies or industries with an accompanying rise in unit costs. Of course, such change is inherent in a dynamic competitive economy.

Advertising expenditures have risen as the economy has expanded. At such times, the absolute increase in sales resulting from higher advertising expenditures need not be accompanied by a loss in sales in other industries. This is particularly true if a new product has been developed and its sales are expanding. In that event, new jobs probably will be created and help to support a higher level of economic activity generally.

The claim that resources devoted to advertising would be utilized more efficiently for other purposes ignores the fact that generally we have a surplus economy. All of the resources used for advertising are not diverted from other alternatives. Rather, it is probable that much of the resources involved would be idle or would be used less efficiently. Even more important would be the failure to provide the jobs which expanding markets create.

Finally, advertising does not take place in a vacuum. It is one of several marketing alternatives. The abandonment of advertising could not represent a net saving to a company or to the economy. Instead, such a development would require a shift to alternative marketing techniques, some of which would be less efficient than advertising since companies do not deliberately adopt the least effective marketing approach. On balance, advertising is an invaluable competitive tool.

NOTES

1. George Leland Bach, *Economics,* Fifth Edition (Englewood Cliffs, New Jersey: Prentice-Hall, Inc., 1966), p. 437. See also Kenneth Boulding, "Economic Analysis," Volume 1, *Microeconomics,* Fourth Edition, Vol. 1 (New York: Harper and Row, 1966), p. 513.

2. Nicholas H. Kaldor, "The Economic Aspects of Advertising," *The Review of Economic Studies,* Vol. 18 (1950–51), p. 6.

3. Joe S. Bain, *Industrial Organization* (New York: John Wiley & Sons, 1959), pp. 390–91. See also *Report of a Commission of Enquiry Into Advertising* (London, England: The Labour Party, 1966), p. 42. The Reith Report defined "substantially advertised products" at 5%.

4. Richard Caves, *American Industry: Structure, Conduct, Performance* (Englewood Cliffs, New Jersey: Prentice-Hall, Inc., 1964), p. 102.

5. "Advertising and Charlie Brown," *Business Review,* Federal Reserve Bank of Philadelphia (June, 1962), p. 10.

6. Stuart Chase, *The Tragedy of Waste* (New York: Macmillan Company, 1928), p. 112.

7. Committee on Advertising, *Principles of Advertising* (New York: Pitman Publishing Corp., 1963), p. 34; and Neil H. Borden, "The Role of Advertising in the Various Stages of Corporate and Economic Growth," Peter D. Bennett, editor, *Marketing and Economic Development* (Chicago, Illinois: American Marketing Association, 1965), p. 493.

8. Lester G. Telser, "How Much Does It Pay Whom to Advertise?", *American Economic Review, Papers and Proceedings* (December, 1960), pp. 203–4.

9. National Commission on Food Marketing, *Grocery Manufacturing,* Technical Study No. 6 (Washington, D.C.: June, 1966), p. 14.

10. Jules Backman, *Advertising and Competition* (New York: New York University Press, 1967), Chapters 3 and 4.

11. George J. Stigler, *The Theory of Price,* Third Edition (New York: The Macmillan Company, 1966), p. 200.

12. George J. Stigler, "The Economics of Information," *The Journal of Political Economy* (June, 1961), pp. 213, 216, 220. See also S. A. Ozga, "Imperfect Markets Through Lack of Knowledge," *Quarterly Journal of Economics* (February, 1960), pp. 29, 33–34, and Wroe Alderson, *Dynamic*

Market Behavior (Homewood, Illinois: Richard D. Irwin, Inc., 1965), pp. 128–31.

13. "General Foods Is Five Billion Particulars," *Fortune* (March, 1964), p. 117.

14. J. K. Galbraith, *The Affluent Society* (Boston, Massachusetts: Houghton Mifflin Company, 1958), p. 156.

15. This total excludes a miscellaneous category of $3.3 billion.

16. For the United Kingdom, the "disputed proportion" of advertising expenditures has been estimated at about 30% of the total. Walter Taplin, *Advertising, A New Approach* (Boston, Massachusetts: Little, Brown & Co., 1963), p. 126.

17. Fritz Machlup, *The Production and Distribution of Knowledge in the United States* (Princeton, New Jersey: Princeton University Press, 1962), p. 265.

18. David M. Blank, "Some Comments on the Role of Advertising in the American Economy—A Plea for Revaluation," L. George Smith, editor, *Reflections on Progress in Marketing* (Chicago, Illinois: American Marketing Association, 1964), p. 151.

19. *The National Income and Product Accounts of the United States, 1929–1965, Statistical Tables* (Washington, D.C.: United States Department of Commerce, August, 1966), pp. 44–49; and *Survey of Current Business* (July, 1967), pp. 23–24.

20. John W. Lowe, "An Economist Defends Advertising," *Journal of Marketing,* Vol. 27 (July, 1963), p. 18.

21. John K. Galbraith, *American Capitalism: The Concept of Countervailing Power* (Boston, Massachusetts: Houghton Mifflin Company, 1952), pp. 106–07.

17 Americans and Advertising: Thirty Years of Public Opinion

Stephen A. Greyser
Raymond A. Bauer

Thus far we have examined the views of individual students or practitioners of marketing, both pro and con. But what does the American consumer think of advertising?

Obviously, the concept "American consumer" is too broad to be entirely meaningful, since in fact, there is no such entity as *the* American consumer. The following article will provide information about how specific proportions of the American public feel about advertising.

The article also sheds some light on the nature of the American consumer—a frequently discussed section of marketing textbooks.

Students of the mechanism and management of advertising will naturally wish to understand how the public views their importance.

Breathes there an American so unopinionated that he has never expressed an opinion about advertising? Probably not, for advertising is a subject that has consistently elicited praise and criticism from the American public. In conjunction with our study of what Americans think about advertising as an institution in our society, we made an historical review of advertising criticism, particularly in twentieth-century America, including an examination of a series of public opinion studies with questions on advertising, dating from the 1930's. Our hope was to learn not only what the public has said it thinks about advertising over this period, but whether the public's opinions have changed over the past three decades.

Streams of Criticism
In twentieth-century United States, advertising has reached ever-higher peaks with respect both to the volume directed at consumers and its commercial necessity for business. In the wake of the increasing amount and pervasiveness of advertising has come consistent criticism of it. This criticism has comprised three major streams.

Stephen A. Greyser and Raymond A. Bauer, "Americans and Advertising", *Public Opinion Quarterly* (Spring, 1966), Vol. 30, pp. 69–78.

The first stream attacks advertising's basic *economic* function and its business role. This particular stream was at a high tide during the Depression years, and linked the idea of advertising as an economic waste and a cost that the American public could not afford to more general ideological condemnation of business, branded goods, and so on. Criticism of the social goals of society, particularly intellectual criticism of the way in which the social order operates, is a separate but related aspect of criticism of our economic system as a whole and its predominant values.

A second stream relates to the techniques of advertising as an extension of selling, incorporating both displeasure over any partisan advocacy of a product and concern over possible manipulation of consumers by propagandists and persuaders. Disdain for selling and disapproval of manipulation are both segments of a *social* criticism of advertising. (Some of the intellectual criticism belongs here too.)

The third stream is criticism of advertising *content* and the *amount* of advertising. This criticism has been among the most persistent of all, focusing on both advertising's ethical aspects (the truth issue) and its aesthetic aspects (the taste issue).

Public Opinion Studies of Advertising's Institutional Aspects — While countless studies have been undertaken of consumer reactions to the advertisements of specific products and firms, a search of the literature and of the Roper Public Opinion Research Center's files in Williamstown reveals only a small number of studies focusing on the public's attitudes toward advertising as an institution. Of these studies still fewer have dealt systematically with a variety of aspects of advertising's image or posed these issues to broad segments of the public. Among these are:

> The 1938–1939 Alpha Delta Sigma study directed by Professor Neil H. Borden in conjunction with his massive study of *The Economic Effects of Advertising*.[1]
>
> George Gallup's "Studies of Consumer Agitation" (1939, 1940) [2]
>
> *Consumer Attitudes toward Distribution* (1946–1947) [3]
>
> Professor Kenneth Dameron's Ohio State Consumer Study (1950) [4]
>
> The Wage Earner Forum's "How the Public Looks at Advertising" (1951) [5]
>
> Field California Polls "The Public Looks at Advertising" (1953, 1961) [6]
>
> Gallup's *Redbook* "Study of Public Attitudes toward Advertising" [7]
>
> Universal Marketing Research's study of attitudes toward advertisements (1960) [8]
>
> American Association of Advertising Agencies' (AAAA) Study of Consumer Judgment of Advertising (1964) [9]

Having reviewed many of the opinion studies made over the past three decades, are there specific institutional facets of advertising that we can examine in perspective, over time? Further, have the public's attitudes toward particular aspects of advertising changed over the past thirty years? And, has the public expressed great concern over particular aspects of advertising?

Unfortunately, despite the accumulation of a number of studies, there is a paucity of good data. Variations in the samples selected, in the wordings of specific questions, and in the general thrust of particular questionnaires all affect our ability to make, and the utility of making, a solid analysis of trends in public attitudes toward advertising.

Nonetheless, there are a few areas in which such an effort can be undertaken. The following discussion treats each of these institutional issues in turn, presenting chronologically data both from the studies mentioned above and, in certain instances, from other isolated efforts to probe individual institutional aspects of advertising.

GENERAL FAVORABILITY TOWARD ADVERTISING: The data presented in Table 1 indicate that Americans are generally favorable toward advertising.

TABLE 1   General Favorability Toward Advertising (in per cent)

Have you any criticisms of advertising? (Gallup, 1939, 1940)*

	1939	1940
Yes, or some criticisms	42	40

In general, do you like or dislike advertising? (Gallup, *Redbook,* 1959)

Like	75
Dislike	15
Can't say	10

General attitude toward advertising (self-coded). (Universal Marketing Research, 1961)

Generally favorable	54
Half and half	25
Generally unfavorable	17
Don't know	3

Attitude toward advertising (coded independently). (AAAA, 1964)

Favorable	41
Mixed	34
Indifferent	8
Unfavorable	14
Unclassifiable	3

* Note that question wording invites a high proportion of criticism.

While they may have specific criticisms of advertising, and need only an invitation or opportunity to express them, over all the public is quite favorable to advertising as part of American life.

TABLE 2   Advertising and the Economy

Statement	Per Cent Agreeing
Advertising tends to stimulate consumers to improve their standard of living. (*Consumer Attitudes Toward Distribution,* 1946)	75
Advertising is a necessary part of our economic system. (*Consumer Attitudes Toward Distribution,* 1946)	75
Advertising has played a large part in creating a high standard of living in America. (Wage Earner Forum, 1951)	90
Advertising helps keep the country prosperous because it creates sales. (Gallup, *Redbook,* 1959)	81
Advertising is essential. (AAAA, 1964)*	89
Advertising raises our standard of living. (AAAA, 1964)	71

* Statements were put in alternate forms to split halves of the sample. Results here are responses to this statement only.

ADVERTISING AND OUR ECONOMY: Unfortunately, relevant data on how the public reacts to advertising as an essential part of our economy dates only from after World War II. It would be enlightening to have information comparable to that outlined below from the 1930's, when advertising was under considerable economic attack.

As can be seen in Table 2, since 1946 roughly three-quarters of the American public has seen advertising as an essential economic feature making specific economic contributions, particularly in the form of an improved standard of living. This fact and the general similarity of the questions in this series allow us to say that attitudes in this area have been rather stable.

ADVERTISING AS A PERSUADER: On this issue, unfortunately, there are very few questions from which to comprise a series. However, despite differences in question wording (especially in the Field California Poll version) and in the samples, it would seem from the data in Table 3 that unfavorable attitudes toward advertising as a persuader have been rather stable over time, much as attitudes have been stable on the favorable economic aspects.

TRUTH AND STANDARDS OF ADVERTISING: Numerous questions in the surveys bear on the matters of truth in advertising and advertising's standards. About half the American public seems to find fault with the truth content of advertising. Table 4 shows this to be true for 1934, 1939, 1946, and 1964. While the question wording and basic approaches of the inquiries may vary, the results seem to hold steady at about the 50 per cent mark.

TABLE 3   Advertising as a Persuader

Do you think advertising leads people to buy things they don't need or can't afford?
(Gallup, 1939, 1940)

	Per Cent Agreeing
1939	80*
1940	81*

Advertising leads people to buy things they don't need or can't afford. (Ohio State Study, 1950)   80

Most advertising just tries to get people to buy a lot of things they don't really need. (Field California Poll, 1953, 1961)

1953	45
1961	59

Advertising often persuades people to buy things they shouldn't buy. (AAAA, 1964)†
                                                                                             73

* Per cent who answered "Yes" or "In some cases."

† Statements were put in alternate forms to split halves of the sample. Results here are responses to this statement only.

However, concerning the standards of advertising, Americans generally think that things are improving; this was so in 1939, 1940, 1946, and 1964. The wide optimism concerning the trend in advertising standards is paradoxical in light of the continuing complaints about truth in advertising by half of the public. This is especially so when one considers the general American tendency to believe that trends in other zones of life are deteriorating.[10] One must consequently interpret opinion data cautiously in the truth and standards areas, and examine the issues jointly rather than singly, as in Table 4.

ADVERTISING'S EFFECT ON PRICES: This theme has been very frequently studied over the years, and more relevant attitude-trend data exist on it than on any of our other topics. Unlike the situation with respect to several of the issues above, we have data on this topic from the 1930's, 1940's, 1950's, and 1960's, and are fortunate to have one major subseries where the same form of question on this issue was put to a nationwide panel six times from 1938 to 1951.

At least two conclusions can be drawn from examining the data in Table 5. First, in studies in each of the four decades under scrutiny here, a majority of the public believed that advertising costs result in increased consumer prices, although there are exceptions. In each case, in Table 5, the percentage of judgments favorable to advertising comes first. This is apparently a particularly sensitive area for advertising; in studies where the public gives

TABLE 4   Truth and Standards in Advertising (in per cent)

A. Truth and Standards in General

Most advertising statements are based on reasonable facts or exaggerated claims. Which do you find most often to be the case? (*Sales Management,* Sept. 1, 1938)

	1934	1938
Reasonable	51	42
Exaggerated	49	58

On the whole, do you believe advertising today is truthful? (*Ladies Home Journal,* May, 1939)

Yes	51

How much advertising is misleading? (*Consumer Attitudes Toward Distribution,* 1946)

Practically all	8
At least half	35
Less than half	35
Practically none	6

Advertisements present a true picture of the product advertised. (AAAA, 1964) *

Generally or partially agree	47

B. Truth and Standards Today and Yesterday

Is advertising more or less truthful than 5 years ago? (Gallup, 1939, 1940)

	1939	1940
More	46	50
Less	21	19

Present day advertising is much better than that of 4–6 years ago. (*Consumer Attitudes Toward Distribution,* 1946)

Yes	62
No	8
Doubtful	20
Don't know	10

Advertising today is more truthful than it was three years ago. (Ohio State Study, 1950)

More truthful	41
Less truthful	15

Would you say that today's standards are higher, lower, or about the same, compared with ten years ago? (AAAA, 1964)

Higher	58
About the same	18
Lower	10
Don't know	14

* Statements were put in alternate forms to split halves of the sample. Results here are responses to this statement only.

its views on a number of issues related to advertising, they tend to be more anti-advertising on this issue than on others.[11]

Second, the proportion of consumers holding this attitude has increased somewhat in recent years, although it is still below the level of the 1930's. This is perhaps most clearly revealed in the trends shown in the Psychological Corporation and Field California Poll series. Furthermore, the AAAA study, which in 1964 used two forms of the question on split halves of the sample ("advertising results in lower prices"; "advertising results in higher prices") shows a slightly higher percentage of the public saying that advertising results in higher prices than saying lower prices. This dual-statement formulation is perhaps the best barometer of opinion on the topic to date.

Conclusion   It would seem clear from the above that even professional researchers can have problems in developing questions to yield meaningful data, especially data that will be comparable and readily interpretable in view of previous research. However, despite variations in question wording and samples, *there seems to be no reason to believe that Americans are particularly more, or less, critical of advertising today than they have been in the past.* The general stability of opinion over time is marked, with respect to *both* favorable and unfavorable attitudes. This stability is reinforced by the general findings of the AAAA study, showing that Americans make distinctions between those aspects of advertising they endorse and those they disparage: few say they are basically opposed to advertising, and few give advertising across-the-board approval.

When we examine these data in conjunction with other historical research, we find that sentiment toward advertising as a basic economic institution in our society seems to reflect the prevailing economic context of the times. During the Depression and immediate post-Depression eras, economic issues were salient, and the costs of advertising were among those clarioned as "excessive" during the heyday of the so-called "consumer movement." When war came, winning the struggle became the supreme objective; in addition, the unavailability of many products resulted in a greatly reduced volume of product or brand advertising. Both these factors tended to diminish wartime antiadvertising sentiment. The postwar era saw not only an end to price controls but the advent of television: economic matters again loomed relatively important to the public, and television became the most intrusive advertising medium ever. Both these factors tended to increase consciousness of, and negative sentiment toward, advertising.

Yet, in spite of all these general tendencies, the public's basic feelings toward advertising and its major institutional elements have remained remarkably stable over the years. While consumers will criticize individual aspects of advertising, they accept it as part of American life and are on the whole favorable toward it.

TABLE 5   Advertising's Effect on Prices (in per cent)

Stores could sell for less money if they didn't advertise so much. (University of Toledo, 1935)*

No	46
Yes	39
Uncertain or don't know	15

Do you believe that you are paying a premium for widely advertised goods, because of the large amount of money spent for advertising by the manufacturer of these goods? (*Advertising Age*, 1936)*

No	49
Yes	51

One pays more for advertised articles than for those distributed without advertising. (*Sales Management*, 1936)*

No	22
Yes	53
Uncertain	25

Do you think products that are advertised widely cost more than products that are not advertised? (*Ladies Home Journal*, 1939)*

No	49
Yes	51

Do you believe that widely advertised mass production articles cost more because they are advertised? (*Sales Management*, 1939)*

No	64
Yes	36

Manufacturers could sell their products for less if they did not spend so much on advertising. (Borden, 1938–1939)*

No	50
Yes	37
Uncertain	14

Do you think that advertising increases or decreases the cost of things you buy? (Gallup, 1939, 1940)

	1939	*1940*
Decreases	15	17
Increases	72	69
Don't know	13	14

Advertising may cause the consumer to pay less for a product than if it were not advertised because it increases sales and makes it possible to cut the cost of production and marketing.† (*Consumer Attitudes Toward Distribution*, 1946)

Yes	52
No	18
Doubtful	20
No answer	10

The consumer must pay more for goods because of advertising. (*Consumer Attitudes Toward Distribution*, 1946)

No	33
Yes	39
Doubtful	17
No answer	11

Do you think advertising increases the cost of the items you buy? (Ohio State Study, 1950)

Yes	65
(Remainder unreported)	

On cigarettes, for example, they spend thousands of dollars for advertising. If they cut out the advertising, they could pass the savings on to the consumer. (Wage Earner Forum, 1951)

No	40
Yes	58
Don't know	2

Do you believe advertising makes the things you buy cost more or less in the long run. (Psychological Corporation, 1938–1951)

	1938	1941	1944	1946	1949	1951
Less	24	29	19	33	30	26
More	40	37	34	37	39	46
Neither	17	15	25	13	19	19
Don't know	19	19	22	17	12	9

In your opinion, does advertising increase or decrease the cost of things you buy? (Gallup, *Redbook*, 1959)

Decrease	11
Increase	57
No difference	20
Don't know	12

Advertising makes things cost more than they would without advertising. (Field California Poll, 1953, 1961)

	1953	1961
No	41	32
Yes	57	64
Don't know	2	4

In general, advertising results in lower/higher prices. (AAAA, 1964)‡

Lower	40
Higher	45
Don't know	15

* Reported in Neil H. Borden, *The Economic Effects of Advertising*, Chicago, Irwin, 1942, p. 790.
† An incredibly worded item!
‡ Statements were put in alternate forms to split halves of the sample.

NOTES

1. Chicago, Irwin, 1942; see especially Chap. 26.
2. Advertising Research Foundation, New York, 1939–1940.
3. Committee on Consumer Relations in Advertising, Inc., New York, 1947.
4. Reported in *Printers' Ink,* March 7, 1952.
5. Macfadden Publications, May 9, 1951.
6. FRC *Footnotes,* October, 1961.
7. *Redbook,* 1959.
8. "An Experimental Study of Public Attitudes Toward Advertising," 1960.
9. "An Analysis of the Principal Findings," AAAA, 1965.
10. See, for example, Hazel Gaudet Erskine, "The Polls: Some Thoughts about Life and People," *Public Opinion Quarterly,* Vol. 28, 1964, pp. 517 ff.
11. That it is anti-advertising to agree that advertising increases prices has long been assumed. It is possible that many people might agree that advertising raises prices, but might simultaneously agree that benefits such as national brands are worth the added cost.

18 What's Ethical? Admen Cast Votes

Among the ethical problems that confront advertising practitioners are some that are not related to the society as a whole. Many significant questions arise that concern the behavior and decisions of the practitioners themselves. In this article some of these ethical problems are presented together with a sampling of the opinions of advertising people themselves.

All self-respecting admen endorse ethics, but they differ on what is ethical.

That is evident from the response to questions about 12 hypothetical cases involving ethics, published in the Feature Section (AA, May 27). For each of the 12 cases, *Advertising Age* asked readers one or several questions about what they thought was proper conduct. Readers were asked to mark their "yes" or "no" answers, with comments, on an accompanying ballot. On none of the questions was the response unanimous, and on some it was divided 50–50, or close to it.

What some admen saw as a legitimate (even if highly competitive) business action, others viewed as betrayal of an agency account or an employer, disloyalty to an associate, or dishonesty in selling one's agency or oneself. A vp and management supervisor at a large New York agency termed some questions "frightening" in their implications.

Generally, disagreement was more pronounced on questions that were more difficult or complex. In one hypothetical case, the supposition was that you were sent by your agency to make an account solicitation, in the course of which you were sounded out and were made a job offer by the prospective client. Do you tell your boss about the offer? A large majority of AA respondents shared a common reaction: 72% said yes, 28% said no.

But a second question, differently worded, brought a different response. Do you tell your boss everything about the presentation except the job offer? On that question, opinion was much more evenly divided: 45% said yes, 55% said no.

Reprinted from "What's Ethical? Admen Cast Votes", *Advertising Age* (September, 1968), Vol. 39, No. 40, pp. 105–108. Copyright, 1968, by Advertising Publications Inc. (now Crain Communications, Inc.).

Among those who believed you should tell the boss about the offer was an agency vp who commented: "Nothing wrong with letting your boss know that someone else thinks you're worth a bundle. You might get a raise." Among the dissenters was an assistant ad manager who maintained: "You have no obligation to reveal competitive job offers."

In another case, you are making a speech to a marketing group and you use the occasion to promote your "hot creative shop" by telling how the expertise led to a $3,000,000 account just landed by your agency. You don't mention that the new president of the client company is your old college roomie. Question: Is that ethical?

This was one case where admen were divided in their opinion almost evenly, with considerable comment (see Case 7, below). It was also a case where advertisers and agency men differed slightly: Among advertisers a bare majority voted yes (seeing nothing particularly wrong with your conduct), while a small preponderance of agency men voted no.

Other ethical questions included what you do about a colleague who drinks too much and another who talks too much (leaking new product information).

AA received 413 ballots on its questions about ethics. From agency men, 203 ballots were mailed in; advertisers, 114 ballots; others (media, suppliers, etc.) 81 ballots. An additional 15 came from students, including 14 from an advanced advertising class at Kent State University, Kent, O.

Reflecting the difficulty or complexity of ethical issues raised, most respondents left some questions unanswered. Generally, the pattern appeared to be: The tougher the question, the lower the response. Sometimes the respondent found his thinking too complex to be indicated simply by marking a yes or no ballot, and his opinions were restricted to his written comments. The balloting was as follows:

Case 1:
Inside Merger
Talks

During his prolonged merger talks with the Hustle & Bustle Agency, Clyde Bonney of the Bonney Shoppe learns all about the H&B accounts, including the fact that the biggest client, Wiltwire Automotives, is shaky. There's a personality clash between the H&B management and the Wiltwire management. Mr. Bonney contacts Mr. Wiltwire and, after a good first meeting, breaks off merger talks with H&B. Later, he gets the Wiltwire account.

Q. A. Did Mr. Bonney handle this situation properly all the way?   A. YES, 10%. NO, 90%.

Q. B. Was it up to H&B to keep the Wiltwire problem secret from Mr. Bonney?   A. YES, 19%. NO, 81%.

The large majority disapproved of Mr. Bonney's conduct, and their feelings are summed up in the terse phrase of a sales promotion manager: "Pure piracy." A marketing manager said, "Matters discussed in merger talks should be considered 'privileged information'." A vice-chairman of an agency plans board was even more emphatic: "It's more a matter of poor judgment to talk to a scoundrel like Bonney in the first place."

An agency president, condemning Bonney's conduct, suggested preventive measures: "H&B should have made an agreement in advance to protect existing accounts of both agencies."

Among the minority upholding Bonney's conduct were these comments: "All's fair in love and the agency business" and "Merger talks don't put you under obligation; it's up to both parties to dig."

Students, generally considered more idealistic than oldsters, appeared less so, (more inclined to "let the merging agency beware") as they parted company with admen on the second question. Unlike the admen, most students voted that it was up to H&B to keep its account woe secret from Bonney.

Case 2:   You're an overworked account exec at the Miff & Mole Agency
Should You   and you know that your pals, Linder & Byrd, have opened a new
Tell?   agency. They have sent out letters to agency execs, advertisers, media people and studios to announce their opening and they promise to pay commissions, based on billings, to anyone who leads them to new business. You know that one of your agency's accounts (but not one that you work on), Callow & Brash Fashions, is unhappy. Do you give Linder & Byrd this information and offer to arrange a meeting?

Q. A. A smart move.   A. YES, 4%. NO, 96%.

Q. B. Smart move, up to a point.   A. YES, 26%. NO, 74%.
     That point is what?

Admen were fairly united on the first question, but showed more disagreement on the second. A creative director expressed the common view of the move: "Inexcusable." An agency president asked, "Whose bread are you eating?"

On the opposite (minority) side, a point most often mentioned was explained this way by an advertising manager: "Tipping off your friends is a smart move so long as you do not become involved in the meeting or let it be known that you started it." Another ad manager spelled it out further: "O.K., but do not offer to set up an appointment." A product manager said, "Yes, but don't get involved in the negotiations."

An advertising consultant advised: "It's all right if you plan to join L&B. Otherwise, you owe loyalty to your employer." An advertiser drew an even finer line: "It's O.K. if the information came from outside your agency contacts and your present agency has failed to do anything to firm up the shaky account." But the majority view was stressed by a sales promotion manager, who rejected the move without qualification: "When you work for a man, you work for *him*."

Case 3:   You're a star salesman on the West Coast and now a big New
Honor Bound?   York company has hired you, moved you (and your family) at
                 a cost of about $2,500. You've agreed, orally, to stay with them
for at least a year. Everything goes along beautifully for five months. At
that time, you receive an offer from another New York outfit—the one
you've had your sights on for years. It's a better opportunity. But . . .
there's that darned promise you made.

Q. A. There is no contract; it's a free   A. YES, 24%. NO, 76%.
country. Move.

Q. B. You stay. You know that, where   A. YES, 73%. NO, 27%.
real talent is concerned, opportu-
nity knocks more than once.

Q. C. Do you offer to reimburse them   A. YES, 58%. NO, 42%.
for all or part of the expense?

In Question A, a creative director circled the phrase, "There is no contract," and wrote, "Yes, there is." He voted no. Echoing that view, an advertiser stated: "The expense money and one-year promise are equivalent
to an unwritten contract—and morally binding." Another asked, "What is
a man's word worth?" The president of an outdoor advertising company
stated, "No, man! Fulfill your obligations, always."

But the minority offered argument. An advertising consultant, who advised moving, asserted, "Many companies would fire you regardless of oral
discussions, if they wanted. Tit for tat." An agency creative vp agreed: "If
the agency suffered reverses, it would let you go with apologies. So apologize and go." A radio-tv producer urged: "Pay 'em back and leave. They
don't want a discontented employe."

A creative chief had a detailed plan: "You accept the job with the provision that you will start work in seven months. Then you tell your employer. If he's smart, he'll let you go—and it won't cost you a dime. Your
employer writes it off to bad luck; you remain honorable."

But the majority voted "stay," with such unequivocal comments as, "A
deal's a deal" and "You are committed for one year. Turn the offer down,
then tell management." And finally: "The reputation that followed you
would not be worth the move."

Case 4:   You want to sell your studio's services to another cosmetics
Client Wants   company. You arrange with the account supervisor on Silver
to Peek   Gold face gel to get the ground tour of your shop and examine
                 your work. Yes, you show him some past efforts your company
has handled for cosmetics companies other than Silver Gold. He asks to
see some newer work. It just happens that you have something new to show
—a new campagn for Frostfire Cosmetics Ltd.

Q. A. Do you show him the Frostfire   A. YES, 3%, NO, 97%.
   work?

Q. B. Can you show him just one   A. YES, 20%. NO, 80%.
   Frostfire ad that you are proud of,
   which you know isn't really typical
   of the entire campaign, and hold
   back the rest of it for ethical reasons?

The no's have it. "A shocking breach of trust," said an agency vp. A vice-
chairman, plans board, stated: "It is not your property; you have no right
to reveal any part of it to a competitor."

Commenting on Question B and voting no, an account executive said,
"The entire campaign in all its parts can be called typical." An exec vp with
an advertiser commented, "Forgetting ethics, Silver Gold, if smart, wouldn't
buy."

Case 5:   In the suburban town where you live, you are active on a com-
Tempting   mittee that seeks to block the Unexcelled Gas Co. from erecting
Account   power lines and a booster station in the town park. Into your
                 agency's office one day comes the Unexcelled marketing vp. Mis-
sion: To assign you a small, one-shot promotional campaign for use in
another district. You ask if he knows of your opposition to his company
back home. He says yes, but he'd still like you to handle this job. He likes
the work your agency turns out.

Q. A. Should you turn him down?   A. YES, 44%. NO, 56%.

Q. B. Should you recommend an   A. YES, 29%. NO, 62%.
   agency friend in a different suburb
   to handle the job?

The vote was pretty close on the first of these. In the modest majority, a
director of advertising who would take the account offered this view: "As
long as you were honest and told the man about your convictions and your
committee, take him on—business is business." An agency president said,
"I'd take the account provided he understood that it would in no way buy
off my opposition in my own town. Other cities' conditions might be different."

But another agency head, who would shun the account, asserted, "This
is a bribe." Voting with him, a manager of marketing services said, "Stick
to principles."

As for Question B, an agency vp of media and programing presented the
prevailing view: "Don't recommend a friend. If you help at all, he's got you
in the bag." An ad consultant concurred: "War is war."

Differing, a radio station manager was less persnickety: "Sure, why not

help a friend? After all, Unexcelled is going to get the job done someplace."
An agency art director agreed: "You must stand by personal commitments;
but it's blind to think no one will handle the account. So, why not someone
worthy and not committed?" That view was outvoted.

Case 6:
A Job Offer

After weeks of trying, you finally line up an appointment with
J. Jones Topdog, *the* media decision-maker at a key prospect.
Your boss is thrilled and orders special material to help you
make your presentation. The big day arrives. To your surprise, Mr. Topdog begins interviewing you and asks, finally, what it will take to get you
to work for his company. He makes a great offer. After this, your presentation is hasty and somewhat distracted. Back at your office, the boss asks
you to tell about the interview in detail.

Q. A. You tell the boss everything.   A. YES, 72%. NO, 28%.

Q. B. You tell him only the part that   A. YES, 45%. NO, 55%.
doesn't involve Topdog's offer.

Most admen favored telling the boss everything but they wavered a little
on Question B. Voting with the majority on both counts was an agency
head who declared: "A boss worth his salt would know good men are subjected to other offers. It's a compliment to him." An account management
supervisor advised: "Tell him of the offer but no details. And decide
quickly."

Tell all, said a director of advertising, adding "Are you man or mouse?"
Agreeing, an account director observed: "How can you lose? You're 100%
honest, and maybe you'll get more dough to keep you from leaving. If not,
take the new job. This doesn't involve ethics at this point."

Case 7:
The Whole
Truth and . . .

You've just landed a $3,000,000 advertising account and now
you've been asked to deliver a speech before the local marketing
exec's club. You use the occasion to promote your "hot, creative shop." You tell of your agency's expertise and cite examples
of skills that led that big account into your agency. You know that the
agency has such skills.

Q. Should you go on like this when   A. YES, 50%. NO, 50%.
you know in your heart that your
new client is your old college
roomie, just elected president of
his company?

On the yes side, an agency president sagely asked: "Would your old college chum have given you the account if you had not demonstrated the
skills?" Also voting yes, a vp-creative said, "It's no problem if the agency is
really good." Others in agreement were a copywriter ("People don't really
select agencies completely on the basis of alma mater; if you think you have

a hot shop, say so"); an advertiser ("Make the speech, make it good, then live up to it"); and an account executive ("Good excuse for promoting your shop. You don't have to go into painful details.")

A copywriter voted no but, showing his creativity like a copywriter should, added, "That (college roomie revelation) does provide a nice twist for an ending, though." An agency vp with the same idea voted yes to the speech: "Yes, if the agency is a hot creative shop, as everyone would know, anyway; but also tell the truth—it would make a terrific punch line."

Voting no was an agency president: "Better not. The audience might also know about your old college roomie." Another said simply, "Be honest." Also, an ad manager who asked, "Who are you fooling?" and a copywriter/producer: "Ethically, if you got the account fair and square, there's nothing wrong with it—but who would believe you?"

Case 8:   One night, over an after-hours drink, you talked with some of
What's Yours? your agency colleagues about two campaigns they were working
                 on. They had some interesting creative ideas and, from time to
time, you chimed in with a few words. Really, though, they had both campaigns pretty well along. Now, here you are, looking for another job and those ads are now in your portfolio.

Q. A. O.K., since you got in on them   A. YES, 6%. NO, 94%.
   at the start, to some extent.

Q. B. Naughty, naughty.   A. YES, 94%. NO, 6%.

Among the dissenting multitude on Question A were at least three creative directors whose comments respectively were: "Yecht!" and "The second oldest sin" and "Stealing is stealing."

But the 6% minority who approved inclusion of the ads in your portfolio came back strong with arguments and a dash of cynicism. Included was a creative director who qualified his stand: "Remember to mention the limited extent of your contribution." An exec vp with an advertiser agreed: "Use them as something you participated in, but not your sole responsibility." A hardbitten ad manager asked: "Scruples? When you're out of work?" An equally skeptical advertiser said, "Come on now, I'll bet half the portfolios in New York are filled with such samples."

Case 9:   Along with Jim Coleman, a brand manager, you are sent to a
Blabber Mouth major food association meeting, where Jim meets an old friend
                 who is assistant sales manager of your company's biggest and
most important rival, and spends a good deal of time with him. On the way home, Jim confesses he may have talked too freely to his friend about your company's forthcoming introduction of a new freeze-dried food line, and asks you not to say anything to your mutual boss. What do you do?

A Summary of the Ballot on Ethics

The consensus among agency men differed somewhat from the consensus among advertisers and other groups on the questions of ethics posed in *Advertising Age*'s "Ballot on Ethics." The breakdown of the "yes" and "no" answers—that is, the number voting "yes" and the number voting "no" on each question among agency men, advertisers and "others" (media men, etc.)—is presented below.

Case 1

(A)

	YES	NO
Agency Men	9	189
Advertisers	12	93
Others	15	48
Total	36	330
Per Cent	10	90
Students	7	8

(B)

	YES	NO
Agency Men	30	159
Advertisers	27	81
Others	12	49
Total	69	289
Per Cent	19	81
Students	10	5

Case 2

(A)

	YES	NO
Agency Men	2	184
Advertisers	9	87
Others	2	63
Total	13	334
Per Cent	4	96
Students	3	12

(B)

	YES	NO
Agency Men	29	144
Advertisers	36	45
Others	13	31
Total	78	220
Per Cent	26	74
Students	7	6

Case 3

(A)

	YES	NO
Agency Men	35	138
Advertisers	24	69
Others	18	33
Total	77	240
Per Cent	24	76
Students	4	9

(B)

	YES	NO
Agency Men	106	45
Advertisers	72	21
Others	36	12
Total	214	78
Per Cent	73	27
Students	12	2

(C)

	YES	NO
Agency Men	81	57
Advertisers	57	37
Others	18	21
Total	156	115
Per Cent	58	42
Students	3	10

Case 4

(A)

	YES	NO
Agency Men	9	192
Advertisers	2	105
Others	0	61
Total	11	358
Per Cent	3	97
Students	1	14

(B)

	YES	NO
Agency Men	30	156
Advertisers	27	72
Others	13	45
Total	70	273
Per Cent	20	80
Students	8	5

Case 5

(A)

	YES	NO
Agency Men	84	101
Advertisers	36	69
Others	33	27
Total	153	197
Per Cent	44	56
Students	5	10

(B)

	YES	NO
Agency Men	68	87
Advertisers	21	54
Others	20	39
Total	109	180
Per Cent	29	62
Students	5	10

Case 6

(A)

	YES	NO
Agency Men	132	54
Advertisers	74	37
Others	44	8
Total	250	99
Per Cent	72	28
Students	10	5

Case 6 (B)	YES	NO
Agency Men	66	69
Advertisers	39	51
Others	11	23
Total	116	143
Per Cent	45	55
Students	4	10

Case 7	YES	NO
Agency Men	96	102
Advertisers	57	53
Others	28	25
Total	181	178
Per Cent	50	50
Students	9	6

Case 8 (A)	YES	NO
Agency Men	11	168
Advertisers	7	63
Others	0	52
Total	18	283
Per Cent	6	94
Students	4	10

(B)	YES	NO
Agency Men	174	10
Advertisers	65	8
Others	55	0
Total	294	18
Per Cent	94	6
Students	11	3

Case 9 (A)	YES	NO
Agency Men	105	70
Advertisers	69	36
Others	35	16
Total	209	122
Per Cent	63	37
Students	9	6

(B)	YES	NO
Agency Men	62	75
Advertisers	27	63
Others	15	31
Total	104	169
Per Cent	38	62
Students	6	9

Case 10 (A)	YES	NO
Agency Men	34	109
Advertisers	16	78
Others	8	38
Total	58	225
Per Cent	20	80
Students	0	14

(B)	YES	NO
Agency Men	161	17
Advertisers	101	11
Others	66	1
Total	328	29
Per Cent	92	8
Students	15	0

(C)	YES	NO
Agency Men	47	99
Advertisers	34	52
Others	13	28
Total	94	179
Per Cent	34	66
Students	9	5

(D)	YES	NO
Agency Men	32	107
Advertisers	5	83
Others	14	30
Total	51	220
Per Cent	19	81
Students	2	12

Case 11 (A)	YES	NO
Agency Men	96	59
Advertisers	64	41
Others	26	14
Total	186	114
Per Cent	62	38
Students	8	6

(B)	YES	NO
Agency Men	76	46
Advertisers	51	22
Others	31	13
Total	158	81
Per Cent	66	34
Students	7	8

Case 12 (A)	YES	NO
Agency Men	5	121
Advertisers	2	67
Others	0	28
Total	7	216
Per Cent	3	97
Students	0	15

(B)	YES	NO
Agency Men	191	7
Advertisers	107	2
Others	63	1
Total	360	10
Per Cent	97	3
Students	15	0

Q. A. Your company and your job   A. YES, 63%. NO, 37%.
mean more. You tell your boss that
the competition may have come
upon this secret information and
what does he suggest?

Q. B. Chances are the secret stuff   A. YES, 38%. NO, 62%.
wouldn't remain a secret for long,
regardless of Jim's spouting off, so
you agree to keep quiet.

"This is the toughest question yet," said an account executive. "Tell the boss, but refrain from revealing the leak source. Chew Jim out yourself!" In similar vein, an agency president said: "This is a tough one." He voted yes to telling the boss but added that it "would depend on how important the secret stuff is."

Many offered the suggestion of an agency vp: "Do not disclose the source." Many of both the no votes and yes votes included the thought that you should reprimand Jim. Voting no on Question A, a product manager said, "Tell Jim he should keep his big mouth shut." Voting yes, an agency research director added: "But tell Jim my feelings and give him a chance to tell the boss himself."

In the minority were the no votes of an advertiser exec vp ("It's not your problem") and an ad manager ("It's not up to you to tell on the mouthy one."). With them was an account executive who commented: "Nothing constructive would result from a 'confession.' The company would certainly not change plans because the competition 'might' know about them. A few strong words to Jim, however."

Case 10:
Drinking
Problem

As an account exec on Go-Go Motors, you've learned that Charley Beaubue is one damned fine account supervisor. Knows everything about the car business and everyone in it. He's a demon on detail, solid salesman for the creative side, an expediter of decisions. He even gets along nicely with the new marketing vp. Only . . . well, how do you say it. Lately, Charley's lunch breaks have been three, four hours long. And when he does turn up at the office, he's in no shape to make decisions. Only a very few people realize this. You're one of them . . . the highest ranking one, in fact. What do you do?

Q. A. Tell management that Charley   A. YES, 20%. NO, 80%.
needs watching.

Q. B. Talk to Charley and try to   A. YES, 92%. NO, 8%.
straighten him out.

Q. C. Talk to Charley's wife. See what   A. YES, 34%. NO, 66%.
she can do.

Q. D. Suggest to management that it   A. YES, 19%. NO, 81%.
give Charley a warning.

The consensus: Don't snitch on Charley, but talk to him yourself. As one adman put it, "Try to help Charley, but don't be a blabbermouth." Said another: "He's worth reforming. Boozers can be healed, you know."

As for telling Charley's wife, the vote was more divided. An account executive said, "Don't tell Charley's wife, unless you know both of them very well. When Charley starts to fall down on the job, management will know."

The attitude of some respondents was: Stay out of it. A woman assistant account executive advised, "Mind your own business." A creative director: "Management will know soon, if it doesn't already." An account executive: "Shut up, but try to find a way to protect yourself if there's a blow-up."

Case 11:
Black and
White

Two fine candidates are under consideration as account execs at your agency. Mr. Smith is white; Mr. Jones is black. Mr. Smith's experience has more depth; his qualifications are more readily apparent. You're sure he can do the job. You know all ten of your clients will approve of him. You also know that one or two clients didn't seem too happy when you mentioned Mr. Jones to them. But, for a variety of reasons, you'd really rather hire him.

Q. A. You hire Mr. Smith. Why look   A. YES, 62%. NO, 38%.
for trouble?

Q. B. You hire Mr. Jones. If trouble   A. YES, 66%. NO, 34%.
comes, you'll stand your ground.

Admen voted and reasoned "practically" on Cases 11 and 12. "Pick the better man," said an agency vp, and that was reflected in most of the comments. "The key is the qualification, not the color of the skin," said a radio station executive.

An advertiser advised: "Hire Mr. Smith on his qualifications, not for the reason, 'Why look for trouble?' " An advertising manager suggested: "You hire the man best able to do the job, not to be company 'nigger.' " Others who would hire Mr. Smith were an assistant ad manager ("You hire Smith because of experience and potential—period") and an agency executive ("Why discriminate in the opposite way?").

Several admen, some voting neither yes or no, suggested, "Hire both."

Among the minority who would hire Mr. Jones were a director of advertising, who asked, "Are you your own boss, or not?" and an agency man who commented, "Run your shop the way you see fit." An account executive agreed, but added a thought voiced by various others, "I hope your reasons for wanting to hire Jones are valid."

Another account executive, supporting Jones, observed: "Smith will find other jobs. Jones probably won't."

Case 12:
Discretion
vs. Valor

Same as Case 11, with two exceptions: (1) Mr. Jones is clearly the smarter, better long-term risk, and (2) one of your ten clients has made it pretty clear that hiring Mr. Jones will simply make the present shaky agency-client relationship considerably more shaky.

Q. A. You hire Mr. Smith. Why look   A. YES, 3%. NO, 97%.
for trouble?

Q. B. You hire Mr. Jones. If trouble   A. YES, 97%. NO, 3%.
comes, you'll stand your ground.

With Mr. Jones tagged as the better man, the vote to hire him was nearly unanimous. The handful of ballots favoring the hiring of Mr. Smith was mostly without comment, although a marketing manager offered this reasoning: "Promote from within to save all faces." A pr manager who voted with him commented: "I need short-term results." An agency vp who voted no to both Smith and Jones said, "Keep looking."

The overwhelming majority who would hire Mr. Jones fell in two camps: Those who would do so on principle and those who offered pragmatic and business reasons. Among the former were a director of advertising ("Good talent has no color"); a creative director ("Hire the best man for the job, even if he's purple with orange polka dots); and a radio/tv producer ("Competency comes in a variety of colors—black, white, brown and yellow—and you must run your business with people as well as for people. So inform that bigoted, shaky client.").

Not inclined toward these sentiments was an ad manager who did not vote on the case but stated: "It's easy to be theoretically valorous. If the account is vital to your survival, forget Mr. Jones and your good intentions."

Favoring Jones, but in the more pragmatic camp, was a copy chief, who said: "No business—especially no agency—is stronger than the people it hires. For every client Jones drives away, he could bring in or keep several good ones." An advertising manager offered strategy to help put over Mr. Jones in his new job: "Hire Mr. Jones. Outline the situation to him. Arrange a three-man dinner date, golf date, or business meeting—whichever will enable Mr. Jones to perform to advantage—and have him primed."

Finally, an ad director commented: "Shaky accounts don't get 'unshakier' if they can tell the agency what to do."

QUESTIONS FOR DISCUSSION

1. It has been said that inducing people to purchase goods by appealing to their sublimated desires is immoral and dangerous. What do you think of this statement? What counterargument would you use to respond to this view?

2. To what extent do *you* think advertising agencies are responsible for the ads that they create and disseminate? What are the agencies' *legal* obligations? How will current developments in the area of product liability affect the producer-advertiser-consumer relationship?

3. Do you think that we have insufficient, sufficient, or too much governmental control over advertising?
4. What do you think the effect upon the nation's marketing system would be if advertising were substantially curtailed or eliminated?
5. The statement that "Advertising expenditures add to the cost of products" has often been made. Is this true? Why or why not?
6. How important is advertising to the "small" businessman as compared to the "big" businessman? What role does advertising play in the marketing mix of small firms versus large firms?
7. A recent major study of the effect of advertising on the nation's business concluded that it increases competition. How could it do this? Would this be true under all normal business conditions, or is such a conclusion limited to certain products, industries, and sizes of firms?
8. Do you think that advertising today is more truthful than it was 50 or 100 years ago? Why or why not?
9. Do you think that there should be a limit placed upon the advertising expenditure for a product, such as 30 percent of the retail price?
10. What do you think is the most important law that should be passed (if any) to regulate advertising in the United States?

SELECTED READINGS

Alexander, George J., *Honesty and Competition* (Syracuse, New York: Syracuse University Press, 1967).

Caves, Richard, *American Industry: Structure, Conduct, Performance* (Englewood Cliffs, New Jersey: Prentice Hall, Inc., 1964).

Galbraith, John Kenneth, *The Affluent Society* (Boston: Houghton Mifflin Co., 1958). See especially pp. 154–159.

"Advertising from a Management Viewpoint", *Experiences in Marketing Management,* No. 2, "Management, Marketing, and Public Policy" (New York: National Industrial Conference Board, 1960). See especially pp. 17 ff.

Kottman, E. John, "Truth and the Image of Advertising", *Journal of Marketing* (October, 1969), Vol. 33, pp. 64–66.

Lyon, David G., *Off Madison Avenue* (New York: G. P. Putnam's Sons, 1966).

Morton, James G., *Taste in Advertising and Marketing,* paper presented at Forum on Taste in Advertising and Marketing, Minneapolis, April 17, 1967, pp. 1–7.

"New Watchdog for the Admen", *Business Week* (February 8, 1967), No. 1955, pp. 86–93.

Telser, Lester G., "Some Aspects of the Economics of Advertising", *Journal of Business of The University of Chicago* (April, 1968), Vol. 41, No. 2, pp. 166–173.

Warne, Colston E., "Advertising—A Critic's View," *Journal of Marketing* (October, 1962), Vol. 26, No. 4, pp. 10–14.

Webber, "Advertising and Product Responsibility", *Business and Society* (Autumn, 1966), Vol. 7, No. 1, pp. 22–32.

section 6 the changing perspective in product liability

A critical problem for both the consumer and those who sell to him is "Who is responsible when the item purchased is defective?" Is the retailer, the wholesaler, or the manufacturer responsible, or is it just tough luck for the consumer—is he "stuck" with the product?

From the time this nation developed its system of laws until about World War I, the answers to these questions were clear. The *only* recourse the consumer had was against the person *who sold the product to him*. Any other individuals or firms in the chain of distribution were considered to be too remote to bear *any* responsibility. From 1916 on, however, the feeling of the courts that dealt with such matters began to change. By 1970, the changes were so substantial that for many classes of goods and services it became permissible to sue *any or all* links in the distribution channel—manufacturer, wholesaler, retailer—and get quite a sympathetic hearing in court.

That the age-old phrase "Let the buyer beware" has changed to "Let the manufacturer and the seller be sued" is dramatically shown by the fact that in 1969 well over 100,000 products-liability cases were introduced in courts.[1]

Many of these cases amounted to "big money", with a number of individual awards exceeding $100,000. Premiums specifically for products-liability insurance are in the neighborhood of $100,000,000 per year.

These important changes in the law and the enormous cost of product liability are significant to all participants in the chain of distribution and consumption. Obviously, if a manufacturer can now get sued for a defect in his product, he must take steps to protect his corporation from the potential for losses big enough to bankrupt his firm. The manufacturer must minimize his potential for liability loss by establishing stricter quality control standards, issuing more carefully worded warranties and guarantees, designing a better product, revising the advertising and sales literature so that any warranties are not unreasonable for the firm to fulfill,[2] keeping better records as to the precautions taken in designing and producing the product, obtaining greater insurance protection, and so forth. The result of undertaking such activities very often requires that the marketers raise their prices—someone has to pay the costs of these products-liability measures. Ultimately, these costs are borne by the consumer, who profits enormously, too, by finally having recourse when his goods and services are not what they should be.

---

[1] *Products liability* is the legal term used to describe those laws and court decisions that pertain to the characteristics of a product that can be challenged in court.

[2] An *express* warranty must be differentiated from an *implied* warranty. The former is either written or oral, and it forms the basis of an understanding between the buyer and the seller; even "sales talk" can be in the "express warranty" category. *Implied* warranties, however, are those that are imposed by the law or public policy, such as that a product is fit for use, that the buyer can rely upon the skill or judgment of the seller, and so forth.

19 The Lengthening Reach of Liability

Normally, product development has included some attention to product testing, at least in theory. Whether there has been sufficient attention to this matter in practice is what the subject of product liability is all about.

There is a long history of litigation on the responsibility of the manufacturer when a product is defective. This article deals with the changes in the courts' views on the subject, the nature of these changes, and their meaning to businessmen.

. . .

I. A Chronicle of Expansion   Historically, manufacturers had no liability except to the specific customer to whom they made a direct sale—unless their products fell in the area of food, chemicals, drugs, and firearms, which could seriously affect human life. Automobiles were not included; a dealer's customer could not sue the manufacturer if the car caused injury, because of the gap between maker and buyer—they were not "in privity," as the law put it.

In 1916, a man named MacPherson bought an automobile; it had a defective wheel which collapsed. MacPherson, who was injured, sued Buick Motor Co., which had bought the wheel from a components maker. In the New York Court of Appeals, Judge Benjamin N. Cardozo ruled that an automobile, if negligently made, was a "dangerous instrumentality," just like drugs or food. Since Buick had not tested the wheel, it could not escape liability simply because the "ultimate purchaser" did not buy directly from it; clearly, the car was not designed solely for the dealer's use.

The so-called MacPherson doctrine was soon adopted by the courts of many states; by last year, Mississippi rounded out the roster.

Bottled Mice   While these cases were being decided, a parallel development brought a great widening of the law on liability for defective food and drugs. Some of the earliest cases concerned mice and other objects turning up rather mysteriously in soft-drink bottles. Under the new interpretations, a plaintiff had only to prove that the bottle had been in the exclusive control of the bottler; he did not have to prove negligence, which the jury was allowed to infer from the presence of the foreign object —and the jury generally did just that. Also, the plaintiff did not have to be the actual purchaser of the bottle. A wife who drank the beverage and found the mouse could sue, even though her husband had done the buying.

It was a short quick step from letting juries infer negligence to eliminating the requirement for negligence altogether. By the 1920s, courts began to hold that makers of food and drugs were absolutely liable for harm caused by their products, no matter how much foresight, testing, skill, and care had gone into the making.

One distinction persisted for a time. The courts continued to require proof of negligence in cases involving such "dangerous instrumentalities" as cars and power tools, no longer necessary for "inherently" dangerous products such as drugs.

Legal Switch   In the years between 1920 and 1960, the courts felt a bit queasy about overturning the centuries of precedent requiring proof of negligence whenever no contract existed, yet at the same time their whole tenor was to widen the reach of liability. To get around the problem, the courts began to shift their approach from negligence—classed as a tort— to warranty—a contract.

This road leading from liability-through-negligence to liability-without-fault actually had three bends:

An express warranty was first required as a basis for liability. If the maker's contract warranted that his product was fit or safe, its failure would make him liable. When contracts offered no express warranties, the courts seized on representations in advertising and on labels. In the early 1930s, when a windshield advertised as shatterproof was broken by a pebble, the owner recovered from the maker, though he had not bought the car directly from him.

"Implied warranties" were the next discovery of the courts, to counter a corporate trend to disclaim liability in every contract, with explicit denials of any express warranty. Implied warranties ended up as a protection provided by the courts for the weaker party to a bargain in which no such warranty was included. With the elimination of the requirement of direct dealing between manufacturer and consumer, the courts felt it was also reasonable to require that the products be free from defects which would "actively" cause injuries.

The implied warranty doctrine turned up first in food and drugs, spread to cosmetics, deodorants, and shampoos, and finally reached automobiles in 1960. The landmark auto case involved a New Jersey housewife who was injured when the family car, bought 10 days earlier by her husband, went out of control and hit a wall. The driver could not prove the manufacturer had been negligent, but the court instructed the jury to bring in a verdict for the plaintiff. The finding was affirmed by the New Jersey Supreme Court, which said: "We hold that under modern marketing conditions, when a manufacturer puts a new automobile in the stream of trade and promotes its purchase by the public, an implied warranty that it is reasonably suitable for use as such accompanies it into the hands of the ultimate purchaser."

A Tort
After All
The final step in the warranty process was to get products liability back into the tort category, which among other things freed it from the often stiffer limits of the statute of limitations as applied to contract cases, and from certain legal notice requirements.

This third step was taken in 1963 when the California Supreme Court ruled that "a manufacturer is strictly liable in tort when an article he places on the market, knowing that it is to be used without inspection for defects, proves to have a defect that causes injury to a human being." In the case at issue, a wife had bought her husband a power lathe; his head was injured when the tool ejected a wooden workpiece.

That same year, the Court of Appeals extended the doctrine to New York State after a defective altimeter caused a commercial plane to crash near LaGuardia Airport. The court held that the mother of a passenger killed in the crash could sue the airline and the maker of the plane—but not the maker of the altimeter—though no carelessness in manufacture and assembly could be proved. Some states would allow the mother to sue the components maker directly; in New York he can be sued in his turn by the carrier and the assembler.

II. How the Law
Stands Now
The rapid churning of judicial development in the products liability field has for now shaken down to three general rules:

A warranty, whether express or implied, runs with the product.

Any product that could be dangerous if made defectively will subject the manufacturer to liability, even if he used the utmost care in producing it, and disclaimed liability in advance.

A manufacturer may be liable for "economic loss" to the purchaser if the product does not perform as it should, even if there is neither injury nor warranty.

The first general rule is already the law in all 50 states, and more than 30 state courts have accepted the second. Even in areas where negligence must still be shown, the requirements for showing it have been eased. In Washington, D.C., a customer in a beauty salon was burned when a plastic comb burst into flames during a heat treatment. The court allowed her to recover from the maker of the comb, although she had not bought it, because the maker had failed to stamp on it a warning that the comb was combustible. Similarly, in a Connecticut case, the plaintiff did not even have to be a user of the product. The case involved a defective parked automobile that careened onto a golf course and killed a player.

The third rule, that of economic loss, has not yet won majority acceptance but it is gaining. In New Jersey, in 1965, the purchaser of a carpet was allowed to sue the manufacturer directly instead of the dealer when the rug he had bought was found to have a wrinkle that could not be removed, and began to shred. The dealer meantime had left the state, and the court was unimpressed by the manufacturer's defense that he had no contract with the customer.

Making Up the Loss   More recently, there have been direct rulings and some hints—from courts in California, Oregon, and Tennessee, among others —that manufacturers may be required to pay the difference between a product's actual value and what it would have been worth if properly made. This sort of recovery is likely to become commonplace as courts interpret the Uniform Commercial Code, which in the past few years has become law in almost every state. The code limits the seller's power to disclaim liability, and so broadens the buyer's right to recover if the product proves defective.

There is a rather complex rationale for this broadening of product liability laws. For one thing, consumers continually come into contact with products that can kill or maim them, and that are too complex for the customer to test their safety. So the law looks to the manufacturer to protect the customer from loss. It has been argued that putting the burden on the manufacturer will lead to more testing and safer products, and that the manufacturer, by his very size, is better able to bear the risk.

III. A Few Defenses   Apart from the protection that the manufacturer can find in insurance against product liability, he has certain other defenses.

For example, he is not liable in the many cases that involve "wrongful use" of the product. No court would hold the maker of a power lathe liable because a purchaser carelessly dropped the heavy tool on his foot.

For liability to exist, the product must have been used for its intended purpose, or one reasonably foreseeable, and in either case one that would be unreasonably dangerous if the product were defective.

In a recent New York case, the manufacturer was absolved of liability for an injury to a worker using an industrial tool that lacked a safety device. The court held that the worker was injured through his own carelessness, not through any lack in the machine. Moreover, the court said, the manufacturer was under no obligation to put in safety devices unless the machine would be unreasonably dangerous without such devices.

Some courts limit liability though conceding a safety lack. Thus a Florida court recently absolved a hospital following an injurious blood transfusion: blood was said to be "unavoidably unsafe."

There are some cases in which the manufacturer's liability is limited. One such is when his product becomes dangerous only because it was put into operation negligently by the installer. Another comes when retailers make warranties or representations that the manufacturer has not and would not authorize. If such representations led the customer to use the product in a way for which it was not intended, the manufacturer may be in the clear—unless a warning could have been placed on the product itself.

Generally, manufacturers seem to be accepting the toughening rules with relative equanimity. The Machinery & Allied Products Institute, in a study [in 1967] on Products Liability and Reliability, made few calls for any easing of rules, and largely confined its suggestions to urging more rigorous testing, and in maintaining meticulous records of the testing against the day when they might be required in court.

What Is the Consumer's Use of the Product?*

The case answers the question of "How safe must a product be?" A defense attorney will usually say, "My client's liability is limited to those uses for which our product was intended or for which it is appropriate. If you used it for some other purpose and injured yourself, it's just too bad."

But, is this really so? In a recent case a manufacturer of doors was sued by a longshoreman who had been unloading them from a ship and hurt his leg. The doors are shipped with an empty space where glass is to be set in when the doors are hung. Covering this cavity during shipment is merely a piece of cardboard. It is the practice of longshoremen, when unloading such doors, to stack them in four-foot piles.

In this case, a longshoreman with a 100-pound sack of flour on his back stepped on the cavity (covered by cardboard) and fell through the empty space. He injured his leg and sued for $80,000.

Should the door manufacturer be responsible? After all, the doors are not intended for use as a support for longshoremen with heavy sacks of flour. Before reading the following solution, analyze this case carefully.

The issue went all the way up to the U.S. Supreme Court, where a lower-court ruling in favor of the longshoreman was affirmed. The Court, responding to the manufacturer's contention that it was a "misuse of my product; he used a door as a floor," said essentially the following: "What difference does that make? You should have known that stevedores stack products such as this, and it was *foreseeable* that such an accident might occur. You should have anticipated it; since you didn't, you're liable for damages."

* This material was prepared by the authors for this book.

20 Product Liability Requires Strict Quality Control

Richard G. Moser

Most states now adhere to the principle of strict liability, that is, the supplier of a product represents *unconditionally* to all prospective users that it is safe and can be used without danger or hardship for the purposes for which it can reasonably be expected to be used. As a result, business executives have instituted a number of changes in the way they conduct the affairs of their firms and in order to protect their enterprises from the prospect of substantial lawsuits.

One of the activities undertaken to minimize the number and size of such suits is the implementation of good quality-control techniques. This article points out that goods of high quality are less likely to provide the basis for litigation, and it presents an excellent illustration of how the courts might look at a defective product in assessing a manufacturer's product liability.

A few years ago a freight train was gently meandering through a quiet Ohio valley. Suddenly, with a loud crash, a boxcar loaded with bags of fertilizer ripped off the tracks and plunged into a highway bridge abutment.

Later, investigation revealed that the cause of the accident was a broken side frame on the truck of the car. When it broke, the axle dropped, and the car plunged off the track. Inspection indicated that the side frame was a defective steel casting.

Here are the catastrophic consequences that followed from that one defective casting.

1. A trainman who happened to be walking along the top of the car was thrown violently to the ground and injured.
2. A large stretch of track and ballast was ripped up.
3. Half of the fertilizer shipment was destroyed or was carried off by Ohio farmers.

4. A piece of cement from the bridge abutment fell to the highway and hit a passing wagon load of wheat, spreading broken wheat sacks along the pavement and injuring the farmer who was driving.

When all of those events were taking place, the president of the foundry that had made the casting was having a leisurely game of golf with his insurance broker, his lawyer, and his psychiatrist. All were relaxed and ignorant of the catastrophe of which they would hear much in the months and years ahead.

The first party to be heard from was the car manufacturer, who said he was being sued by everyone. The railroad was suing him for damages to the car and the stretch of the track. The shipper was suing for loss of his load of fertilizer. The trainman was suing for medical bills, pain and suffering, and loss of consortium. The farmer was suing for loss of his wagon and load of wheat, and the State of Ohio was suing for damage to the bridge. The car manufacturer said he intended to enjoin the foundryman as a defendant and to shift the liability involved to him.

Everyone in that golf foursome benefited from the catastrophe except the foundryman. The lawyer was retained to defend the foundryman, a job for which he eventually received a substantial fee. The psychiatrist tended the foundryman and his wife through three long years of litigation. The insurance broker received commissions on substantially increased public and product liability insurance premiums.

The Defense   The foundryman's lawyer asserted a number of defenses. Let us cover them one by one.

First, he argued that the casting was made according to good foundry practice, that due care was exercised in its manufacture and inspection, and that the foundryman should not be held liable unless negligence on his part could be shown. This doctrine of due care used to be the law, but it no longer is. Until recently the basis of this kind of liability was proof of negligence.

In the last 20 years, however, there has been a galloping reversal of this principle, and the courts or legislatures of 38 states have adopted what is known as the principle of strict liability. In 30 states it applies to products of every kind. In eight states it is limited to food products or drugs and other products that affect the human body. There is no doubt whatever that in due course the remaining states will also fall in line.

This rule is based on the philosophy that a loss should be borne by those best able to afford it. Simply stated, the rule is that when a supplier of any product places it on the market, he unconditionally represents to all prospective users that it is safe and suitable for all purposes for which it reasonably can be expected to be used.

Thus, our unfortunate foundryman, in the vast majority of the states, could not hide behind the shield of due care when sued by any plaintiff involved in the chain of reasonably expected use. That chain, in the case cited, would include the carbuilder, the railroad, the shipper, and the trainman. Each of them normally would be expected to make some use of the boxcar.

The rule would not include the State of Ohio as owner of the bridge or the farmer. Both would have to prove negligence to win because they were not users of the car. The trainman as an employee of the railroad would be covered by the workmen's compensation laws, but that fact would afford no protection for the foundryman.

The second defense was that the side frame casting was made according to the carbuilder's specifications and that if the accident was due to faulty design, the foundryman was not responsible.

This sounds like a pretty good defense, but it not always is. If the design is so clearly faulty that the foundryman knows that as designed it would not be suitable for use on a boxcar, he has a duty to say this to the carbuilder and perhaps ask the carbuilder to assume responsibility for the design.

The third defense was that the casting when sold was in rough form with substantial machining required and that as sold, it was not in a condition intended for use. The foundryman's lawyer would argue that it was the carbuilder's responsibility to complete the casting and see that it was suitable and safe. This defense would be a good one provided that the defect lay outside the casting process. If the casting broke because of improper melting, pouring, cooling, or heat treating, the foundryman could not shift the blame to those who did the machining.

The fourth defense was that the boxcar was overloaded. If it was, this would be a good defense under the strict liability rule because the manufacturer's only responsibility is to assure that the product is safe against dangers that can be reasonably anticipated.

On the other hand, if a certain amount of overloading was a generally accepted practice in the railroad industry, the foundry would be expected to allow for such overloading by reasonable tolerances.

The foundryman's final defense was that the casting had been delivered ten years ago and that he had no duty to guarantee that it would be safe for so long a time. But the jury would be told that this point alone does not protect the foundryman against liability if the jury finds that it is not reasonable to expect side frames to last as long as the car itself.

Case Was Lost   As you might imagine, our foundryman lost the case, and every plaintiff was awarded a large verdict by a jury that believed that any plaintiff is entitled to something. The ones who recovered the most were the trainman and the farmer because they were the least able to absorb the loss.

The one bright aspect of the story was that the foundryman himself did not have to pay the damages. He was fully covered by public liability and

FIGURE 1.   A "traditional" warranty. Reprinted by permission from: Monsanto Biodize Systems, Inc.

products liability insurance. But the next year his rates and the rates of every other steel foundry in the country went up.

The fate of this foundryman could be yours. High-pressure pumps, cranes, oil rigs, steam shovels, road-building equipment and a hundred other products contain castings that could cause serious accidents and heavy damages to people and their property if they proved defective. The foundryman never knows when his casting will be the culprit.

Picture a supersonic aircraft carrying 500 passengers that crashes because of a defective casting. A jury might think that each passenger was worth $100,000. That could cost someone $50 million. Think of a crane on a ship unloading explosives that drops a load because of a faulty cast hook, blowing up a whole ship and perhaps a whole town.

Quality Control Vital   The principle of strict liability, which is expanding by leaps and bounds in the field of product liability, places a heavy load on those responsible for quality control. You must be prepared to prove that your casting was suitable for the purposes intended and safe to use under all reasonably anticipated conditions. This means that you must chart your quality control course not just toward good castings, but toward perfect castings. This task is not an easy one, but it's becoming an inescapable fact of business life.

I do not recommend that you lie awake at nights worrying about the number of lethal weapons your foundry has placed in the hands of the public. I do, however, urge you to bear down heavier than ever on quality control.

21 Seals of Approval

Bess Myerson Grant

"Seals of approval" (for example, *Good Housekeeping*) concern several important aspects of marketing practice. To begin with, there is an assumption when such a seal appears that the product has been thoroughly and appropriately tested and is ready and safe for use. This in turn rests on an assumed process of standardization, that is, standards have presumably been set, based on consumer needs, by which the product can be judged. Third, once the seal appears, it becomes a promotional item so that one can say "Approved by ————".

The National Commission on Product Safety has conducted hearings on a number of aspects of safety, including an investigation of "seals of approval". Such seals apparently are widely regarded by American consumers as reliable guarantees of a product's fitness and the producer's and seal-giver's willingness to stand behind those products. But is the consumer making a reasonable assumption? This selection by New York City's Commissioner of the Department of Consumer Affairs shows that such seals really do not provide the consumer with the protection that he seeks.

. . .

Ever since Ralph Nader raised the standard of the consumer movement, Americans everywhere have become aware of the substandard quality and safety controls existing in today's product market. Naïve assumptions were pushed aside. We discovered that though we could purchase meat in a local supermarket with relative assurance that ptomaine poisoning would not ensue, we could not purchase an automobile with any guarantee that minimal standards of safety would save our lives in the event of an accident.

The world has taken several revolutions round the axis of consumer awareness since that time. Yet the basic inadequacies of safety control devices, in most consumer markets, still abound.

How is it that Americans have permitted this disgraceful and dangerous state of affairs to continue? Why have consumers not stood up to demand that the products we buy are safe? That they have been tested for safety?

Reprinted from Bess Myerson Grant, *Seals of Approval*, Report to the National Commission on Product Safety (1969), pp. 1–9, by permission of the author.

That the tests were designed to check the adequacy of those products against safety standards? That those standards are good, true and genuinely precautionary?

One of the reasons may be the seals of two magazines—*Good Housekeeping* and *Parents'*. These magazines cater to a readership of women 18–35 years of age; these are women with families, and they constitute the major group of buyers in this country. A survey conducted by officials of the New York City Department of Consumer Affairs showed that a substantial portion of women in this group believe in product seals—and that they believe many things which are not true.

The Department of Consumer Affairs surveyed 200 persons. (The survey itself and the total results are included on pages 190–191.) The survey asked the person interviewed to circle the reproduced seals which were familiar to him and answer questions based on his familiarity. One question asked the person to identify the seal which means the product is safe. Another asked which seal was issued by the federal government and another asked whether seals meant a product meets federal safety and quality standards. The seals included were, of course, *Good Housekeeping* and *Parents'* and also American Gas Association, U.S. Testing, Power Tool Institute, OPEI, and Underwriter's Laboratory, and a fabricated seal inserted as a control device. The person interviewed was asked the meaning he attributed to a seal identified, and if the meaning was "guarantee," what he interpreted that word to mean.

Judging by the results of our study, the public thinks very highly of the *Good Housekeeping* seal, the *Parents'* magazine seal, and their imitators. Here is a sample of what we found:

29% of those responding to the survey believed that the seals which they recognized signified that the product met federal quality and safety standards;
90% of the respondents recognized the *Good Housekeeping* seals, and 60% recognized the *Parents'* seal—but no one interviewed recognized that the seals were given to advertisers alone;
33% believed that the two leading seals meant that a product is "safe";
15% believed that the seal entitled a customer to bring suit against the seal giver, if injury resulted from use of the product;
50% of all those surveyed stated that they rely on seals in purchasing consumer products.

Thus, it is clear that the leading seals are highly prized by the public. Therefore, it is clear why they are highly prized by advertisers, why hundreds of major national advertisers are willing to pay the price *Good Housekeeping* and *Parents'* demand for the seals—what the magazines represent as the cost of investigating the product, plus an amount of advertising which is "consistent with the advertiser's schedule in other consumer media and sufficient to accomplish the objective."

Unfortunately, however, the great faith which innocent consumers and trusting readers place in these seals is quite without justification.

What in fact do the seals given by *Good Housekeeping* and *Parents'* mean?

In the case of *Good Housekeeping*, a seal can realistically be understood to mean these three things:

First, that the product is advertised in *Good Housekeeping*;
Second, that *Good Housekeeping* has "satisfied" itself that the product is "good," and that claims explicitly made about the product in the magazine are truthful;
Third, that, if the product turns out to be "defective," then the magazine will guarantee the customer a refund or replacement—apparently, at the magazine's discretion.

That is what the *Good Housekeeping* seal *does* mean. What does it *not* mean?

It does not mean that the product meets any predetermined and public standards, federal or otherwise;
It does not mean *Good Housekeeping* represents to the public even those minimal qualities which it asserts that it has "satisfied" itself about—that the product is "good," whatever that means, and that advertising claims are truthful;
The seal does not mean that *Good Housekeeping* has necessarily satisfied itself that the product is in anyway superior or equal to other competing products, or that it is safe.
The seal does not mean that *Good Housekeeping* will stand behind the product to which it has granted its seal, except to the limited extent of promising a refund or replacement, if the product is defective. *Good Housekeeping* will not provide refund or replacement, if the product turns out to perform below the customer's legitimate expectations, or if it performs below the advertiser's claims—i.e., . . . if it is not as useful as represented. *Good Housekeeping will not compensate any customers for injuries to person or property sustained by the product.*

Parents' magazine attempts to make its seal even more meaningless than the *Good Housekeeping* version. Its statement of policy asserts only that seals are granted when the Consumer Service Bureau of the magazine considers such action "merited"—but there is nothing to indicate that this decision will depend in any way on the merit of the product. From all one can discover in the magazine's description of the standards it applies, the *Parents'* seal may be granted or withheld on a wholly arbitrary basis. *Parents'* does not even represent that its own management is satisfied that products covered by its seal are "good," or that advertising claims are true.

Indeed, *Parents'* magazine must have no faith in the products they permit their seal to be associated with. *They undertake to provide refunds or replacements for defective products "only for claims made within thirty (30) days from the date of purchase."*

Thus, even more than *Good Housekeeping, Parents'* magazine tries to double-cross the housewife and mother, who trusts the seals they confer on products for her home and whose trust attracts advertisers to the magazines. These seals ought either to mean what the public thinks they mean, or they should not exist at all. The companies which confer seals on products ought to stand behind those products all the way, or else they should not grant any product the benefit of their apparent approbation.

The fraud on the public inherent in *Good Housekeeping* and *Parents'* seals had not escaped the attention of the Federal Trade Commission. It has, however, unfortunately, managed to escape any effective corrective action from the Commission—as seems to be too often the case.

In 1941, the FTC issued a cease and desist order against the Hearst Corp., the publishing empire which owns *Good Housekeeping*. The order instructed the magazine to stop calling its seal a "seal of approval," since it was too cautious actually to represent to the public that it had "approved" a product.

In 1966, the FTC issued a similar cease and desist order against *Parents'* magazine, which forbade it from further use of its "commendation" seal, which also inaccurately held out to readers that products had been "approved."

Sadly, however, the FTC's actions have not done much for consumers. Their principal benefits have been for the lawyers retained by *Good Housekeeping* and *Parents'*. The lawyers have now written disclaimers of liability into the small print of the magazines' policy statements about the seals, which make it much harder than it ever was before for misled consumers to recover money lost because of their reliance on the seals.

Both magazines have now substituted what they call "guarantee" seals for the old "approval" and "commendation" seals. They guarantee replacement or refund. They do not represent approval by the seal-giver to the public.

A member of the staff of the Department of Consumer Affairs asked the Director of *Parents'* magazine's Bureau of Consumer Services—the bureau responsible for deciding what advertisers "merit" the seal and which ones do not—why *Parents'* changed the contents of its seal. The answer was that "The FTC was down our backs about the commendation seal."

We asked the *Pareents'* magazine official whether the new guarantee seal would satisfy the objectives of the FTC's order. "We don't know," she said. "But it will take them a long time to do anything about it," she added.

Remarks such as that do not build confidence in the integrity of the seal-and-private-testing system associated with the seal programs of *Good Housekeeping* and *Parents'* magazines. Even less do such remarks lead to respect for the effectiveness of present regulatory controls on the seals.

We can accept as a given fact that a true service magazine, with a policy of satisfying itself that the product is a good one or that it is suitable for families with children, will meet this obligation to its readers by employing standards of evaluation and methods of investigation suitable to that policy. But so long as no uniformity of standards exists, and so long as no uniformity of testing methods prevails, the reasonableness of the evaluation procedures will always be subject to criticism, and an understanding of those procedures will never be available to consumers.

The answer to the problems is not to dispense with seals but rather to establish some measure of uniformity in testing to lend credence to them.

What is needed is a federal Department of Consumer Affairs, one of whose principal concerns would be the establishment of safety standards. The function of both establishing standards and approving industry standards where they already exist cannot be given to any existing regulatory agency. They must be the sole domain of an agency which is genuinely and totally committed to the interest of consumers. A federal Department of Consumer Affairs could set standards rigid enough to disallow the willfully disobedient; standards flexible enough to withstand the test of technical time. Those standards must be the law, and compliance with them would entitle a manufacturer to a seal from the government.

Where does this leave *Good Housekeeping* and *Parents'* magazines? Until a Department of Consumer Affairs is created at the federal level to establish standards of evaluation and testing, *Good Housekeeping* and *Parents'* magazine seals will continue to provide the main source of information on product safety to many consumers.

Yet it is clear that the substantial reliance of those consumers on seals is not founded upon any concrete information. Surely, if *Good Housekeeping* and *Parents'* continue to offer their seals, they have a responsibility to publish their standards of evaluation and investigation.

Consumer reliance on the seals of *Good Housekeeping* and *Parents'* is clearly founded on serious misunderstandings of the meaning of the seals. Although *Good Housekeeping* has not had a seal of approval since 1941, most readers of the magazine, by *Good Housekeeping*'s own admission, still refer to its "seal of approval." Readers believe that the magazines stand behind the products for which they grant seals—they believe that these products are guaranteed by the seal givers to be fit and safe for use whether or not they develop actual "defects," whether or not they develop defects in thirty days or thirty months. It is unconscionable that these magazines should be permitted to allow public faith to persist, to profit from advertisers perceptions of the market value of the public's naïveté, and still escape all risks which the trusting consumer unwittingly undertakes—because of that faith.

In order to call a halt to this disgraceful ploy aimed at the innocence and naïveté of consumers, the following steps seem to me to be in order.

First, neither the *Parents'* nor the *Good Housekeeping* seal should be permitted to exist, unless standards for evaluating products and for the design of testing procedures are developed and adhered to by the companies— *and until these standards are made available to the public*;

Second, neither *Parents'* nor *Good Housekeeping* should be permitted to disclaim liability for personal and property injuries, where the injury results from any condition of a product which is inconsistent with the claim implicit in the existence of these seals—that the product is safe and fit for the use for which it was intended;

Third, *Parents'* and *Good Housekeeping* should both be required to state any limitations on the meaning of and liability risked by their seals in a full page, easy-to-read disclaimer;

Fourth, all products which use the *Good Housekeeping* and *Parents'* seals in advertising *outside the magazine* should be required to carry a conspicuous statement, wherever the seal is used in advertising, that these seals contain no representation about the safety, quality, or merchantability of a product, and are granted only to advertisers in the magazine.

I therefore recommend that the Federal Trade Commission immediately take the following steps to ensure that public faith in these seals is not misplaced:

First, the FTC should require *Good Housekeeping* and *Parents'* to adopt and publish standards applicable to determining whether to grant seals to products which they advertise. The Commission should review these standards and reject them if they are not meaningful. If the magazines refuse to adopt and publish meaningful standards, the Commission should order them to cease and desist from further use of their seals.

Second, the FTC should require both magazines to print their disclaimers as a full page near the front of each issue of the magazine. Further, smaller, but nevertheless conspicuous, versions of the disclaimer should be required to be carried in every advertisement, regardless of where it appears. The disclaimer ought to read:

[*Parents'*/*Good Housekeeping*] seal is granted only to advertisers in the magazine, who agree to place a prescribed number of advertisements each year. The seal does not constitute a guarantee of the safety, quality, or merchantability of a product. The magazine will not provide compensation for injuries to person or property arising from use of products covered by the seal. The magazine will not assure replacement or refund, unless the product actually develops a defect. In other words, the customer has no remedy against the magazine, if the product functions in an ineffective or unsafe manner without developing any specific defects.

Third, the FTC should order *Parents'* magazine to cease and desist altogether from limiting refund and replacement to claims made within thirty days of purchase.

If the FTC refuses to afford consumers the minimal protections contemplated by these recommendations, then the courts must do the Commission's job for it. With or without FTC action, it is unconscionable for the magazines to make money from these seals and yet quietly restrict their liability as narrowly as they attempt to do. Courts should therefore refuse to honor the magazines' disclaimers of liability for injury, unless disclaimers are carried with advertisements wherever they appear, and unless the disclaimers are given a full page in the magazines themselves. Courts should altogether reject *Parents'* magazine's outrageous thirty-day limitation of its obligation to provide replacement or refund; this device is inherently unconscionable.

Total Results

1. Do you recognize any of the following seals?
   a—AGA   7
   b—US Testing   56
   c—PTI   5
   d—*Parents'*   149
   e—*Good Housekeeping*   163
   f—Fictitious   63
   g—OPEI   10
   h—UL   69
   None—   38

2. What meaning do you associate with the seals you know?
   a—good   67
   b—safe   68
   c—the best available   5
   d—the safest available   16
   e—tested by seal giver   98
   f—approved by seal giver   129
   g—liked by seal giver   28
   h—guaranteed by seal giver   46
   i—no better or worse   36
   j—given to all advertisers   5
   k—given only to advertisers   13

3. Do you look for seals when you buy a product?
   YES   75
   NO   116

4. If a seal guarantees the product, do you think that means . . .
   a—seal giver will replace product if defective   86
   b—seal giver will refund the price of product if defective 71
   c—seal giver will replace product if you are dissatisfied with it   33
   d—seal giver will refund price if you are dissatisfied with product   23
   e—seal giver can be sued if you are injured by product   37
   None—   63

5. Which of above symbols means that the product is safe?*
   a—   83
   b—   37
   c—   70
   d—   41
   e—   34
   f—   10
   g—   72
   h—   52
   None—   16

*Refer to a–h in question 1.

6. Which of above symbols are issued by an agency of the federal government?*

a—	28
b—	87
c—	1
d—	1
e—	2
f—	5
g—	21
h—	8
None—	45

*Refer to a–h in question 1.

7. Does a seal mean the product meets federal safety and quality standards?

YES	55
NO	135

Thank you, Mr. Chairman, for giving me this opportunity to express the views of the New York City Department of Consumer Affairs on this matter, which deserves prompt attention from federal authorities concerned with the welfare of the American consumer.

22 Court Opens the Door for Suit Against Issuer of Product Seal

An entirely new pattern in product litigation may be established in U.S. District Court for Delaware this fall. Judge Edwin D. Steele, Jr., has decided that Allen A. Hempstead can sue not only the manufacturer of the fire extinguisher that allegedly cost him the sight of an eye when it exploded but also the testing laboratory whose seal of approval it carried.

Now Hempstead can sue Underwriters' Laboratories, Inc., the testing organization, as well as General Fire Extinguisher Corp.

Far-Reaching Effect Judge Steele's ruling breaks new ground in product litigation. According to Arthur G. Raynes of Philadelphia, one of Hempstead's two attorneys, "This is the first case that I know of, and that the court knew of, where a testing company was held to have a duty to the public and could be found in negligence for injuries flowing from a breach of that duty." He sees a "staggering" potential significance in this precedent.

"In a case where a product bears the seal of approval of UL, *Parents' Magazine, Good Housekeeping,* or any of the other testing companies," Raynes says, "the plaintiff now stands in the enviable position of enlisting expert testimony in his favor from a most unimpeachable, palatable, and persuasive source.

"If the product is in fact defective, or if the manufacturer has not complied with the regulations of the testing company, then the plaintiff will find himself sitting between two responsible defendants with high-powered experts taking pot-shots at one another. The end result is that the plaintiff will benefit, whichever expert the jury believes."

Reprinted from "Court Opens the Door for Suit Against Issuer of Product Seal", *Product Engineering* (September, 1967), Vol. 38, No. 20, p. 104, by permission of the publisher.

Court Ruling   In upholding Hempstead's right to make UL a co-defendant, Judge Steele said: "It is straining at words to say that Underwriters' does not approve the design of a product. The design may originate with the manufacturer, but when Underwriters' lists it, it tacitly impresses its approval upon the design."

In his opinion, Judge Steele also notes that UL's seal was "unquestionably of aid" to General in selling its extinguisher to the owners of the Arlington (Va.) apartment house where the explosion occurred. The county's fire prevention code, the judge says, not only requires installation of fire extinguishers but also specifies that they must be approved by a recognized testing authority such as UL.

How Much   According to Hempstead's complaint, "the fire extinguisher ex-
Inspection?   ploded because the stainless steel body was improperly brazed
                   to the bronze collar and cap." UL contended that the manufacturer had failed to adhere to the UL-approved design. But Steele's written opinion points out that UL permitted the manufacturer to label the extinguisher: "Tested 500 pounds . . . Underwriters' Laboratories, Inc.— Inspected."

Not every product so labeled is individually tested by UL, but the lab regularly inspects products on the line in manufacturers' plants. Periodic inspection is a basis for continued listing of approved items. As Judge Steele interprets the relationship:

"The arrangement between General and Underwriters' contemplated that the latter would prescribe standards of construction and of materials which would render fire extinguishers safe for use. . . . Underwriters' knew, or should have known, of the type of construction and materials which would be required if the hazards involved . . . were to be avoided."

Among the authorities Steele cited in his opinion is the American Law Institute's Restatement of Torts. The Law Institute statement has been influential in guiding more and more state courts and legislatures toward giving broader relief for injuries through negligent product design or manufacture. And, Judge Steele says in his opinion, it in no way excludes testing organizations or other nonmanufacturing agencies from liability in damage suits.

QUESTIONS FOR DISCUSSION

1. What is the significance to the marketing manager (or advertising manager, production manager, sales manager, product manager, customer service manager, long-range planners, or legal department) of the recent changes in products liability law?

2. Extrapolate the changes of the past three decades in products liability law to the next 30 years.
3. If you were a manufacturer of small consumer appliances (toasters, broilers, radios, and the like), what product safety and warranty policies would you set? Why?
4. How can you measure the cost of running a good warranty policy?
5. How can you determine the effectiveness of your warranty policies?
6. Can you disclaim a product warranty? Justify your answer.
7. Do you think that contributory negligence on the part of a product's user is still a valid defense against products liability suits?
8. What will be some probable effects upon a firm's suppliers of the recent changes in products liability?
9. Do you think that it will be necessary for suppliers to raise prices because of the additional cost of liability insurance, greater quality control, and so forth?
10. What do you think of the research methodology employed by Bess Myerson's staff? Is it likely to produce an unbiased response? Are the questions, sample size, and so forth, reasonable?

SUGGESTED READINGS

Employers Insurance of Wausau, *ABC of Product Liability Loss Control* (Wausau, Wisconsin, 1900).

"Engineers Alone Can't Stop Product Liability Suits", *Product Engineering* (June 19, 1967), Vol. 38, pp. 113–114.

Gray, Albert W., "Product Defects, Injuries, and the Law", *Purchasing* (July 16, 1966), Vol. 61, pp. 81–92, 112.

————, "Products Must Match Vendor Claims", *Purchasing* (June 27, 1968), Vol. 64, pp. 57–58.

————, "There's a Limit to Vendor Liability", *Purchasing* (December 29, 1966), Vol. 61, pp. 51, 62–63.

Morris, John D., "Nixon Consumer Aide Criticized for Built-in Conflict of Interest", *New York Times* (February 15, 1969), p. 15.

"Quality Men Face Up to Liability Threat", *Steel* (September 2, 1968), Vol. 163, pp. 37–40.

Roach, Colleen, *Product Liability: Guides for the Corporate Manufacturing Executive* (Milwaukee, Wisconsin: Defense Research Institute, Inc., 1966).

Rooney, R. O., "Developments in Product Liability and What Can Be Done About Them", *National Underwriter* (September 1, 1967), Vol. 71, pp. 18–22.

Schultz, G. V., "What the Product Liability Crisis Means to You", *Factory* (April, 1968), Vol. 126, pp. 67–74.

Southwick, Arthur F., Jr., "The Disenchanted Consumer—Liability for Harmful Products", *Michigan Business Review* (January, 1966), Vol. 18, pp. 5–11.

"Strict Liability Suits Pile Up for Auto Makers", *Business Week* (August 23, 1965), No. 1878, pp. 30, 32.

"Warranty Hassle", *Chemical Week* (November 21, 1964), Vol. 95, pp. 40–42.

Wise, Clare E., "Products Liability", *Machine Design* (March 28, 1968), Vol. 8, pp. 20–24.

section 7 the social consequences of product innovation

The importance of the new product and the new product container is evident to any resident of the United States today. Indeed, for the consumer in America this is probably the most obvious aspect of the vast technological revolution that defines the twentieth century. The significant idea of the rising standard of living is in part, at least, related to the flood of product innovations.

We have already glimpsed the social results of this tide. The new "un-necessities" have accentuated the need for selling efforts and elevated marketing to its present importance in modern business. Product innovation has extended the role of fashion and status in the field of consumer goods and intensified obsolescence and competition in industrial goods. What Jean Shepard has jokingly amalgamated as the "newmproved" product is a major marketing development in our time.

As in so many cases, the useful and stimulating aspects have been accompanied by disadvantages. The effects of business and particularly the marketing part of business have become serious social issues. In this section we examine some of the significant social consequences of product innovation, specifically the tendency to replace old products, whose useful lives may not yet be over, with new products and the problems of waste disposal generated by product and package alike.

The first issue that we shall examine in connection with product innovation re-lated to the problem of obsolescence. When a product is invented or developed or improved, it most commonly offers a competitive way of doing something done previously by another product. There are some, but relatively few, inventions that are entirely new. Inventions are often the result of needs to carry out jobs already done in a faster or better way. Even before the great historical inventions—the power loom, the spinning jenny, the cotton gin, the reaper, the sewing machine—textiles were spun, woven, and sewn, and cotton bolls were cleaned.

The new product is bound to raise some questions about the usefulness of the old. In functional cases, such as those just mentioned, the new product and its technology are manifestly superior to the old. With consumer goods, however, novelty marks a line between what is new and what is old. What is new is generally exciting and interesting just because of its freshness, and what is old loses some value when the new appears. The new makes the old less desirable by "antiquating," or in the more common term, "obsolescing," it.

Since manufacturers are as aware of this as the rest of us, they have put a great premium on novelty and innovation because it tends to promote interest in the products they are prepared to create. Thus, if people like and prefer the new, manufacturers are prepared to invest heavily in product innovation, and when they invest in product innovation, they automatically generate product obsolescence. If the time between new and old is relatively short, the old product is psychologically obsolete but physically still functional. Therefore, some critics charge that innovation is destroying perfectly acceptable and useful products.

Some critics of business have also forcefully argued against "planned obsolescence," the *deliberate* introduction on the part of manufacturers of a "new model" or "style" that makes the existing product obviously old. The following three articles examine the arguments concerning this issue.

23 Planned Obsolescence: Rx for Tired Markets?

Martin Mayer

In planning and developing a new product, the question of how good it should be is inescapable. A tire jack to be put into a car does not have to be good enough to serve a truck, but that fact sets only an outside limit.

In fact, manufacturers nowadays give considerable thought to what might be called minimum quality levels, frequently emphasizing product obsolescence. How does planned obsolescence actually operate? In what way is it advantageous to the manufacturer? What is the consumer interest in this subject?

In this article Martin Mayer explains the answers to these questions and provides insight into industry's attempts to deal with the relation between product quality and innovation.

We see before us a most perplexed person, a man who is wondering how he ought to feel at this moment. He is the controller of a large corporation which makes electrical products, mostly big-ticket items, for the consumer market. And he is visiting the home of a friend, who is just now showing him the kitchen. Over against the wall, he sees an electric stove which his company made more than twenty years ago when electric stoves were a relatively new idea. The stove gleams. It is obviously in steady use and carefully kept up. Somebody loves it.

"That was one of ours, wasn't it?" says the controller.

"Yes," says his friend happily. "It's a wonderful stove."

The controller's automatic reaction is a feeling of pride in the quality of the product his company turned out twenty years ago—but then a sudden shaft of gloom descends upon him. All that money spent on planning wall ovens, automatic controls, clocktimers, griddles, deep-fat fryers—all that money spent on advertising the remarkable new product features, styling, choice of colors. Why does his friend still *want* the old stove? Has he no feeling for progress? How could the company survive if everyone were happy with an old stove?

Goods, as J. K. Galbraith has recently pointed out in his book, *The Affluent Society,* are produced to be consumed—and "consumed," in this case, has a specific meaning. Once something has been "consumed," the value is gone out of it. Paintings in a museum can't be consumed by the patrons of the museum, because the paintings are as good as ever after the art lover has looked at them. However, what is left of a steak after you have eaten it isn't much use to anyone but a dog.

Between the imperishable work of art and the evanescent beef steak, there is, in a highly-developed community, a wide range of "durable" goods. The more durable the item, the more slowly it will be consumed and the fewer units any one consumer will require over a period of time. Coffins, to take a special case, are one to a customer. Manufacturers of durable goods must, therefore, sell most of their output to a limited market of first customers.

Theoretically, it would seem, there is nothing the manufacturer can do to remedy this situation. Once an item is produced and sold, its rate of consumption depends upon the use the consumer makes of it. Obviously, a manufacturer can't hope to make a five-year-old refrigerator or automobile as valueless as an eaten ice cream cone or a combusted gallon of gasoline. But a manufacturer *can* hope to increase the *apparent* rate of consumption of a durable item—and thus automatically increase his replacement market —if he makes his older product seem "obsolete." The trick isn't foolproof, but it ought to work a good part of the time—and perhaps it can even be planned, assuring the manufacturer of a large, steadily increasing replacement market. Such planning could proceed in three directions:

1. FUNCTIONAL OBSOLESCENCE: Refrigerators are a good example. New refrigerators with effective, self-contained freezer compartments—and trouble-free automatic defrost mechanisms—make older refrigerators far less valuable, despite a great continuing consumption-potential. The addition of a new function and a new convenience are persuasive reasons for the market to discard old units still in perfect working order. The more important the new function—or the more important it can be made to seem by advertising—the closer to "obsolete" the old units become, and the more willing consumers will be to replace what they have. When television sets with 21-inch screens first became available, many people discarded relatively new 17-inch sets.

2. STYLE OBSOLESCENCE: The ladies' garment industry was, of course, the pioneer in this area. And the automobile industry has followed in its high-heeled footsteps, developing a kind of style obsolescence by social pressure. Upper-income elements of the market have been encouraged to believe that they are socially declassed if they are seen driving an old automobile. To make sure that the age of a car can be dated at a glance, models have been changed—superficially in most cases—every year. And the technique un-

questionably has been effective in certain markets. There are communities in this country where a wealthy man can get a reputation for stinginess simply by driving an older car. It must be kept in mind that this situation is exclusively American. Citroen, in France, made an automobile that was exactly the same on the outside from 1938 to 1956. It is not possible to date a Jaguar, a Mercedes, a Rolls-Royce, or even a Volkswagen, simply by the appearance of the vehicle. In France, England, and Germany, productive capacity has remained below effective demand for automobiles. Thus the manufacturer has had no reason to attempt to heighten the consumption rate of his product.

3. MATERIALS FAILURE: Obviously, one way to increase the replacement market for durable goods would be to make products in such a manner that they would function less well as they got older. This area of possible planned obsolescence is so highly charged emotionally that it is virtually impossible to get accurate evidence of actual procedure—and positively libelous to suggest possible examples. Items which are made to wear out more quickly than they must are, by definition, shoddy goods. A manufacturer who puts his name on shoddy goods risks a destructive reaction from the market which could more than offset his possible gains from increased consumption.

Durability Still Sells   There are some areas, indeed, where durability is regarded as a major selling point. Fountain pens are still guaranteed "for life" or even "forever." One of the most effective advertisements appearing [in 1958] was for Zippo cigarette lighters, which offered free, unlimited repair service. The advertisement contained a strong appeal for social approval of craftsmanship for its own sake, and all the attendant value connotations of honesty, responsibility, and so forth.

Placing such subjective judgments to one side for the time being, it is clear that a pattern of successful style obsolescence must eventually be reinforced by a decrease in the durability of the product. There was a time in rural America when considerable quantities of clothing were passed down from mother to daughter. Certainly, women's garments could be made to be more durable than they are today. But if a dress is to be obsolete in five years, there is no sound economic reason to make it durable for ten. Indeed, under these conditions, the achievement of maximum durability for the product would be wasteful. If the decreased cost of making the less durable product is passed on to the consumer in the form of lower prices—which is likely in most situations—the "shoddy" product will be more attractive, not only in the market, but also by standards of community interest.

Such an analysis assumes that all members of the community feel style obsolescence at the same rate—an assumption which is not valid. There must be women somewhere who would be content to wear older fashions if the clothes held out. To the extent that the majority sense of obsolescence diminishes the durability of the available product, these women are discriminated against. It is this minority, presumably (there is also a political element here) that voices the complaints about defective workmanship which are fairly often lodged against the clothing industry.

Fins, Fashion, and Craftsmanship   Where such complaints are common, it is at least possible that goods are not being made for maximum durability. Thus the charge against the automobile industry is worthy of a hearing—especially since the evidence indicates that European cars, which are not produced under conditions of repeated style obsolescence, tend to give somewhat longer service. Except for the Rambler, which has done a minimum of restyling in recent years, no American make of automobile stresses durability as a major selling point. Dodge once concentrated its promotional fire in this area, but the 1959-model Dodge is being sold with the bald argument that "the old must make way for the new." The theoretical conditions necessary for the calculated use of materials failure to reinforce campaigns of style obsolescence are present in the industry.

Nevertheless, it seems unlikely that the automobile companies are, in fact, using such an approach. The brand names of automobiles are probably better known than the brand names of any other product, and a proved accusation of shoddiness could be competitively catastrophic. Again, while very few women would wish to be seen in any but the latest fashions, a large section of the community still desires a durable automobile, and is quite willing to drive something old. (The existence of an active used-car market still is vital to the selling of new automobiles.) If social philosophers find the contemporary American automobile less durable than might be ideally desirable, the blame is less likely to lie in the shoddiness concomitant with style obsolescence than in the difficulties of maintaining high standards of quality control when the labor force is strongly unionized.

Functional obsolescence and style obsolescence are also very closely related. Even in the area of quickly-consumed goods—drugs and toiletries, for example—modern marketing procedure calls for a change in style whenever there is a change in function to heighten awareness of the "new" product. Again, a style change will be far more effective in creating obsolescence if an improvement in function can be associated with it. Thus Chrysler advertised the "aerodynamic" values of fins, and electric stove manufacturers found reasons why wall ovens do a better job of roasting turkeys. In the advertising of consumer durables, the most important single task is to convince those who already own such goods that the new styles are functional, not just decorative.

Chance Takes
a Hand

Not everything that happens in the world is necessarily "plan-ned." Artificial obsolescence is clearly in the self-interest of the durable goods manufacturer, and its occurrence in the market-place is plainly visible. The fact that things happen as an intelligent manu-facturer would wish them to happen argues strongly that there is an *intent* toward obsolescence. But intentions and plans are greatly different breeds of cat.

Continuing reactions to continuing changes in market conditions could create patterns of "planned obsolescence" with no more long-term planning than that performed by, say, a football coach. It is always hard to determine whether or not a given business achievement was really *planned* to happen as it did. A great deal of on-the-spot decision-making is involved even in a thoroughly planned operation, and only someone who has lived with the situation can say for sure how greatly these small decisions made under the impact of market conditions have influenced the course of the larger plan. And when these lucky experts come to speak, one usually finds that the notoriously selective human memory has interpreted past actions by the value of present results. If the operation was a failure, luck was bad; if the operation was a success, the planning was splendid.

A Case
in Point

One of the clearest examples of intended obsolescence in recent years was the introduction of the "stereo" phonograph record and associated playing equipment. The change from conven-tional records and phonographs was functional. Though a considerable tech-nological change was involved, no alteration in the appearance of either record or playing equipment was required. The new technique involved an undoubted potential for improving accuracy in the recording and the repro-duction of sound, and it could honestly be maintained that stereo made ex-isting equipment "obsolete."

Economically, some considerable functional advance was much to be de-sired by the manufacturers of phonographs. Despite the popularity of "high fidelity," the rate of increase in the market had slowed, and by the Winter of 1957–58, the pipelines from factory to consumer were well clogged with slow-moving items. Stereo offered manufacturers the chance to build a new replacement market and also to force rapid, sales-price disposal of stock-in-being on distributors and retailers.

The first successful demonstrations of stereo records and playing equip-ment were performed in the Fall of 1957 by Decca Records (Britain) in London and by the Westrex Corporation in New York. Almost immediately, the larger manufacturers proclaimed their intention to proceed as quickly as possible with the manufacture of stereo goods. The fact that the tech-niques had been developed by relatively small companies (Westrex was a subsidiary of Western Electric, but AT&T had agreed to divest itself of the subsidiary as partial answer to an antitrust problem) meant that secrecy was out of the question. Manufacturers, in this case, didn't want secrecy anyway, because part of their aim was to use the threat of obsolescence to push existing goods through the channels at increased speeds.

An initial delay developed because the two systems, British and American, were different in several details. Two meetings of the engineering staffs of all the potentially important producers of stereo phonograph records were held in January and February of last year. (The meetings were not publicized because of a well-founded fear that the Justice Department might take an interest.) Significantly, the meetings failed to produce general agreement on the best technical approach to stereo. Nevertheless, the largest single company in the market—RCA Victor—decided to go ahead with the Westrex system as refined by its own engineers. All the other companies shortly fell into step behind the leader in the approved fashion, and marketing departments prepared to introduce stereo to the public in the Fall.

Many a Slip   No engineering department in the industry was really happy with the decision to market stereo in the Fall of 1958—although, as the head of the largest such group said, "We'll get through it all right. We've learned to invent on schedule." Marketing departments, however, were convinced that delay increased the danger of the competition coming in first and slicing off an unduly large share-of-market. This fear was well-founded. Even before the policy decisions had been made in executive offices, one of the smaller record companies had come out with a line of stereo records (though the equipment on which they could be played did not yet exist, even in prototype). In the early Spring of 1958, one of the larger phonograph manufacturers held a press showing of its new stereo line and even advertised to the public that its stereo equipment was now on sale in the stores. If any appreciable demand had been stirred up by this announcement, the company would have had explanations to make to both its dealers and the public because the production lines were not yet in operation. But the gamble paid off. The company managed to tie its name to the new development without arousing the ire of disgruntled prospective purchasers.

All Off Schedule   In the end, nobody met delivery dates. RCA Victor engineers refused to release their designs for production on the deadline day. Westinghouse stylists were still unable to decide on cabinetry as late as mid-June, although introduction was scheduled for a trade fair in July. General Electric, which had manufactured the largest-selling quality "pickup" for conventional high fidelity installations, did not even begin production on its stereo pickups until the last week in September. As the result of the rush to meet release deadlines, the first stereo phonographs on the market were not—to put it mildly—of the quality expected from their eminent manufacturers. Moreover, phonograph dealers, noting that the stereo items were not coming through on schedule, refused to be hustled into store-wide inventory sales, so that the anticipated clean-up of older models was not achieved.

Time will not only heal these wounds; it will turn them into battle ribbons. In two or three years, when stereo is solidly established, authorities will look back on the frenzied days in Spring and Summer 1958, and cite the introduction of stereo records and phonographs as an example of "planned obsolescence." And fair enough, too, for the obsolescence of conventional phonographs was certainly the industry's *intention*. But nobody who sat up with the patient through the feverish preintroduction nights—as I did —could ever honestly say that the obsolescence was *planned*.

Planning   One of the oddest features of the current business thinking is
vs. Flexibility   the prestige which the word "plan" has achieved among men
                      who are most vocal in their loyalty to the concept of a free market economy. It was only a few years ago that Peter Drucker assured the nation that deep recessions were no longer possible because the essential cause of serious economic setbacks was a decline in business investment, and that long-range planning had now made such declines inconceivable. Nevertheless, the recession of 1957–58 was characterized by a very severe slash in business investment in reaction to prior overproduction of capital goods. (Partly due, by the way, to an unsuccessful pattern of artificial obsolescence in the capital goods market, especially in equipment for the manufacture of steel, nonferrous metals, and automobiles.) Planning, which is unresponsive to the market conditions, would be indistinguishable from the socialist administration of business. But Mr. Drucker thought such planning was a good thing, a sign of the maturity of our business leaders and the excellence of our present semi-competitive business structure.

The genius of capitalism is, in point of fact, its ability to react swiftly to market changes, and to the extent that any "planning" tends to lengthen that reaction time, it places the company involved at a severe competitive disadvantage. Notwithstanding the virtues of long-range planning as taught in business schools and reported at management conferences, it is unlikely that corporate policy-makers will carry the concept of long-range planning to the point of renouncing all flexibility of corporate action and reaction. Rigid long-range planning would be an especially severe handicap if it were applied to withhold innovation until some later time. The more one studies the question of "planned obsolescence," the more certain it seems that the phenomenon occurs because business men react to changing conditions, rather than because they plan.

Competitive   The introduction of stereo illustrates some of the problems in-
Free-for-All   volved. Even technical discussion on an industry-wide basis was
                         regarded as risky under the antitrust laws, and any large-scale
agreement on marketing procedures would surely have called down the
wrath of the Federals. Without a better espionage system than most businesses are willing to support, therefore, no company can be entirely sure
how its competitors are proceeding with any innovation. The safest course
is to rush ahead, full speed, and get your own version on the market as
quickly as possible. Even where an entire industry starts with everybody at
scratch—with a public announcement of a new process available to all by
license, as the Westrex announcement of its stereo devices—each company
scrambles forward at full tilt. The scramble gets even more frenzied when
an individual company's research department comes up with something new
and has no way of knowing for sure whether the competition has hit upon
the same idea.

Haste Can   "Planning," if the word means anything at all, implies that some-
Be Risky   thing is held back for the future. In a competitive consumer mar-
                         ket, holding back can be profitable only if the item in question
is not yet perfected—or, to put the matter more precisely, if it cannot be
made to function properly when produced in large quantities. (RCA Victor
gained nothing whatever by being first on the market with a gremlin-ridden
color television set.) Otherwise, the overriding marketing necessity is to be
early. Each year, as technical advances are made, companies vie with each
other to be the first to get their new products before the public. Such a
process is the essence of competition, but it prohibits meaningful planning.
    Style obsolescence is more subject to planning than functional obsoles-
cence—partly because it is less dependent on the accidental timing of technical innovation, partly because the discontinuance of a style tends to
frighten the market (as Chrysler found out in the 1930's), and may even
lead prospective purchasers to cherish rather than to disdain what they
already own. Even here, however, the trick is to arrive at the preferred
style ahead of the opposition, and the market researchers must work with
the stylists to determine how quickly appearances can be altered.
    The disastrous 1958-model automobiles led critics to wonder whether
obsolescence, as a marketing device, had not finally lost its place in the
American economy. Such a development, while not inconceivable, would be
revolutionary and thus surprising. The feeling that last year's furniture is
now "obsolete" has deep roots in the American past, in the psychology of
mobility, the love for the frontier, the belief in progress. If ten years of depression did not interfere with the American notion that the new is better
than the old, it seems unlikely that a one-year recession, however deep, can
wield such influence.

**The Case
Against
Obsolescence**   Regarded critically, patterns of obsolescence show many unfortunate facets. The discarding of "perfectly good" used wearing apparel and machinery is a well-known sin-and-shame. Nobody likes waste. Constant stress on the importance of newness diminishes respect for craftsmanship. It would be sad to think, as *Time* magazine does, that Americans are now buying cheap rather than good wrist watches because they wish to have something they can discard painlessly when fashions change. (One could also argue that high-priced watches have simply been losing ground to other big-ticket items in a period when consumers have had to think twice about major expenditures.) And within industry itself the need to get there first with anything new may produce diminished quality and some strikingly odd product features—like the first refrigerator cold controls, which were not connected to anything.

Nevertheless, the market wants newness, and producers must react to the market. Perhaps there would be less uproar over "planned obsolescence," from both conservative and radical social critics, if business men stopped stressing the very minimal amount of true planning that can, in reality, be applied to the problem of enlarging replacement markets.

24 Competitive Aspects of Planned Obsolescence

Edward M. Barnet

The concept of planned obsolescence has its defenders as well as its critics. This selection cites specific reasons why planned obsolescence is good for society.

The demand for obsolescence is not to be considered from the point of view of Stuart Chase's shrieks about "economic waste," but more usefully in terms of high level consumption. . . .

. . . Goods should be good, *but not too good*. Ecko Products saw this in opening a cutlery factory in the textile center of England. There, unemployed textile workers did not know enough to try to make kitchen knives that would last ten generations, as did the workers in Sheffield. Ecko thus supplies the customers of Woolworth's in England with kitchen knives at a shilling a piece, while Sheffield still offers heirlooms in the form of kitchen knives at one pound per knife. Who needs a kitchen knife that will be passed on to one's great-great-grandchildren?

The competitive demand for continued obsolescence and planned obsolescence stems from both a physical short life and a psychological short life. In the one case it has been accused of bringing about induced perishability, and in the other case it has been accused of bringing about forced-fashion.

But there is an economic question at stake as to whether people need to have a kind of durability built into products that are primarily based on the desire of the consumer for variety and change.

This is particularly true in the apparel field and in women's wear more than men's. But even in the appliance field it is quite apparent that one cannot ignore the economic recognition of the fact that most of us in the United States today . . . are members of an employee society, where our success as earners and maintaining a job is perhaps more significant than

Reprinted from Edward M. Barnet, "Competitive Aspects of Planned Obsolescence", *Advancing Marketing Efficiency* (Chicago: American Marketing Association, 1959), pp. 40–44, by permission of the author and the American Marketing Association.

worrying about what real income means in terms of thrift—in the sense that led to the sponsoring of early cooperatives in Europe.

Today, people in our employee society need jobs more than low prices. It is quite conceivable that obsolescence is one of the necessary evils which maintains employment. . . .

.   .   .

It is pointed out that in terms of razor blades, the lack of standardization forces people to be repeat purchasers. Not only lack of standardization in types of blades but innovations in types of razors themselves necessitates change. Also, it is contended that the sharpness and durability of the edge of the blade is far less than it might be.

Heaven knows that nylon hose for women have been so constructed to a degree of sheerness that supposedly is intended to flatter women's need for translucency; it certainly does not satisfy her need for durability, but it is contended that she prefers the quality in the sense of sheerness to long life.

.   .   .

In point of fact, there is a real question of whether this is cheating or achieving what the consumer really wants, which is not paying for quality that is excessive. Excessive quality makes a product last longer than techno-logical or fashion changes make the product desirable.

I think it is very significant to note that the success of Sears, Roebuck & Company in the appliance field is based on the avowed policy of Mr. T. V. Hauser when he was Vice President in Charge of Merchandising, that "We at Sears," said he, "will give the customer the best for the money, but not necessarily the best." This definition of quality has much to do with the issue of purposeful obsolescence.

To what degree must a product be rendered obsolete to be an improve-ment? Every writer who challenges this seeming demonstration of economic waste always inserts the proviso that *real* innovation, *real* technological im-provement should not be stopped; and yet how does one distinguish between what is called pseudo-innovation, and pseudo-perishability, and what is real?

This in many cases is a matter of taste and gets into the area of emotion, and psychological need, and has nothing to do with an engineer's viewpoint as to long life and durabiilty. Anyone who has studied the economics of fashion is familiar with the fact that in our time people may be bored and people may suffer from an acute need for excessive variety. But whether the consumer needs variety or not, the fact remains that salespeople them-selves become dull and stale and that a great deal of so-called pseudo-obsolescence is designed to keep a sales organization alive with something fresh to talk about.

.   .   .

In an era where the use of the word "competition" connotes so many different things to so many different people, when imperfect competition and "handicap" competition have been displaced by innovistic competition, there is little question that the purposes of competition are to obtain a favorable advantage over one's competitors by obtaining products of differentiations which justify people's replacing items already in their home stocks with new items.

With the compulsion on the manufacturer to convert his fixed capital in a limited time, with a constant threat of other technological improvements from organized research in the hundreds of millions of dollars, there is no question at all as to whether he must indulge in this kind of competition.

If you wish to charge him with an attempt to avoid price competition, that is a very old accusation which has probably been valid for many a century. No competitor has ever contended that his article was not better than someone else's, even if offered at the same price. The advantages of being made by a particular person . . . has always been a fact in the market place. Today the intensity of this kind of avoidance of price competition has forced the injection of a series of novelties in every kind of merchandise.

Whether or not this is economic waste is not entirely debatable since what is social and economic waste that compels people to trade in an automobile that still has thousands of miles of life in it because a new model has a new strip of chrome or a new kind of ashtray. It is not necessarily to be regarded as waste to society if it opens the market to those in lower income groups where they have access to *used* cars that they could not otherwise afford. This kind of discussion has raged in the journals for many a year and will, no doubt, continue to do so.

The distinction between real innovation, namely the constructive, the builder kind of innovation, and the negative kind, the purposeful obsolescence with implications of falseness conducted by the wreckers, is in no way a distinction that holds much validity since the wreckers are those who create purposeful obsolescence, in fact, pave the way to further experimentation in improvements that are really constructive. And whether they are really constructive or only a flash of artistic design, if it enhances the life of the owner of the product, who is to say that this in itself is wrong or wasteful?

The fact is that competition by innovation—a positive view of planned obsolescence—is no longer optional. It is a necessity. Innovistic competition threatens even the most firmly entrenched quasi-monopoly. It is but the newest and most aggressively defensive fashion in the evolving forms of competition.

25 Why the U.S. Is in Danger of Being Engulfed by Its Trash

In the preceding part of this section we reviewed the inevitable relationships between innovations and obsolescence. We were especially interested in the controversy surrounding the so-called "planning" of obsolescence.

A Yankee proverb counseled: "Use it up, wear it out, make it do." Older Americans can still remember when this slogan was meaningful. Only 50 years ago, a man's trousers were cut down when they wore out at the knees so that junior could wear them. When other holes appeared, the pants became rag rugs. Flour was bought in large sacks that were transformed into work shirts. Collars were reversed when they wore out. When the shirt could no longer be used, it became one or several dishtowels or cleaning rag. Shoes for children were invariably larger than required since the child's feet were expected to grow. The same was true of their clothing. In the words of one observer*:

> Things didn't wear out; they gave up in exhaustion. Even our patches eventually found their way into quiet patterns.

But with the new attitude toward product innovation on the part of both business and consumers, the above adage doesn't apply any more.

Whatever may be the psychological and economic consequences of obsolescence, the physical effect of obsolescence has become increasingly evident and troublesome. Product obsolescence means more and more rubbish. The fate of the obsolete product is to move through whatever second-hand markets exist to the trash baskets and garbage dumps. As product innovation increases in velocity, so also appears the nagging question—what are we going to do with all the excess that nobody wants?

To be sure, product innovation alone does not account for the entire problem. The multiplication of population, affluence (wealthy people consume more goods), urban concentration, as well as other factors play an undeniable part. But product innovation, including the new packaging revolution that has cut down reuse of containers, are prime reasons behind the "waste explosion." Thus, marketing practice appears as a central agent in one of the looming public issues of the time. Industry's realization of this fact and its assumption of the responsibility for needed correction will constitute a significant challenge to business for the balance of the century. The "waste problem" is being called a national disgrace, and new solutions are being sought, as shown in the following article.

Reprinted from "Why the U.S. Is in Danger of Being Engulfed by Its Trash", *U.S. News & World Report* (September, 1969), Vol. 67, No. 10, pp. 64–66. Copyright 1969 U.S. News & World Report, Inc.

*From *Homebrew and Patches*, by Harry J. Boyle, © 1963 by Clarke, Irwin and Company Limited. Used by permission.

Americans, their health threatened by air and water pollution, are disturbed by warnings that they also face the danger of being engulfed in trash.

Mountains of waste are building up around the major cities. Space for disposal is running out. Garbage-dumping is poisoning water supplies. Inefficient incineration further fouls the air.

The problem is not just household and commercial waste. Worn-out automobiles and tires are dumped by the millions. Bottles, cans and paper containers litter streets, highways, rural roads and parks. Industrial and farm refuse piles higher and higher.

The country now has to deal with 3.5 billion tons of solid waste each year, and that figure keeps growing. This includes 360 million tons of household and commercial trash.

It costs cities $4.5 billions a year to collect and dispose of this refuse.

. . .

Richard D. Vaughan, director of the Bureau of Solid Waste Management of the U.S. Public Health Service, notes:

"The most convenient means for disposal—usually an open-burning dump—was, and unfortunately still is, most frequently employed. However, it is becoming increasingly obvious that such a casual approach to solid-waste management—which may have been acceptable in an earlier day— can no longer be tolerated in a country of over 200 million persons, 70 per cent of whom live in urban areas."

. . .

Now: 5.3   According to Mr. Vaughan, in 1920 an average of 2.75 pounds
Pounds Each   of waste was collected daily from each person in the U.S. Today,
                this figure has grown to 5.3 pounds, and it is estimated that by
1980, the per capita waste collection will be 8 pounds a day.

. . .

Incineration is not the final solution because burning leaves a 20 per cent residue of ash, in addition to pollution of the air. New high-temperature furnaces, however, may reduce the ash content to 10 per cent.

Some big cities, notably San Francisco and Philadelphia, have been dickering with railroad lines to freight their trash many miles away to otherwise useless land or abandoned mines, but costs and other problems have delayed these programs.

Another idea being considered is compressing rubbish in containers, taking it out to sea and jettisoning it in deep water. This method presumably would benefit only seaboard cities.

From Dump   The major innovation in waste disposal so far has been develop-
to Park   ment of the "sanitary landfill" system. Trash is hauled to an
                  open area and put into trenches. Then it is covered with soil.
When filled, the dump is converted into a park or recreational facility.

This is being done at a site in Washington, D.C., where open burning
was practiced a few miles from the Capitol. A few months hence, dumping
will stop and conversion of the area into a 300-acre park will begin.

The sanitary-landfill system, says the Public Health Service, makes a
dump rodent-proof and odorless. It is only slightly more costly than
burning.

Why is trash becoming such a big problem? The answer, in part, is the
steady introduction of more conveniently packaged consumer items. Increasingly, too, many items still reach the buyer in containers that do not
deteriorate quickly or at all.

It has been estimated that Americans, in a typical year, throw away 48
billion cans, 26 billion bottles, more than 30 million tons of paper, 4 million
tons of plastics, and 100 million rubber tires weighing a million tons.

Use of disposable bottles, to be tossed away rather than returned for a
refund, is spreading. Aluminum cans, which unlike steel cans do not rust
away when discarded, are growing in popularity. More and more items
come in plastics which do not decompose and cause noxious fumes when
burned.

A recent survey of litter along a one-mile stretch of two-lane Kansas highway turned up these items: 770 paper cups, 730 empty cigarette packs, 590
beer cans, 130 soft-drink bottles, 120 beer bottles, 110 whisky bottles and
90 beer cartons.

The collection also included everything from bedsprings to shoes.

One firm, the Reynolds Metal Company, is trying to make a small dent
in all this litter. It is offering a half-cent bounty for each aluminum beer can
turned in at depots in Los Angeles and Miami, Fla.

Mr. Vaughan gave a viewpoint of the Bureau of Solid Waste Management when he said:

"I sometimes don't understand Americans. In Europe, you almost never
see anyone discard anything in the street. In the United States, I've seen
DON'T LITTER signs practically covered with litter. Americans are litterers.
The problem is so bad that we have sociologists working on the problem,
trying to find out why Americans have such an untidy streak."

Dead-Traffic Jam Another headache for the officials dealing with solid waste is the
                      increasing number of scrapped autos. One estimate is that, by
1980, Americans will be discarding 10 million motor vehicles a year.

With an introduction in recent years of new methods of steelmaking,
there is almost no demand for baled steel scrap.

Under the old method, cars were put into a hydraulic press, squeezed into blocks about the size of a small trunk and fed to steel-plant furnaces.

Now some old cars are being chewed up by huge machines that turn them into shavings and chunks for reprocessing into steel. But one of these machines—and there are only a few in the country—can dispose of only about 1,000 car shells a day, after these have been stripped of tires, seats, engines, windows and transmissions.

As for the 100 million worn-out tires that are thrown away every year, experts are seeking ways to make them into something more useful than bumpers on boatyard docks.

.   .   .

New Gold Rush?   Another Bureau of Mines project has literally found gold in rubbish piles. A study of ash residue in incinerators turned up both gold and silver from lost or castoff costume jewelry, coins and photographic negatives. The minerals were discovered to assay at $14 per ton of ash.

Although the trash problem primarily is a local one, the Government has stepped in to lend assistance. Under a 1965 act of Congress, the Bureau of Solid Waste Management was created. Two-thirds of its budget of 15 million dollars goes in grants to State and local agencies, universities and a few private companies for experiments to find better ways of handling trash.

One research project at the University of Pennsylvania is examining the possibility of using pipeline techniques for collection and removal of household solid waste. Researchers have designed a pilot-scale removal system that would pipe away solid wastes that had been mixed with water.

"Recycling and reuse" is another concept that is being investigated. A limiting factor in this process at present is that it must start with hand separation of different types of trash. The Stanford Research Institute, under a Government grant, is working to develop a separator that would use air pressure to sort out five different types of materials, some of which could be processed for reuse.

Jobs for   Mr. Vaughan believes that, in 10 to 15 years, all but 5 to 10 per
Housewives?   cent of household garbage will be reclaimed.

"It would be nice," he says, "if the American housewife could be persuaded to sort out garbage into about 15 different piles. Then all the plastic bottles and aluminum cans could be gathered and melted down for reuse. Well, my wife isn't about to take on such a job of garbage-sorting, and I doubt that many other wives would."

.   .   .

Composting of household and restaurant garbage on a commercial scale for sale as fertilizer has been tried, but has not been notably successful.

Farmers and gardeners find it easier to pick up a bag of chemical fertilizer at the local hardware store, and most of the compost firms have closed.

The dream of most experts in the solid-waste-disposal field is a concept called "total recycling." This would eliminate trash because nothing would ever be thrown away. It would be used again in some way.

An automobile, for example, would be designed and built so its unworn parts could be retrieved for reuse when its usefulness was ended. Only irreducible scrap would remain, and that could be salvaged. But the experts agree that the time when such a system may evolve is not now in sight.

What Mr. Vaughan calls "one of the most promising engineering concepts in solid-waste management" is a combustion power unit being developed under contract by the Combustion Power Company of Palo Alto, Calif. This is basically a special incinerator that burns household and commercial trash at high pressure to produce hot gases to power a turbine, which in turn drives an electrical generator.

As designed, the unit should produce approximately 15,000 kilowatts of electric power while burning 400 tons of municipal trash daily.

The incinerator-generator units could be installed at strategic points in urban areas, reducing hauling distances. For example, five such units could handle all the refuse from San Francisco, while about 40 units would be required for New York City.

The Loathsome Train   For a time, it appeared that one answer to the problems of major cities in disposing of their trash would be to cart it away in trains. The fact is that close-in urban land has become too valuable for dumping and long-haul trucking costs are too high to dump at sites farther away. Trains could provide a cheaper service.

.   .   .

New York considered a rail-haul plan for its waste several years ago, but the idea never got off the ground. A Philadelphia plan is stalled because of official doubts about the sanitary aspects of using old mines for disposal.

Denver and Milwaukee considered similar programs, but dropped them because of economic obstacles.

Chicago and Detroit are experimenting with equipment that compacts trash into blocks. The Japanese tried to use such blocks as building material. This failed because of decomposition, but experiments continue in use of the block to fill swampy land.

Rising Costs   As the piles of trash climb higher, so does the expense of removal. Fees to householders in some of Washington's suburbs exceed $45 a year. In Milwaukee, annual rubbish-removal charges went up in 10 years from $26 to more than $35. New York officials estimate it costs $30 to dispose of a ton of trash.

.   .   .

QUESTIONS FOR DISCUSSION

1. How would you define a "new" product?
2. Suppose that product innovation could somehow be stopped. To the best of your ability describe the results.
3. In what sense is obsolescence "planned"?
4. What are the negative effects of planned obsolescence?
5. Do you believe planned obsolescence has any positive results?
6. Would you favor legislation to restrict product obsolescence? Why or why not?
7. Investigate the proposals currently under consideration for handling waste. Which of these are particularly related to product innovations?
8. For what reason(s) do manufacturers introduce innovations in packaging?
9. With reference to packages, what standards would be useful to consumers? Should the government determine allowable package sizes and forms?
10. Do you believe that clothing designers and manufacturers "make" consumers buy?

SUGGESTED READINGS

Berg, Thomas L., and Abe Schuchman, *Product Strategy and Management* (New York: Holt, Rinehart and Winston, 1963).

"Is *Waste Makers* a Hoax? Why Packard Did It", *Printers Ink* (September 30, 1960), Vol. 272, pp. 20–29.

Kuehn, A. A., and R. L. Day, "Strategy of Product Policy", *Harvard Business Review* (November–December, 1962), Vol. 40, No. 6, pp. 100–110.

Lasagna, Louis, "The Pharmaceutical Revolution: Its Impact on Science and Society", *Science* (December 5, 1969), Vol. 166, No. 3910, pp. 1227–1233.

Main, Jeremy, "Industry Still Has Something to Learn About Congress", *Fortune* (February, 1967), Vol. 75, No. 2, pp. 128–129, 191–194.

Packard, Vance O., *The Waste Makers* (New York: David McKay Co., 1960).

"Planned Obsolescence—Is It Wrong—Is There a Better Way?" *Printers Ink* (May 26, 1961), Vol. 275, No. 8, pp. 25–31.

Robinson, Dwight E., "Fashion Theory and Product Design", *Harvard Business Review* (November–December, 1958), Vol. 36, No. 6, pp. 126–138.

Shaw, S. J., Behavioral Science Offers Fresh Insights on New Product Acceptance", *Journal of Marketing* (January 1965), Vol. 29, No. 1. pp. 9–13.

Stewart, John B., "Planned Obsolescence", *Harvard Business Review* (September–October, 1959), Vol. 37, No. 5, *passim*.

section 8
the social
implications
of company
pricing
policies

The classical economists, writing in the eighteenth and nineteenth centuries, saw prices as responses to market conditions. They believed, when the supply of a product is large compared to the demand for it, the price will fall. When the demand is large relative to the supply, the price will rise.

In this view of price behavior the individual firm or seller is not supposed to have any important freedom or discretion. Modern business, however, has cast doubt on this belief. The situation is not as simple as the elementary theory of supply and demand suggests. For one thing, the "product" is usually far more complex than it was in classical economics. Product brands are competitive but not identical. Moreover, large producers and sellers try to influence buyers to believe that their brands are superior to those of competitors.

If the prices are not "automatic", and if companies do in fact have a certain amount of discretion in pricing the brands and varieties they offer consumers, then certain implications emerge for consumers. Consumers may ask whether the price charged is "fair." Similarly, the question of whether consumers can recognize the quality differences that price differentials are supposed to reflect may arise.

Let us first examine the relation between price and quality. The old saying "You get what you pay for", was an essentially correct precept in an earlier time, when staple products were well known to consumer and producer. The growth in the complexity and number of products for sale has made it more difficult to get what you pay for. The result is to raise two closely related questions: (1) Are price and quality in fact correlated? (2) Are consumers really interested in and capable of estimating in any exact way the relationship between price and quality?

In general, national manufacturers naturally argue that their products are of high quality and are therefore high in price. Less well known manufacturers often argue that their materials are high in quality and relatively low in price. Retail discounters take a similar position. Less partial observers, such as consumer testing agencies, however, tend to indicate that the relationship between price and quality is far from close.

In this section we shall take a look at several aspects of the questions raised.

26 Why Corporations Find It Necessary to "Administer" Prices

Robert F. Lanzillotti

Under "pure" or "perfect" competition, as defined by economists, prices were supposed to be decided "automatically," that is, by the interaction of demand and supply. In practice, in twentieth-century America, however, it has been evident that sellers have price policies or, one might say, they "administer" prices rather than merely waiting for demand and supply to act.

In the article that follows, Robert Lanzillotti attempts to make us understand how and why this happens. Note that he also raises the crucial question of how this phenomenon relates to the public interest.

Some 25 years ago the distinguished economist Gardiner C. Means coined the term "administered prices" to describe certain industrial goods whose prices are typically rigid, at least for a period of time, and whose sales fluctuate with demand at the rigid price. In contrast to what are sometimes called "market prices," i.e., those that are determined *automatically* by the interaction of demand and supply forces in the market, "administered prices" are formulated in executive offices of companies as a matter of operating policy and financial planning by corporate officials.

The distinctive feature of an administered price situation is that firms, whether acting individually or cooperatively with competitors, have a kind of plenary power to set prices within a considerable range. Market forces, of course, limit the range within which an administered price may be set, but they do not *determine* the price. There is nothing in the supply and demand situation that will *force* a particular price to result.

This condition, where firms enjoy measurable discretion over prices, is found whenever the number of firms in a particular industry or market is small, or wherever one or two firms account for a predominant share of the market and act as strong price leaders. Typical examples are such industries as automobiles, steel, aluminum, rubber, chemicals, petroleum and electrical equipment.

Reprinted from *Challenge: The Magazine of Economic Affairs*, published by Institute of Economic Affairs, New York University (January, 1960), Vol. 8, No. 4, pp. 45–49.

While recognizing the undesirable competitive implications of these situations, many economists—including Dr. Means—regard administered prices as an *inevitable and indispensable* part of our modern economy. Harvard economist John Kenneth Galbraith goes even further and says: "It is equally inevitable that a great many industries will be conducted by a comparatively small number of large firms. That is the nature of capitalism wherever it is found. A large amount of price administration is thus part of our economic system. Those who deplore it are wasting their breath."

There are other economists of note who contest the validity of this view and hold that administered prices are symptomatic of excessive market power that should be brought under some type of social control. But there is no general agreement among economists regarding either the need or desirability of such measures.

Greater Awareness   Almost all students of the subject, however, seem agreed on one point: The nature of administered prices is not fully known or understood by policy-makers and the public. In order to formulate appropriate and effective national economic policies regarding inflation and full employment, there must be a greater awareness of the way in which administered prices are determined and the nature and extent of their impact on general economic processes.

The limited information available on the actual pricing process suggests that many factors motivate and influence corporate managements. A recent Brookings Institution study of big corporations, whose pricing falls in the administered price category, discloses that corporate objectives underlying price decisions vary from company to company within and among different industries. Most large companies were found to have rather specific long-term goals, such as the desires to:

Attain a particular "target profit" rate on capital invested in the company.
Stabilize industry prices, margins and profits.
Attain a specific percentage or "penetration" of a market.
Meet or minimize competition.
Follow the price leader.

A National Industrial Conference Board survey of 155 companies confirms the Brookings finding: "Representative is the statement by a vice president of a general industrial machinery concern that "the basic policy is to establish prices that will return a predetermined volume of sales."

General Motors officials, for example, have indicated in several appearances before Congressional committees that it is their policy to set prices to yield a profit of 15 to 20 per cent *after* taxes on investment. In practice, this means that even though GM output should fall below the company's normal volume (as in 1957–58), or consistently above (as in the 1950–56 period), suggested list prices established at the beginning of the model year will remain unchanged. This is the prototype of administered prices.

Long-range and Inflexible   There are two main sets of factors that explain why managements think in terms of relatively long-range, inflexible prices.

First, a firm falling in the administered price group usually will be characterized by one or all of the following features: It is one of a few large producers; it is a price leader; and it sells products in a market or markets that are more or less protected by virtue of the magnitude of capital requirements, the influence of trademarks, brand names and patents, and the control of strong retail organizations.

A second set of special influences is found in the nature of the product, production costs, customer preferences, problems of internal management, control and various public pressures. More specifically, administered prices are traceable to:

A high capital-to-sales dollar ratio.

Relatively constant unit costs over wide ranges of output and over long intervals of time (up to a year).

Rigidity of wage rates and prices of some semifinished materials and intermediate goods.

Customer preference for stable (rigid) prices that simplify pricing and production planning.

High cost of frequent price changes for the company.

Increasing pressure on managements to resort to capital budgeting and profits planning in order to allocate available capital funds to competing uses and to provide for necessary plant expansion. (Projects that offer the best promise of reaching the predetermined profit target over the long term are likely to be given priority in the use of funds.)

The guarantee of the Full Employment Act of 1946. (Firms, like wage earners, have a reasonable assurance that government action will be taken to maintain incomes and production. Hence, decreases in demand are viewed as temporary, and decreases in price dangerous and unnecessary.)

Management conception of the corporation as an industry leader vested with responsibilities akin to those of a public utility. (A U.S. Steel official confided that he was "unable to understand or properly describe the corporation's pricing policy except as something like the approach of the public utilities.")

This tendency toward public utility thinking is reinforced by the disposition of the community and government officials to appeal to such firms as "pattern setters" for industry generally. In pricing they are expected to restrain themselves from taking full advantage of immediate profit opportunities.

Uniformity of prices among competitors also is typically found in conjunction with administered prices, which means that the force of competition is channeled along lines other than price. This is why profit targets are crucial—to provide a steady flow of funds to help maintain company position in the industry, as well as to mollify stockholders. Plant expansion will be planned with some "built-in" excess capacity so that the company can compete for customers by guaranteeing supplies in times of peak demands.

Thus, administered prices are regarded as necessary to protect producers from the temptation of cutting prices as a means of stimulating sales and operating closer to capacity—an action which corporation executives generally regard as self-defeating.

The wisdom of this thinking, of course, depends upon the responsiveness of industrial and consumer demands to price cuts. It is plausible that in times of declining demand both industry and consumers will postpone those purchases that are postponable; hence, price reductions would not greatly alter the purchase of these buyers. The magnitude of price cuts (i.e., token vs. large cuts) and their impact on buyer expectations must also be reckoned with, however. Experts are divided on this question, and managements feel an administered (rigid) price policy, on balance, is "safer" in terms of their long-run objectives.

Misleading Emphasis   It needs to be noted, therefore, that the expression "administered prices," while an accurate and vivid description of the kind of pricing under discussion, carries a misleading if not faulty emphasis. It would be more accurate and more useful, both to an understanding of management thinking and a guide to public policy, to speak of "administered profits." By doing so, attention would be focused on the fact that our big corporations are *interested in and have the economic power to make administrative decisions that will fully utilize, or underutilize, industrial capacity as necessary to meet profit objectives.*

Even a brief discussion of the problem of administered prices and inflation requires more than just a mention of the importance of the rigidity of costs—and wage costs, in particular. The persistent inflation of the post-World War II period, at times side-by-side with recession, raises the question of whether our economy has developed a new kind of inflationary track as contrasted with the old-fashioned monetary variety.

Although the problem of administered prices would exist even in the absence of unions, the development of strong labor blocks has complicated the problem. The ability of management to administer its prices, on the one hand, has meant less resistance to union demands and, on the other, the level of profits resulting from administered prices has made labor more militant in its demands.

Since the end of the Korean conflict especially, both management and labor appear to have taken advantage of the administered price mechanism to escalate cost and price increases upward in a "staircase" pattern. The rather large area of price discretion available to certain companies has afforded a means by which both management and labor interests could attain their private objectives. The administered price mechanism has provided a rationale for explaining the result to the public.

The decision of the steel companies to "bow their backs" against union demands in the 1959 negotiations was due, no doubt, to concern about the high levels steel prices had already reached and the increasing threat of foreign steel. There is reason to believe, however, that the prolonged stalemate and costly strike was also due in part to the belated recognition by government officials of the administrative nature of wage-price adjustments in our major industries and a desire to do something to bring this inflationary mechanism under control.

The resort to admonitions, pleas and threats at the only real point of susceptibility—prices—reflects official concern over administered prices, but apparent inability to make them serve the economic system. It remains to be seen whether this strange administrative process that has served management and organized labor so well in the past decade will be harnessed and directed in the public interest.

27 The Psychology of Pricing

Benson P. Shapiro

Price theory has usually assumed that the demand for a product will vary inversely with the price for that product. But when this idea is tested in the market, one finds that the opposite may also be true, that is, the higher the price, the higher the demand. How and why this can happen is the concern of the article that follows.

Scientific investigators have carried out a number of experiments dealing with consumer perceptions relating to prices and quality. This article is a summary of the resulting psychological information and is equally valuable to the marketing executive and to the intelligent citizen. It also indicates why pricing policy can become a social issue.

. . .

The literature of marketing and economics includes several significant studies of the psychology of pricing, and I shall review them in this article. I shall place most of the emphasis on the role of price as an indicator of quality to the consumer, because this has been a very neglected concept that may prove quite useful to retailers and manufacturers.

Price Consciousness   Determining the level of consumer price knowledge is an important part of determining the meaning of price. Two studies, one by an industry group and the other by two scholars, are helpful here. They tell us something about the number of people who remember price variations, the relation of such price knowledge to social class, and other factors.

The *Progressive Grocer* study (performed in conjunction with Colonial Stores) covered 60 frequently advertised and highly price-competitive brand items.[1] Several thousand customers were shown these items and asked to state the price of each. In addition, each customer was asked if he or she used each item, and to supply information about his or her age, income, and size of family. Price consciousness was found to be quite high for *some* products but varied greatly. For instance:

> The correct price of Coca-Cola six-packs was remembered by 86% of the respondents, and 91% named a price that was not more than 5% off the right figures.
>
> On the other hand, only 2% could recall the exact price of a shortening; 34% were within 5% of the right figure.
>
> The median items were Ivory bar soap with 17% exact recall and 32% in the plus-or-minus 5% range, and Scott towels, with 16% exact recall and 24% in the 5% range.

In this study, the sex, age, and income of respondents appeared to make little difference.

A rigorous experiment by Andre Gabor and C. W. J. Granger casts more light on the question of price consciousness.[2] A sample of 640 English housewives was chosen at random within stratified areas. Only 15 commodities were used, and the respondents were interviewed by 44 University of Nottingham volunteers who were given careful oral and written instructions. The students successfully completed 428 interviews.

In addition to demonstrating, as the *Progressive Grocer* study does, that price consciousness is quite high for some products, the Gabor-Granger research suggests a relationship between social class and price consciousness. Housewives in the highest social class were more willing than housewives in lower classes to *name* a price for a commodity, whether the price was correct or not; but the percent of correct prices recalled tended to be greater the lower the social class of the respondent. For the seven commodities for which prices were stable over time and consistent between stores, 51% of all respondents knew the correct price, 28% guessed incorrectly, and 21% did not name a price at all. (To indicate the range: in the case of tea, 79% of the answers were correct; in the case of breakfast cereals, only 35% were correct.)

Connotations of Quality   Now let us turn to the role of price as an indicator of the quality of a product. Here is where we begin to find very practical (and sometimes surprising) implications for manufacturers and retailers.

Two studies deserve our attention—one done in 1954 by Harold J. Leavitt, and the other in 1966 by Gabor and Granger, the same scholars who conducted the research on price consciousness described earlier. Both studies conclusively show that customers *do* use price as an indicator of quality, and that the strength of this phenomenon varies with socioeconomic class, product type, and retail outlet.

New
Correlation

The Leavitt study, "A Note on Some Experimental Findings About the Meaning of Price," dealt with four products: floor wax, razor blades, moth flakes, and cooking sherry.[3] Leavitt used 60 subjects—30 Air Force officers (majors and lieutenant colonels) and 30 male and female graduate students, most of them in their thirties and forties. Two brands of each product were offered, and four sets of prices were developed for each product pair. (For instance, Brands A and B of one product were priced at 68 cents and 72 cents, 66 cents and 74 cents, 62 cents, and 78 cents, and 52 cents and 88 cents; similarly, 4 pairs of prices were given for each of the other 3 products.)

The choice situations were on paper; no physical product or brand was presented. The price combinations (one for each product) were distributed among the subjects in no special order. A subject had to choose Brand A or Brand B for each product. He also was asked to answer a question regarding satisfaction with the choice, and to rate the product in terms of quality differences he believed to exist among brands based on his previous experience.

The subjects often chose the higher-priced products. Leavitt reports:

"When faced with choices between two brands of floor wax, 57% of our subjects selected the higher-priced brand [all pairs of prices are pooled here]; 30% of the subjects chose the higher-priced razor blades; 24% the higher-priced moth flakes; and 21% the higher-priced cooking sherry." (Page 208.)

The question on satisfaction yielded another interesting result: when the subject believed that there was a difference in the quality between brands, he felt a psychological conflict. Leavitt observed that the subjects tended to have more doubts when they chose the lower-priced brands than when they chose the higher-priced brands. Further, the greater the perceived quality difference, the greater the uncertainty about a choice. Thus, the competing brands of floor wax were believed to have the greatest difference in quality (the cooking sherries had the least difference); many more of the subjects indicated doubt about their selection in this product category than any of the others, and the percentage of doubt was greater among those choosing the lower-priced floor wax than those choosing the higher-priced one.

Leavitt sums up his findings by emphasizing that increased price may cause increased demand:

"These findings suggest that demand curves may not invariably be negatively sloped, that price itself may have more than one meaning to a consumer, and that a higher price may sometimes increase, rather than decrease, his readiness to buy. One might guess that a high price may be an attracting instead of a repelling force for particular brands of many different brands of items." (Page 210.)

The Leavitt work can, I believe, be criticized on two obvious points. First, his sample is small and not very broad; also, the subjects appear to be similar in age, education, and social class. Second, and more important, the simulated purchase procedure is quite contrived—the subject does not have to spend his money. This would, of course, bias the results in favor of the higher-priced product.

The results, however, seem so strong that these shortcomings do not detract from the conclusion that some consumers judge the quality of some products by their prices. The question of *which* consumers and *which* products will be considered later, but let me observe now that the number of consumers using price as an indicator of quality may be substantial.

"Reverse"   In 1966, Gabor and Granger reported on another study of price
Demand Curve   perception.[4] The study was detailed, complex, and mathematically rigorous. The experimental work was based on a simulated purchase situation using six different products. Essentially, the investigators probed to determine the consumer's "too cheap" and "too expensive" curves, and, from those, the buy-response curve. Two methods of questioning were used. Gabor and Granger found that "considerable proportions of the subjects trusted price rather more than the evidence of their senses." The authors observed:

"What is interesting is not so much the fact that consumers exist who would not be deterred by a very low price for a given article, but rather that this phenomenon is not ubiquitous. . . . We felt that [price would be an indicator of quality for] a wide range of commodities, such as textile products, simply because their quality cannot be ascertained by sight and, owing to constant changes in technology and fashion, past experience is of little use in this respect. The reputation of the manufacturer, the brand and the shop do, of course, matter, but it would be difficult to deny that a reputation for high quality and high price generally go together." (Page 50.)

Although this careful study has the weakness of dealing with a simulated purchase situation in which the customer "buys" at no cost to himself, it is of great significance because it provides (1) a concept of the meaning of price and its effect in the purchase decision, and (2) a means for quantifying data in this area—a kind of framework on which to hang numbers. This work will, if applied adroitly, provide a base for marketers and market researchers to use the concept of price as an indicator of quality. The "reverse" demand curve can be quantified, and the normal demand curve can be better understood (and possibly better quantified at the level of the individual consumer). Although many of the conclusions are tentative, the thinking is a starting point for further rigorous analysis.

Some marketers are already using the concept of price as an indicator of quality. Alfred R. Oxenfeldt's "Multi-Stage Approach to Pricing" provides several examples. He writes:

"Among producers one finds Patou boasting that its Joy perfume is the most expensive, and Chock-Full-of-Nuts implying much the same thing about its coffee. Without being explicit, some retailers seem to claim that no store charges more than they—and, strangely, this image is a source of strength." [5]

One of the best examples of the strength of psychological pricing comes from an article by Oswald Knauth:

"In one case a retailer was able to purchase hosiery, having a normal market value of $2.00 per pair, for about 65 cents a pair, and offered it at $1.00. A mere handful of customers responded. Why? Reasons were searched; the values were unquestioned, the advertising forceful, the day fair. But the price of $1.00 suggested just that value, as this is a normal price for medium-grade hosiery. Two weeks later, the same goods were advertised at $1.14, which suggested higher value, with an enormous response." [6]

.   .   .

Judging Quality by Price   The important role of price in indicating the quality of many products can be explained in four ways.

1. EASE OF MEASUREMENT: In a paper delivered to the American Marketing Association, Donald F. Cox offers a useful way to look at pricing. He views a product "as an array of cues" and states that the "consumer's task in evaluating a product is to use cues [information] from the array as the basis for making judgments about the product." A cue can be evaluated on two dimensions: predictive value and confidence value. Cox states:

"Predictive value is a measure of the probability with which a cue seems associated with [i.e., predicts] a specific product attribute. . . . Confidence value is a measure of how *certain* the consumer is that the *cue* is what she thinks it is." [7]

Price is a concrete, measurable variable for the shopper. In most retail outlets price is fixed—not subject to bargaining. If the shopper were to buy in a store where bargaining over price is the usual practice, he or she would not view price in the role described.

Since price is concrete and measurable, the consumer views it with much confidence. He trusts it more than most cues directly concerned with quality (e.g., quality of technical components and yarn strength). The difficulty in using variables other than price is emphasized by Tibor Scitovsky:

"Today, the consumer is no longer an expert shopper. The rise in the standard of living has greatly expanded the range and variety of consumers' goods and increased the share of complex technical commodities in the consumer's budget. . . . More and more, therefore, the consumer of today has to judge quality by indices of quality. The size of a firm, its age, even its financial success are often regarded as indices of the quality of its produce. . . . Another important index of quality is price." [8]

Willard W. Cochran and Carolyn Shaw Bell concur in their book, *The Economics of Consumption*. They observe that "the constant stream of new and altered goods and services makes the problem of considering available alternatives a continuous occupation." [9] Furthermore, the increasing emphasis on self-service shopping makes it difficult for the customer to obtain product advice from sales personnel.

2. EFFORT AND SATISFACTION: In his article, "An Experimental Study of Customer Effort, Expectation, and Satisfaction," Richard N. Cardozo finds that consumer satisfaction with a product depends, at least in part, on the amount of effort which the consumer expends to obtain the product. He states: "The effort invested in shopping may, under specifiable conditions, contribute [positively] to the evaluation of the product." [10] The Cardozo study refers to effort expended by the buyer and to her evaluation of the product. However, it seems reasonable to believe that, in a sense, an expenditure of money may be viewed by the consumer as similar to an expenditure of effort. Some economists, in fact, consider money as stored expended effort. It also seems reasonable to assume that when a consumer is choosing a product, she is likely to predict and consider her feelings after purchase.

Thus, if expenditure of money is similar to expenditure of effort, and if, while choosing a product, a consumer considers how she will feel about it after buying it, the Cardozo work helps to explain why a consumer uses price as an indication of quality. The more she spends for a product, the more she has invested in it and the more she probably will like it.

3. SNOB APPEAL: In 1899 Thorstein Veblen raised the idea of "conspicuous consumption" in his classic, *The Theory of the Leisure Class*.[11] Tibor Scitovsky uses the same general notion to explain the consumer decision process:

"Another basis for price discrimination is the premium some people put on certain goods and services merely for the sake of their expensiveness. A person may know that the more expensive model is no better than the cheaper one and yet prefer it for the mere fact that it is more expensive. He may want his friends and neighbors to know that he can afford spending all that money, or he may feel that his prestige and social position require that he should always buy the most expensive of everything." [12]

To the extent that high price indicates scarcity (as in the case of diamonds and gold), it may convey the impression of individuality. In a society with as high an economic standard of living and as high an emphasis on material wealth as ours, it is likely that scarcity and prestige are factors in many buying decisions.

4. PERCEPTIONS OF RISK: Another explanation of the price-quality relationship has to do with risk. The prospective buyer balances (a) the dollars-and-cents amount of the extra cost of a higher-priced product against (b) the possibility of losing out because of the assumed lower quality of the lower-priced product. Leavitt states:

"If price sometimes has more than an economic meaning, if it also carries with it some implications about quality or good value or social propriety, then we would expect (1) that the consumer would feel some 'conflict' in making a choice and (2) that he would in some cases make the higher-priced choice. The pressures toward the lower price, in other words, deriving from his concern about spending his money, might be balanced, or even overbalanced, by his concern about getting good quality or the 'right' product." [13]

To reduce the risk of choosing a product of significantly poorer quality, the consumer chooses the higher-priced brand.

The buying situation itself is a factor. Many consumers, for example, view the purchase of a gift differently from the purchase of an item to be used by themselves. They choose the gift more carefully and spend more to ensure that it will be appropriate and "good." In a sense, this explanation is similar to the prestige concept just discussed; in both cases, the buyer's attitude is influenced by the possibility of public display or exposure.

Because risk is involved in the process, it seems likely that self-confidence, generalized and specific, might also be involved. Donald F. Cox and Raymond A. Bauer have done some significant work in this area.[14] Judging from their findings, women who are self-confident are least likely to feel the need to use price as an indicator of quality.

The concept of apparent justification is related to risk. If a product is priced low, it is common practice for the retailer to give a reason such as an end-of-season closeout, "seconds," and stocktaking. It also seems appropriate for higher-than-normal prices to be accompanied by better packaging, class advertising, and so forth, which reduce the customer's perceived risk by bringing the product image and the price into congruence.

The cost and quality of a component part also have a bearing on the consumer's attitude toward risk. The less important the cost of a component in the finished product, and the more important the quality contribution of the component, the more likely the consumer is to buy a high-priced component to ensure that the finished product will be acceptable.

Finally, pressure to conform is a factor. In a sense, the consumer who purchases a product priced higher than what she would pay normally is reducing risk by conforming. She is accepting the judgment of other people who, she perceives, think that the product is worth a higher price. The pressure to conform is strong, as we all know.

Responsive Consumers   Different segments of the population will respond differently to the pricing approach described. For example, Scitovsky states, "Well-to-do people can afford to be more casual and careless in their purchases than the poor." [15] But many people are not in this category. In particular, those who are not capable or confident of their ability to choose a product on its merits will tend toward the use of price. In the camera market, for example, the expert will not need to use price as an index of quality, whereas the novice, without other advice, will tend to use price rather than attempt to understand a morass of technical information. In addition, the prestige-conscious and the risk-averse are likely to use price as an indicator of quality.

Unfortunately, it seems that the poor and the uneducated are highly susceptible to price connotations. They would be the least capable of analyzing most products, and they would be strongly risk-adverse.

.   .   .

The pricing approach known as "creaming" a market can be understood in the terms described in this article. If a new product is introduced at a high price, the product may gain an image of quality and prestige. Then the price can be lowered and a broader market tapped. As the price is lowered, many consumers will consider the new price a bargain because it is below the old price, which is perceived as "fair." In addition, the product may retain its image of quality and prestige. In a sense, the high initial price has legitimatized the product.

A fine example of this pricing approach was Du Pont's introduction of Corfam to compete with leather. After introducing it to the high-priced shoe market, the company slowly moved Corfam down into the mass market for shoes. Markdowns illustrate the same principles, and so do price-off deals, such as the soap sold at a permanently reduced price with the "original" price conspicuously marked on the package.

.   .   .

NOTES

1. "How Much Do Customers Know About Retail Prices?" *Progressive Grocer*, February, 1964, pp. C105–C106.

2. Andre Gabor and C. W. J. Granger, "On the Price Consciousness of Consumers," *Applied Statistics*, November, 1961, p. 170.

3. *Journal of Business*, July, 1954, p. 205.

4. "Price as an Indicator of Quality," *Economica*, February, 1966, p. 43.

5. Alfred R. Oxenfeldt, "Multi-Stage Approach to Pricing," *HBR*, July–August, 1960, p. 129.

6. "Considerations in the Setting of Retail Prices," *The Journal of Marketing*, July, 1949, p. 8.

7. "The Measurement of Information Value," *Emerging Concepts in Marketing*, Proceedings of the Winter Conference, 1962, edited by William S. Decker (Chicago, American Marketing Association, 1963).

8. "Some Consequences of the Habit of Judging Quality By Price," *The Review of Economic Studies*, Vol. XII (2), No. 32 (1944–1945), p. 100.

9. New York, McGraw-Hill Book Company Inc., 1956.

10. *Journal of Marketing Research*, August, 1965, p. 248.

11. New York, The New American Library, Inc., 1954.

12. Scitovsky, *op. cit.*, p. 103.

13. Leavitt, *op. cit.*, p. 207.

14. See, for example, "Self-Confidence and Persuasibility in Women," in *Risk Taking and Information Handling in Consumer Behavior*, edited by Donald F. Cox (Boston, Division of Research, Harvard Business School, 1967), p. 394.

15. Scitovsky, *op. cit.*, p. 103.

28 When Is the Price Too High?

Alfred R. Oxenfeldt

Several times during the past few years, "housewives' revolts" have developed. Such revolts have normally been responses to sharp rises in retail prices. Consumer resentment, particularly on the part of low and middle income families, is natural when such price rises occur. Directing their resentment at the retailers, the businessman with whom they are in immediate contact, housewives express their feelings by "strikes" against the retailer. Frequently, the housewife sincerely believes that the rise in price is a kind of malicious action taken by the retailer to extort more money from her family.

Consumer feelings about high prices do not necessarily square with those of academic experts. Professor Oxenfeldt concludes, on the other hand, that prices "are too high when very little can be sold because of price." Even here, however, we are cautioned that by high pricing General Motors, for example, may be driving customers away from Cadillacs but it is quite content to do so. Thus, to Professor Oxenfeldt it is an involuntary or unexpected inability to sell goods because of price that makes the price high.

The persistence of inflationary pressures makes this situation a serious one for both the nation in general and business in particular. The question "Who or what is responsible for high prices?" represents a serious and vital social and economic issue. Unfortunately, not all textbook discussions of "pricing" include this perspective.

. . .

Prices are too high when very little can be sold because of price. Here . . . we run into the difficulty of expressing verbally the concept of a demand schedule. Loosely expressed, however, a price is too high when a seller repels most customers by the price he asks. Actually, of course, the Cadillac division of General Motors consciously repels most potential automobile buyers; however, since enough buyers pay the price it asks, so that it attains approximately the sales volume it seeks, its price cannot be considered too high. In contrast, the price of Chevrolets would be too high, even though only a fraction of the Cadillac's price, if Chevrolet's sales were far below what the company was set up to sell.

Reprinted from Alfred R. Oxenfeldt, *Executive Action in Marketing*, pp. 274–275, by permission of the publisher. © 1966 by Wadsworth Publishing Company, Inc., Belmont, California 94002.

If a slight reduction in price would increase sales greatly, it is likely (though not certain) that price is a little too high. Conversely, if a very substantial price reduction would be required to stimulate sales very slightly, price almost certainly is not too high. However, one cannot decide whether price is too high on the basis of demand conditions alone. Various other business considerations are involved.

Only when a firm is making virtually no sales, and when customers state that they are not buying because of the high price, can one be certain that price is too high. Relatively few sales can also result from the fact that a product is not known to potential customers because of poor communication and distribution arrangements. Imperfections in the product might also explain a lack of sales; it might not be purchased no matter what price was asked for it. Confusion arises here because imperfections in a product or even in its method of distribution can ordinarily be overcome by reducing its price. For example, a consumer might be willing to buy a television set of relatively poor design if he were offered a $50 saving. The low sales of this product should be attributed, however, to its poor design rather than to the fact that an excessive price was asked for it. The confusion mounts when we observe that once a product is poorly designed, it may be an additional mistake to maintain the original price.

Accordingly, we can conclude only that prices are excessive when buyers' resistance is extremely high and when it cannot be attributed to defects in product or service or to poor methods of distribution. We should recognize, however, that sellers always consider it difficult to find customers, and it is perhaps for this reason that most salesmen complain that the home office is charging too much. Consequently, this subjective test of too high a price is difficult to apply. A better test is lacking, unfortunately.

.   .   .

29 Break for Drivers:
Gas-Price Wars

Price wars occasionally occur, and the consumer is the beneficiary. Generally, such price behavior is an attempt to remain competitive in the face of a vigorous attempt by one supplier to increase his share of the market. The following article provides some insight into gas-price wars.

Price cutting at the gas pump is proving to be a boon for millions of motorists—but an embarrassment to major oil companies.

Motorists living in price-war areas are able to fill their tanks at 5 or 10 cents per gallon below normal costs. But some big oil companies find themselves on the spot because they raised gasoline prices late in 1970, saying an increase was long overdue. Now they haven't been able to make that increase stick.

The average price of regular gasoline, including taxes, fell from 36.09 cents a gallon in December to 34.48 cents in March in 52 cities surveyed weekly by "The Oil and Gas Journal."

Further weakness in gasoline prices was indicated in recent days when many big refiners in the Midwest dropped wholesale prices by an average of ¾ of a cent.

Oil-industry economists say that a surplus of gasoline is the root cause of the price wars, and a veteran oil jobber adds that price-cutting now is the most widespread that he has seen in 40 years in the business.

Says George Watters, executive director, Nebraska Petroleum Marketers:

"People must think we are a bunch of kooks when they buy gas for 40 cents one day and 30 cents the next. They know we can't sell below cost and stay in business, so they think the oil industry is really gouging them at the higher price."

Whatever motorists think, they are taking advantage of the price cuts.

In Los Angeles, where price wars are a way of life with service station operators, one motorist says:

"I get the tank filled when the price war breaks out, and keep it topped off until prices go back to normal. Then I nurse the car along, buying a

Reprinted from *U.S. News & World Report*, April 19, 1971, p. 47.

dollar's worth at a time, waiting for the stations to start cutting each other's throats again."

Breaking
a "Truce"   On a recent Saturday in Los Angeles, a "truce" that had pre-vailed in the price war for several weeks suddenly gave way.

Typically, the owner of a service station on Beverly Boulevard got word of a wholesale-price reduction late Friday afternoon. First thing Saturday morning, he put out a large "Gas War" sign and rolled back the prices on his pumps by 2 cents. From there, price cuts moved swiftly up the street as other dealers followed suit.

But that reduction was minor compared with many across the country.

In Chicago, a motorist was having his car's tank filled when the dealer came out and set the price on an adjoining pump back by eight cents.

Said one station operator: "There's a standing joke around here that the computers in the pumps are wearing out because prices change so fast."

Prices in the Chicago area have varied from a low of 32.9 cents a gallon to 43 cents, including all taxes.

In Detroit, said by some industry officials to be the "worst gasoline-marketing area" in the nation, a price war has been going on for two years. Current price for a gallon of regular at one independent station is 21.9 cents, compared with 26.9 cents at stations of major companies.

Among Southeastern cities experiencing price wars lately were Charlotte, N.C., Jacksonville, Fla., and Atlanta.

In Jacksonville, prices dropped from 36.9 cents at large oil companies' stations to 25.9 cents for regular grades. The "war" ended after about six weeks in Charlotte and Jacksonville, but is continuing in parts of Atlanta.

In Trenton, N.J., one industry official says gasoline is being sold there "at a price lower than the normal wholesale price in other areas."

Why the Cuts?   Most oil-industry experts agree that the basic cause of price wars is the surplus of gasoline. During the 1970–71 winter season, this surplus has been larger than in past years because of heavy demand for fuel oil.

To produce the needed fuel oil, refinery runs were stepped up. But crude oil, when refined, produces gasoline as well as fuel oil and other products. Thus the gasoline surplus grew.

Another reason for gasoline price wars is the wide margin between wholesale and retail prices. An oil-company official explains:

"Wholesale price of gasoline is at the same level today it was 15 years ago. During that time, retail prices have increased about 50 per cent because of rising costs, mainly labor. This wide margin offers maverick dealers who stress volume rather than service a chance to cut prices.

"Sometimes they will cut the price for a time to where they are losing money, hoping to win customers.

"To remain competitive, other dealers are forced to reduce prices. And major oil companies, to protect their dealers, are forced to sell gasoline to service stations at lower cost."

This is good news for car owners, but a growing headache for the companies. Says "The Oil and Gas Journal":

"The industry needs an image of sound business conduct as never before —not one of reckless management as shown by price fights."

QUESTIONS FOR DISCUSSION

1. Explain how supply and demand are supposed to work in determining prices, according to classical economists.
2. A consumer says "Prices are too high." Explain the possible meanings of such an assertion.
3. A corporate executive says "Prices are too low." Explain the possible meanings of such an assertion.
4. Compare your answers to Professor Oxenfeldt's criteria shown in Article 28.
5. What is meant by monopoly? Oligopoly? How do these relate to the idea of administered pricing?
6. Select a particular product. Consult a consumer rating service showing the brand prices and the quality rating given by the service. List each brand, its price, and its quality rating. Do these correlate closely in your judgment? Explain.
7. A cosmetic product is introduced at a fairly low price. It fails to sell well. It is repackaged in a more elaborate container and the price is tripled. It now sells far better. Explain why the raised price does not reduce demand.
8. How do you explain the fact that some retailers reduce the "list" prices set forth by manufacturers?
9. Secure prices of several product brands for both 1970 and the present. Compare the prices. Explain why they have either changed or not changed in relation to changes in the general price level.
10. "Bait advertising" combines pricing policy and advertising. Explain (a) the meaning of this statement, (b) whether you consider it objectionable, (c) if not, why, and (d) if "yes," why and what could be done about it.

SUGGESTED READINGS

Backman, Jules (ed.), *Price Practices and Price Policies* (New York: Ronald Press Co., 1953).

Brown, F. E., "Price Image Versus Price Reality", *Journal of Marketing Research* (May, 1969), Vol. 6, No. 2, pp. 185–191.

Kaplan, A. D., J. B. Dirlan, and R. F. Lanzillotti, *Pricing in Big Business* (Washington, D.C.: The Brookings Institution, 1958).

Myers, John G., "Determinants of Private Brand Attitudes", *Journal of Marketing Research* (February, 1967), Vol. 4, No. 1, pp. 73–81.

"Pocketbook Pinch", *U.S. News & World Report* (May, 1970), Vol. 66, No. 20, pp. 64–66.

Tull, D. S., R. A. Boring, and M. H. Gonsior, "A Note on the Relationship of Price and Imputed Quality", *Journal of Business* (April, 1964), Vol. 37, No. 2, pp. 186–191.

Udell, Jon G., "How Important Is Pricing in Competitive Strategy?", *Journal of Marketing* (January, 1964), Vol. 28, No. 1, pp. 44–48.

section 9
marketing
to the
poor

In the past several years a good deal of attention has been devoted to the marketing problems of the poor. Most of the studies undertaken were specifically concerned with retail prices—especially food prices—in ghetto areas, as compared to those prices in other locations. Food prices are not the only interest in a marketing study of the poor, however; the quality of merchandise offered for sale is also significant. But food prices are easily measurable and quite important; thus, convenience and necessity provide strong inducements to perform such studies. A summary of recent food price studies among the poor is given in Table 1.

Congressional committees, the Federal Trade Commission, the Bureau of Labor Statistics, and other agencies as well as individuals have all conducted hearings or research projects on marketing to the poor. The results clearly show that many marketing problems do exist for the poor and for those who sell to them.

Many of the studies clearly indicate that "the poor pay more"; others "prove"

that prices are *not* higher for the poor. In addition, some of these studies show that the reasons for the higher prices and reduced quality are not primarily the result of venality, but often are a direct consequence of the nature of the market structure that interacts with the poor. Specifically, when prices are higher in the poor areas, it is often because:*

1. Merchants cannot get insurance—especially after riots—or are paying very high premiums; the higher prices are needed to pay for their losses.
2. There is often greater theft by employees, customers, and suppliers.
3. There are additional costs of protecting the retail premises against damage, theft, and so forth; that is, burglar and fire detection systems and guard service are sometimes employed at extra cost.
4. Land costs in inner-city areas are often considerably higher than in the suburbs. Hence, rent is higher.
5. Errors in check-out stations always occur, sometimes more often in inner-city stores because the help used by some of these stores is not very well trained or otherwise qualified, and the small store owners cannot afford training programs.
6. There are proportionately more "mom and pop" stores** in poor areas, and such retail outlets always have inefficiencies and added costs when compared to modern supermarkets, such as lower turnover, smaller order quantities, and more credit sales.[1]

Most of these reasons are equally applicable in explaining why merchandise quality is sometimes lower in those establishments that sell to the poor.

---

* Robert J. Lavidge, "The Ghetto Challenge", paper presented at the 14th Annual American Marketing Association Public Utilities Seminar, Detroit, Michigan, May 3, 1968, pp. 7–12.

** "Mom and pop" stores are those small, underfinanced retail establishments that are operated by the members of a family.

30 Consumer Practices of the Poor
Louise G. Richards

Studies of consumer behavior and consumer spending frequently generalize about consumers as though one could characterize *all* consumers by single statements. In recent years, marketer and marketing analysts have become more cautious. They divide consumers not only into demographic classes (age, income, sex, population centers) but by psychographic categories (personality, spending pattern).

Currently much attention is being centered on those people whose condition of poverty or minority status creates special consumer problems for them.

The poor—34 million people according to the U.S. government's criteria for poverty—are consumers with unique characteristics. They use more credit relative to their gross incomes than do other market segments, lack product information, purchase more of their goods in "neighborhood" stores, and so on. An understanding of the market characteristics of the poor is essential to a successful effort to provide them with goods and services of quality at reasonable prices. This article presents an overview of the "Consumer Practices of the Poor."

To the economist, being poor means having an income below a certain figure—a figure that represents the minimum amount necessary for a decent life in America today. To the behavioral scientist, being poor means a number of characteristics found to be associated with low income: patterns of family life, health care, education, and general outlook on life. To the poor person himself, however, being poor may mean different things depending on how his money is spent. This report is a summary of research findings on those consumer practices. The report covers not only how money is spent by the poor, but also what kinds of behavior—shopping, methods of payment, and the like—go along with income disbursement.

Few would quarrel with the judgment that an income of $3,000 is too low for a family to live on today. Hardly anyone would suggest that even the best consumer practices would solve the problem of poverty. Many would agree, however, that good consumer practices might alleviate some of the worst aspects. Knowledge of actual practices of the poor can suggest new areas for education and action.

Louise G. Richards, "Consumer Practices of the Poor", *Low Income Life Styles*, ed. Lola M. Irelan, U.S. Department of Health, Education and Welfare (August, 1967), pp. 67–86.

One writer on the topic of consumer practices of the poor has concluded that they are irrational in their buying behavior.[1] Some of the evidence for that conclusion is included in this report. To indict poor consumers as irrational is too simple an explanation, however. Moreover, it provides no handles for action. Much of the evidence for irrationality should be considered in the light of other explanations that make equally good sense. The particular social and demographic characteristics of the poor must be taken into account. The inflexibility of low income per se must be kept in mind. And, finally, the possibility that apparent irrationality may stem from the very conditions of poverty must be dealt with. These explanations will be discussed more fully in a later section.

For practices to be labeled as irrational there must be a standard for judging their rationality. Many people would subscribe to the idea that there are good, common-sense rules for stretching income. Many of those who knew poverty during the Thirties, and those who have known severe reverses since then, would avow that such rules helped them keep their heads above water in difficult times.

.   .   .

Very simply, the traditional rules for good consumership can be stated as follows:

1. Spend first for necessities and last for luxuries. Although many individuals disagree on how to classify specific goods, few would dispute that food, shelter, basic articles of clothing, and health should have priority over recreation and other categories of expenditure.

2. Buy the best quality of goods for the lowest price. This means that costly extra features—high styles, non-seasonal treats, store services, and above all, the cost of installment buying—should be avoided. In order to follow this rule, a person needs to shop widely and keep up with information about goods, prices, and sources.

3. Another rule stems from recognition of the fact that it is not easy to suppress desires for luxury goods and extra features: Budget small incomes carefully and plan purchases in advance. If possible, one should save for (or insure against) future emergencies to prevent insolvency.

4. Another rule covers the thousand-and-one suggestions for home production of needed goods: Try to get what is needed or wanted without spending money, or by spending only for raw materials. Home preservation of food, home sewing, self-building and self-repairing of homes, are a few of many recommended money saving practices.

5. Take advantage of certain benefits available to persons with limited incomes. Surplus food (and Food Stamps), legal aid, scholarships, day care for children, public housing, and medical and dental clinics are examples of such benefits provided through legislation or private funds.

Most detailed advice to consumers could be put under one of these five rules. Together they provide a backdrop for viewing actual consumer practices of the poor. In reporting the findings, these five rules will be referred to specifically. Before turning to those findings, we need to review what is known about the different kinds of people that constitute the poor population today, and the different kinds of studies that provide the facts.

Population Characteristics of the Poor

Several writers have pointed out that the poor as a group are neither homogeneous nor strictly representative of the population as a whole.[2] The *majority* of low income families are white, non-farm, and headed by a male between twenty-five and sixty-five years old. Compared with the general population, however, poor families tend to include more non-whites, fewer earners, more families with female heads, larger families, and more old or young persons. The poor more often reside in rural farm areas or in cities (and less often in rural non-farm or suburban areas). Above all, poor people have completed fewer years of schooling than the rest of the population. Almost every family or individual below the poverty line can be characterized by at least one of these facts. These differences between the poor and the general population are important in interpreting research findings about their consumer habits.

·   ·   ·

Consumer Practices

Turning now to consumer practices in the framework of the above-mentioned rules for good consumership, here is the evidence:

Do Low-Income Families Buy Necessities First, and Luxuries Last?

For the most part, "Yes." When consumer goods and services are classified according to their survival value (beginning with Food and ending with Recreation), the poor spend more of their income than others do on the basic needs. When goods are classified as durables (automobiles, equipment, furniture, and the like) and non-durables, we find that the poor, on the average do not buy durables as frequently as higher income families do. When we look at the poor who do purchase one or more durable goods in a given year, however, we find that a startlingly high proportion of their income is spent for those goods.

One weak spot in the poor family's purchasing behavior appears to be this over-spending on durable goods. Since most durable goods are relatively expensive items, it is not hard to see why the purchase of a durable good makes heavy inroads on a small income. Moreover, it is difficult to judge whether or not a given durable good should be considered a luxury for a poor family. (One could argue that an automatic washing machine is not a luxury for a large family in which the mother's time is at a premium.) However, when purchasing families with incomes less than $2,000 spend almost half of their income on durable goods, we need to look for an explanation.

The durable goods that take the largest bites from poor families' incomes are large household appliances and radios, television sets, and phonographs. These are household items that can be considered part of the standard package of American consumption. According to one writer, these home items are especially significant to working-class wives who aspire to the role of the modern, efficient American housewife. Also, of course, much effort and money are devoted to the advertisement of these and other items in the standard package. The poor are no less vulnerable than others are to persuasive selling. Such pressure may be particularly hard for the Negro poor to resist, since traditionally they have been denied access to other forms of social status.

There are other, less subjective factors in the purchase of durable goods than role image and vulnerability to advertising. Young families and those with large numbers of children spend more on durables, regardless of income. Since the poor include proportionately larger numbers of young, large families, we can attribute some over-spending to heavier need in newly formed households with more demand for labor-saving devices. Another factor in some poor neighborhoods is the incidence of merchandizing practices that result in higher prices than those found for the same goods in middle-income shopping areas.

We have made some general statements about how the poor spend their incomes, and have provided some brief explanations of the patterns found. Some of the findings that support those statements are given below.

CATEGORIES OF SPENDING: Food, shelter, and medical care take larger shares of the poor family's consumer dollar than they do in families with higher incomes, on the average. Clothing and transportation take smaller shares, on the average. Household operation (including furnishings and equipment) and other expenses (recreation, personal care, and education) take about the same share as in higher income families.[3]

The above findings compare average proportions spent annually by different income groups, whether all families in a group made purchases in the category or not. In a given year, most families do buy food, shelter, and at least a few articles of clothing. They probably also pay at least one medical fee. We know from other data that in a given year fewer low-income families make purchases of automobiles, furniture, and household appliances. What is the share of income spent by poor families who do purchase a major durable in a given year?

Among those in the lowest income group (under $2,000) who bought a major durable in 1962, an average of 48% of their income was spent on such purchases. In the next higher income group ($2,000 to $4,999), the share was 28%. These percentages are high compared with the shares of income spent by the poor on "needs," and startlingly high compared with the shares spent on durables by families in other income groups. (In the category that included median family income ($6,000 to $7,499) in 1962, the share spent for durables was only 14%.)[4] The durables that take the largest shares of poor families' income are large household appliances and radios, television sets, and phonographs. High consumption of these same items, and furniture, is reported in Caplovitz' study of low-income families in New York: 95% owned television sets, 63% owned phonographs, and 41% owned automatic washers.[5]

EFFECTS OF CLASS AND ETHNIC VALUES: The special importance of household appliances, television, and furniture to the working class was discussed in some detail in Rainwater's analysis of the working-class wife. According to that author, appliances and furniture mean something different to working-class wives from what they mean to middle-class wives.[6] The difference in values is a subtle one, but may be an important contribution to overspending.

Working-class wives' lives revolve around home and housework to a greater extent than the lives of middle-class wives. The working-class wife knows that housework is inevitable, and she dreams of a home (especially a kitchen) that symbolizes the role of the modern, efficient American housewife. She also tends to associate the new with the beautiful. The middle-class wife, on the other hand, is interested in labor-saving appliances that free her as much as possible from the role of housewife so that she may enjoy the social, intellectual, and aesthetic pleasures of upper-middle-class life. These differences suggest that the working-class wife sees household durables as an end in themselves, rather than merely as means to other ends.

One sociologist describes another pattern of spending in terms of the symbolic value of certain products. Negroes underspend in four major areas —housing, automobile transportation, food, and medical care. On the other hand, a number of Negro women are more interested than white women in "high fashion," even in the Under-$3,000 income group. And Negro families report buying Scotch whiskey, a high-status drink, twice as often as white families do.[7] One theorist writing on the subject of "conditions for irrational choices" suggests an explanation: Irrational choice making occurs when "something . . . [is] . . . repressed among a large number of individuals in a specific segment of our society with a distinctive subculture."[8]

THE EFFECT OF YOUTH AND SIZE OF FAMILIES: In one analysis of frequency of purchase of selected durables, it was found that the rate for young married couples with incomes under $3,000 increases after the birth of their first child, whereas the rate for couples with incomes over $3,000 decreases.[9] Caplovitz' study also showed that family size among his low-income public housing tenants affects durable goods' ownership (or aspirations for ownership) regardless of the size of income.[10]

These facts and the much cited findings by Caplovitz about high-priced durables in poor neighborhoods provide the evidence for our answer, "Yes, but . . ." to the question on whether the poor spend their incomes on basic needs. We do not want to leave the impression that the poor are profligate spenders on special goods, however.

There is some evidence that they do not have much desire for all kinds of special purchases. In one nationwide study, their desires for "special expenditures" were found to be less frequent than those expressed by middle and upper income families.[11] Although poor families may not dream of as many new purchases as other families do, they do appear to be eager to acquire the standard package.

Do Low-Income Shoppers Try to Get the Best Quality for the Lowest Price? Available evidence indicates that the answer is "No." Lower income consumers are not more deliberate in their shopping, more wide-ranging in their search for good buys, more price conscious, nor more informed on the characteristics of products than families with higher incomes. If anything, they are less apt to carry out these practices than others. Neither are low-income consumers more apt to buy used articles, to buy "separate items," nor to pay cash for their purchases.

On three counts, poor people do exhibit more economical practices. They tend more often to negotiate special deals on durables, especially through relatives or friends. The *very* poor tend to buy goods on sale more often than others. And, although there is just as much use of credit by low-income families as by others, fewer of the poor have installment or mortgage debt. Among those who do have installment debt, however, the effect on family solvency may be ruinous.

On the basis of strict rationality, one would expect low-income consumers to be more deliberate, searching, price-conscious, and informed than high-income consumers. The low level of education of many poor people goes a long way in explaining why they are not, and indeed, why they fall below other income groups in the frequency of some of these activities. Knowledge of the immense variety of goods on the American market is not easily acquired. Especially in the case of appliances, knowledge of technical features is highly specialized. Knowledge of the intricacies of credit agreements or consumer rights is not easy to acquire, either. The best that a poorly educated person can do, perhaps, is to rely on a known dealer, buy what a relative has bought, or try to negotiate a special deal. These are the very practices that many poor families follow.

Research findings also suggest that shopping practices are affected by length of exposure to urban American ways. The Puerto Ricans are an example of a newly arrived group that prefers traditional, personal stores rather than more bureaucratic, price-competitive outlets, and so do Negro migrants from the rural South. It is reasonable to expect that the longer people live in proximity to modern, depersonalized outlets, and the more they are exposed to knowledge about the urban world (through education or experience), the more often they will conduct wide-ranging searches of stores, and be price-conscious.

One reason for lower frequency of installment or mortgage debt among the poor is their ineligibility for loans under legal credit requirements. It is also possible that some poor families actually prefer not to be in debt. Among those families who are in debt for installment purchases, however, there is a large percentage of young, large families. Again, the pressing needs of this group probably account for some of the extremes of insolvency found among the poor.

The findings that support these views are:

DELIBERATION IN BUYING: In a nationwide sample of families, the poor were found to be neither higher nor lower than others on a scale of deliberation in durable goods purchases. On three deliberation activities in the scale, however, they were less active than others: They were less circumspect in seeking information, less concerned about the several features of the item and somewhat more dependent on brands. The poor families were no different from others in the extent of their enjoyment of "shopping around," an attitude found to be positively related to high deliberation.

Extent of formal education was more strongly associated with deliberation in buying durables than was income, in the study described above. The higher a person's level of education, the more he or she tended to score high on the deliberation scale. An interesting exception was in buying sport shirts, however: The less well-educated were more deliberate. Thus, the extent of deliberation may be influenced in some groups by the type of purchase.[12]

SHOPPING SCOPE: Several findings point to the tendency of the poor to use nearby stores rather than distant ones, and to prefer personal buying situations (the peddler as an extreme form), rather than "bureaucratic," impersonal ones. The poorest housing tenants in the New York Study used independent neighborhood stores, chain stores, and peddlers more frequently than department stores or discount houses, for buying durable goods. Among these low-income families, it was the poorest who had the narrowest shopping scope. And it was those who bought from the neighborhood stores or peddlers who paid more for the goods, especially for television sets.[13] In a Chicago study, the personal buying situation also was found to be more appealing to the upper-lower-class than to the lower-middle and upper-middle classes.[14]

In a study of urban families in Wisconsin, the preference for independent and neighborhood stores (rather than chain stores) was related to motives concerning the store and its personnel, rather than to motives concerning price, and was more typical of rural migrants to the city than of natives or urban migrants.[15] Caplovitz also found narrow shopping scope more typical of those who had been a short time in New York or any other city, and more typical of those with less education. He found, for example, that the Puerto Ricans in the study were narrower in shopping scope than Negroes or whites.[16]

Another factor in shopping scope, according to Rainwater, is the discomfort felt by working-class women in "downtown" stores:[17] ". . . [Clerks] . . . try to make you feel awful if you don't like something they have told you is nice and they would certainly think it was terrible if you told them you didn't have enough money to buy something."

INFORMATION ABOUT PRODUCTS: According to several studies, formal education appears to be the key characteristic of the informed consumer. Income is slightly related to use of consumer rating magazines (the poor use them less often), but education is strongly related.[18] Education is also clearly related to consultation of any kind of reading material (including advertisements) as a source of information about products.[19]

These are formal channels of communication about products, and it is not surprising that those with skills and experience in formal communication are more active. Those with little education do make more use of relatives (though not necessarily more use of all other people) as a source of information about durable goods. Relatives were found to be a fruitful source of information for poorly-educated people in decisions on a model for a subsequent purchase of a durable. Other interesting differences between those with lower and higher levels of education have been found. In one study, the latter tended to buy a different model from the one seen at someone's house, whereas the former more often bought the same model.[20] In another study, high-income persons were found to be more critical of features of goods, including obsolescence.[21] Education apparently induces a more critical attitude and less reliance on reference groups in the choice of consumer goods.

PURCHASE OF USED GOODS AND SEPARATE ITEMS: The tendency of low-income families in New York to buy new appliances and furniture (especially sets) was mentioned by Caplovitz,[22] but no nationwide data are available to confirm this finding. The only nationwide figures found on the purchase of new vs. used items concern automobiles; the evidence is clear that the poor tend less often to buy new autos and more often to buy used ones.[23]

On the topic of buying sets of furniture and other items sold as preselected groupings, one unpublished study indicates that low-income households purchase living room suites less often than higher income households. No difference was found in frequency of purchase of other kinds of sets by income group. There was a slight tendency for low-income respondents in that study to *prefer* suites, and some other types of set, however, compared with respondents in higher-income households.[24]

If lower-class consumers do tend consistently to prefer sets of furniture to separate pieces, two factors may be at work; one cultural, and one economic. There may be a true class difference in taste for the strictly harmonious room: More interest on the part of the working class.[25] It is possible also that low-priced sets may be more numerous than separate items in furniture outlets located in poor neighborhoods.

USE OF CREDIT AND INSTALLMENT BUYING: Half or more of the poor families over the nation use consumer credit of some kind. (81% of the New York City tenants in Caplovitz' study used it.) [26] Poor families nationwide who had installment debt in 1962, however, were a smaller proportion—between one-fourth and one-third of all families below the poverty line. This proportion can be compared with half or more families with higher income who had installment debt in 1962.[27]

Mortgage debt is also carried by a smaller proportion of the poor than of higher income families over the nation—only about one-fourth of the former owed on mortgages in 1962, compared with half or more of families in higher income brackets. Another kind of debt—money owed to doctors, dentists, and hospitals—was owed by a small proportion of poor families (about 17%), and this proportion is similar to that reported for families with higher incomes.[28] It is not so much whether poor people buy on credit, however, as what it does to their financial situation that interests us. The ratio of debt to annual income is considerably higher for the poor than for others—about twice as high as the ratio among better-off families.[29] (Also, debt is clearly responsible for a shaky financial status in many poor families, as described in the section below.)

There is conflicting evidence on whether the poor actually prefer buying on credit. On the one hand, findings from a nationwide study show that in general low-income consumers do approve of installment buying.[30] On the other hand, the majority of Caplovitz' respondents said they thought that credit is a bad idea, although some felt that buying on time is easier than trying to save cash for large purchases.[31]

Only persons with high income or a college education are well informed on the real cost of credit, according to one nationwide study.[32] Added to this fact are two others reported in the New York City study: (1) Credit costs were higher for goods bought in the very sources that many poor families use—peddlers and neighborhood dealers; and (2) A majority of the families did not know where to go if they should be cheated by a merchant. Thus, many factors seem to converge in making installment debt an especially pressing problem for the poor.

Do Low-Income Families Budget Their Incomes and Plan Their Purchases?   One proof of good financial management in families—whether or not they manage to stay solvent—suggests that poor families do not score very well. Few have many assets, and a sizable minority have negative net worth. (In other words, these families' debts exceed their assets.) Poor families who are insolvent are not complacent about it, however.

As a group, the poor save very little and are not often covered by insurance. Moreover, when they do save or invest, they tend to be less "modern" in their pattern of saving than higher income groups. Also, their views on the value of life insurance are more traditional.

The central place of installment debt in many poor families' insolvency was described earlier. Regardless of kind of debt, cultural factors may affect this proclivity to be in debt. Solvency as a moral obligation is not strong in all cultures. Thus, we might expect differences among ethnic groups in tightness of control over family finances. We might also expect changes in ethnic groups' state of solvency as they acquire education and higher status occupations in the American setting.

Again, education is an important factor in explaining low efficiency of planning among the poor. Education can affect not only the amount of knowledge one has about financial matters, but also one's mode of thinking about money. The ability to think of money as a long-range, abstract value, rather than as concrete visible amounts, may allow educated consumers to weigh purchases and income more effectively. For the concrete thinker, it is easy to "Buy now" with a small portion of the weekly paycheck, and hard to see in advance how difficult it will be to "Pay later."

Hardly anyone would expect families on $3,000 or less income to save or buy insurance. Furthermore, since there are high proportions of families with no major earners among the poor (as high as 72% in the Under-$1,000 group), savings and insurance plans supported by employers or unions are often out of reach.

.   .   .

Do Low-Income Families Meet Some Needs Through Home Production?   Evidence on home production by the poor is sparse, but what there is points to less, not more, production in two areas: food growing, and home repairs. However, since these types of home production are also affected by the extent of home ownership (known to be lower among the poor), these facts about the effect of income must be considered tentative.

In the one study consulted, it was interesting to note that those with the highest average amount saved through home production had training beyond high school (though not a college degree). Those with twelve grades of school or less, and those with a bachelor's degree or more, were below average in amounts saved through home production.[33]

Those findings bear out our hunch that many home production activities will not be attempted, nor be successful, unless someone in the family has had special training or experience in these skills. Often, expensive tools and understanding of technical instructions are necessary for the success of a home project. This means that the poor, and the poorly educated, may be unable to improve their situation very much through this means.

Do Low-Income Families Take Advantage of Consumer Benefits Available to the Poor? The existence of many successful programs in legal aid, medical and dental clinics, and similar facilities, testifies to the variety of ways the poor could cut their cost of living if they took advantage of them. A summary of evaluations of so many diverse programs cannot be included in this report. Many experienced workers would agree, however, that there is need for greater coverage or utilization. The unmet health needs, the legal predicaments of the poor, and the great educational losses of poor children, are cases in point.

Whether coverage is adequate or not, the lack of full success by established programs often is justifiably attributed to apathy on the part of the people who need them most. Apparently, it is not enough to offer the service. It has to be carefully planned to conform to attitudes, schedules, and locales of poetntial recipients. Also, the availability of the service has to be communicated directly and simply, and the preliminaries have to be carried out quickly and smoothly. Thus, we must conclude that the poor do not use these resources to the full for easing their income situation.

Adding the Score How do consumer practices of the poor compare with the recommended rules of financial management? On almost every count, we have found that the poor fail to use what many would call the rational solution:

1. Although they spend most of their income on basic needs, those who buy durable goods make serious inroads on their incomes.
2. Most do not use more deliberation, consult more sources, or shop more widely, to get the best buys. Instead, many depend on known merchants or relatives for judgments of what to buy.
3. Few have savings of any size; most do not have life insurance; and only about half are covered by medical insurance.
4. It is doubtful whether many carry out home production activities to supplement cash purchases.
5. Many probably do not make full use of the programs established to provide services and goods free or at reduced rates.

Explanations of some of these apparently irrational consumer practices can be found in the special needs and characteristics of concentrated subgroups of the poor. We have mentioned the concentration of young, large families, in connection with the problems of durable goods purchases, heavy installment debt, and insolvency. We have also mentioned the concentration of recent migrants (from within or outside the United States), in connection with findings about narrow shopping scope and preference for personal treatment in stores. A third group, one that undoubtedly includes many more of the poor, consists of those with little formal education. The lack of education shows up as an important factor in low level of

TABLE 1 Recent Food Price Surveys Undertaken with Respect to Low- and Higher-Income Areas

Survey Source	Dates	Cities	Number of Stores	Number of Items' Prices Checked	Findings with Respect to Discrimination
Government studies: Bureau of Labor Statistics[1]	February 1966.	Washington, D.C.; New York, N.Y.; Chicago, Ill.; Atlanta, Ga.; Houston, Tex.; and Los Angeles, Calif.	30 stores in each city, including chain and independent stores.	18 items in each store.	Higher prices on the average in small independent stores, which constitute a larger portion of food sales in low-income areas. No significant differences in chainstore pricing as between low- and higher-income areas.
U.S. Department of Agriculture[2]	February 1968.	Six unnamed cities.	24 chainstores in each city, in most cases, 12 from each chain.	Do	No significant differences between low- and higher-income areas in chainstore pricing. However, substantial mispricing rates apply in many chains—ranging from 4.1 per cent up to 31 per cent.
Scholarly studies: Carlton E. Wright, professor of consumer education, Cornell University, for the New York City Council on Consumer Affairs, testimony of October 1967.[3] (This study was done for the New York City Council on Consumer Affairs.)	Summer, 1967.	New York, N.Y.	1,400 stores, including independent and chainstores.	25 items in each store.	A preliminary report by Dr. Wright indicated some price discrimination against low-income areas, although the pricing pattern of three large chains failed to reveal such discrimination. Then in subsequent testimony (October 1967) Deputy Mayor Costello summarized the data as revealing no general price discrimination by chainstores. However, higher prices were found in smaller stores, which were more important in low-income pattern of neighborhoods.
Marcus Alexis and Leonard S. Simon, University of Rochester, "The Food Marketing Commission and Food Prices by Income Groups," Journal of Farm Economics, May 1967.	Spring, 1966.	Rochester, N.Y.	31 stores, including 16 chainstores.	Not available	Higher prices were found in small, independent stores. To the extent less mobile, low-income families do more of their shopping in independent stores, they would tend to pay more for food.
Charles S. Goodman, professor of economics, Wharton School, "Do The Poor Pay More?," Journal of Marketing, January 1968.	Summer, 1965.	Philadelphia, Pa.	A public housing area with only independent stores.	Do	The great majority of low-income consumers in the surveyed public housing area did their major grocery shopping in chainstores located outside the area. Lower prices in the outside chainstores motivated low-income purchasing patterns.
Donald F. Dixon and Daniel J. McLaughlin, Jr., "Do The Inner City Poor Pay More for Food?," Economic and Business Bulletin, Temple University, Spring, 1968.	November 1967.	Do	87 supermarkets and 153 neighborhood stores.	20 items in each store.	A larger share of low-income food shopping is carried on in smaller stores with typically higher prices. However, the average level of prices in small stores in both low- and higher-income areas was roughly comparable, with slightly higher average prices in higher-income areas.
Civic and local government surveys: United Planning Organization.	September 1965.	Washington, D.C.	21 stores, including 15 chainstores.	30 items purchased on Tuesday, Sept. 28, 25 items purchased on the weekend of Sept. 30.	Tabulated data indicated the existence of higher prices in a low-income area store of 1 chain (chain D). 18 of the 30 weekday prices and 12 of the 25 weekend prices were higher for this store than for the medium-income area store surveyed in this chain. Overall, this study found that chainstores provided greater availability of quality items at lower prices. However, remoteness from shopping centers or lack of transportation limited the low-income consumer's ability to shop in chainstores. The small neighborhood stores filled a need, offering credit, delivery, and other services. "Of course, high carrying charges on groceries, and exorbitant prices (were) the other side of the coin."

TABLE 1 (Cont.) Recent Food Price Surveys Undertaken with Respect to Low- and Higher-Income Areas

Survey Source	Dates	Cities	Number of Stores	Number of Items' Prices Checked	Findings with Respect to Discrimination
Civic and local government surveys:—Continued Better Business Bureau of St. Louis.	November 1967 to February 1968.	St. Louis, Mo.	64 stores of 5 chains.	18 items in each store.	No pattern of discrimination was evident in the summary pricing data published, although a 5 per cent mispricing rate applied to the total of all stores surveyed.
Metropolitan New York Consumer Council.	Fall 1966 to Spring 1967.	New York, N.Y.	40 supermarkets, including some independents.	Observed generally for prices, quality, and advertising for 26 weeks.	Wide variations in pricing were observed, but no pattern of price discrimination against low-income areas was found in chainstores. However, small stores with higher prices are more frequent in low-income areas, and therefore indicate higher prices paid on the average by low-income area residents. Some quality discrimination was found along with generally poor compliance with weights and measures. Advertised, low-priced specials were generally not adequately stocked in chainstores.
Project Summer Hope, sponsored by the New Detroit Committee.	Summer 1968.	Detroit, Mich.	278 chainstores, and 63 independents.	18 items in each store.	Wide variations in pricing were observed, and significant price discrimination was found against low-income areas in both chain and independent stores.
Baltimore Community Relations Commission.	March 1968.	Baltimore, Md.	5 different chains throughout the metropolitan area.	7 items in each store.	A "paucity" of chainstores was found in inner-city areas, but no systematic differences in prices between low-income and higher-income sections were noted in the area as a whole.
Consumer group surveys: Ad Hoc Committee on Equal Pricing[4]	September 1967.	Washington, D.C.	9 stores of 1 chain.	9 items in each store.	Some price discrimination was found against low-income area shoppers.
Consumer action program of Bedford-Stuyvesant, Inc.[3]	November 1967.	New York, N.Y.	5 chainstores.	20 items in each store.	Do
MEND consumer education program[3]	August 1967.	Do	2 stores of 1 chain, 4 stores of another chain.	15 items in each store.	Do
			1 store of 1 chain and 6 stores of another chain.	10 to 16 advertised items in each store.	Some price discrimination was found against low-income area shoppers, together with greatly reduced availability of low-priced specials.
News media surveys: WRC-TV reporters[4]	October 1967.	Washington, D.C.	3 stores of 1 chain, 2 stores of another.	10 items in each store.	Do
St. Louis Post-Dispatch reporters[3]	Do	St. Louis, Mo.	20 stores, including chains and independents.	40 to 50 items in each store.	Do

[1] Retail Food Prices in Low- and Higher-Income Areas, Bureau of Labor Statistics, U.S. Department of Labor, February 1966. This is also available in Technical Study No. 10 of the Special Studies in Food Marketing, National Commission on Food Marketing, June 1966, pp. 121–144. The same BLS data were also analyzed independently with some cost information as Chapter 17 in Organization and Competition in Food Retailing, Technical Study No. 7, National Commission on Food Marketing, June 1966.

[2] Comparison of Prices Paid for Selected Foods in Chain Stores in High- and Low-Income Areas of Cities, Consumer and Marketing Service, U.S. Department of Agriculture, June 1968.

[3] Based on published testimony in hearings, "Consumer Problems of the Poor," subcommittee of the Committee on Government Operations, House of Representatives, 90th Cong., 2d sess., Oct. 12, and Nov. 24–25, 1967.

[4] Results were reported to the Federal Trade Commission during investigational hearings conducted by the staff.

Source: U.S., Cong., House, Committee on Government Operations, Economic Report on Good Chain Selling Practices in the District of Columbia and San Francisco, 91st Cong., 1st sess., July 1969, pp. 43–44.

knowledge about the market and the economy, and in inadequate conceptual tools for planning and making decisions.

Other kinds of explanations point to objective conditions (in sociological terms, to the social structure) that account for existing consumer practices by the poor. Three examples of such conditions are: the credit system, with its risk-cost formula and inexorable penalties that work against the poor; merchandising practices in some low-income area stores; and the fluctuating nature of employment in occupations followed by many low-income earners.

One purely economic explanation also deserves attention: the effect produced by low income, per se. The size of an income determines to some extent whether any "economies of scale" can be employed by a family. A small income has to be disbursed in smaller amounts than a large income, regardless of the different ways families now spend incomes. Thus, low-income families can less often take advantage of low prices for quantity purchases. On the other hand, some products and services are available in standard units that cannot be divided into smaller ones. Thus, large outlays (such as one month's rent in advance) are greater disturbances to a small than to a large income.[34] Since there is less possibility for flexibility in the disbursement of a small income, there is more possibility of imbalance.

Finally, we come to the psychological explanations proposed by a number of writers for explaining consumer practices of the poor. Among the traits or values that are said to dispose the poor to behavior different from the middle and upper classes are: an attitude of fatalism; a preference for immediate gratification of impulses; a low level of aspiration and low need to achieve; an unclear view of the higher social structure; a concrete style of thinking; and over-concern with security.

Often the psychological differences attributed to the poor are discussed as if they were "givens," [35] in much the same way as the idea of irrationality seems like a "given." However, these same differences are discussed by other writers as possible outcomes of objective social and economic conditions of the lower class.

One set of research findings indicates, for example, that a child's preference for immediate gratification is related to the absence of a father in the home. Another finding indicates that continued delay in reward can induce this same preference in children.[36] In a like vein, it has been said that "splurges" by lower-class people are natural reactions to past deprivation and insecurity about the future.[37] Still another writer argues that low ambition in the lower class is more apparent than real: Lower-class people have ambition, but since it is unrealistic for the poor to aspire to the same goals as the middle class, their goals only seem less ambitious.[38] Thus, we have explanations that range from the social characteristics of the poor, through purely economic and purely psychological factors, and finally back to the environment of the poor. What does all this mean for planners of programs to improve their consumer practices?

At first glance, the problem seems to be so severe, and the explanations so deeply rooted in far-reaching social problems that it may seem futile to attack it at all. It is instructive, however, to look at some consumer programs that have been successful, and at some recommended programs based on the New York study. Examples of recent successful programs are described in some detail in the 1965 report of the President's Committee on Consumer Interest, "The Most For Their Money." [39] Recommendations based on the New York study are found in the final chapter of Caplovitz' book.[40]

In general, the successful programs and the recommended actions employ unorthodox, "backdoor" methods that capitalize on the very differences in the poor that we have described. They may use informal methods of education carried out locally in poor neighborhoods. They may attack problems of financial management indirectly through appeals to material interests rather than by teaching abstract principles. They may provide for intervention at the top in dealing with problems that stem from rigidities in the market itself. Finally, they may concentrate efforts on special groups of the poor who seem particularly vulnerable to buying mistakes or insolvency.

If the apparent irrationality of poor consumers can be dealt with in these realistic ways, we have some hope of softening the worst effects of a hand-to-mouth existence.

NOTES

1. Martineau, Pierre, "Social Classes and Spending Behavior," in Martin Grossack, ed. *Understanding Consumer Behavior*. Christopher Publishing House, Boston, Massachusetts, 1964.

2. Pennock, Jean L., "Who Are the Poor?" *Family Economic Review*. Consumer and Food Economics Research Division, Agricultural Research Service, U.S. Department of Agriculture, March, 1964.

3. Holmes, Emma G., "Expenditures of Low-Income Families," *Family Economic Review,* Consumer and Food Economics Research Division, Agricultural Research Service, U.S. Department of Agriculture, March, 1955; also LIFE, *Study of Consumer Expenditures: A Background for Marketing Decisions,* Vol. 1, Time, Inc., New York, 1957.

4. Katona, George, Charles Lininger, and Richard Kosebud, *1962 Survey of Consumer Finances.* Monograph No. 32, Survey Research Center, Institute for Social Research, Ann Arbor, Michigan, 1963; also Katona, George, Charles Lininger, and Eva Mueller, *1963 Survey of Consumer Finances.* Monograph No. 32, The University of Michigan, Survey Research Center, Ann Arbor, Michigan, 1964.

5. Caplovitz, David, *The Poor Pay More*. The Free Press of Glencoe, New York, 1963.

6. Rainwater, Lee, R. Coleman, and G. Handel, *Workingman's Wife*: Oceana Publications, New York, 1959.

7. Bauer, Raymond, "The Negro and the Marketplace," paper read before the American Psychological Association, Los Angeles, California, September, 1964.

8. Rose, Arnold M., "Conditions for Irrational Choices," *Social Research.* Vol. 30, No. 2, Summer, 1963.

9. David, Martin H., *Family Composition and Consumption.* North Holland Publishing Company, Amsterdam, 1962.

10. Caplovitz, 1963, *op. cit.*

11. Katona, George, *The Mass Consumption Society.* McGraw-Hill, New York, 1964.

12. Mueller, Eva, "A Study of Purchase Decisions," in Lincoln Clark, ed., *Consumer Behavior.* Committee for Research on Consumer Attitudes and Behavior, New York University Press, New York, 1954.

13. Caplovitz, 1963, *op. cit.*

14. Stone, Gregory, "Sociological Aspects of Consumer Purchasing in a Northwest Side Chicago Community," *Unpublished Master's Thesis,* University of Chicago, Chicago, Illinois, 1952.

15. Harp, John, "Socio-economic Correlates of Consumer Behavior," *The American Journal of Economics and Sociology,* Vol. 20, No. 3, April, 1961, pp. 265–270.

16. Caplovitz, 1963, *op. cit.*

17. Rainwater, 1959, *op. cit.*

18. Sargent, Hugh W., *Consumer-Product Rating Publications and Buying Behavior.* University of Illinois Bulletin No. 85, Urbana, Illinois, 1959.

19. Mueller, 1954, *op. cit.*

20. *Ibid.*

21. Katona, 1964, *op. cit.*

22. Caplovitz, 1963, *op. cit.*

23. Katona, Lininger, and Mueller, 1964, *op. cit.*

24. Unpublished data from the author's study, "Cognitive Structure and Consumer Behavior," under a grant from Consumers Union, Mount Vernon, New York, 1961–1962.

25. Rainwater, 1959, *op. cit.*

26. Caplovitz, 1963, *op. cit.*

27. Katona, Lininger, and Mueller, 1964, *op. cit.*

28. *Ibid.*

29. *Ibid.*

30. Katona, George, *The Powerful Consumer.* McGraw-Hill, New York, 1960.

31. Caplovitz, 1963, *op. cit.*

32. Katona, 1964, *op. cit.*

33. Morgan, James, Martin David, Wilbur Cohen, and Harvey Brazer, *Income and Welfare in the United States.* McGraw-Hill, New York, 1962.

34. Willie, Charles V., Morton O. Wagenfeld, and Lee J. Cary. "Patterns of Rent Payment Among Problem Families," *Social Casework,* October, 1964, pp. 465–470.

35. Martineau, 1964, *op. cit.*

36. Mischel, Walter, and Ralph Metzner, "Preference for Delayed Reward as a Function of Age, Intelligence, and Length of Delay Interval," *Journal of Abnormal and Social Psychology,* Vol. 64, No. 6, 1962, pp. 425–431.

37. Lazarsfeld, Paul, "Sociological Reflections on Business," in Martin Grossack, ed., *Understanding Consumer Behavior.* Christopher Publishing House, Boston, Mass., 1964.

38. Keller, Suzanne, and Marisa Zavalloni, "Ambition and Social Class: A Respecification," *Social Forces,* Vol. 43, No. 1, October, 1964, pp. 58–70.

39. President's Committee on Consumer Interest. *The Most for Their Money.* A Report of the Panel on Consumer Education for Persons with Limited Incomes, Washington, D.C., U.S. Government Printing Office, 1965.

40. Caplovitz, 1963, *op. cit.*

31 Comparing the Cost of Food to Blacks and to Whites—A Survey

Donald E. Sexton, Jr.

One of the aspects of "price" receiving a good deal of attention in the past several years is that of the cost of goods purchased by minority groups. Are prices higher in the ghettos? Do blacks, American Indians, and Chicanos pay more? Do the poor pay more?

Many studies have been undertaken to shed some light upon these and related questions. Unfortunately, the results are frequently ambiguous and of doubtful statistical validity. Professor Sexton analyzes a number of studies and attempts to clear up some of the confusion surrounding these vital price issues. His article is of particular relevance to those studying retailing, pricing, or marketing ethics.

Do black families pay more for grocery products than white families? If the answer is yes, then food price differences may be a contributing factor to urban unrest and should be a concern of public policy. If the answer is no, research effort should be directed to other markets (such as housing, jobs, transportation, and education) in order to identify factors more significantly involved in the urban crisis.

Several studies have focused on the comparative prices of food to blacks and to whites. The majority of the findings suggest that blacks are not charged or do not pay more than whites in stores of the same type. However, these results seem to have had little unified impact on the public debate of the question, "Do blacks pay more?" Community groups and politicians continue to claim that blacks (and the poor) pay more for food. In part, this may reflect the lack of an adequate summary of these studies. However, it is more likely that discrepancies exist between what a researcher means when he says blacks are not charged more and what an inner city resident means when he says he pays more for food.

This article attempts to summarize and clarify the current state of knowledge concerning the comparative costs of food to blacks and whites. The

Reprinted from Donald E. Sexton, Jr., "Comparing the Cost of Food to Blacks and to Whites—A Survey", *Journal of Marketing* (July, 1971), Vol. 35, pp. 40–46.

methodology and findings of each study are briefly described, their limitations are discussed, and their implications are explored.

The Price   The price studies vary enormously in their statistical credibility.
Studies   Some are so seriously flawed that their results are not discussed
in detail in this survey. These studies generally consist of surveys undertaken by ad hoc consumer groups and by the news media. Such organizations have often been in the vanguard of those examining differences in prices charged by stores. (Studies by consumer groups and newspapers in Washington, D.C., St. Louis, and New York were prominent during the 1967 Congressional Hearings concerning chain store pricing policies.[1]) The author is familiar with six price studies conducted by consumer groups or the news media.[2] With but one exception (*St. Louis Globe-Democrat*), these studies have concluded that inner city residents are charged more for grocery products than are whites, or the more affluent who reside in other city areas or in the suburbs.

The conclusions of such studies, though, must be viewed with extreme caution due to methodological difficulties such as inadequate sample sizes, casual sample design, and selective and inaccurate reporting. For example, all but the *St. Louis Post-Dispatch* study are based on sample sizes of nine or fewer stores.[3] In one three-day study of Safeway stores in Washington, D.C. (Ad Hoc Committee on Equal Pricing), bias might have been present since just one housewife gathered the prices from three of the stores.[4] In a New York study by MEND, a New York social-action group, selective reporting appeared to be part of the research design since one of the researchers declared ". . . we wanted to have the most striking differences apparent. We have thrown out surveys in relation to some chains in which we found as many items to be higher priced as lower priced, and this has happened." [5] In addition, controls on reporting errors were not apparent in some of these studies. For example, stores in Washington, D.C., Safeway study were misclassified into low- and high-income areas, and prices were quoted for brands not stocked,[6] while in a St. Louis study by the Human Development Corporation over 60% of an alleged price difference between high- and low-income area stores was due to a single likely price reporting error.[7]

The more methodologically sound studies have been conducted by the federal government, civic groups, and academics and are discussed in detail below. Because there is a relatively high correlation between race and income in cities, most of these price studies do not clearly distinguish between whether they are answering the question, "Do blacks pay more?" "Do the poor pay more?" or "Do the poor and black pay more?" While this distinction may seem to be a pedantic point, a priori it seemed to be a useful basis for classifying the studies. However, the author could not employ this classification method since the demographic focus of most studies was not sharp due to the use of aggregate statistics. Instead, the studies are presented according to the city or cities involved: Buffalo, Chicago, Detroit, Los Angeles, New York, Philadelphia, St. Louis, and various other groups of cities. This system of organization has the advantage that the consistency of findings within a particular city can be judged.

Buffalo   In the Greater Buffalo area, Teach compared the cost of a 120-item market basket among stores in the urban core, in other areas of the city, and in the suburbs. The brand and size of each item were designated. The prices were gathered by volunteer students between Thursday and Saturday in each of three weeks. Teach could not unequivocally conclude either that the poor did or did not pay more since his five statistical tests yielded different results.[8]

Chicago   Frank, Green and Sieber used 1961 *Chicago Tribune* panel data and regressed the mean price paid for each of 44 grocery products against several socioeconomic and purchasing behavior variables, including race of the purchasing household. They concluded that, "Whites tend to pay higher prices per unit than do nonwhites," but furnished no further details of their results with respect to race.[9]

The author examined mean prices paid by approximately 120 black and 600 white families who were members of the *Chicago Tribune* panel.[10] Three products were considered: two during 1960 and one between the fall of 1963 and the spring of 1966. He compared prices for the same brand (three brands for each product) purchased in stores of the same affiliation (five store categories—three different chains, one affiliated independent organization, and the unaffiliated independents); that is, he compared across areas the prices corresponding to each of 45 different brand-store categories. For all the brands purchased in chain stores, whites living in white sections of Chicago were found to have paid on the average 1% more than whites in the suburbs, and blacks living in black sections of Chicago on the average 1% more than whites in the white sections of Chicago. For all the brands purchased in the independent stores, the Chicago whites on the average paid 6% more than the suburban whites, and the Chicago blacks on the average paid 9% more than the Chicago whites. Although these results showed blacks typically paid more than whites, they did not necessarily indicate price discrimination against blacks. This is because the estimated differences in average package sizes purchased by whites and blacks and in operating costs among stores could explain about 6% of the price differences between the suburbs and the white section of the city and approximately the same amount between the white and black sections of the city. These results were generally the same (within 1%) for both the chain stores and the independent stores. In fact, the figures implied that chains may discriminate in favor of blacks.[11]

In 1969, the Task Force on Public Aid of the Church Federation of

Greater Chicago concluded that a 45-item market basket cost most, on the average, in the black inner city areas and successively less as one moved through the white inner city areas to the outer city areas and then to the suburbs. The results were based on a survey of 108 stores conducted by volunteer shoppers in February and March of 1969. Each shopper was asked to record the price of the cheapest brand of each of the 45 products. For many products a particular package size was specified; for others a small range (e.g., 7–8 oz.) of package sizes. These volunteers shopped on whatever day they wished. Included in the inner city store sample were proportionately more small independent stores because that was ". . . where large numbers of public aid recipients could reasonably be expected to shop." [12]

Detroit   Grocery and drug prices and services among stores in the Detroit metropolitan area were compared in 1968 by Focus:Hope, Inc., a civic group sponsored by the Detroit Catholic Archdiocese. The food price survey covered 44 items, identified by brand and size. Four hundred inner city and suburban housewives, after six hours of instruction, visited 340 chain and independent stores to gather the price information. In the report, complete results were presented for only nine items. Generally, these items cost the most in inner city small independent stores (the Mom and Pop's), and successively less in inner city larger independents, suburb independents, and suburban chain stores. Aspects of stores such as parking and courtesy were rated by the housewives on a four-level scale (excellent, good, fair, poor). The independent stores in black and in poor areas were generally found to fall one level below similar stores in white or more affluent areas. [13]

Los Angeles   Marcus compared prices of 86 food items in 33 stores in Watts with those in 16 stores in Culver City, a more affluent, white suburb. Brand and size were specified for each item. If the particular brand was not available, the least expensive brand of the product found in the store was included in the survey. Marcus found that meat and produce prices were about the same in the two areas, but that for both chain stores and Mom and Pop stores grocery prices were higher in Watts than in Culver City. [14] He believed that the quality of meat and produce was lower in Watts than in Culver City and concluded that Watts residents in effect paid more for these items.

New York   In the summer of 1967, the price of a leading brand (depending on the brands available in the store) for each of 37 food items was collected in about 25 stores in 45 neighborhoods. Weight was specified for each item—for most, a specific weight, for a few, a limited range (e.g., 9–10 oz.). This survey was performed by about 35 Urban Corps workers (college students), and the data were used in studies by Wright and Alcaly.

Wright compared the cost of a 20-item food basket across five areas. He concluded that, "If it is true that chains charge higher prices for identical commodities in their stores in poor areas, it did not show up in this survey." [15]

Alcaly concluded that:

> . . . the means and standard deviations of the price charged, distributions of the individual items were generally found to be not significantly related to neighborhood income and racial composition. . . . In those cases in which significant relationships were discovered—mostly in the smaller independents and among the fresh food items—the mean prices and standard deviations were almost always positively related to neighborhood income.[16]

Alcaly's principal means of analysis were linear regressions across 20 neighborhoods for all stores, for chain stores and affiliated independents only, and for small independents only. The dependent variables used were the mean, the standard deviation, and a measure of the skewness of the distributions of prices charged for each commodity in each neighborhood. The independent variables were 1960 median income and percentage of nonwhite residents for each neighborhood. These regressions were made for each of 31 commodities and for a market basket of products.

Philadelphia   In Philadelphia, Dixon and McLaughlin compared the prices of stores in the North Philadelphia inner city with those in higher income areas throughout the city. During one week in 1967, the cost of a 20-item market basket (composed mainly of staples such as flour and eggs) in supermarkets was found to be higher in the latter areas. Similarly, the cost of the market basket in small stores was observed to be higher in the higher income areas. These patterns were consistent over all the items in the market basket.[17]

Goodman studied the stores frequented by families in a low-income area (about 60 blocks) of Philadelphia as well as the price levels in those stores. For a 72-item market basket, he found that prices in supermarkets were generally higher than those in medium-sized independent stores, but that they were generally lower than those in small independent stores. From a survey of 520 residents of the area, he estimated that 92% of families in the low-income area left the neighborhood to do their principal shopping. He concluded that, "Because they shop at competitive stores, going outside their residence area to do so if necessary, the poor do *not* pay more for food in this area." [18]

St. Louis   In 1967, Conway examined a pair of stores for each of four chains—one store in the inner city and one in the suburbs. Each store was visited nine times over a six-month period on Thursday, Friday, or Saturday. Prices were gathered for each of 50 items. Conway concluded that, "No unequivocal statement can be made that national food chains charge different prices in poverty area stores as compared to nonpoverty area stores." [19] In fact, the cost of a 50-item market basket in a given chain on a given day was found to be higher in the nonpoverty area store more frequently than in the poverty area store.

To examine the charges raised in St. Louis in 1967 by consumer groups and newspapers, the Better Business Bureau of Greater St. Louis made an extensive study of retail food selling in that metropolitan area. Over a five-month period, 64 chain stores, including 30 in poverty areas, were shopped a total of 238 times (169 shopping trips were made to poverty area stores) by 19 shoppers. The prices charged for 18 items specified by brand and package size were collected. For three of four major chains, no pattern of price differences was found between stores of the same chain located in poverty and in nonpoverty areas.[20] The prices charged in the seven poverty area independent stores surveyed were generally higher than those in the nearest poverty area chain store on the same day. The Better Business Bureau further concluded that "There appeared to be no consistent pattern of difference between the quality of produce offered in the poverty areas of the suburban areas," and reached a similar conclusion about meat.[21]

Groups of Cities   In 1966, the Bureau of Labor Statistics compared the prices of 18 food items in food stores sampled from high- and low-income areas of Atlanta, Chicago, Houston, Los Angeles, New York, and Washington, D.C. They:

> . . . found no significant differences in prices charged by food stores located in low-income areas versus those charged by stores in higher income areas when the same types of stores (chains, large independents, small indipendents), the same qualities of food, and the same sizes of packages are compared. Prices are usually higher, however, in the small independent stores which are most common in low-income neighborhoods, than in large independents and chain stores which predominate in the higher income areas.[22]

The Department of Agriculture surveyed the prices of two brands for each of 17 food products in two chains selected in each of six cities. A total of 134 stores were visited in areas classified as high or low income. The study made comparisons only between stores of the same chain in a given city. They discovered ". . . no identifiable patterns of differences between sample stores of the same chain operating in high- and low-income areas." [23]

The conclusions of the 1969 Federal Trade Commission study of Washington, D.C. and San Francisco were based on two surveys. The first survey covered 137 stores and included about 65 items usually advertised by food stores. The second survey consisted of 166 stores and compared the cost of a market basket of items across the low- and high-income areas. The FTC found that food prices were generally higher in low-income areas. The primary explanation was that, "Many foodstores serving low-income, inner city areas are small, less efficient, and have higher prices." [24] Chain store prices were often found to be higher in low-income areas than in high-income areas, but the FTC discovered no policy of intentional discrimination against low-income areas. Overall, no significant quality differences in products were discovered between the low- and high-income areas.

Discussion of Studies   Of the 15 studies based on relatively sound methodology, only five found that consumers in black or in low-income areas either paid or were charged more for food products. The ten remaining studies found that the black or the poor did not pay or were not charged higher prices. Although they do not represent an overwhelming majority, the findings of these latter studies must be respected as the consensus of the current literature. However, these results need to be tempered—first by their methodological limitations and second by the scope of their conclusions.

Methodological Limitations   A careful reading of these studies has disclosed three general types of limitations: (1) commission of errors in statistical methodology; (2) failure to allow for differences in commodities; and (3) impropriety of price data.

Statistical Errors   The 15 studies by the federal government, civic groups, and academics were generally free of statistical errors as far as the author could assess from their reports. An exception is the Conway study which was based on a small sample size—eight stores. The six studies by ad hoc consumer groups and the news media were plagued by the statistical errors discussed earlier.

Commodity Differences   When prices for products are compared, care must be taken to ensure that they correspond to the same package of goods and services. In particular, the same brand, store affiliation, and package size should be used in the comparisons.

If the average price for a product is calculated from a subset of the brands on the market (e.g., Focus:Hope, Church Federation of Greater Chicago, and Teach) as an estimate of the cost of food to residents of a particular area, it is biased to the extent they do not buy those brands. In particular, if private brands are not included in the study (as in Alcaly and Wright, the resultant average prices are biased toward equality since the prices of national brands are higher and have less variation over time than those of private label brands.[25] In the Alcaly, Marcus, and Wright studies, more than one brand comprised the data for a given product, resulting in averages that are not strictly comparable.

Bias may also occur in the results when average prices are computed if various chains, affiliated independents, and unaffiliated independents are not considered separately, since services vary among stores. Studies such as Alcaly, Focus:Hope, Marcus, and Church Federation of Greater Chicago did not indicate that different chains were examined individually.

As shown in the Sexton study, package size is an important factor determining price per standard unit. Some of the items included in the Church Federation of Greater Chicago, Alcaly, and Wright studies varied in package size.

The directions of the biases caused by these omissions vary by study. If private brands, chain stores, or large packages are relatively overrepresented in a sample, the resulting price average is biased low; if underrepresented, it is biased high.

Propriety of
Price Data
All but two (Frank and Sexton) of the studies discussed are based on price data collected in a sample of stores on one or a few days. These data are pertinent to the question of whether the market prices faced by blacks are higher than those faced by whites. However, they only provide an adequate answer if brands and stores of different affiliations are considered separately, or if the sample is weighted according to the relative prominence of the brands and store affiliations in the marketplace. For example, if an average price is based on a sample of four stores, including three chain A stores and one chain B store, and if blacks shop at chain A stores 90% of the time, then average price does not represent the prices blacks typically face. In studies such as Teach, Church Federation of Greater Chicago, Focus:Hope, Marcus, Bureau of Labor Statistics, and Alcaly, data from different chains may have been mixed together without considering where and relatively how often blacks and whites shopped.

The Frank and Sexton studies are based on panel data. These price data are relevant to the question, "Do blacks pay more?" With these data, though, the researcher must account for differences in consumer behavior. In particular, if consumers differ in the amount of effort they expend on search, average prices calculated from panel data are biased—low for consumers who search, high for those who do not. Both of these studies did attempt to allow for search effort. In particular, Sexton included several variables in his analysis in an effort to account for opportunity costs of time, price expectations, and quantities purchased. Even after including these variables, blacks were found to have paid more than whites.

Miscellaneous
Limitations
While the price data for the Alcaly and Wright studies were being collected, daily radio broadcasts reported the prices found in low- and high-income neighborhoods, and this publicity may have decreased any existing price differences. In the surveys of the BLS study, chain store managers were advised a week before their stores were

surveyed—again a case where publicity may have biased prices toward uniformity.

Scope of   While the above reservations may suggest a reevaluation of the
Conclusions   conclusions of some of the studies, they do not go far in explain-
                  ing their lack of impact in answering the question, "Do blacks
pay more?"

One reason this question is still a source of controversy may stem from the possibility that inner city residents shop relatively more in independent stores. If prices in these stores tend to be higher than those in chain supermarkets, then the poor or black consumer does pay more for grocery products. That is, perhaps many price studies have focused on individual store types rather than upon the entire market structure—where people shop and why. As Dixon and McLaughlin point out, "The *prices charged* by chain supermarkets are not a measure of the *prices paid* by the urban poor who do not shop in supermarkets." [26]

Generally, prices in independent stores have been found to be higher than those in chain supermarkets. Each of 13 studies known to the author reported that prices in independent stores were higher than those in chain supermarkets.[27]

Moreover, independent stores seem to be relatively more prevalent and chain stores relatively less accessible in the inner city (see Federal Trade Commission, Focus:Hope, and Sexton). For example, Sturdivant wrote:

> The ghetto retailing crisis is basically structural in nature. That is, the retail communities in most ghettos are characterized by an atomistic structure with numerous small, owner-operated establishments serving the poor. Such firms lack the managerial sophistication, capital, and capacity, to service their market effectively.[28]

In short, for the same brand in stores of the same type, researchers can find equal prices charged in black and in white areas, or equal prices paid by blacks and whites. However, blacks may still have to pay more than whites because the (lower-priced) chain stores are not as accessible to them. The inner city housewife has the choice of shopping at the independents with their higher prices or of paying for transportation to shop at a chain store. Goodman found that blacks did travel to larger stores to avoid the higher priced neighborhood stores. Sexton discovered that independent stores had a similar market share among blacks and among whites and that supermarkets were relatively less dense, per capita, in the black areas of Chicago than in the white areas; these findings are consistent with those of Goodman.

The other reason for the lack of impact of these studies appears to be that while answering the question, "Do blacks pay more?" they generally ignore the deeper and more important question, "Are blacks the victims of price discrimination?" To answer that question, one must consider quality and service differences among stores. One way to undertake that investigation is to examine operating-cost differences among stores. Only Sexton and the FTC have attempted such an effort, and neither concluded that there was price discrimination against blacks.

Future Research   The findings of available food-price studies are both too equivocal and too restricted for marketing researchers to ignore this area of investigation. Future studies of price differences among blacks and whites must take more care in comparing identical commodities. Operationally, such care consists of comparing prices for the identical package size, brand, and store affiliation. Only from such careful research can unequivocal answers to the question, "Do blacks pay more?" be expected.

But the real need for research in this area lies in expanding the scope of price-comparison studies to answer the question, "Are blacks the victims of price discrimination?" There are two major gaps in the present research that deny answers to that question. First, service and quality differences among stores need to be estimated. A start on that estimation consists of thorough examinations of operating-cost variances among chain and independent stores in different areas. Generally, store operating-cost data across areas are nonexistent with the exception of the National Commission on Food Marketing study.[29] Second, the stores patronized by blacks and whites and the reasons for such patronage need to be investigated. If price discrimination is empirically established, then legislative solutions may be considered; knowing where people shop and why is crucial to an understanding of the possible effects of such legislation. For example, suppose a law were proposed that would remove most Mom and Pop grocery stores from low-income areas. If these small stores provided services necessary to many residents, but were unavailable in supermarkets (e.g., assembling shopping lists for small children whose mothers work full-time), then implementation of such a law might be disastrous to low-income area residents.

Summary   Fifteen price-comparison studies have been discussed, and the consensus of their findings appears to be that inner city residents do not pay more. However, these findings are generally not unequivocal because of methodological reservations. Moreover, they are narrowly focused and typically fail to consider the reasons for price differences or shopping patterns. More research concerning comparative food prices is needed to provide clearer insights for consumers, retail grocery store executives, and legislators.

NOTES

1. United States Congress, House, Subcommittee of the Committee on Government Operations, *Consumer Problems of the Poor: Supermarket Operations in Low-Income Areas and the Federal Response, Hearings* (Washington, D.C.: Government Printing Office, 1968).

2. Joan F. Dames, "Food Prices Found Higher in Slum Areas," *St. Louis Post-Dispatch* (November 30, 1967), pp. 1, 15; Human Development Corporation, *Initial Report on the Survey of Food Prices in the St. Louis City and Surrounding County* (St. Louis, Mo.: Human Development Corporation, November 1, 1967); "Globe Survey of Supermarkets—Poverty Area and Suburb Food Prices Identical," *St. Louis Globe-Democrat* (January 18, 1968), p. 3; and other studies described in same reference as Note 1.

3. Federal Trade Commission, *Economic Report on Food Chain Selling Practices in the District of Columbia and San Francisco* (Washington, D.C.: Government Printing Office, 1969).

4. United States Congress, House, Subcommittee of the Committee on Government Operations, *Consumer Problems of the Poor: Supermarket Operations in Low Income Areas and the Federal Response — Report* (Washington, D.C.: Government Printing Office, 1968).

5. Same reference as Note 1, p. 142.

6. Same reference as Note 4.

7. Same reference as Note 4, p. 210.

8. Richard Teach, "Supermarket Pricing Practices in Various Areas of a Large City," *Working Paper No. 53,* State University of New York at Buffalo, 1969.

9. Ronald E. Frank, Paul E. Green, and H. F. Sieber, Jr., "Household Correlates of Purchase Prices for Grocery Products," *Journal of Marketing Research,* Vol. IV (February, 1967), pp. 54–58.

10. Donald E. Sexton, Jr., "Do Blacks Pay More? A Comparison of Prices Paid for Grocery Store Commodities by Black and by White Families," unpublished doctoral dissertation, University of Chicago, 1970.

11. Same reference as Note 10.

12. Task Force on Public Aid of the Church Federation of Greater Chicago, "Summary of Results of Food Pricing Survey," press release, June, 1969.

13. Focus:Hope, Inc., *Comparison of Grocery and Drug Prices and Services in the Greater Detroit Area* (Detroit: Catholic Archdiocese of Detroit, 1968).

14. Burton H. Marcus, "Similarity of Ghetto and Nonghetto Food Costs," *Journal of Marketing Research,* Vol. VI (August, 1969), pp. 365–368.

15. Carlton E. Wright, "Summer Participation in the Program of the N.Y. City Council on Consumer Affairs," unpublished report, Cornell University, 1968.

16. Roger E. Alcaly, "Food Prices in Relation to Income Levels in New York City," unpublished paper, Columbia University, June, 1969.

17. Donald F. Dixon and Daniel J. McLaughlin, Jr., "Do the Inner City Poor Pay More for Food?" *The Economic and Business Bulletin,* Vol. XX (Spring, 1968), pp. 6–12.

18. Charles S. Goodman, "Do the Poor Pay More?" *Journal of Marketing,* Vol. 32 (January, 1968), pp. 18–24.

19. Edward B. Conway, "A Comparison of Retail Food Prices in Food Chain Outlets—Poverty Area Versus Non-Poverty Area Stores," unpublished master's thesis, St. Louis University, 1967.

20. Better Business Bureau of Greater St. Louis, Inc., *Comparative Study: Food Prices and Quality Practices of Major Chains in the St. Louis, Mis-*

souri *Metropolitan Area* (St. Louis: Better Business Bureau of Greater St. Louis, Inc., 1968).

21. Same reference as Note 20, p. 6.

22. United States Bureau of Labor Statistics, *Retail Food Prices in Low and Higher Income Areas* (Washington, D.C.: Government Printing Office, 1969).

23. United States Department of Agriculture, *Comparison of Prices Paid for Selected Foods in Chainstores in High and Low Income Areas of Six Cities* (Washington, D.C.: Government Printing Office).

24. Same reference as Note 3, p. 3.

25. National Commission on Food Marketing, "Retail Food Prices in Low and Higher Income Areas: A Study of Prices Charged in Food Stores Located in Low and Higher Income Areas of Six Large Cities, February, 1966," *Special Studies in Food Marketing*, Technical Study No. 10 (Washington, D.C.: Government Printing Office, 1966).

26. Donald F. Dixon and Daniel J. McLaughlin, Jr., "Do the Poor Really Pay More for Food?" unpublished paper, Temple University, Philadelphia, Pennsylvania, 1969.

27. Marcus Alexis and Leonard S. Simon, "The Food Marketing Commission and Food Prices by Income Groups," *Journal of Farm Economics*, Vol. XLXIV (May, 1967), pp. 439–440; Better Business Bureau, same reference as Note 20; Einar Bjorklund and James L. Palmer, *A Study of the Prices of Chain and Independent Grocers in Chicago* (Chicago: University of Chicago Press, 1930); Dixon and McLaughlin, same reference as Note 17; Federal Trade Commission, same reference as Note 3; Focus: Hope, Inc., same reference as Note 13; Werner Z. Hirsch, "Grocery Chain Store Prices—A Case Study," *Journal of Marketing*, Vol. 21 (July, 1956), pp. 9–23; Bob R. Holdren, *The Structure of a Retail Market and the Market Behavior of Retail Units* (Englewood Cliffs, N.J.: Prentice-Hall, 1960); Marcus, same reference as Note 14; Richard D. Millican and Ramone Jean Rogers, "Price Variability of Non-Branded Food Items Among Food Stores in Champaign-Urbana," *Journal of Marketing,* Vol. 18 (January, 1954), pp. 282–284; Lois Ann Simonds, "A Study of the Variation in Food Costs in Four Cities in Ohio," unpublished doctoral dissertation, The Ohio State University, Columbus, Ohio, 1967; U.S. Bureau of Labor Statistics, same reference as Note 22; and Wright, same reference as Note 15.

28. Frederick D. Sturdivant, "Retailing in the Ghetto: Problems and Proposals," in *Marketing and the New Science of Planning*, Robert L. King, ed. (Chicago, Ill.: American Marketing Association, Fall, 1968).

29. National Commission on Food Marketing, *Organization and Competition in Food Retailing*, Technical Study No. 7 (Washington, D.C.: Government Printing Office, 1966).

32 Some Consumption Pattern Differences Between Urban Whites and Negroes

James E. Stafford
Keith K. Cox and
James B. Higginbotham

Even within the market segment that can be characterized as "poor" there are consumption-pattern differences that cannot be attributed to income. Those who assume that Negro and white households purchase alike simply because their income categories are equivalent are mistaken. Because society's pressures and cultural traditions have been different for poor whites and poor Negroes, their buying patterns are also different.

Marketing texts dealing with "Consumer Behavior," as well as "Consumer Behavior" chapters in general marketing texts, deal with a *broad range* of consumer characteristics which interact with the marketing process. In this article the results of a survey shed *specific* light upon consumption-pattern differences between urban whites and Negroes.

During the past 20 years, the "Negro Market" has been virtually ignored in the United States, except by a few farsighted companies. Most mass-market-oriented firms assumed that the advertising message, as well as the product itself, reached the Negro, even though both were directed almost exclusively at the white audience. As a result, few companies have realized their potential with Negro consumers, and many opportunities have been overlooked. In recent years, however, increased political, social, and economic pressure has forced more companies either to consider for the first time, or to re-evaluate, the nature of the Negro market.

A very basic question being asked is, "Does a Negro market really exist?" The answer appears, on the surface, to be a simple and straightforward "yes." If the problem is carefully delineated, however, it is found that there are several sides to the question, and they must be uncovered, evaluated, and integrated before a definitive answer can be stated. Several studies, for example, have noted that the Negro market is a distinct geographic, social,

Reprinted from James E. Stafford, Keith K. Cox, and James B. Higginbotham, "Some Consumption Pattern Differences Between Urban Whites and Negroes", *Social Science Quarterly* (December, 1968), Vol. 49, pp. 619–630, with permission of the author and the Social Science Quarterly.

and psychological reality based not only on certain physical characteristics, but also on common experiences of exclusion and deprivation.[1] Similarly, from an economics standpoint, there is little doubt that Negroes constitute a segment of the population separate from the majority of whites. The Negro's relatively low economic status is clearly demonstrated by the fact that 35% of Negro families had incomes below $3,000 in 1965, compared with only 14% of white families. At the other end of the spectrum, 42% of the white families had family incomes greater than $8,000, while only 16% of the Negroes had comparable family incomes.[2] When these facts, plus other enlightening economic comparisons, are coupled with the severe educational and housing deprivations suffered by Negroes, it should be no great revelation to learn that, on an aggregate basis. Negroes have distinct consumption patterns, relative to whites.[3] Some of these same economists, however, have argued that even when income discrepancies are controlled statistically, comparable Negroes and whites still allocate their incomes differently. The alleged difference in spending behavior of Negroes and whites is attributed to the economic and social discrimination which has been part of the Negro heritage. Not being able to live, relax, or dine where they please, American Negroes are said to have developed aggregate consumption patterns different from those of their white counterparts.[4]

It is apparent from the foregoing discussion that Negroes, as a group of individuals having certain characteristics and behavior patterns in common with—yet distant from—whites, could be viewed as a "market." To marketers, however, such a segment exists only to the extent that Negroes *behave differently* from whites *as consumers.* A group of individuals with certain characteristics in common does not, in itself, constitute a realistic market segment. Only when people have common characteristics as consumers may they be thought of as a market segment.

Marketers, therefore, are basically concerned with determining if consumption-pattern differences exist between Negroes and whites and, if they do, whether they are attributable to income differentials, racial differences, or other factors often overlooked.[5] It may be that race, for example, is secondary to income as an influence on purchase behavior; in fact, it is conceivable that 100% of the consumption-pattern differences between Negroes and whites could be accounted for by income and other sociodemographic differentials. Klein and Mooney reach somewhat the same conclusion when they state that "this explanation of racial differentials is not solely adequate" to explain consumption differences. They go on to say that the "effects of [socio]demographic variables have been found to be statistically significant . . . but not clear in direction." [6]

In the study reported here, the authors hoped to shed light on the problem of Negro-white consumption-pattern differences over and above that shed by earlier studies. . . . More specifically, the purposes of the present study were (1) to determine if there existed between Negroes and whites consumption-pattern differences which were not accounted for by income differentials, and (2) to specify, where possible, the nature or possible origin(s) of those differences.

Methodology

Sample

The consumption-pattern data for both Negro and white housewives was taken from a large-scale commercial survey conducted in the Houston Standard Metropolitan Statistical area in 1967. A probability sample of 1,546 housewives was obtained through personal interviews in the respondents' homes. This sample survey was cited by Advertising Research Foundation as conforming to the standards set forth in ARF's *Criteria for Marketing and Advertising Research.* With no substitutes allowed in the sample survey, a completion rate of 80% was achieved by the researchers, who made up to eight call-backs to housewives who were not at home. The accuracy of the field interviewing was verified by ARF, which conducted a 100% verification of the field interviewing, using FACT (Field Audit and Completion Test).[7] Because of the procedures used in this survey, the usual problems of sampling errors (and non-sampling errors due to interviewing) were considered to be minimal.

Limitations

Due to the nature of the original proprietary survey, several limitations were imposed on this study. First, since the search objectives of the company conducting the project were much broader in scope than a simple study of Negro-white consumption patterns, they made no attempt to be all-inclusive in the product categories chosen. As a result, the present study was restricted to a survey of only a small list of household product purchases. Second, even though the Negro sample selected was unusually large (see Table 1), it was still not large enough to permit a completely satisfactory breakdown of income classes, particularly at the middle ($3,000–$6,000) and upper ($8,000 plus) levels. Similarly, multiple cross-classifications by income and other sociodemographic characteristics were impossible, due to inadequate cell sizes. Isolation of the impact of these other sociodemographic characteristics on consumption patterns was limited to inferences drawn from Table 2. Great care, however, was taken by the authors not to become over-enchanted with implying cause and effect relationships relative to these characteristics. Finally, any generalizations from this study must be tempered with the realization that the data were collected from one large urban metropolitan area located in a Southern state.

Results

While of general interest to marketers, aggregate income-allocation differences do not provide any information about actual product- or brand-choice comparisons, which are so vital to marketing strategy decisions. It may be, for example, that even though Negroes spend more money on food, their product and brand choices are very similar to

TABLE 1   Sample Breakdown by Income Classifications

Income	Whites		Negroes	
	N	Per Cent	N	Per Cent
Under $3,000	151	11.3	86	40.8
$3,000–5,999	236	17.7	77	36.5
$6,000–7,999	298	22.3	26	12.3
$8,000 and Over	650	48.7	22	10.4
	1,335[a]	100.0	211[a]	100.0

[a] These are the base numbers used hereafter in each of the tables except where stated differently.

those of whites in comparable circumstances. In this study (see Table 3), specific usage comparisons were made between Negroes and whites for ownership of a selected number of household products (by holding income constant). An evaluation of brand preferences will be left to a future study.

Differences Consumption   ① FOOD PRODUCTS. Table 3 clearly demonstrates that, at every income level, Negroes consumed more butter than did whites. In fact, Negroes at the lowest income level (under $3,000) spent more on butter than did whites at the highest level of income ($8,000 and over). Obviously, factors other than income must account for these variations, but none of the sociodemographic characteristics shown in Table 2 seem to provide any substantial clues.[8]

Nondietary soft drink consumption varied drastically across income classes between the two groups. Negro usage was double that of whites at the lowest income level, but then tended to decline with increasing wealth. Among whites, consumption followed somewhat a reverse trend, with usage rising as income increased. Consumption differences at the low-income level can be attributed primarily to dissimilarities in occupations between the groups. The data in Table 2 indicate that the 77% of the low-income whites were retired, as compared to only 30% of the Negroes. As a result, the low-income Negro families were considerably larger and had more children than the average low-income white families. Why Negro consumption of nondietary soft drinks was so erratic in the high-income brackets is difficult to answer.

Dietary soft drinks were more popular with Negroes until the highest-income bracket was reached. At this point, usage among whites was almost double that among Negroes. Again, the larger size of Negro families probably is sufficient to explain large consumption patterns in the low-income groups. At the highest income level, it may be that Negroes are less diet-conscious than are whites and, as a result, have turned their attentions to other "drinks."

2. LIQUOR. Negroes, in every income bracket but the highest, purchased more liquor than did whites. For both groups, however, liquor consumption rose steadily with increases in income. Scotch whiskey was preferred to a substantial degree by Negroes in almost every income group, when compared with whites. This observation supports the findings of several other studies, which indicate that Negroes drink at least 25% of the Scotch consumed in the United States, although they represent only 12% of the population.[9] Scotch, among all consumers, has always been thought of as a "quality," high-class product. Therefore, it appears likely that, among Negroes, drinking Scotch has become associated with high status. Bauer also found that "those Negroes who see themselves as moving upward self-perceived mobility from their fathers' position in society are most likely to . . . regard Scotch as a 'status' drink, and are most likely to report being regular Scotch drinkers." [10]

3. PERSONAL HYGIENE PRODUCTS. In 11 of 12 possible income groupings, Negroes purchased more deodorant, toothpaste, and mouthwash than comparable groups of whites. Negroes, on the other hand, did not purchase as much shampoo, although the differences were slight in most cases. More household disinfectants were used by Negroes, except in one income group.

The bulk of the differences, particularly at the lower income levels, can be attributed to larger Negro families with more children. Higher rates for usage of household disinfectants by Negroes probably result from the difficulty of keeping their average substandard housing facilities clean.

4. MAJOR HOME APPLIANCES AND HOME OWNERSHIP. A very striking point was that, except for the lowest income bracket, almost as many Negroes owned their own home as did whites. The difference at the lowest income level can be explained by the occupational discrepancies mentioned earlier.

Substantial differences in ownership of various major appliances were noted between the two groups at all income levels. Ownership differences for washing machines, clothes dryers, and dishwashers were particularly apparent. Part of the reason for these differences is income; for example, ownership of washing machines among Negroes increased across each income level until it was fairly close to the white ownership level. Another reason which helps explain the differentials is that many of the dwellings occupied by Negroes, regardless of income, are not equipped with the plumbing and electrical connections necessary for installation of those appliances. The additional installation cost makes it impractical or impossible to purchase washers and dryers. A further comment on automatic dishwashers is in order, since ownership variances are so prominent, even at the highest income level. The reason for these variances is that the majority of dishwasher sales are made to home builders who install them in new

TABLE 2 Total Sample Breakdown by Income and by Various Sociodemographic Characteristics (in per cent)

Sociodemographic Characteristics	Annual Family Income							
	Less than $3,000		$3,000–$5,999		$6,000–7,999		$8,000 or more	
	Whites	Negroes	Whites	Negroes	Whites	Negroes	Whites	Negroes
Occupation								
Prof/semi-prof/tech	—	—	4	4	8	8	19	9
Prof/mgr/official	—	—	6	1	9	11	22	14
Clerical/sales/kindred	3	5	16	6	15	11	16	18
Craftsmen/foremen/kindred	6	3	24	25	34	8	26	23
Operatives/service	10	48	24	49	26	31	12	14
Farm/laborers	3	14	8	8	2	19	1	9
Retired	77	30	18	6	5	8	3	9
Others/not reported	1	—	—	1	1	4	1	4
Total	100	100	100	100	100	100	100	100
Education								
Less than high school	48	53	28	26	15	19	7	9
Some high school	22	23	26	30	23	23	15	9
High school grad.	18	17	26	31	34	31	27	14
Some college	9	3	15	9	18	8	25	32
College graduate	2	1	2	—	7	8	17	23
Graduate or prof. training	1	—	1	—	3	8	9	9
Not reported	—	3	2	4	—	3	—	4
Total	100	100	100	100	100	100	100	100
Sex—head of household								
Male	40	48	77	83	94	88	96	91
Female	60	52	23	17	6	12	4	9
Total	100	100	100	100	100	100	100	100
Age of household head								
Less than 24 years	3	9	14	6	9	4	2	9
25–34 years	1	10	16	27	31	31	21	32

35–44 years	7	26	16	32	27	31	33	27
45–54 years	10	19	19	22	18	22	26	23
55–64 years	18	20	18	13	11	8	15	9
65 years or older	60	14	16	–	4	–	3	–
Not reported	1	2	1	–	–	4	–	–
Total	100	100	100	100	100	100	100	100
Total living in household								
1	44	17	11	4	2	–	1	–
2	43	32	33	20	21	15	22	14
3	7	13	25	22	23	20	21	36
4	3	13	11	18	26	23	27	14
5–7	3	19	18	23	26	38	27	32
8 or more	–	6	2	13	2	4	2	4
Total	100	100	100	100	100	100	100	100
Total no. employed in household								
None	75	17	14	3	4	4	2	5
1	21	50	64	47	70	46	58	18
2	4	29	19	44	24	50	33	68
3	–	2	2	5	2	–	6	9
4 or more	–	–	1	1	–	–	1	–
Not reported	–	2	–	–	–	–	–	–
Total	100	100	100	100	100	100	100	100
Stage in life cycle								
Younger children only	3	12	18	14	25	11	12	23
Younger and older children	1	16	15	26	21	27	17	27
Older children only	9	23	16	35	29	35	36	18
None—head less than 45	3	15	10	10	7	8	7	9
None—head over 45	31	14	27	9	16	19	24	18
None—single head over 45	52	19	14	4	2	–	3	5
Not reported	1	1	–	2	–	–	1	–
Total	100	100	100	100	100	100	100	100

TABLE 3 Percentage of Negroes and Whites Who Had Recently Purchased or Who Owned Various Household Products

| | Annual Family Income | | | | | | | |
| | Less than $3,000 | | $3,000–5,999 | | $6,000–7,999 | | $8,000 or more | |
Products	Whites	Negroes	Whites	Negroes	Whites	Negroes	Whites	Negroes
Food Products[a]								
Butter	6.6	23.3	8.0	31.2	7.7	26.9	14.1	45.4
Margarine	58.3	61.6	63.6	72.7	69.8	57.7	69.5	81.8
Frozen vegetables[b]	30.5	31.4	28.0	50.6	39.6	34.6	47.1	54.6
Canned vegetables[c]	20.5	35.6	35.6	44.5	37.9	40.4	40.6	43.2
Dietary soft drinks	7.3	17.4	11.9	23.4	20.8	23.1	25.5	13.6
Nondietary soft drinks	26.5	60.5	55.5	71.4	62.4	23.1	67.1	45.4
Liquor								
All respondents[d]	15.2	26.7	29.7	39.0	39.3	46.2	56.5	54.6
Scotch[e]	3.3	9.3	4.2	22.1	7.7	34.6	19.7	27.3
Bourbon[e]	7.3	15.1	20.3	23.4	29.2	7.7	40.9	40.9

Personal Hygiene Products[f]							
Shampoo	42.4	41.9	59.3	52.0	74.5	65.4	72.6	50.0
Deodorant	39.7	65.1	56.8	79.2	74.5	92.3	76.6	81.8
Toothpaste	48.3	76.7	75.0	89.6	86.9	88.5	89.1	86.4
Mouthwash	43.7	61.6	58.5	75.3	56.7	88.5	63.5	86.4
Disinfectants	52.3	69.8	56.4	80.5	70.1	61.5	68.6	86.4
Home Appliances[g]							
Auto. washing machine	47.4	19.8	57.6	29.9	78.6	50.0	85.5	72.7
Auto. clothes dryer	12.6	5.8	16.5	7.8	34.2	15.4	54.9	27.3
Auto. dishwasher	2.0	–	5.5	–	14.1	3.8	33.8	–
B&W television	87.4	91.8	89.5	98.7	83.7[h]	97.9[h]	–	–
Color television	3.3	0.6	5.7	1.9	24.3[h]	6.2[h]	–	–
Home Ownership							
Own home	68.3	39.5	49.4	57.1	70.8	73.0	81.5	77.3

[a] Purchased within the past seven days.
[b] Includes all types of frozen vegetables.
[c] Includes canned corn, peas, green beans, and tomatoes.
[d] Percentage to total respondents purchasing some alcoholic beverages within past 12 months.
[e] Percentage of Scotch and Bourbon purchases among total respondents.
[f] Purchased within past 30 days.
[g] Percentage "having" in the home.
[h] Last two income classes were combined because of small number of respondents.

homes. Since even higher-income Negroes have had limited opportunity to purchase new homes, it should not be surprising that dishwasher ownership is so low.

Color television ownership was much higher among whites at every income level, although the reverse was true for black-and-white television. No simple explanation is available for this phenomenon, unless Negroes: (1) do not care much about color TV, or (2) cannot afford or are not willing to replace a working black-and-white TV for a new color set.

Consumption
Similarities
A major finding of this study was that, for many household products, consumption-pattern differences were small both in number and magnitude. In fact, many similarities existed. For example, purchases of margarine, frozen and canned vegetables, and bourbon were nearly identical for both groups. Even among those products for which group differences existed, there were similarities in overall consumption patterns (for example, high total usage of personal hygiene products in both groups) as well as expanding usage as income rose.

Discussion   Most of the earlier economic studies were concerned with comparing and analyzing aggregate consumption-pattern differences between Negroes and whites. They concluded that, essentially, the consumption differences were a reflection of the greater need of Negroes to save, rather than a result of cultural differences. This type of aggregate analysis, however, tends to conceal any internal variations in consumption which might exist within each group.

Although extensive consumption-pattern differences were found for a variety of household products, most of the discrepancies could be explained by income and/or other sociodemographic differentials between the two groups. Consider, for example, major home appliances, for which ownership appears to be primarily a function of income and a lack of proper utility connections. Even though a large portion of the consumption differences could be attributed to economic and sociodemographic considerations, usage patterns for several products—particularly Scotch, butter, soft drinks, and frozen foods—could not be so explained.

One reason behind the varying consumption patterns in the Negro market versus the white market is in the Negro's narrower spectrum of choice:

> The Negro has less selectivity in the purchase of a home, of a vacation, of travel, dining, entertainment, etc. This results in a greater expenditure per unit in the things that are available to him. Whites have more places to put their discretionary income while Negroes, even in the same income level as whites, use their dollars differently because of their narrower selectivity.[11]

Another reason for consumption differences is that minority groups today are apt to engage in compensatory consumption. Most Negro families have little opportunity to base their self-respect on occupational, educational, or other accomplishments. This poverty of opportunity tends to reinforce for these families the significance of consumption as at least one sphere in which they can make progress toward the American dream of success. Appliances, automobiles, and a home of their own can become compensations for blocked social mobility.[12] Bullock agrees and notes that "the main criterion for determining social class in many urban Negro communities of the South is overt consumption rather than wealth, family background, or church affiliation." [13] Similarly, Negroes who are insecure in their status or who believe their status is not widely accepted may participate in conspicuous consumption. "For instance," according to Broom and Glenn, "those who have recently improved their economic standing may buy conspicuously expensive items to communicate the fact that they have 'arrived.' " [14]

Because material goods have such an important symbolic role in American society, their acquisition symbolizes to the Negro his achievement of full status. Yet, this often creates a dilemma for the Negro consumer: whether to strive against odds for middle-class values, as reflected in material goods, or to give in and live for the moment.[15]

Summary and Implications   A probability sample of 1,335 whites and 211 Negroes was interviewed in Houston, Texas, to determine if, and to what extent, consumption patterns varied for a selected list of household products. The results for both groups were broken down and analyzed across four income categories. Sample variations for other sociodemographic characteristics were noted and utilized in explaining the resulting product-usage differences.

For the five product categories evaluated—food, soft drinks, liquor, personal hygiene products, and major home appliances—variations in consumption were found between Negroes and whites. A substantial portion of these differences, however, were explainable more in terms of income or sociodemographic variations than by purely "racial" influences. The evidence, in fact, disclosed as many similarities as differences in consumption patterns. There were, however, certain products for which unexplained differences in consumption patterns still existed between Negroes and whites even after an attempt was made to separate out the influence of income and other sociodemographic factors. Two such examples were butter and Scotch. No economically "rational" explanation exists why Negroes at every income level consume more of these products than do whites. The two most likely reasons put forth by this and other studies are compensatory consumption and status or conspicuous consumption. Unfortunately, too few products were studied to ascertain accurately which types of people or products would most likely be subject to these influences.

In conclusion, it can be said from a businessman's point of view that a

Negro market does exist, not so much identifiable by color as by patterns of consumption. Marketers who assume that product buying in Negro households is roughly a match for that in white families of similar economic circumstances are far from correct. A combination of societal constraints; cultural traditions; and differences in values, preferences, and psychological needs have led Negroes not only to spend a larger proportion of their incomes on food, drink, clothing, and home entertainment than do whites, but also to vary their expenditures across different products and, probably, brands compared with whites.[16] However, as the Negro continues to climb the economic and social ladder, some of these patterns of consumption will undoubtedly change, as the more prosperous persons raise their sights from compensatory spending to financing nice homes, education, medical care, and travel. In other words, it is likely that a smaller percentage of the Negro's income will be channeled into traditionally popular product categories—food, clothing, liquor, and entertainment—while there will be an increase in forms of consumption which heretofore have been either unattainable or unwanted. This means that opportunities will continue to expand very rapidly for companies willing to cultivate the Negro as a market. If this is to be, then marketing must keep up with the changes occurring inside and outside this market.

NOTES

1. See T. F. Pettigrew, *A Profile of the American Negro* (Princeton, N.J.: D. Van Nostrand Company, 1964); Talcott Parsons and K. B. Clark, eds., *The American Negro* (Boston, Mass.: Houghton-Mifflin Company, 1966); Henry Bullock, "Consumer Motivations in Black and White," *Harvard Business Review* (May–June, July–Aug., 1961), pp. 89–104, 110–124; L. E. Black, "The Negro Market," *Sales Management*, 91 (Oct. 4, 1963), pp. 42–47; Raymond Bauer *et al.*, "The Marketing Dilemma of Negroes," *Journal of Marketing*, 29 (July, 1965), pp. 1–6; and Leonard Broom and Norval D. Glenn, *Transformation of the Negro American* (New York: Harper & Row, 1965).

2. U.S., Bureau of the Census, *Current Population Reports*, Series P-60, No. 53, "Income in 1966 of Families and Persons in the U.S.," (Washington, D.C.: U.S. Government Printing Office, 1967), p. 19.

3. Horst Mendershausen, "Differences in Family Savings between Cities of Different Size and Location, Whites and Negroes," *Review of Economic Statistics*, 22 (Aug., 1940), pp. 122–137; Dorothy Brady and Rose Friedman, "Savings and Income Distribution," *Studies in Income and Wealth*, 10 (New York: National Bureau of Economic Research, 1947), pp. 247–265; J. Duesenberry, *Income, Saving and the Theory of Consumer Behavior* (Cambridge, Mass.: Harvard University Press, 1949); Marcus Alexis, "Some Negro-White Differences in Consumption," *American Journal of Economics and Sociology* (Jan., 1962), pp. 11–28.

4. Alexis, *ibid.*, p. 11.

5. At least one writer argues very strongly that most studies to date have de-emphasized the consideration that many factors other than race influence the determination of consumption patterns. In fact, he con-

cludes that because of the number of uncontrolled variables, "the concept of race as a factor in the statistical analyses of group economic behavior . . . has no more validity than lefthandedness, eye pigmentation, or height." B. E. Sawyer, "An Examination of Race as a Factor in Negro-White Consumption Patterns," *The Review of Economics and Statistics,* 44 (May, 1962), p. 220.

6. L. R. Klein and H. W. Mooney, "Negro-White Savings Differentials and the Consumption Function Problem," *Econometrics* (July, 1953), p. 455.

7. Pilot Study of FACT, Arrowhead Study No. 4 (New York: Advertising Research Foundation, Inc., 1968).

8. Among other possible explanations, two stand out as likely sources of influence. The first is "status." Bauer, in a recent study, stated that Negroes are extremely interested in quality and are "even more concerned with the symbolic value of goods than are whites." (Bauer, "Marketing Dilemma," p. 2.) The possibility exists, therefore, that a certain amount of status usually is associated with highly conspicuous goods—clothing and automobiles. A more likely explanation is that Negroes are compensating for their narrower spectrum of choice relative to potential uses of their income. In other words, since the Negro has less selectivity in the purchase of a home, of a vacation, etc., he spends more per item on the things that are available to him.

9. "The Negro Market, Accent on Quality," *Media-scope* (April, 1964), p. 77.

10. Bauer, "Marketing Dilemma," p. 3.

11. "Is There Really a Negro Market?," *Marketing Insights,* Jan. 29, 1968, p. 14.

12. David Caplovitz, *The Poor Pay More* (New York: The Free Press, 1963), pp. 12–13, 181.

13. H. A. Bullock, *Pathways to the Houston Negro Market* (Ann Arbor, Mich.: Edwards Brothers Publishing Co., 1957), p. 190.

14. Broom and Glenn, *Transformation,* pp. 28–29.

15. Bauer, "Marketing Dilemma," p. 3.

16. Marketers should keep in mind, however, that the indications in this study are that the Negro market is not completely homogeneous. Even as Negroes at the top income levels find the lines separating them from the rest of America becoming less of a barrier, those at the bottom income level still find themselves essentially isolated from their total environment. As a result, there has been increasing economic and cultural stratification within the Negro community which, among other things, has led to internal consumption-pattern variations.

33 Better Deal
for Ghetto Shoppers   Frederick D. Sturdivant

A good deal of thought has been given to the question "How can we solve the retailing problems of the ghetto?" One answer lies in the realm of economics; we must make it *worthwhile* for retailers to operate efficiently. This means that national or regional firms must be induced to compete with the "mom and pop" stores that are so ubiquitous in poor areas, insurance coverage against riot damage must be provided, managerial training must be instituted, and so forth.

This paper, by Frederick Sturdivant, provides a solution to the problem of the ghetto marketers' high entrepreneurial risk and at the same time reviews some of the problems and practices of retailers who operate in economically depressed areas.

Over a period of two years, more than 2,000 interviews were held with consumers and merchants in these two poverty areas,[1] numerous shopping forays were conducted, and price-quality comparisons were made with stores serving the more prosperous sections of Los Angeles and surrounding communities. Although there were a number of interesting differences between the findings in the two areas (the differences were based for the most part on cultural factors), the evidence points to two basic flaws in local retailing which were present in each of the areas:

1. The prevalence of small, inefficient, uneconomical units.
2. A tendency on the part of many stores to prey on an undereducated and relatively immobile population with high-pressure, unethical methods.

These findings, I believe, apply rather generally to the retail segments serving disadvantaged areas in U.S. cities. Let us look at each of them in more detail.

Inefficient "Moms and Pops" One of the cruelest ironies of our economic system is that the disadvantaged are generally served by the least efficient segments of the business community. The spacious, well-stocked, and efficiently managed stores characteristic of America's highly advanced

Reprinted from Frederick D. Sturdivant, "Better Deal for Ghetto Shoppers", *Harvard Business Review* (March–April, 1968), Vol. 46, No. 2, pp. 130–139, *passim*, by permission of the publisher. © 1968 by the President and Fellows of Harvard College; all rights reserved.

distribution system are rarely present in the ghetto. The marvels of mass merchandising and its benefits for consumers normally are not shared with the low-income families. Instead, their shopping districts are dotted with small, inefficient "mom and pop" establishments more closely related to stores in underdeveloped countries than to the sophisticated network of retail institutions dominant in most of the U.S. economy.

With the exception of one outdated supermarket, no national or regional retailing firms were represented on the main street of Watts before the 1965 riots. Following the riots, when 103rd Street was dubbed "Charcoal Alley," not even that lone supermarket remained. On Brooklyn Avenue, the heart of the poorest section in east Los Angeles, one found such establishments as Factory Outlet Shoes, Nat's Clothing, Cruz Used Furniture, Villa Real Drugs, and Chelos Market, ranging in size from 315 square feet to 600 square feet. Of the 175 stores in the shopping district (this figure excluded service stations), only 5 were members of chain organizations, and 2 of these firms traced their origins back to a time when the neighborhood was a middle-class district.

Lacking economies of scale and the advantage of trained management, the "moms and pops" muddle through from day to day and, in the process, contribute to the oppressive atmosphere of such neighborhoods. Their customers generally pay higher prices, receive lower-quality merchandise, and shop in shabby, deteriorating facilities.

Inflated Prices   The most controversial of these conditions is pricing. The phrase,
and . . .   "the poor pay more," was popularized by Columbia University
                       sociologist David Caplovitz's widely read book with that title.[2]
Unfortunately, in addition to being an eye-catching title, it describes reality. While the small, owner-operated stores do not have a monopoly on high prices in the ghetto, they contribute significantly to the inflated price levels. Consumers in Watts, for example, can expect to pay from 7% to 21% more for a market basket of 30 items if they shop for groceries in one of the small local stores than would a family shopping in a supermarket in affluent Beverly Hills. Similar or even greater price differentials prevail in most merchandise categories.

Comparative pricing analyses of the disadvantaged areas and the more prosperous sections in a city are very difficult to make because of quality differences. When national brands are carried by a ghetto appliance dealer, for example, he generally stocks only the lower end of the line. Retailers in higher income areas usually concentrate on the middle and upper price ranges of the product line. Furthermore, off-brand merchandise tends to make up a substantial part of the ghetto dealer's line. Since these lines are not carried in other areas, direct price comparisons are impossible. In food stores, the problem is particularly acute with respect to meat and produce items. Commercial grades of meat are generally carried by ghetto stores, and visual comparisons reveal major qualitative differences in the produce carried, but precise measurements of these quality distinctions are impossible.

· · ·

Parasitic   While the deteriorated condition of shopping facilities obviously
Merchants   does little to attract shoppers from outside the area, the ghettos
                       do act as magnets for high-pressure and unethical merchandisers
who become parasites on the neighborhoods. Take New York, for example.
Because of the predominance of parasitic merchants in the ghettos of Manhattan, Caplovitz describes business communities there as "deviant" market systems "in which unethical and illegal practices abound." [3]

TABLE 1   Ghetto Shoppers Pay More for Appliances

	Price		
Product	Watts Area	East L.A. Area	Control Area
1. Zenith portable TV (X1910)	$170	—	$130
2. Olympic portable TV (9P46)	$270	$230	—
3. RCA portable TV (AH0668)	$148	—	$115
4. Zenith portable TV (X2014)	—	$208	$140
5. Emerson portable TV (19P32)	$210	$200	$170
6. Olympic color console TV (CC337A)	—	$700	$630
7. Zenith clock radio (X164)	—	$42	$19
8. Eureka vacuum (745a)	—	$35	$30
9. Fun Fare by Brown (36 in. free standing gas range)	—	$200	$110

Note: Prices for items 1–4 are averages computed from the shopping experiences of three couples (Mexican-American, Negro, and Anglo-White) in three stores in each of the three areas. The three couples had nearly identical "credit profiles" based on typical disadvantaged family characteristics. The stores located in the Mexican-American and Watts areas were selected on the basis of shopping patterns derived from extensive interviews in the areas.

Items 5–9 are the only prices obtainable on a 24-item shopping list. One low-income Anglo-White couple shopped 24 randomly selected stores in the disadvantaged areas.

All prices are rounded.

The parasitic merchant usually deals in hard goods and emphasizes "easy credit." He stocks his store with off-brand merchandise, uses bait-switch advertising, offers low down payments and small installments, employs salesmen who are proficient at closing often and fast, and marks up his merchandise generously enough to assure himself of a very good return for his effort. Again, direct price comparisons are difficult because of brand differences, but *Exhibit I* reflects the higher prices paid by ghetto shoppers compared with store prices in a middle- to lower-middle class suburb of Los Angeles.

Data gathered on markups further confirm the presence of exploitation. The major furniture store serving the Watts area and its unaffiliated counterpart in east Los Angeles both carried Olympic television model 9P46. This model wholesales for $104. The retail price in the Watts area store was $270, a markup of 160%, and $229.95 in east Los Angeles, a markup of 121%. The latter store also carried a Zenith model number X1917 priced at $269.95, or 114% above the wholesale price of $126.

Are such substantial markups justified because of the higher risks associated with doing business in a ghetto? It would seem that such risks are more than offset by the interest charges on the installment contract. The rates are highly volatile, but never low. A Mexican-American couple and a Negro couple with virtually the same "credit profile" shopped a number of furniture and appliance stores in the two disadvantaged areas as well as stores in the middle-class control area. An "easy payment" establishment serving south central Los Angeles applied the same high-pressure tactics to both couples, who shopped for the same television set. The retailer charged the Negro couple 49% interest on an 18-month contract, while the Mexican-American couple really received "easy terms"—82% interest for 18 months!

Charges of this magnitude go well beyond any question of ethics; they are clearly illegal. In California the Unruh Retail Installment Sales Act sets the maximum rate a dealer may charge on time contracts. For most installment contracts under $1,000, the maximum service charge rate is ⅚ of 1% of the original unpaid balance multiplied by the number of months in the contract. Accordingly, the legal rate for the television set selected by the two couples was 15%.

While it is true that most ghetto merchants do not exceed the legal limits, their customers still pay higher credit charges because of the inflated selling prices on which the interest is computed.

How They Get   Parasitic merchants are attracted to disadvantaged areas of the
Away with It   cities by the presence of ill-informed and generally immobile
     consumers. Operating from ghetto stores or as door-to-door credit salesmen, these merchants deal with consumers who have little understanding of contracts or even of the concept of interest. Given their low-income status, one dollar down and one dollar a week sounds to the buyer like a pretty good deal. The merchants are not at all reluctant to pile their good deals on their customer with the prospect of repossessions and garnishments.

Comparative shopping outside his own neighborhood would, of course, provide a ghetto resident with a vivid demonstration of the disadvantages of trading with the local merchants. Unfortunately, the idea of comparing prices and credit terms is little understood in the ghetto. And for those residents who can appreciate the advantages of comparative shopping, transportation is often a barrier. In Watts, less than half of the households studied had automobiles. The public transportation facilities, which are inadequate at best throughout the city of Los Angeles, are archaic. Infrequently scheduled, time-consuming, and expensive bus services are of little value to the area's shoppers.

In east Los Angeles, the Mexican-Americans have greater mobility; 73% of the households studied had an automobile, and bus services were better than in Watts. The Mexican-Americans also have relative proximity to modern shopping facilities. However, there are strong cultural ties that encourage residents to forgo shopping advantages offered in other areas. They choose, in effect, to be reinforced continually in the existing cultural setting by frequenting stores in the disadvantaged area where Spanish is spoken. Whether for reasons of transportation problems or self-imposed cultural isolation, the local merchant enjoys a largely captive market.

Shunning Depressed Areas   Not all merchants in disadvantaged areas are there for the purpose of exacting all they can from a neighborhood of undereducated and poor consumers. As noted before, many of the small shops offer their customers higher prices and lower quality because of inefficiency, not by design. The great villain, say the retailers, is the cost of doing business in disadvantaged areas. For example, it is said that small merchants normally cannot afford insurance protection. Of the merchants interviewed in Watts, fewer than 10% had insurance before the riots. Retailers in slum areas have always paid higher insurance rates. According to California's insurance commissioner, rate increases of 300% following the riots were not uncommon. In this respect, the riots throughout the country have only magnified the problem of good retail service, not relieved it.

Since so few small merchants attempt to insure their businesses, the major effect of the abnormally high rates is to deter larger organizations from investing in ghetto areas. An executive responsible for corporate planning for a retail chain would be hard pressed to justify building a unit in Watts or east Los Angeles when so many opportunities and excellent sites are available in fast growing and "safe" Orange County (in the Los Angeles area). A parallel could be drawn with building in the South Side of Chicago as opposed to the prosperous and rapidly expanding suburbs on the North Shore, or in virtually any central city slum area contrasted with the same city's suburbs. Large retailers not only are frightened away by insurance costs, but also point to personnel problems, vandalism, and alleged higher incidences of shoplifting in disadvantaged districts.

This is not to suggest that there are not profits to be made in such areas. Trade sources, especially in the supermarket industry, have pointed to unique opportunities in low-income neighborhoods.[4] The managements of supermarket chains such as Hillman's in Chicago and ABC Markets in Los Angeles admit that, while there are unique merchandising problems associated with doing business in depressed areas, their profit return has been quite satisfactory. It might also be noted that companies that do a conscientious job of serving the needs of low-income consumers are highly regarded. For instance, interviewees in Watts were virtually unanimous in their praise for ABC Markets. Perhaps the most dramatic affirmation of the chain's position in the community came during the riots: not one of the company's three units in the area was disturbed during the week-long riots.

My interviews with executives of Sears, Roebuck and Co. and J. C. Penney indicate that these companies have been highly successful in adapting to changing conditions in transitional areas. Those of their stores located in declining neighborhoods have altered their merchandising programs and the composition of their work forces to adjust to the changing nature of the market area. The result has been profits for both firms.

Yet, in most cases, such opportunities have not been sought out by large retailers, but stumbled on; they have been happily discovered by older stores trying to readapt themselves in areas where the racial and economic makeup is changing. New stores are built only in trading areas where the more traditional competitive challenges are to be found. As one executive said, "Our target is the mass market, and we generally ignore the upper 10% and the lower 15% to 20% of the market." The upper 10%, of course, can be assured that Saks Fifth Avenue, Brooks Brothers, and a host of other such firms stand ready to meet their needs. The poor, however, are left with "moms and pops" and the easy-credit merchants.

A Workable Solution   Most critics of business-consumer relations in disadvantaged areas have called for legislation designed to protect consumers and for consumer education programs. Indeed, laws designed to protect consumers from hidden and inflated interest charges and other forms of unethical merchandising should be passed and vigorously enforced. Consumer economics should be a part of elementary and secondary school curricula, and adult education programs should be available in disadvantaged areas. However, these approaches are hardly revolutionary, and they hold little promise of producing dramatic changes in the economic condition of the disadvantaged.

A crucial point seems to have been largely ignored by the critics and in the various bills introduced in the state legislatures and in Congress. This is the difficulty of improvement so long as the retailing segments of depressed areas are dominated by uneconomically small stores—by what I call an "atomistic" structure. Indeed, many legislators seem eager to perpetuate the system by calling for expanded activities by the Small Business Administration in offering assistance to more small firms that do business in the ghettos. Another common suggestion is for the federal government to offer low-cost insurance protection to these firms. This proposal, too, may do more to aggravate than relieve. If the plight of the ghetto consumer is to be dramatically relieved, this will not come about through measures designed to multiply the number of inefficient retailers serving these people.

Real progress will come only if we can find some way to extend into the ghettos the highly advanced, competitive retailing system that has so successfully served other sectors of the economy. To make this advance possible, we must remove the economic barriers that restrict entry by progressive retailers, for stores are managed by businessmen, not social workers.

How can these barriers be removed?

Investment Guarantee Plan   Since shortly after the close of World War II, the federal government has had a program designed to eliminate certain barriers to investment by U.S. corporations in underdeveloped countries. In effect, the government has said that it is in the best interest of the United States if our business assists in the economic development of certain foreign countries. In a number of Latin American countries, for instance, the program has protected U.S. capital against loss through riots or expropriation. The investment guarantee program does not assure U.S. firms of a profit; that challenge rests with management. But companies are protected against the abnormal risks associated with building facilities in underdeveloped countries. If a guarantee program can stimulate investment in Colombia, why not in Watts or Harlem?

I propose a program, to be administered by the Department of Commerce, under which potential retail investors would be offered investment guarantees for building (or buying) a store in areas designated as "disadvantaged." A contract between the retail firm and the Commerce Department would guarantee the company full reimbursement for physical losses resulting from looting, burning, or other damages caused by civil disorders as well as from the usual hazards of natural disasters. In addition, the contract would call for compensation for operating losses sustained during periods of civil unrest in the area.

To illustrate: A Montgomery Ward store established in the heart of Watts would, under this program, be insured for the book value of the establishment against damages caused by natural or human events. If the firm emerged from a period of rioting without suffering any physical damages, but was forced to cease operations during the period of the riots, Montgomery Ward would be compensated for operating losses resulting from the forced closure.

COSTS AND RESTRICTIONS: The costs to a company for an investment guarantee would be minimal in terms of both financial outlay and loss of managerial autonomy. An annual fee of 0.5% of the amount of insured assets would be charged. There is no actuarial basis for this rate; rather, the fees are charged to cover the costs of administering the program and building a reserve against possible claims.

There would be no restriction on either the size of the investment or the term of the guarantee contract. The contract would be terminated by the government only if the firm violated the terms of the agreement or if the economic character of the area improved to the point that it was no longer classified as disadvantaged.

In addition to paying annual premiums, the participating companies would be required to conform to state and local laws designed to protect consumers (or minimum federal standards where local legislation is not in effect). A participating retailer found guilty of violating state law regarding, let us say, installment charges, would have his contract terminated.

In effect, the ethical merchandiser would find no restrictions on his usual managerial freedom. So long as he abided by the law, his investment would be protected, and he would have complete freedom in selecting his merchandise, setting prices, advertising, and the other areas of managerial strategy.

Enlarged
Investment
Credit

The guarantee program would offer the manager maximum discretion, but it would not assure him of a profit. The guarantee phase of the program merely attempts to place the ghetto on a par with nonghetto areas with respect to investment risk. The final barrier, the high costs associated with doing business in such areas, would have to be offset by offering businesses enlarged investment credits. Credits of perhaps 10% (as compared to the usual 7% under other programs) could be offered as an inducement to outside retailers. Firms participating in the guarantee program would be eligible for such investment credits on all facilities constructed in disadvantaged areas.

The more generous investment credits would serve as a source of encouragement not only for building new facilities, but also for expanding and modernizing older stores that had been allowed to decline. For example, the Sears Roebuck and Penney stores located (as earlier mentioned) in transitional and declining areas would be likely targets for physical improvements.

Key to
Transformation

Perhaps the most important characteristic of the investment guarantee and credit program is the nature of the relationship that would exist between the government and the business community. The government is cast in the role of the stimulator or enabler without becoming involved in the management of the private company. The program is also flexible in that incentives could be increased or lowered as conditions warrant. If the investment credits should fail to provide a sufficient stimulus, additional incentives in the form of lower corporate income tax rates could be added. On the other hand, as an area becomes increasingly attractive as a retail location, the incentives could be reduced or eliminated.

If implemented with vigor and imagination, this program could lead to a dramatic transformation of the retail segment serving ghetto areas. While size restrictions would not be imposed, the provisions of the program would be most attractive to larger retail organizations. Thus, the "atomistic" structure of the retail community would undergo major change as the marginal retailers face competition with efficient mass distributors. The parasitic merchants would also face a bleak future. The study in Los Angeles revealed no instance in which a major retail firm was guilty of discriminatory pricing or inflated credit charges. In addition, the agency administering the investment program could make periodic studies of the practices of participating firms, and use these investigations to prod companies, if necessary, to assure their customers of equitable treatment.

．　　　．　　　．

NOTES

1. A Negro area in Los Angeles (Watts) and a Mexican-American area in east Los Angeles.
2. New York, The Free Press, 1963.
3. *Ibid.,* p. 180.
4. See, for example, "Supermarkets in Urban Areas," *Food Topics,* February, 1967, pp. 10–22.

34 Questions to Improve Marketing Services in Low-Income Areas

U.S. Department of Commerce

Check lists can serve a very valuable purpose by providing for the consideration of all vital factors whenever certain decisions have to be made. Their use to low-income consumers is no exception, as the following check list shows. Its guidelines were prepared by a Task Force of the National Marketing Committee to assist those interested in improving marketing services to the people living in low-income areas.

1. Will there be adequate demand for the goods or services which will be made available to low-income consumers?

    Is there a realistic expectation that what is offered will fit the desires of the people to whom it is offered?

2. Will low-income consumers have a better range of choice in facilities, goods and services?

    Will they have more real alternatives to choose among? Will the probability be increased that they will find, and be able to afford, goods and services that truly fit their wants and needs?

3. Will low-income consumers get more for their money?

    It is alleged that the poor pay more for some types of products and services.

4. Will low-income consumers get more satisfaction from their marketing experiences?

    Consumer satisfaction does not depend solely on lower prices. Deeply-felt desires of low-income citizens are psychological and sociological as well as economic. Development of increased self-esteem, dignity and feelings of involvement with the local community and with society as a whole, which are sought and are needed, are influenced by the marketing facilities and services available to all consumers, including those in low-income areas.

Reprinted from the National Marketing Advisory Committee to the Secretary of Commerce, "Questions to Improve Marketing Services in Low-Income Areas," *Marketing Information Guide* (January 1970), pp. 18–19.

5. Will the people to be served be involved in the planning?

Experience has demonstrated the importance of participation by residents of low-income areas in the planning of marketing programs in their areas. This involvement can play an important role in overcoming suspicion as well as in properly designing the program to fit the community.

6. Will helpful marketing information be more available and be put to better use?

Given the limited resources of low-income consumers, it is especially important that they have, and use, adequate market information to get the most benefit from their expenditures. There is a need for programs which incorporate imaginative means of increasing low-income consumers' familiarity with, and use of, sound buying practices. The importance of genuine involvement of the consumers in these programs must be recognized. Just making information available is not enough.

7. Will unethical business practices be reduced?

Low-income consumers have been victimized by unethical, sometimes illegal, business practices. Examples are overcharging, underweighing, misrepresentation of quality or quantity, mislabeling, false and misleading advertising, and bait-and-switch advertising. Such practices have bad psychological, as well as economic, effects.

8. Will the physical facilities in low-income areas be improved?

Improving the quality of marketing facilities in low-income areas demands changes in appearance as well as in operation. While appearance changes may seem only superficial, they can affect the satisfaction consumers derive from their marketing experiences. They also can have a good effect on community pride. Further, the upgrading of commercial facilities in a locality often stimulates improvements in other facilities nearby.

9. Will the financial resources needed for marketing facilities in low-income areas be expanded?

Capital limitations have been a major problem restricting the improvement of marketing services in low-income areas. Programs are needed to attract investments which will help build the community, rather than merely offer a quick profit to the investor.

10. Will the drain of resources out of the low-income araes be reduced?

Money earned by low-income area residents often passes quickly into higher-income areas. Low-income communities can benefit from activities which increase the use of resources within those areas. Emphasis should be on positive programs to increase the circulation of money within such areas rather than on the erection of barriers which would make it more difficult for responsible outside businesses or individuals to provide services of value to the area residents.

11. Will improved use be made of existing facilities?

Quicker results often can be obtained by expanding or improving established facilities than by creating new facilities. The use of existing facilities also may enhance the sense of participation of residents of the area and increase their acceptance of new marketing services.

12. Will employment and job-training opportunities for residents of low-income areas be expanded?

Marketing activities which provide jobs for poverty-area residents and which require little or no extended training or remedial education have obvious merit. There may be even greater value in practical projects which provide opportunities for low-income citizens with adequate skills to assume managerial and enterpreneurial positions. In low-income areas, marketing programs, as well as others, should include specific, positive plans for at least some of the higher-level jobs associated with them to be filled by residents of the areas served.

13. Will needed managerial skills be provided?

The best looking store with the widest selection of merchandise will fail unless it is properly managed. Projects which do not provide for adequate management should be avoided.

14. Are the costs of operating in low-income areas being considered realistically?

Among the elements contributing to high cost and risk in low-income areas are a relatively small volume of purchases per shopper, the use of costly selling methods, expensive credit administration, high insurance costs, pilferage and damage. Programs and experiments aimed at cutting these costs are highly desirable. While such costs exist, they should be taken into consideration in planning new ventures in order to avoid failures which will result in a drain on the low-income areas rather than a contribution to them.

QUESTIONS FOR DISCUSSION

1. What demographic characteristics differentiate the poor from the affluent?
2. Do low-income families take advantage of consumer benefits available to the poor?
3. Are the poor more deliberate in making purchasing decisions?
4. Do low-income families try to get the best quality at the lowest price?
5. In what ways do the poor buy "unwisely"?
6. What consumption similarities and differences characterize Negro and white consumers? How do these characteristics change as the income of each group increases?
7. What do you think about the allegation that chain stores increase their prices and decrease the quality of their merchandise in poor neighborhoods?
8. What recommendations would you make to improve the market structure in poor neighborhoods? What can the federal government do to improve the market structure of poor neighborhoods? What can entrepreneurs do? What can the poor accomplish?
9. Do you think that store owners should be compensated for any losses caused by civil strife? If so, by whom? How?
10. Make a comparative shopping tour for several items and compare prices between low- and high-income neighborhoods.

SUGGESTED READINGS

Caplovitz, David, *The Poor Pay More* (New York: The Free Press of Glencoe, 1963).

Comparative Study: Food Prices and Quality Practices of Major Chains in the St. Louis, Missouri Metropolitan Area (St. Louis, Missouri: Better Business Bureau of Greater St. Louis, Inc., 1968).

"Consumer Credit and the Low Income Consumer", preliminary report prepared for the Urban Coalition by William G. Kaye & Associates, Rockville, Maryland, November, 1969.

Dixon, Donald F., and Daniel J. McLaughlin, Jr., "Do the Poor Really Pay More for Food?" *Business and Society* (Autumn, 1968), Vol. 9, No. 1, pp. 7–12.

Goodman, Charles S., "Whither the Marketing System in Low-Income Areas?" *Wharton Quarterly* (Spring, 1969), pp. 2–10.

Groom, Phyllis, "Prices in Poor Neighborhoods", *Monthly Labor Review* (October, 1966), Vol. 89, pp. 1085–1090.

Irealan, Lola M. (ed.), *Low-Income Life Styles* (Washington, D.C.: U.S. Department of Health, Education and Welfare, August, 1967), pp. vii +65.

Kassarjian, Harold H., "The Negro and American Advertising, 1946–1965", *Journal of Marketing Research* (February, 1969), Vol. 4, pp. 29–39.

Lavidge, Robert J., "The Ghetto Challenge", paper presented at the 14th Annual American Marketing Association Public Utilities Seminar, Detroit, Michigan, May 3, 1968, pp. 7–12.

Oladipupo, Raymond O., *How Distinct Is the Negro Market* (New York: Ogilvy & Mather, Inc., 1970).

Sturdivant, Frederick D., "Business and the Mexican-American Community", *California Management Review* (Spring, 1969), Vol. XI, No. 3, pp. 73–80.

———, *The Ghetto Marketplace* (New York: Free Press of Glencoe, 1969).

———, and Walter T. Wilhelm, "Poverty, Minorities, and Consumer Exploitation", *Social Science Quarterly* (December, 1968), Vol. 49, No. 3, pp. 643–650.

Taira, Koji, "Consumer Preferences, Poverty Norms, and Extent of Poverty", *Quarterly Review of Economics and Business* (Summer, 1969), Vol. 9, pp. 31–44.

U.S., Congress, House, Thirty-Eighth Report of the Committee on Government Operations, *Consumer Problems of the Poor: Supermarket Operations in Low-Income Areas and the Federal Response,* House of Representatives, H. Res. 1981, 90th Cong., 2d sess., August 7, 1968, pp. 7–8, 27–40.

U.S., Congress, House, *Economic Report on Food Chain Selling Practices in the District of Columbia and San Francisco,* House of Representatives, 91st Cong., 1st sess., July, 1968, pp. 1–12.

U.S., Department of Commerce, Business and Defense Services Administration, *Bibliography on Marketing to Low-Income Consumers* (Washington, D.C.: U.S. Government Printing Office, January, 1969).

section 10
salesmanship:
the social
and ethical
perspective

Two thousand years ago Roman jurists proclaimed *caveat emptor*—let the buyer beware! Since ancient times, in fact, the reputation of those who sell or trade goods has not been very good.

On the American scene the image of the salesman as a fast-talking, hard-pushing, not entirely scrupulous individual is strongly entrenched in our folklore, even though many individual salesmen do not conform to that stereotype. Salesmen are still being accused of deceiving or "high-pressuring" customers, especially in door-to-door selling to ultimate consumers. The charge is frequent enough to merit some attention when we are considering the social impact of marketing practices.

Obviously, most salesmen have some advantages when "confronting" the potential customer. In addition to having such personal characteristics as persistence, verbal ability, and aggressiveness, they come prepared with reasonably thorough knowledge of the product and frequently of human behavior as well. Pitted against this is the prospect's potent ability to say "no." The view of the sales interview as a contest or conflict is held by many. Needless to say, in a very large number of sales interviews, especially with executive, professional, or industrial buyers—the salesman offers real services to the potential buyer.

Essentially, most current complaints against salesmen originate with "direct" selling, that is, salesmen calling on or selling to final customers. In some communities "Green River" ordinances forbid door-to-door calls. Recent legislation also gives buyers in some states a "cooling off" period, usually 72 hours after signing contracts, during which the buyer can revoke the contract.

In this section we shall examine some of the evidence and concern that surround allegedly deceptive and high-pressure salesmanship.

35 The Salesman Isn't Dead— He's Different

Carl Rieser

The unfortunate stereotype of the salesman as a pathetic, servile, and conniving individual is far from realistic. In the following article—which is still quite accurate although written in 1962—Carl Rieser dispels some erroneous notions about this vital link in our marketing system.

There is no more abused figure in American life than the salesman. One group of critics scorns him for certain qualities that another group sneers at him for losing. To many novelists, playwrights, sociologists, college students, and many others, he is aggressively forcing on people goods that they don't want. He is the drummer, with a dubious set of social values—Willy Loman in the Arthur Miller play. The second group of critics, which includes the Secretary of Commerce and many business executives all over the U.S., charges the salesman with lacking good, old-fashioned, hard-hitting salesmanship. . . .

Both sets of critics are swatting at a target that doesn't matter much any more. The plain fact is that, as one Boston sales executive recently said, "The old drummer type of salesman has gone by the board." Nor are his talents especially needed in today's economy. To be sure, there are plenty of aggressive, hard-hitting salesmen still around, and there will always be a place for their brand of selling. But this kind of man is no longer the archetype.

From bits and pieces of evidence in all sectors of U.S. business, it is now possible to discern the emergence of a new dominant type, a man with a softer touch and greater breadth, a new kind of man to do a new—much more significant—kind of job. Whereas the old-time salesman devoted himself primarily to pushing a product, or a line of products, the new-era salesman is involved with the whole distribution pipeline, beginning with the tailoring of products to the customer's desire and extending through their promotion and advertising to final delivery to the ultimate consumer.

Carl Rieser, "The Salesman Isn't Dead—He's Different", *Fortune*, Vol. 66, No. 5 (November, 1962), pp. 124–127.

The salesman has been cast in his new role by "the marketing concept," a term that originated at General Electric around 1950 and has gained wide currency recently. It means essentially that companies are orienting their organization and effort toward the market, toward the ever changing needs of the customer, and the ever shifting calculations of their own production costs and opportunities. The emphasis is less concentrated on the isolated point-of-sale; it is spread forward, into the buyer's operations, and backward into the seller's operations. The profound consequences of this trend have been suggested by Orm Henning, marketing manager of industrial products at Texas Instruments:

"One should remind oneself that selling is only part of marketing—particularly in the scientific-industrial world. Marketing is communicating back to your factory your individual customer's needs and particular problems. When you realize and practice this, you open an entirely new vista in the area of sales. You cannot afford to sell a product, a static product—not in our business."

.   .   .

The great change in selling affects practically all industries and all kinds of goods, whether they are what the marketing profession calls "pull-through" or "push-through" products. Pull-through refers generally to mass-produced consumer items, where a sort of siphon is already working. Pull-through products and services are presold by the manufacturer to the final consumer by mass advertising and promotion, which in effect creates a demand that almost literally pulls the goods through the distribution pipeline. Push-through products are wholly new consumer goods for which the siphon has not yet begun to work or, more commonly, they are industrial materials and equipment. Since the latter are usually highly technical in nature, they must be explained to the buyer and they require more personal selling so as to generate in the buyer the idea that he needs the product.

The distinction between pull-through and push-through is becoming less important. The retailer now stocks Kleenex tissues, for example, because he is persuaded that Kimberly-Clark Corp. will maintain public recognition of the brand and will see to it that thousands of boxes are siphoned rapidly and profitably right through his warehouse and off his store shelves. The job of the Kimberly-Clark salesman is to service the account so that the buyer will keep buying. He expedites and consolidates the shipments, keeps track of the retailer's inventory, sees that the goods get the greatest display and promotion possible, keeps himself available in case of any trouble or emergency. The job of the man who sells computers is much the same. The computer is one element in a whole system of mechanical devices and programing techniques, which is sold on the basis of what the customer is persuaded it can do for him.

The salesman's responsibility becomes greater as technology advances and producers offer products of ever mounting complexity. "We are tending toward the marketing of systems and services," says James Jewell, marketing vice president of Westinghouse. "The customers want to buy greater production—not equipment. We take the full responsibility for engineering and installing, and we are moving further into servicing."

This orientation toward the customer's needs is pointed up in a recent book that has received wide attention in the trade—*Innovation in Marketing*, by Theodore Levitt, a management consultant and a member of the faculty of Harvard Business School. Levitt, who speaks for a new generation of believers in "the marketing concept," states flatly that "a strictly sales-oriented approach to doing business can be suicidal. The difference between selling and marketing is more than semantic. Selling focuses on the needs of the seller, marketing on the needs of the buyer. Selling is preoccupied with the seller's need to convert his product or service into cash; marketing with the idea of satisfying the needs of the customer by means of the product or service and by the whole cluster of customer-getting value satisfactions associated with creating, delivering, and finally consuming it."

In this quotation Levitt seems to be oversimplifying the contrast between selling and marketing. Any implication that "the marketing concept" isn't motivated by the seller's desire for profits is, of course, mistaken. While his motives remain the same, the seller now sees marketing as a more elaborate link between production and consumption, a link that has to be carefully constructed and maintained.

Two situations may illustrate the change. In the past, a factory would overproduce the market and unload on the sales force the responsibility for unloading the goods on the customers. In the other situation, the salesmen kept their volume up by selling those products in their line that were easiest to sell—even those that were the least profitable. The incidence of both these cases tends to be diminished by the new trend with its more delicate alignment of markets and production, and its careful analysis of product profitability. The salesman is less often stuck with the necessity of a fast, hard sell. But he is steadily pressed to make the sales where the profit lies.

•   •   •

The Mirror of the Markets   There is little doubt that the impact of "the marketing concept" has reduced the stature of the sales manager in scores of companies. He has lost his former autonomy and now reports to the marketing vice president rather than directly to the president. He has less say over such vital matters as pricing and credit policies. The sales force must fit its work into an over-all corporation marketing policy. Furthermore, over the decade, the autonomy of the sales manager has been further trimmed in many companies by the creation of the job of product manager, who has both line and staff authority for a given product or group of products and coordinates production with advertising, research, and field selling.

The marketing concept has had very decided and significant structural effects on sales forces. This can be seen very clearly at General Electric, father of the marketing concept. G.E.'s salesmen used to be essentially product specialists, each selling only the line of a specific manufacturing department, even though it went into a variety of markets. It took time for G.E. to orient its sales forces toward markets rather than products, but this process finally began seven years ago in the company's electrical-apparatus business. Instead of specializing in one product, e.g., cord sets, fan motors, push buttons, the salesman began selling a whole group of products to a particular market—for example, the air-conditioning industry. . . .

Recently, Westinghouse reorganized its entire 13,600-man field sales organization along somewhat similar lines, in accord with what the company calls the "province concept." The company wants to be represented wherever possible by a "Mr. Westinghouse" rather than by a confusing bevy of different salesmen from various production divisions. (Significantly, in reorganizing, Westinghouse also seized the opportunity to put more salesmen in jobs where they actually meet customers and eliminated virtually an entire "staff" layer of some 104 sales managers who never called on customers.)

The same kind of reorganization has gone on in scores of companies in such diverse fields as motor trucks and optical equipment. At American Optical Co., for example, salesmen who used to be product specialists now sell a line that includes every piece of furniture and equipment for the doctor's office, from lenses to tables.

Thus the kind of man needed for this new kind of sales job has to be a generalist. The trend is away from the "sales engineer," the technically trained salesman, of a few years ago. His successor is a man capable of absorbing stacks of information churned out by the marketing department, and of applying it to his customers' problems. He goes forth armed with a tremendous amount of data on his customers' needs, their products, their corporate organizations, and their supply and delivery schedules.

He is also a man with more executive ability than the salesman of yesterday. A Boston sales manager describes the new salesmen as simply "businessmen who travel." One Milwaukee executive notes that increasingly the new salesman is being given the authority and stature to make important decisions in the field without having to go back to corporate headquarters for an O.K. General Foods has adopted a new title of prestige for its senior salesmen, each of whom lives with one food-chain customer and attends to its needs. They are called "account executives" and they command the services of junior salesmen, who do the routine housekeeping chores of servicing the customers' stores.

In the new order of things there is obviously still a need for hard-selling, aggressive salesmen to open up new accounts, to introduce new and untried products, to sell the wares of new companies that have no national reputation. Since the service-oriented sales staff has turned away from this kind of pioneering effort, the door has been opened to a new kind of specialist, typified by a New York firm called the George N. Kahn Co. This company provides a crew of highly aggressive young salesmen who open up new territories for companies that don't want to retrain their own sales forces for such sporadically necessary missions. (Kahn is not a manufacturer's representative; it works on a flat-fee basis rather than a commission and, after pioneering the sale of a product, expects that the manufacturer will take it back for handling by his own sales staff.) There is now some thought in the top management of a number of companies that the way to deal with this basic problem is to set up special sections of sales staffs with the specific function of going after new business. Thus what has been commonly thought of as the primary function of all salesmen is now becoming the specialty of a few.

The Service Troops
The new salesman has a tremendous advantage over his predecessors. Not only does he have access to much more information about his customers, but he is also backed up by formidable technical and other kinds of assistance. For example, in reshaping its inorganic-chemical sales recently, FMC Corp. (formerly Food Machinery & Chemical Corp.) has beefed up the number of its technical people directly behind the salesmen by some 20 per cent. The present ratio: one technical man to every four salesmen. The great pioneer in this development was du Pont, which years ago saw the close connection between selling and customer service. Today, at Chestnut Run, outside Wilmington, du Pont has an impressive $20-million, campus-like complex of laboratories and workshops, employing 1,700 scientists, technicians, and others devoted to providing sales literature, solving technical problems, providing all kinds of services for customers or potential buyers of du Pont products, and otherwise aiding the sales effort. Companies selling all kinds of goods have developed similar assistance, though, naturally, the more complex the technology, the more elaborate the technical backup.

The development of sophisticated electronic data-processing systems, which was described earlier in this series, is revolutionizing inventory handling, ordering, warehousing, and other physical aspects of marketing. This in turn, relieves the salesman of a great deal of detail that used to absorb valuable hours of his time—writing up orders and reports, checking whether goods are available and how soon they can be delivered, and performing other niggling drudgery.

At the same time, the computer also introduces an element of impersonality in the relations between a seller and a buyer. Much of today's ordering of goods and materials, from packaged foods to industrial chemicals, is done, as it were, by a computer, which tells the buyer when to reorder; the transaction is handled routinely and a salesman never enters into it. This disencumbering of the salesman releases him to function on a new level of performance, to use his time more creatively. At Allis-Chalmers, which has just set up a department of marketing, an executive says, "Now our salespeople won't get bogged down in a lot of detail that goes hand in hand with selling, like the preparation of presentations, charts, convention exhibits, and whatnot. We'll do all the work, including the training of salesmen, in cooperation with company divisions."

"You Lose One of the Big Babies . . ." The rise of the new salesman is the result of changes in the marketplace that have drastically altered the relationship of buyer to seller. One of the most significant developments has been the growing importance of the big customer. In almost every line of business, fewer and bigger customers are responsible for an increasingly large part of any given company's sales. Twenty-five years ago, when independent grocers were an important factor in food retailing, food processors did the bulk of their business with thousands upon thousands of chains and stores. Today, with the concentration of business in the hands of a relatively few big chains, some 300 buying offices throughout the U.S. account for 80 per cent of all food bought at wholesale. Preoccupation with the "key customer" affects every industry, from steel to office supplies. Sighs an officer of the Acme Chemical Co. in Milwaukee, "You lose one of the big babies and you're in trouble."

This whole trend is building up momentum as smaller buyers band together to increase their purchasing power and efficiency by buying cooperatively. It affects suppliers of school equipment, for example, because schools are consolidating on a county basis. Independent hardware stores and even hospitals are doing it.

How this has affected the food business has been fully explored in a new book with a provocative title, *The Vanishing Salesman*, by E. B. Weiss, a New York marketing specialist in the consumer-goods field. Actually, Weiss does not believe that the salesman is vanishing; his point is that the shift to the service-oriented sales function has so greatly altered the nature of personal selling that companies are faced with entirely new conditions in the hiring, training, and organization of salesmen. Weiss also notes that as retail food chains have become bigger and bigger, and their purchases have reached stupendous volume, the position of the individual buyer, once regarded as the salesman's opposite number, has greatly diminished. The buyer in a food chain used to be an important figure; he made the decisions on what the chain was going to buy. Now his power has been usurped by buying committees. The buyer has become merely a technician who interviews the salesmen from the food processor and passes on his findings to his superior. Says Weiss: "Members of the buying committee tend not to be buying specialists. Moreover, they make decisions covering the entire range of merchandise inventoried by the organization. Since they tend to be at executive levels considerably higher than that of the buyer who appears before them, they are more apt to depend on their own judgment than that of the buyer. And, by the same token, the buyer is not apt to put up much of a battle. . . . In buying committee sessions, it is presumably the majority that rules. But since it is traditional in large organizations for so many committee members to vote with the head of the table, the majority rule prevails more in theory than in fact."

So the man that the seller must get to is the man at the head of the table. And this is true not only in the food field. Throughout U.S. industry, key buying power has steadily risen up through the corporate structure to higher echelons of authority. In industrial selling, an increasing number of purchasing decisions tend to involve bigger and bigger outlays of capital. In large part this is the result of the rise of what is now commonly called *systems selling*. Instead of buying components from many suppliers, a company often buys a whole integrated system, be it a system for heating and air conditioning, protecting a plant from theft and fire, automating a production line, or handling materials. As technology becomes more complex, users, intent on eliminating technical headaches, are ever more anxious to buy such systems, while suppliers, intent on greater profit, are ever more anxious to design and sell a whole package. Naturally, the final approval for such an expenditure or commitment moves up the line, from the plant superintendent or manager, to the corporate controller or treasurer, perhaps all the way to the president or board chairman.

"The President's Project" Not only has this created the need for salesmen with sufficient stature to talk to the customer's top management, but it has also drawn top executives more directly into the selling act. In company after company, higher officials now make a very determined effort to get out in the field and call on the big customers, and even to do considerable pioneer work with potential customers. This kind of thing, of course, is not new. Many companies were built by star salesmen at the top, a very good example being the late Thomas J. Watson Sr. at I.B.M. ("What my father used to do when people began to talk about the great complexity of the products," says Tom Watson Jr., the present head of the company, "would be to sweep his hand and say, 'It's all so simple. All it does is add, subtract, and multiply!' ") And in industries where enormous capital investment is required, such as the utility business, intimate and continued contact between seller and buyer at a high level has always been important. But now personal selling by top executives is becoming much more common. Raytheon, for example, has divided up its list of big customers among managers and officers of the company, and assigned each the responsibility of keeping in touch with a few accounts, with a view to bolstering the salesman's efforts.

General Foods was one of the pioneers in this. When Charles Mortimer was president of the company, he started "The President's Project," a series of meetings with customers all over the country. "In the beginning the meetings started out 100 per cent social," explains Wayne Marks, now president of the company. "They were strictly for pleasure—and we invited more than one customer to a meeting. But we found that nothing *happened*. Except that we got acquainted. We didn't find out what to improve in our business operation. So the format was quickly changed."

Now Marks's office sets up his customer-visiting schedule at least a month in advance. The customer is requested to have all his key people at the meeting, and several weeks before the encounter, G.F. sends along a "questionnaire" to elicit comments on G.F.'s performance and suggestions for items to discuss. In the past eighteen months Marks, accompanied by a team of executives and salesmen, has visited fifty-four customers throughout the U.S.

Marks has found the customers "avid" for this kind of contact. Not only does G.F. come out of these encounters (some of them lasting for five or six hours over dinner and drinks) with a fuller idea of what it should be doing—but the customers learn a great deal about their own organizations that they weren't aware of. Says Marks: "Many a meeting, at the end the boss man will say, 'Why don't *we* go out and find out what's happening in our own stores?' At the end of a recent meeting the top man told me, 'I've been frank with you and told you what I don't like about your operations. Would you be willing to report back to us on what you think of us?' "

The "Sellingest" Firm   Personal selling is now a company-wide endeavor, and the contact with the customer takes place at many levels in an organized, formal way. The best illustration of how this has changed fundamentally the relations between buyer and seller is offered by National Cash Register, long known as perhaps the "sellingest" firm in the country. N.C.R.'s founder, the late John H. Patterson, has been called the father of many of the standard techniques of modern selling. He established the first formal training courses for salesmen, the first yearly sales quotas, the first guaranteed sales territories for salesmen, the first annual sales convention. Patterson's earlier sales methods were comparatively crude; cash registers were sold to storekeepers by appealing to their fear that dishonest clerks were pocketing money out of the till. But over the years the company refined its appeals, and forty years ago, when it began selling accounting machines, it even evolved a primitive kind of systems selling. But its big leap came about five years ago when the company introduced, somewhat belatedly as compared with the competition, its first electronic computer.

N.C.R. had to set up a whole new sales force for the computer, and in doing so it made a profound discovery: it was not easy to make a salesman of accounting machinery into a computer salesman. Says one N.C.R. senior salesman: "It was the death of salesmen like Willy Loman. At N.C.R. a few were left behind. They couldn't make the switch. It wasn't that they were too old—some were in their forties. But men's intellectual capabilities get set at various ages, and some *were* too old at that age." The company also found that it had to alter its time-honored compensation system. Normally, the N.C.R. salesman collects an advance that is charged against the commission he makes on his sales. Says marketing director Harry Keesecker, "Computer selling is still incentive selling, but due to the kind of product— sometimes the long time between sales—we have to compensate the salesmen by salary plus commission."

At the same time N.C.R. set up an elaborate organization to give the salesmen technical support. This now includes 325 mathematicians and technical people; the number has doubled in size in the past twelve months. They develop manuals and presentations, help the customer define his problems, train his computer operators for him, set up his E.D.P. system, and produce the programing for it. The support organization also trains the computer salesman, a departure for N.C.R., which years ago built its whole sales-training program around the use of experienced salesmen, borrowed from the field, as instructors. (The total computer sales and support staff numbers about 500 people, as against 2,100 in accounting machines, but the company is supplementing the small computer force by training as many of the accounting-machine men as possible to sell both kinds of equipment.)

The Willy Lomans Are No Longer Feasible
The difference between the old and new eras at N.C.R.—and in salesmanship in general—is dramatically illustrated by the story of how the company landed a rather sensational contract for the sale of a computer to the Dime Savings Bank of Brooklyn, New York, the country's second-largest mutual savings bank. The bank and the company had longstanding ties dating back to 1929, when the Dime bought its first N.C.R. posting machines for the tellers' windows. In subsequent decades the bank bought other N.C.R. equipment. In those years the chief link between the two was an N.C.R. salesman, Anthony de Florio, now district manager of sales for accounting and computer systems, and Karl Stad, who is now vice president of methods and systems at the Dime. The relationship was a cordial one, and N.C.R., which is mainly known for its experience in retailing and banking, was solidly in with the Dime.

In the late 1950's, however, there was a sudden change in the old easygoing ways. The bank decided, in 1957, that it was time to think about tying its entire bookkeeping operations into a computer to keep up with its bounding growth, and Stad was told to set up a task force to study the entire field and to recommend the "ideal" system. De Florio observes, "This was the beginning of group selling. The salesman had to understand the problems and systems of the customer. The staff at the bank had to define what was required. And we at N.C.R. had to be sure that the bank wasn't running away from us in know-how." (To N.C.R., as to many another company, the growing sophistication of the buyer has become an important factor to reckon with.) N.C.R. also had to reckon with competition; every other computer manufacturer came in for the kill at Dime. For the next two years Stad and his team studied the field and enlarged their expertise. By 1959 they had winnowed the choice down to four systems, including N.C.R.'s, and asked the competitors for feasibility studies. (Says de Florio: "By the time you get to feasibility studies, the Willy Lomans are no longer feasible.")

Now the contacts between the company and the bank multiplied. N.C.R. sent teams of technical people from Dayton headquarters to confer with Stad—they submitted a technical proposal two inches thick—and Stad went out to Dayton to talk to N.C.R.'s research people. He was put up at N.C.R.'s plush Moraine Farm, the estate of a former board chairman, which the company now uses to entertain groups of customers and potential customers. (Like du Pont and other companies, N.C.R. uses its factories and laboratories as a sales showcase.) By the end of 1959, Stad decided that N.C.R.'s 304 computer, then just being delivered to the first purchasers, was the one for the Dime.

Thereupon the Dime's board of trustees decided that Stad's decision ought to be second-guessed by an independent consultant in the electronic data-processing field. This, of course, opened up the whole matter again, and brought the competitors back in. Fortunately for N.C.R., the consultant confirmed the decision, and the affair between the bank and the company again resumed, in a deliberate and measured way. The Dime's board selected a committee of three trustees to study the proposal. They went out to Dayton—staying at an even more posh N.C.R. guest house, the old home of Orville Wright—and they talked with everyone from technicians to N.C.R.'s president, R. S. Oelman, and its then board chairman, S. C. Allyn. On the way back in the plane, the trustees decided to sign with N.C.R. It was an $800,000 decision, and it was a key one not only to the bank but to N.C.R., which closed some other bank contracts on the strength of the Dime's decision.

N.C.R. was in the middle of a training program for the Dime's employees when, early in 1960, a crisis arose. N.C.R.'s technicians reached the chilling conclusion that the 304 computer would not have the capacity to do what the Dime eventually would require—i.e., a direct linkage from the posting machines at the tellers' windows to the computer without the intermediate use of tabulating equipment. The next model in the design stage, the 315 random-access computer, would do the job—but not the 304. De Florio had to come clean with the bank. "I called up Karl and said, 'Let's have lunch at the Brooklyn Club,'" recalls de Florio, still wincing at the ensuing conversation. De Florio offered to tear up the contract for the 304. The Dime's board accepted the proposal, and the whole computer question was back in the soup again.

Rival manufacturers had another chance to make presentations, and N.C.R. had to start all over again selling its 315 model, then two years from delivery. De Florio kept pounding on one main point: the bank already was using N.C.R. machines at its windows, and any company that finally got the computer contract would have to tie in to N.C.R.'s equipment. In the end the argument prevailed; Stad recommended the 315 computer on the grounds that it would be "just as good" as other computers—though no better—and that N.C.R. had "window experience." Along with the computer, the bank also agreed to use other N.C.R. equipment in its integrated system, so the total package came to $2 million. Says de Florio, looking back on the whole transaction, "In this kind of selling you can't see everything you buy. A lot has to be bought on faith. Therefore a company likes to work with big companies. Come hell or high water, they have to deliver."

One of N.C.R.'s brightest and most successful young computer salesmen recently expanded this doctrine. "A salesman is important," he remarked, "because the policy makers today come from a previous generation of doing business. They don't have the technical equipment necessary to make a decision about a computer that requires technical sophistication. So the salesman has to take the language of the computer man and turn it into language his customer understands. I used to think that those decisions would be made on a scientific basis—but it's a gross act of faith." The salesman's job, he said, is "to create an environment in which an act of faith can take place."

The "Foot Soldiers" Need Upgrading   There is doubtless still plenty of faith in sales transactions. But as the Dime Savings Bank affair shows, there is a great deal more. And this is the fact that salesmen do not seem to realize when they talk about their jobs. They are still trained to have a kind of emotionalism about their craft, and they carry with them a heavy load of outworn notions about their role. They view selling as both warfare and love, hostility and benevolence. They see themselves as "the men on the firing line," and "the foot soldiers of democracy." The combative nature of selling is stressed in almost every book on the subject, as in one of the most famous and widely sold of all books on selling, *Open the Mind and Close the Sale*, by John M. Wilson, who recently retired as N.C.R.'s sales manager. Wilson speaks of the "tension in every buyer-seller relationship," of the "challenge" in each encounter, of the need for "handling" the customer—though, of course, "in the way he wants to be handled."

This lag in the recognition of what has happened to selling is harmful, because the sales profession is still held in low esteem by the public. Just how low was indicated recently in a survey by *Sales Management* magazine of college students and their attitude toward selling. Selling ranked a very poor fourth, after teaching, law, and medicine, as a choice for a career. Only 6% of the students favored it. (Of seventy-one students whose fathers are in sales, only *five* wanted to go into selling.)

The students did not particularly object to the working conditions in selling; relatively few said they were put off by too much traveling, for example. Nor did many feel that the financial reward was inadequate. The chief objections to a selling career (some even denied that selling *is* a career) were these: "I don't want to force people to buy things they don't need." "Job security is poor." "I'm not extrovert enough." "Selling has no prestige."

One student unwittingly put his finger on the ironic predicament business faces. He remarked that selling simply does not require "a college education or intelligence." The main feature of the new kind of personal selling, of course, is that it does require men who are able and intelligent; the new salesman, quite obviously, must be recruited from among the better college graduates. But how are they going to be recruited if the better college graduates think selling is beneath them? The experience of Scott Paper illustrates the difficulties business has in luring these men into selling. The company prides itself on the fact that 95 per cent of its sales staff are college graduates. Each year, to keep the staff replenished, its interviews some 2,000 students, invites about 100 of these men to visit its Philadelphia headquarters, makes offers to about seventy-five—and lands thirty-five or forty of them.

The trouble is that business has signally failed to get across the idea that there has been a tremendous change in selling. (The *Sales Management* poll shows that this generation of students has not grasped one of the simplest and most fundamental changes—i.e., that by and large salesmen are no longer paid on commission but are salaried.) Business has a massive educational job to do. Perhaps as a start it might throw away a lot of the old inspirational literature on selling and let the facts of the new situation do the inspiring.

36 Consumer Sales Protection Act

U.S. Senate, 90th Congress

Door-to-door sales regulation has long been sought by many individuals. Some states have such laws; others are considering them. Obviously, federal legislation can help to create uniformity out of what otherwise might become a complex and unwieldy stew of 50 states' laws. Firms that operate nationally would have problems conforming to so many variations of a similar law.

Proposed legislation to regulate door-to-door sales—known as S. 1599, or the Consumer Sales Protection Act—involves a regulation that will permit the purchaser who buys in his own home to rescind the purchase agreement within a stated (and brief) interval of time. This extract gives some of the highlights of the Senate's Commerce Committee Report on the proposed Act.

. . .

Report The Committee on Commerce, to which was referred the bill (S. 1599), to assist in the protection of the consumer by enabling him, under certain conditions, to rescind the retail sale of goods or services when the sale is entered into at a place other than the address of the seller, having considered the same, reports favorably thereon with amendments and recommends that the bill as amended do pass.

Purpose S. 1599, as amended, would permit a consumer who has entered a substantial sale or contract of sale with a seller, at a place other than the seller's place of business, to rescind that sale or contract of sale if he mails (by certified mail) or delivers a notice to the seller, informing him of his intention to rescind, within 2 business days. It would also require that the seller deliver to the buyer, at the time of the sale, or at the time that the buyer signs the contract, a receipt which contains the seller's name and address, the details of the transaction, and a prominent notice informing the buyer of his right to rescind.

Reprinted from U.S. Congress, Senate, Committee on Commerce, *Report Number 1417, Consumer Sales Protection Act*, 90th Cong., 2d sess., 17 July 1968, pp. 1–4, 10–14.

Need

The Consumer Sales Protection Act is designed to provide a consumer with some meaningful and readily available relief once he has succumbed to a high pressure sales pitch of a door-to-door salesman, but has subsequently had time to mull over the transaction and realize that he has made an unwanted purchase, paid an unconscionable price, or unnecessarily burdened his family with a major long-term expenditure.

To be sure, the vast majority of door-to-door sellers honestly perform a constructive and useful function in conveniently bringing their products to the doors of millions of housewives. But a brief examination of the selling techniques too frequently employed in door-to-door selling indicates how urgently some regulation is required, for no individual preys upon the elderly, the poor, the ignorant, the gullible, or the softhearted as much as the unscrupulous door-to-door salesman of products ranging from encyclopedias, magazines, and kitchenware to sewing machines, vacuum cleaners, furniture, and siding.

There are two varieties of unethical sellers in this industry. The first, and most common, is the one-shot, hit-and-run salesman who operates in nearly every neighborhood. His mission is to sell a story, not a product, so his pitch and approach are carefully rehearsed and perfected so as to disarm his unsuspecting victim. He does not hesitate to play on sympathy, shame, or the buyer's conscience, and to capitalize on the ignorance or lack of understanding of certain customers, the language difficulty of the newly arrived immigrant, the confusion of the harried housewife, or even the fear of the elderly lady or single girl living alone, in order to make his sale.

The second variety of unethical salesman is less common. His goal is to cultivate a permanent customer, most frequently one in a lower income area. He does this by instilling in the customer a feeling of personal loyalty subtly underscored by a sense of obligation, again rather than emphasizing the virtues of his product. His apparent concern with the customer's personal problems, his "friendly" weekly calls, which oddly enough, are also convenient for collecting installments and pushing new products, and his occasional favors, frequently merely delaying collection of an installment, are all designed to establish this special rapport. This type of seller can be particularly successful, for many buyers, especially the elderly or the newly arrived immigrant or urban dweller, may be intimidated by the prospect of shopping in a large downtown store and therefore are particularly appreciative of his personal attention. Younger buyers may also enjoy the convenience of buying from a peddler or the availability of his easy credit terms. Nevertheless, many purchasers come to regret these dealings when they subsequently realize how much his merchandise has actually cost them. For invariably his products are grossly overpriced, and this high cost is carefully concealed. Eventually thousands of consumers discover that it may be difficult to say "no" to such a "friend," but it frequently will be very expensive not to.

This bill is designed to provide an immediate remedy for the large number of consumers who have unpleasant dealings with the first variety of fast talking and faster disappearing door-to-door salesman. It will have no impact, however, on those consumers who deal with the second type of salesman and who crave personal attention or convenient buying and are willing to pay a high price for it. With expanding social programs in recent years designed to break down the feeling of alienation which individuals develop in our increasingly complex and impersonal society, with increased emphasis on consumer education, and with the availability of local legal advice, we can expect, however, that in the future a greater number of those consumers who deal with the latter type of salesman will also find the provisions of the bill an important weapon with which to combat those sellers who are charging unconscionable prices for their wares.

Although direct selling provides a valuable means for promoting and marketing hundreds of products, there is also little doubt that selling abuses are common in this method of merchandising. Magazine sales and home improvement and maintenance schemes, both of which rely quite heavily on door-to-door solicitation, annually lead the better business bureau's listing of categories in incidence of complaint, although only an unspecified portion of those complaints deal with the method of selling. Nearly every major encyclopedia company is subject to a Federal Trade Commission order for deceptive selling practices employed in the home, and one company has paid two civil penalties for violation of its order. Fifteen per cent of all consumer complaints in Chicago relate to door-to-door sales, as do 40 per cent of the complaints received by the Rhode Island Consumers' Council. And officials at Project Moneywise in the Department of Health, Education, and Welfare have learned from their students that peddlers in low income areas are charging five and six times the amount that local merchants charge for standard consumer items—usually by failing to disclose the total purchase price which will be paid for the merchandise.

In New York, $400 sets of encyclopedias have been sold to Puerto Rican parents who cannot read English, by salesmen who have posed as school officials and told the parents that their children would be forced out of school if they did not buy. In public housing units, salesmen, who have pretended to be employees of the housing authority, have installed cabinets and then asked the resident to sign a "receipt" which turns out to be an installment contract. And for many years, youthful magazine salesmen have been collecting "points" toward exotic vacations or college scholarships for sales in which the buyer pays "only the postage."

This bill will provide a consumer with some simple and absolute relief. To assure that he will be aware of it, the bill requires that the salesman furnish the buyer, at the time of the sale, with a receipt which bears a conspicuous notice informing him of his right to rescind and which also sets forth the seller's address and the details of the transaction. The buyer, therefore, will be able to sit down that evening with his or her family and consider more carefully and calmly exactly what they have purchased. Should they decide that the purchase was hasty or ill considered or that the salesman deceived them as to the nature or value of the product, this bill will provide them with some immediate recourse.

In a few instances, of course, legal remedies already exist today, but too frequently the buyer is unaware of their availability. Where he knows of their existence, the time and expense of litigating and the uncertainty of obtaining adequate relief deters him from exercising those rights. Similarly, complaint to the Federal Trade Commission, which may result in a cease and desist order against the seller, only helps prospective customers. It does not pay the victimized buyer's bills. This bill, however, will provide a method for obtaining relief which can be immediately exercised by any consumer—without burdening the Federal Government with the administration of a costly program.

Although, without doubt, unethical sales techniques are employed in all methods of retailing, the committee has limited this bill to direct selling. This is partially because of the indications the committee has received (and cited earlier) that a disproportionate number of door-to-door sales involve misleading or high-pressure sales tactics, and partially because of certain of the unique characteristics of direct selling which seem to leave the consumer particularly vulnerable: The buyer has not made a conscious decision, as by entering a store, to expose himself to a sales pitch, for the seller's call is normally unsolicited and the salesman has frequently failed to indentify himself accurately. The buyer has no way of screening the type of salesman who comes to his door, as he does in choosing the stores in which he shops. The buyer may feel intimidated into making a purchase from a salesman within the home, for there is no place to which he or she can readily escape. The buyer, suddenly exposed to a pitch for a product which he had contemplated buying, has no opportunity for comparing value. And finally, the selling company does not have the same opportunity to police the conduct of its salesmen and their representations in the buyer's home, as it does when they operate within a store.

Although six States have already enacted cooling-off legislation to deal with door-to-door sales, Federal regulation has two major advantages. First, national companies need comply with only a single set of uniform regulations in all their sales transactions. Second, it enables law enforcement officials to deal with fraudulent operators, who successfully operate for long periods of time by fleeing each State's jurisdiction just before local officials catch up with them, by eliminating the necessity for serving process on that person in the same State where he violated the law.

The committee believes that this bill will provide an effective instrument with which to combat the unscrupulous salesman, while at the same time it will not greatly burden the vast majority of ethical direct sellers. Field Enterprises, the only major encyclopedia company which has no serious complaints for unethical selling filed against it, has voluntarily offered its customers a right of cancellation which is comparable to that provided in the bill. It has also prominently informed its buyers of this right to cancel. Nevertheless, today it is the leading company in encyclopedia sales. Based on that experience, the committee believes that this bill will provide an effective, but not indiscriminate, method of combating the unscrupulous.

. . .

37 Hearings on Door-to-Door Sales Regulations

U.S. Senate, 90th Congress

In 1968, before the committee report on S. 1599 was issued, hearings were held. At these hearings the problem of door-to-door sales regulation was discussed, and both advocates and opponents of such legislation were given the opportunity to speak before the subcommittee. Two dozen witnesses were heard, over 100 written statements, letters, and articles were read into the record, and 326 pages of rather small print were amassed.

The extract that follows, which contains a practical description of the high-pressure salesmanship discussed in the previous articles, is drawn from these hearings as an illustration of the sort of door-to-door sales activity that is responsible for S. 1599.

. . .

Huntington Beach
California
March 4, 1968

Re: my complaint of unethical sales tactics by Orange County Kirby, Inc. (Savevio C. Quarantello, President), Santa Ana, California.

Hon. Thomas H. Kuchel
U.S. Senate
Washington, D.C.

Sir:

Please read the attached copy of my complaint filed with the Better Business Bureau of Orange County. The BBB has informed me that they have other complaints on file against this same dealer.

My husband did some library research and it seems that this dealer is one of about 1,000 franchised dealers throughout the U.S. that primarily

Reprinted from U.S. Congress, Senate, Committee on Commerce, *Hearings Before the Subcommittee on Door-to-Door Sales Regulations*, 90th Cong., 2d sess., 4 March 1968, pp. 298–299.

engage in house to house sales of Kirby vacuum cleaners. They are franchised by the manufacturer: Scott & Fitzer Company (J. A. Kemper, President), Cleveland, Ohio.

From all that I have been able to learn I have no protection against a salesman entering my home under false pretenses and forcing me to sign under duress—unless I am able to spend a great deal of money for a lawyer.

If you are not a member of a committee working for consumer protection laws, will you please make this letter available to a Senator that is? I am also writing Betty Furness of the Consumer Advisory Council.

I want you to know that I will fully appreciate any time you may give this matter and any advice you may have for me.

Very truly yours,

Mrs. Susan M. Presley

Complaint of Unethical Sales Activity   Complainant: Susan M. Presley, 7622 Juliette Low Drive, Huntington Beach, California 92647.

Store Charged: Orange County Kirby, Inc. (Savevio C. Quarantello, Pres.), 1254 S. Main St., Santa Ana, California.

On 2-20-68, a lady phoned me and asked me some misc. household questions.

On 2-23-68, the same lady phoned back and said that because I had previously answered the questions correctly, I had won a free rug shampoo for my home. I said that I was not buying anything and that I did not want any salesman calling. She replied that there was absolutely nothing to sell and positively no obligation or charge.

On 2-26-68, at about 10:30 AM, a man (Alan Petrasek) arrived at my door and said that he was here to shampoo my rug. He entered my house with a new Kirby vacuum cleaner with rug shampoo attachment and proceeded to demonstrate and sales talk the machine. He did not shampoo the rug (except a demonstration area) and he did not leave when I told him I was not buying anything. Instead he commenced to brow beat me until I was completely cowered by him and finally at about 1:00 PM, I blindly signed a sales contract he pushed in front of me. He then took my old vacuum and left, leaving the new machine.

During this 2½ hours I repeatedly told him that I was not buying anything and that he should leave and return when my husband was home. As time went on his belligerent behavior intensified and he began waving his arms and shouting over and over, "you're going to buy it!" "you're going to buy it!" "you're going to buy it!" My nerves knotted up in the back of my neck and I was thunderstruck.

On 2-28-68, at about 7:30 PM, my husband and I returned the new vacuum to the store (Orange County Kirby, Inc.) and left it with the store sales manager. (I am not sure of his name but it sounded like Nolan.) I recounted my ordeal to him and requested my old machine back that had been removed without my permission. The manager refused to return my old machine and explained something about the life of a salesman is never appreciated but they are the life-blood of the U.S. economy. He said that Alan Petrasek has been one of his top salesmen for over three years—and while he basically believed my story, he asked me (and this is the clincher) what could I do for him (the manager)? My husband and I then left and made a full report to the police dept. At about 9:00 PM we returned home and found our two children upset. They said about 15 minutes earlier they heard a strange clamor in our garage and upon investigating they saw two wild looking teenagers inside—the teenagers left the new vacuum we had just returned to the store and ran off. (My husband and I have since received phone calls from a Mr. Crews, manager of Liberty Loan Corporation of Santa Ana, who says that the sales contract having a face value of $330.00 was sold to him and that he wants us to understand we must pay him regardless of any circumstances or my husband's wages will be garnished.)

I have seen my family doctor and I have recounted my ordeal to him—with the resulting extreme pain I have since felt from my knotted nerves in the back of my neck, the pressure in the back of my head and the blackout spells I am having. After his examination he ordered me on medication and to lie down as much as possible. He said it is clear that due to the ordeal I am on the verge of a nervous breakdown.

· · ·

38 Statement of Stephen Sheridan, Vice-President, Electrolux Corporation

U.S. Senate, 90th Congress

At the same hearings for S. 1599, industry representatives were also heard in defense of direct-selling operations. The following selection is the statement of an executive of one of the most important direct-selling companies in the United States, the Electrolux Corporation. It presents an industry reaction to attempted regulation of high-pressure salesmanship in door-to-door selling.

My name is Stephen Sheridan and I am vice-president of Electrolux Corporation of New York City.

I want to thank you first for your generous opening remarks about the integrity and ethics of the majority of the major direct sellers and also for your rational explanation of why this bill apparently is against door-to-door sales.

I expect that my statement will be responsive to the points that you raise in your opening remarks.

As one of the best known companies engaged over a longer period of years in home retail selling, we express our unequivocal opposition to S. 1599 in its present form.

In its present form the proposal creates more mischief than it was designed to alleviate; it fails by a wide margin to protect consumers from the abuses it decries; and it foists a discriminatory and intolerable burden upon those companies that are innocent of those practices it seeks to curtail.

We urge you to withdraw this bill or to modify it, logically and equitably, to extend its coverage to all retail sales across the boards whether made in a home or in a store; further to require that during the so-called cooling-off period that the goods either be kept in the seller's sealed carton or else the buyer's right to cancel shall be lost.

S. 1599 taints our sales, or salesmen, and our company with an aura of

Reprinted from U.S. Congress, Senate, *Hearings Before the Consumer Subcommittee on Door-to-Door Sales Regulation*, 90th Cong., 2d. sess., 4, 5, 20, 21 March 1968, pp. 92–96.

rascality that has no basis in fact and invites our customers to cancel a contract that our employees have diligently sought and honestly obtained. Ours are not marginal, or fly-by-night, or high-pressure operations. We are qualified to do business in, operate established places of business in, and pay taxes in all of the continental United States except Alaska.

We do not mislead our customers with market surveys, or deceive them with referral sales plans. We do not sell our contracts to banks or other financial institutions but carry them ourselves. We sell the highest quality products and have a national reputation for the quality of our products, our sales, our service, and our integrity.

When an installment sale is made the contract is explained to the customer; the sale is verified with the customer by our branch store; our regional administrative office confirms with the customer the terms of the contract.

If we allow a purchaser to cancel a contract, and we do, and many stores do, this is a matter of good business practice. We cannot survive, however, when our customers are invited to cancel their contracts—even though they may have used our product for several days—on the theory that there is something inherently fraudulent or devious about it, while at the same time the contracts of our competitors and other merchants are accorded a grace and sanctity that may have no relation to reality. The unfair selectivity of S. 1599 makes it not so much a protective regulation as punishment without crime in many cases.

On behalf of Electrolux and other companies like Electrolux, I respectfully request your deepest consideration of the inequities and the shortcomings in S. 1599, and the needless damage likely to result from S. 1599 in its present form.

There are abuses in retail stores. There is no evidence that there are abuses in all retail stores or with respect to all retail store companies. Of course, there are abuses in door-to-door sales. There is no evidence that there are abuses in all door-to-door sales or with respect to all direct selling companies. The rascal who preys upon the unwary from the privileged sanctuary of a store front would be aided and abetted by S. 1599, while a decent direct seller of quality and integrity is demeaned, penalized, and perhaps destroyed.

There are direct sellers who are deceptive or high pressure. There are store sellers who are both deceptive and high pressure. If there are abuses to be curbed, then they should be curbed by an even-handed approach to the issues. If the consumer should be protected from impulsive or impetuous purchase—and as to the necessity of this, reasonable men may differ—then the consumer should be protected by an equally protective law applying to purchases in store and in home. The rascal should be curbed—in store or in home—by an equal application of the law. The legitimate merchant—in store or in home—should enjoy an equal competitive position with respect to other legitimate merchants.

I do not intend to impugn the morality of store selling, nor to extoll and ennoble door-to-door selling. Simply, I urge you to consider that abuses in selling should be attacked instead of capriciously and selectively targeting a form of selling.

Although a store customer may have made a conscious decision to enter a store and expose himself to a sale, he may not have. He may have been enticed into that action; he may have been conned into it. Although a store customer may have entered a store for one purpose, he may be lured, diverted, or misled into another. It is not the locus of the sale so much as the focus and intent of the seller that should be at issue.

American merchandising is resourceful and imaginative. The variety of ingenious stratagems to influence the consumer into a purchase he never sought range from permissible whimsy to illegal fraud. A deceptive purveyor can exploit his customers by perverting acceptable sales practices—in either a home or in a store.

The persuasive advertising of sophisticated copywriters is geared to influence purchasers into a sale. This has long been an accepted American practice. However the downright deceptive advertising of fraudulent rascals is aimed at inveiglement and entrapment at the point of purchase. The switch and bait lures are naked swindles. None of such sales may have been sought by the purchaser. The ingenious solicitation is implicitly in these wily stratagems and many such sales are consummated in stores.

Impulse buying has become a store merchandising art, stimulated by point of sale displays and massed arrays of goods. Loss leaders are vital to the traffic flow in supermarkets and department stores. That traffic flow is not sought for the volume sale of loss leaders, but to engage the attention of otherwise disinterested persons to oral or visual sales presentation of other merchandise.

Is a purchaser in his own home more captive than a browser in a store "turned over" from salesman to "assistant manager" to "manager"? "Sandbagging" in a "shlock" store is so general as to give rise to its own vernacular, and enriches our vocabulary while it fleeces its victims.

In the Congressional Record dated Monday, March 18, there is an insertion by Senator Proxmire, in which he quotes an article written by Robert C. Maynard, in the Washington Post, dealing with the Federal Trade Commission's survey of retail practices.

"Is the purchaser in the home more captive?" This is from page S. 2980 of the Record. "Mrs. Selman said recently that she had not intended to buy furniture from Tops that day. 'I was just looking around,' she said. A visit to any one of the nearly two dozen high credit stores in any of the city's principal slums will make it easier to understand how difficult it is to leave without signing a contract for something."

The honest merchant—in a store or in a home—conducts his business honestly. He does not want remorseful buyers. Perhaps the honest merchant can survive a cooling-off period that is evenly applied across the boards. But he may not, if he is a house-to-house seller, survive S. 1599 in its present unfair form.

By failing to include store sales within the scope of S. 1599, the bill sanctifies abuses in stores and penalizes honest dealing in homes. It exposes consumers to raids by the unprincipled on good contracts that are only tentative, to be locked into bad contracts that are binding. A switch and bait artist can make his oily solicitation from his hallowed store front, or telephone; can reassure his dupe that marvelous buys are still available to him —just cancel that door-to-door contract and come into my parlor. The victim can be had.

On the other hand, the badly stung buyer of a grossly inferior product— if purchased in a transient tent—must live with that purchase. He cannot change—cannot buy from a legitimate merchant in store or home. Yet if all sales, in home and in store, are subject to S. 1599, the bill becomes nondiscriminatory. The consumer is provided with a cooling-off period to reconsider all sales. The honest merchant is neither tainted nor discriminated against. When all sales are subject to the same restraints, no sales are tainted. No seller is at competitive disadvantage.

By limiting its contemplation to door-to-door sales, S. 1599 ignores and thus condones rampant abuses elsewhere, compounds the vulnerability of consumers, and capriciously strikes down legitimate business enterprise. Logically, equitably, ethically, morally, S. 1599, if adopted at all, should be extended across-the-board to all forms of retailing.

Thank you.

SENATOR BREWSTER: Mr. Sheridan, I thank you. I am sure that the committee is completely familiar with the excellent corporation that you represent here today. I know we have your product in our own house.

MR. SHERIDAN: We are very glad to have you as a customer, sir.

SENATOR BREWSTER: I notice that the Senate District Committee contemplates a 3-day, cooling-off period on door-to-door sales here in the District of Columbia.

I have earlier pointed out that some six States have cooling-off periods and some 10 other legislatures are considering cooling-off proposals.

So you have a situation where you have a great variety of cooling-off periods across the Nation. Your company does business in all America.

MR. SHERIDAN: Yes.

SENATOR BREWSTER: Doesn't this variety of regulations impose some difficulty on your company and on the training of your sales personnel?

MR. SHERIDAN: The variety of regulation is not quite so burdensome as the existence of this type of discriminatory regulation, although we would prefer, frankly, Federal legislation on the issue.

SENATOR BREWSTER: You anticipated my question. Do you believe, because of the action of so many State legislatures, that there is a need for the Federal Government to preempt this field?

MR. SHERIDAN: I would prefer to see the Federal Government preempt it. On the other hand, Senator Brewster, I cannot envision this wave of State legislatures rushing into this fray. I believe that thus far this year, although possibly nearly a dozen States have contemplated this legislation, as we are approaching the end of the legislative season, not a single bill has emerged. I am hoping it is the weight of these arguments that is persuasive.

QUESTIONS FOR DISCUSSION

1. Formulate a definition of high pressure selling.
2. Describe a recent sales interview that you saw or that you participated in. Explain how you felt about the salesman.
3. Do you believe that Mrs. Presley's description of her encounter with a salesman is an accurate one? If not, how do you account for her story? If you do believe her description, what do you believe can or should be done about her complaint?
4. Evaluate Mr. Sheridan's testimony to the congressional committee.
5. Some argue that the principle of *caveat emptor* should still govern the seller-buyer relation. What arguments can be advanced in favor of this?
6. Show how the demands of customers may produce ethical problems for a salesman.
7. "No one can benefit from a product until the salesman enters the picture." Do you agree with this statement? Why or why not?
8. How does one reconcile the statement in number 7 with "Salesmanship is lacking in a moral and ethical basis."

SUGGESTED READINGS

Baker, Richard W. Jr., and Gregg Phifer, *Salesmanship: Communication and Persuasion* (Boston: Allyn and Bacon, Inc., 1960), pp. 95–109.

Bearden, James H. (ed.), *Personal Selling—Behavioral Science Readings and Cases* (New York: John Wiley & Sons, Inc., 1967).

Belasco, James A., "The Salesman's Role Revisited", *Journal of Marketing* (April, 1966), Vol. 30, No. 2, pp. 6–8.

Bursk, Edward C., "Low Pressure Selling", *Harvard Business Review* (November, 1947), Vol. 25, No. 2, pp. 227–242.

McGarry, Edmund D., "The Contactual Function in Marketing", *Journal of Business* (April, 1951), Vol. 24, No. 2, pp. 96–113.

"Sales Ethics: Truth and Taste Needed?", *Printers Ink* (June 7, 1962), Vol. 279, No. 9, pp. 25–28.

Schwartz, David J., "Salesmanship and Professional Standards", *Atlanta Economic Review* (September, 1961), Vol. 11, pp. 15–19.

Tosdal, H. R., *Selling in Our Economy* (Homewood, Illinois: Richard D. Irwin, Inc., 1957).

Weiss, E. B., *The Vanishing Salesman* (New York: McGraw-Hill Book Co., Inc., 1962).

section II antitrust legislation affecting marketing

As one might expect, the range of federal legislation affecting marketing activities is considerable. There are laws concerned with the price at which a manufacturer will sell his goods to competitors (for example, Robinson-Patman); laws concerned with a manufacturer's ability to set the retail price of his products (Fair Trade); and other bits of legislation that bear upon such activities as mergers, acquisitions, packaging, and unfair competition. A comprehensive list of all such legislation and the guidelines of regulatory agencies would be extensive.

Like many laws, those affecting marketing are subject to considerable variation in interpretation and enforcement over a period of time. Republicans em-phasize different aspects and espouse different views of the laws than do Democrats; the Supreme Court changes in composition and tends to be either more or less liberal or conservative as a consequence of its members' inclinations; and the personal views and motivations of the civil servants charged with interpretation and enforcement of the law determine to a significant extent what is to be considered "acceptable" marketing practice.

The effect of these variables on marketers and consumers is considerable. Marketers must tread cautiously at times, lest they place their firms in violation of a law; consequently, they must always be aware of the many legal constraints that are relevant to their activities. Consumers, too, can profit from awareness of the network of federal regulations; they can become better and more effective consumers and thus maximize their satisfaction or minimize their costs.

Since federal regulation of marketing is such a vast field, this section can only be indicative, not definitive. It attempts —by case histories, citations of the law, and reports of various experts—to paint a broad picture of the nature and scope of a few laws and regulations that govern only one aspect of governmental control: antitrust.

39 Policies for the Regulation of Competitive Behavior

John R. Moore

The subject of antitrust cuts across the entire marketing area as well as dealing with the financing and organization of business enterprise as a whole.

However, antitrust regulation is tied closely to pricing policy and to a lesser extent to sales practices that build business by coercive means.

A useful summary of antitrust legislation and enforcement appears in the extract that follows. Although reference is made here to agricultural marketing, the ideas advanced apply to all marketing.

A society can take one of three general approaches to preserving competition within a private free enterprise system. One approach would involve taking the steps necessary to preserve a competitive market structure through such measures as reducing market concentration, barriers to entry, and product differentiation, without consideration as to how the market structure developed. A second approach would involve regulating the methods by which firms compete, through such measures as delineating the types of actions or specific acts that are anti-competitive, and thus defined as illegal. Prohibited action includes such things as price fixing, market sharing, tying arrangements, and certain mergers. A third approach would involve regulating firms and industries on the basis of their performance. This would be more in accordance with the workable competition approach. In general, no steps would be taken against firms if they were reasonably progressive, provided a good product at a reasonable price, and in other ways performed satisfactorily.

Of the three general approaches that might be taken to ensure competition, the second, that aimed at regulation of firm behavior, has been relied upon most heavily in the United States. Upon examination the reason for this is fairly clear: It has fewest disadvantages.

The market structure approach to antitrust has several drawbacks. Some

Reprinted from John R. Moore, "Policies for the Regulation of Competitive Behavior", ed. Vernon L. Sorenson, *Agricultural Market Analysis* (East Lansing, Michigan: Bureau of Business and Economic Research, Graduate School of Business Administration, Michigan State University, 1964), pp. 275–285, by permission of the author and the publisher.

of these include: the sometimes nebulous relationship between market structure, behavior and performance, particularly when there are several market structure variables interacting, the inapplicability of the same economic standards to different industries or to the same industry over time, the difficulty of writing laws in terms of such things as market concentration, barriers to entry, and product differentiation, the mass amount of information on industry conditions that would be needed to enforce the law, the difficulty of resolving the conflict between market concentration and economies of scale, and the difficulty firms would have in knowing when they were violating the law. For example, such an approach would be blind to a situation in which a firm may end up as a monopoly due to the demise of a rival.

The market performance approach to regulation of competition has its drawbacks as well. Its standards would have to be written in terms of such things as progressiveness, efficiency, innovations, profits, product variety, output, employment, growth, stability, and prices, some of which are rather vague. Consideration of the effects of such outside factors as changes in technology and long-run demand would also be very difficult. Enforcement, at best, would still result in making changes in either market structure or behavior or, at worst, if the free enterprise system were thought important *per se,* might lead to direct public regulation or ownership.

The market behavior approach to antitrust may not be perfect but it offers several advantages. In the first place, it looks at the core or essence of competition, rivalry among firms. Second, this approach can be written into a reasonably definite law that can be interpreted without too much vagueness, particularly after judicial precedents have been set. Third, in most cases it takes a positive act to violate the law and these acts can often be proved in court. The need for an overt act to violate the law explains why the largest firms in an industry are sometimes left alone while their smaller competitors are prosecuted for their mergers.

The Development of Antitrust Legislation Antitrust policy in the United States developed over a long period of time. Prior to the passage of our first federal antitrust statute, the Sherman Act of 1890, antitrust action was largely a state matter and was enforced in state courts using English common law precedents. Some American courts invalidated corporate combinations and consolidations if the participating corporations acted beyond powers granted in their charter.

The Sherman Act provided for a coordinated prosecution which was lacking at the state level and was without precedent in other countries. In fact, few countries outside of Canada and the United States had any antitrust legislation prior to World War II, and such legislation as existed is now in part breaking down. In 1914 the two additional antitrust laws were passed, the Clayton and Federal Trade Commission Acts.

The Sherman Act has two substantive sections directed toward firm behavior. Section 1 is aimed primarily at conspiracies among firms that restrain competition, while Section 2 applies mainly to the attempts of individual firms to monopolize markets on their own.

Though the Sherman Act was a substantial step forward in the regulation of competition, it was soon found to have certain weaknesses. These included its inability to strike at monopoly in its incipient stages, thus preventing Sherman Act violations from occurring in the first place, and its use to curb collective bargaining by labor and agriculture. It was also felt that an administrative agency of antitrust experts should be established to help in the enforcement of any broadened antitrust laws. It was primarily for these reasons that the Clayton Act and the Federal Trade Commission Act were passed in 1914.

The Clayton Act prohibits four major types of activities or practices that might lessen competition or tend toward monopoly. These are price discrimination, tying clauses and exclusive dealing arrangements, certain types of mergers and interlocking directorates.

The Federal Trade Commission Act was designed primarily to provide an expert administrative body to speed up the enforcement of the Clayton and Sherman Acts. It also provides for the regulation of false and misleading advertising, wool products labeling, misrepresentation, disparaging competitors or their products, using lottery devices, and a number of other things.

Enforcement of the Antitrust Laws
Enforcement of the antitrust laws has run hot and cold since the passage of the Sherman Act in 1890. It took fourteen years, despite a gigantic wave of mergers, before the first dissolution, ordered in 1904, resulted in separation of the Great Northern and Northern Pacific railroads.

The government antitrust program was considerably more active in the next ten years, however. Antitrust highlights of the period include the dissolution of the American Tobacco and the Standard Oil companies in 1911 and the passage of the Clayton and Federal Trade Commission Acts in 1914.

Antitrust in the United States reached its lowest ebb between 1915 and 1935. In this period U.S. Steel was left intact because it was a "good" trust and did not abuse its power. The decision was seconded in the International Harvester case of 1927. The lowest point in antitrust enforcement was reached in 1933, when the antitrust laws were suspended for industries which had a government-approved NRA code of fair competition. Businessmen and others felt that too severe competition was reducing prices and wages.

Antitrust enforcement picked up considerably after 1935. The Robinson-Patman Act was passed in 1936, and in 1938 Thurman Arnold started a bold antitrust campaign as chief of the antitrust division. The Temporary National Economic Committee was set up in the same year. In 1945 the

U.S. Steel precedent was reversed when it was held in the Alcoa case that monopoly was illegal even when it was not abusive.

In 1946 the courts "brought wholly tacit, nonaggressive oligopoly within the reach of the conspiracy provisions of the Sherman Act" in their decision in the second American Tobacco case. This was a victory for the "new breed" of imperfect competition theorist. In 1950 the Celler-Kefauver amendment to the Clayton Act made the acquisition of the assets of a competitor subject to antitrust action. Only the acquisition of a competitor's stock had previously been subject to the Clayton Act.

Application of Antitrust Laws to Agriculture   The antitrust laws have been applied to agricultural marketing firms from the early antitrust period to the present, and with relatively high frequency. The first agricultural case involved the American Sugar Refining Company in 1892. Several new ones come up each year.

The following is a discussion of the type of antitrust cases being brought against agricultural marketing firms. Emphasis is on recent cases, but reference is made to some of the more important ones historically. The cases are divided into single and group firm (conspiracy) cases and then subdivided into those brought because of actions that tended to reduce rivalry among firms directly, and those brought because of overly competitive actions that tended over time to eliminate rivals and lessen competition.

Application to Actions Directly Lessening Competition (Single Firm)   Over the years the courts and antitrust officials have settled upon several types of firm behavior which they believe restrict business rivalry and thus under certain circumstances violate the antitrust laws. These include: acts that reduce the number of rivals and increase market concentration (such as mergers and interlocking directorates), acts that restrict a rival's access to one's customers (such as tying arrangements, exclusive dealing contracts, full line forcing and long term supply contracts), acts that restrict rivalry among the resellers of a supplier's product (such as resale price maintenance), and acts limiting the amount and timing of product sales in an industry (such as surplus purchasing). Most of these types of practices have been used by firms in the agricultural industries, some much more than others. Some examples follow.

MERGERS: One of the more interesting antitrust periods was from 1904 to 1920, when the early trusts, formed largely between 1890 and 1910, were brought under attack. Several of these trusts were within the agricultural industries. The industries involved included sugar, corn products, tobacco, meat, tin cans, and farm machinery.

The government lost the sugar trust case, brought in 1892 to dissolve the American Sugar Refining Company, which had acquired 90% of the industry's capacity, because the court ruled that sugar manufacturing was not commerce, an interpretation that has since been reversed.

In 1916 the government obtained a decree dissolving part of Corn Products Refining Co., which had acquired control of all the glucose plants and 64% of the starch production in the United States in 1906.

In 1911 the government obtained a divestiture of the American Tobacco Company, which had acquired 90% of the industry's sales in 1890 through merger. The company's direct tobacco manufacturing assets were divided among four firms, the American Tobacco Co., the R. J. Reynolds Tobacco Co., Liggett and Myers, and P. Lorillard Co.

No actual meat trust was ever formed but one was nearly consummated in 1903. It failed because of the financial panic of that year. The assets that had been acquired in preparation of the trust were distributed to the firms involved in the formation of the trust, Armour, Swift, and Morris, after threat of an antitrust suit.

The government lost in its efforts to break up the "tin can" trust in the form of the American Can Company, because its share of the market had dropped from almost 100% to less than 50% in 15 years.

The harvester trust, in the form of the International Harvester Company, entered a consent decree in 1918 requiring them to dispose of their three lesser harvesting lines, Osborne, Milwaukee, and Champion and to eliminate all but one of their representatives or agents in any town or city.

The early trust cases are interesting in two respects. In most cases the trusts had lost considerable market share before antitrust action, in spite of their initial dominant position. This fact was used in their defense. The government achieved some success in breaking them up in all cases except sugar and metal containers. The government's success against mergers declined after the U.S. Steel decision in 1920 and the decision that the law applied only to stock acquisition and not to the acquisition of assets. This latter ruling was changed with the passage of the Celler-Kefauver Act of 1950 amending Section 7 of the Clayton Act.

Since 1950 the government has initiated about a dozen suits for mergers by agricultural firms, several of which have been decided at least at the lower court or Federal Trade Commission level. These include the order for Pillsbury Mills, Inc., to divest itself of assets acquired from Ballard Company and Duff Baking Mix Division of the American Home Foods, Inc.; a consent order requiring Continental Baking Co., the nation's largest commercial bakers of white bread, to sell Omar, Inc., of Omaha, Nebraska, which at the time of its acquisition in 1958 was the nation's eighth largest bread baker; a consent judgment against United Fruit requiring it to create a new competitor out of its own assets with 35% of United Fruit's 1957 volume; a consent judgment requiring Minute Maid to dispose of or discontinue two frozen juice concentrating facilities; a consent order in 1962 requiring National Sugar Refining Company, the second largest refiner, to divest itself of Godchaux Sugars, Inc., the nation's seventh largest cane refiner; a consent order requiring National Dairy Products Corporation to divest two large fluid milk and ice cream firms and limit acquisitions for ten years; and an order requiring Foremost Dairies to divest ten acquisitions.

INTERLOCKING DIRECTORATE: Interlocking directorates, where one man serves as a director for two or more competing firms, logically may tend to lessen competition. Prosecution of interlocking directorates is relatively rare. One example was a consent judgment enjoining existing interlocking directorates and officers among certain dairies in Minneapolis. This civil action was in conjunction with a criminal action charging price fixing to which the defendants had pleaded *nolo contendere*.

TYING ARRANGEMENTS, EXCLUSIVE DEALING, FULL-LINE FORCING AND LONG-TERM CONTRACTS: There are at least four trade practices that have been determined to be unfair under certain circumstances because they tend to exclude rivals from normal access to customers. These practices are tying arrangements, exclusive dealing, full-line forcing and long-term contracts. None of these practices has received a great deal of attention from antitrust officials with respect to firms in the agricultural industries, though a few cases have occurred.

In 1946 American Can Company and Continental Can Company were charged by the Department of Justice with leasing their can-closing machinery at a low rate to canning companies on the condition that the lessees purchase their total requirements of containers from the leasor and for refusing to sell the machines at all. This prevented can manufacturers without comparable machines from competing for these accounts. A decree was entered in 1950 enjoining the defendants from entering into long-term requirements contracts with canners for cans, from refusing to lease or even sell closing machines to accounts not using their cans, and from allowing quantity discounts in the sale of cans.

A second case of alleged exclusive dealing involved three large manufacturers of farm machinery, J. I. Case, International Harvester, and Deere and Company. The government alleged their dealership contracts prohibited their dealers from handling other lines of equipment and thus restrained competition. The complaints were dismissed in 1951, when the government failed to show appreciable coercion, unreasonable restraint on commerce or a tendency to substantially lessen competition and to create a monopoly.

RESALE PRICE MAINTENANCE: Processors with a unique product may try to ensure the profitability of the item for their customers and thus the stability of their wholesale prices by trying to fix the price at which their customers may resell the item. This tends to eliminate competition among retailers on the item at the expense of consumers. For this reason retail price maintenance is contrary to antitrust philosophy, though it is permitted by law in some states. Only a few cases of this type have been brought against agricultural processing firms. One involved a breakfast cereal manufacturer who tried to enforce resale price maintenance by printing the following notice on its packages.

> This package and its contents are sold conditionally by us with the distinct understanding, which understanding is a condition of the sale, that the package and contents shall not be retailed, nor advertised, nor offered for sale at less than 10 cents per package. Retailing the package at less than 10 cents per package is a violation of the conditions of sale, and is an infringement on our patent rights, and renders the vendor liable to prosecution as an infringer.

This resale price maintenance plan was held illegal and perpetually enjoined.

Application to Overly Competitive Practices   Individual firms may engage in practices that are overly competitive and thereby eliminate competition and lessen competition. Control of these types of practices was the main emphasis for the passage of the Clayton and Federal Trade Commission Acts and their amendments.

Many types of activities are in the overly competitive category. Some of the more important include discrimination, sales below cost, false and misleading advertising and disparagement of competitor products.

DISCRIMINATION: This is the offense most frequently cited in antitrust cases. It is thought to injure competitors in two ways. It injures the competitor who loses the account or who would otherwise gain it from his rival and it injures firms trying to sell in competition with firms who have been favored by the discrimination.

Discrimination takes many forms. The simplest is to give one customer a lower price than another for a product of like grade and quality. Discounts can also be provided in the form of promotional allowances, brokerage fees and providing customers with services, facilities, and extended credit. Discrimination is a difficult charge to prove because of the many defenses a defendant may offer. These include assertions that a competitor's price had to be met, that the goods sold at different prices were of unlike kind and grade, that competition was not injured, and that price differences reflected differences in cost of production or distribution.

Charges of discrimination have been levied at firms in nearly all the agricultural industries. The examples that follow involve fluid milk, feed and grain, grocery retailing, fruits and vegetables, and flour and baking.

In 1957, Chestnut Chevy Chase Dairy was ordered by the Federal Trade Commission to cease giving promotional allowances to wholesale customers on a discriminatory basis in the Washington, D.C. area. Over an 18-month period their allowances per retailer ranged from $3.08 to over $16,000 and the allowances were not given on a proportional basis.

Three large-scale feed mixers recently consented to cease and desist from offering such sizeable discounts to their largest dealers that their smaller dealers could not compete with them. The quantity discounts for one of the mixers, for example, ranged from $0.25 to $2.50 per ton.

In 1938 the Federal Trade Commission ordered the Great Atlantic and Pacific Tea Company to cease accepting brokerage allowances from suppliers for groceries it purchased on its own account. This was one of the first cases testing Section 2-c of the newly passed Robinson-Patman amendment to the Clayton Act. The Commission rejected the respondent's defense that the allowances were justified since the respondent gave advice to their suppliers, aided them in disposing of their surpluses, and saved them the cost of employing brokers.

Most of the discrimination cases involving firms in the fruit and vegetable industry have been filed against shippers of citrus fruit for allegedly making illegal brokerage payments to favored customers. Forty-five of these were filed after the Commission's first use in 1960 of the broad powers of Section 6 of the Federal Trade Commission Act to conduct an investigation by mail on an industry-wide basis. All the complaints resulted in consent orders to cease and desist from the alleged practice. The industry-wide questionnaire was viewed by the Commission as the most equitable way of halting an unlawful practice common throughout the industry.

Illegal brokerage fees usually arise in one of the following two ways. A broker will take shipment of produce from a packer, deduct a brokerage commission from the invoice price, pay the packer for it at the deducted rate and then sell the produce on his own account at a higher price. Or the packer will bill the favored buyer (usually a large one) at the price normally billed brokers, but bill nonfavored buyers a price that includes the broker's normal commission.

Price discrimination takes several forms in the flour and baking industry. The most common form is a larger discount to favored purchasers. Other methods include giving larger promotional allowances to some retailers than others, even though they may have the same amount of sales, and discriminating in demonstrator services.

Prior to 1962, the Federal Trade Commission had filed fifteen cases alleging price discrimination in the flour and baking industry, which were concluded in orders or consents to cease and desist. Ten cases of the same type were pending in 1962, indicating that activity is being stepped up considerably in this area.

SALES BELOW COST: Setting prices below cost can be an effective device for accomplishing two objectives, particularly by a large diversified firm. It can be used to squeeze out weaker rivals in a market; it can be used to discipline competitors using selling practices that a dominant firm finds objectionable, such as failure to follow its price leadership, discrimination hurting the dominant firm, and introduction of new products and nonprice inducements.

Sales below cost can violate both the Sherman Act and the Robinson-Patman Act, the former where it tends to create a monopoly, the latter where it is discriminatory but not covered by the former. A few examples follow. In 1959 Fairmont Foods Co. of Wisconsin pleaded guilty to Sherman Act charges of selling milk to a distributor in Houghton County, Michigan, at prices lower than they sold for in Wisconsin and at prices below Fairmont's cost of doing business. In 1955 the government charged Safeway Stores, Inc. with attempting to monopolize grocery retailing in Texas and New Mexico by selling below cost. The defendants pleaded *nolo contendere* and were fined $187,500. This was the first time the maximum penalty under the amended Sherman Act had been imposed. In 1956 the Maryland Baking Co. was ordered to cease and desist from engaging in predatory price cutting in the sale of rolled sugar cones.

FALSE AND MISLEADING ADVERTISING: Occasionally a firm will attempt to mislead buyers with false claims about its product or its type of business. This violates Section 5 of the Federal Trade Commission Act. Examples of these cases include a firm representing its citrus as coming from Indian River when in fact it came from elsewhere, a firm representing itself as a growers' exchange when in fact it was not, a firm falsely advertising that its feed is highly effective in elimination of Bang's disease, and a firm misrepresenting the calorie content and therapeutic properties of bread.

DISPARAGING COMPETITORS' PRODUCTS: Disparaging competitors' products is an unfair trade practice, though the charge is rarely brought, presumably because the offense seldom takes place. No examples involving firms in the agricultural industries were found in a review of antitrust actions against firms in these industries.

Application to Group Action (Conspiracy Cases)   The basic objective of antitrust law is to preserve and maintain free competition in open markets. It logically follows that any agreement among firms not to compete violates the spirit if not the letter of the antitrust laws. Most types of agreements restricting competition among firms are in violation of the antitrust laws. These include price fixing, some trade association activities and cartel arrangements, basing point pricing, market division, nonsolicitation of competitors' customers, group boycotts, and surplus purchasing. A discussion of these violations and some examples in the agricultural industries follow.

PRICE FIXING: Price fixing takes two basic forms: explicit agreement not to charge below a certain price, and tacit price agreement or conscious parallelism. The former is more frequently found in antitrust suits; however, the latter doubtlessly is the more commonly practiced.

Price-fixing agreements seem particularly prevalent in industries with few sellers or buyers and a homogeneous product such as the wholesale market for fluid milk and bakery products. Numerous cases of both types have arisen. One of the more recent in the dairy industry was a case of alleged rigging of bids for milk for government installations by three Nebraska dairies to which two defendants pleaded *nolo contendere*; a third was found guilty.

There have been seven antitrust cases involving price fixing in the baking industry in which the defendant bakers were fined, or ordered to cease and desist. In six of the cases, the defendants pleaded *nolo contendere*. In each case, two or more bakers allegedly agreed on one or more matters such as prices to be charged for certain types of bakery products, discounts to be allowed buyers, prices to be bid on government contracts, whether or not to give prizes and premiums, and disposition of day-old bread.

Examples of price fixing in other agricultural industries include: four cases of alleged price fixing among cheese assemblers for the cheese they bought and sold and two cases of alleged price fixing by butter exchanges.

In the feed and grain industry the government obtained some relief in two cases. They were for alleged attempts of the Washington Cereal Association, and the Oregon Cereal and Feed Association, to coordinate the exchange of prices and terms of sale by its members to which the members were required to adhere, and the Michigan Bean Shippers Association's alleged attempt to fix rates for functions performed by middlemen and to publish "close" prices.

The leading antitrust case of conscious parallelism involved the largest tobacco companies. The government alleged they had combined to control the marketing of leaf tobacco as well as the cigarette distributing system. Leaf tobacco marketing was allegedly controlled by buyers refusing to bid unless all the other buyers were present and by setting ceiling prices on tobacco in advance of the sale. The strongest support for the government's charge of controlling the cigarette distribution system was a uniform price rise for cigarettes by the largest manufacturers in the depths of the Depression in 1931. They later dropped their prices to regain a large share of the market which they had lost to the so-called "10 cent" brands after the price increase.

The case resulted in fines of $312,000. It was not followed up with a civil suit that would enjoin any particular practices. As a consequence the defendants were left in some doubt about which of their practices were legal and which were not.

.   .   .

40 The Art of Self-Defense in Price Discrimination

Ronald M. Copeland

One of the basic legal foundations of marketing behavior is the Robinson-Patman Act, which requires that similar classes of customers be charged the same price by any one manufacturer. If, however, the manufacturer can *prove* that he saves money by selling to a specific customer, then the saving—and no more— can be passed along to that customer without the threat of prosecution on the grounds of price discrimination by the federal government. This selection presents an approach that marketing managers might use in establishing acceptable cost defenses.

Many price managers believe that legal price discrimination is the only expedient marketing remedy for pressures generated by today's competitive marketing structure and selling conditions. Unfortunately, even valid, well-intended use of price discrimination may lead to complications with the Robinson-Patman Act, which provides that it is unlawful to discriminate in price between different purchasers of commodities except for "differentials which make only due allowance for differences in the cost of manufacture, sale or delivery." Therefore, price managers must have a working familiarity with this law in order to enjoy the fruits of discrimination without incurring the risk of lengthy and expensive litigation.

The threat of litigation may be met in several ways; management could stop discriminating, do nothing, or prepare one of several defenses. The most practical and available defense against charges of price discrimination is the cost defense.[1] Much has been written about the cost defense, especially with reference to certain heavily litigated court cases. Although considerable advice is offered to potential users of cost justification, few articles explicitly state a general approach for employing accounting information for cost justification purposes. Most helpful to businessmen, however, is an overview that places accounting methodology in its proper perspective.

Reprinted from Ronald M. Copeland, "The Art of Self-Defense in Price Discrimination", *Business Horizons* (Winter, 1966), Vol. 9, pp. 71–76, by permission of the author and the publisher.

Robert A. Lynn has evaluated the current status of the cost defense by analyzing selected cost justification cases and, from his observations, has synthesized accounting procedures useful for preparing such a defense.[2] The specific accounting practices described have either won general acceptance or proven totally unacceptable to the Federal Trade Commission for verifying cost differences between different customer classes. These and additional practices have also been identified by other investigators of past Robinson-Patman cases, and are available in most business libraries.[3]

However, lists of accepted practices and studies of particular accounting procedures are insufficient as guides for price managers interested in protecting policies of price discrimination. First of all, no two firms are identical with respect to time, place, person, and process. Each firm would have to implement a unique defense. Second, additional questions besides the "what to do" must be asked. Still unanswered are the "where, when, and why" questions. A manager facing potential legal involvement must consider a more inclusive approach to a cost defense than is available in the current literature.

Strategy for a Defense

Whenever businessmen engage in price discrimination, they should be prepared to receive inquiries from the FTC. Answers to these inquiries must be based on factual data. To obtain information for answering inquiries, a strategy for defense should be prepared. A strategy is a predetermined course of action deliberately focused on winning an advantageous position over an opponent and calculated to counteract actions taken by the opponent.

A Robinson-Patman strategy would provide information adequate for the defense of price discrimination charges. At a minimum, it would recognize the following interrelated aspects of a Robinson-Patman defense:

Objectives of the defense must be explicitly understood.
The price differences are justified by cost differences.
The price differences do not injure competition.
The price differences are not related to goods of like grade or quality.
The price differences are not related to goods traded in interstate commerce.
The price differences are related to goods in a deteriorating market situation.
The lower price just meets the price of a competitor.

Methodology used to gather data must be implementable.
Data are gathered as part of the regular routine using the existing information system.
Data are gathered by special analysis of existing information system.
Data are gathered by special analysis using an auxiliary information system.
Data are gathered using a combination of the above.

Timing of effort must be predetermined.
Data are gathered before charges are filed.
Data are gathered after charges are filed.

Data are gathered both before and after charges are filed.

Data are prepared for use early in administrative procedure.

Data are prepared for use late in administrative procedure.

Financial aspects of the defense must be considered.

The expected benefits to be derived from fighting the charges must be estimated.

The expected costs to be incurred in fighting the charges must be estimated.

Only by considering all of these critical variables will a businessman have sufficient insight to make an intelligent business decision. The criterion used most often to judge a decision is whether it has a positive net effect on the firm's earnings or on the stockholder's wealth. The decision to fight charges of price discrimination on principle is an ethical one and, as such, is not subject to a business decision analysis.

Given this overview, lists of accepted accounting practices prepared by Lynn and others may be used more effectively. While accounting matters are still left in the hands of accountants, executive decision makers can place methodology in its proper perspective: more attention must be given to the timing and financial considerations directly related to any decision.

Timing of Cost Justification Effort   DATA COLLECTION: There are two aspects of timing cost justification effort. The first relates to the time for collecting justification data and has implications for the design of the data gathering system. Most often, the information system must be designed to record, summarize, and retain required data until it is needed. The data system may be ignored only if data are to be gathered by special studies after charges are filed; these reconstructions are often less detailed or reliable than currently collected data.

A second aspect of defense timing concerns the time for presenting cost data to the FTC. This timing implication can only be understood in terms of the administrative procedures used to process Robinson-Patman charges. ADMINISTRATIVE PROCEDURES: [4] Any interested party may ask the commission to initiate a Robinson-Patman proceeding simply by submitting a signed request for action. No special form or procedure is required. Also, the commission itself may institute an investigation upon its own initiative.

The commission may not act on all requests. However, after finding sufficient information to indicate a violation, it may proceed in one of three directions: the respondent may be given an opportunity to dispose of the matter on an informal, nonadjudicatory basis; he may be allowed to enter a consent order; or he may be subjected to a formal hearing. If the respondent signs a consent order, he must admit the jurisdictional facts, stop the alleged practice, and waive his rights to further procedural steps. However, even if he wishes to accept a consent order, the commission may proceed with an adjudicatory examination.

After hearing testimony and examining evidence, the hearing examiner will reach an initial decision. This decision automatically becomes final in thirty days unless the respondent appeals or the commission elects to review the case. If the respondent still thinks that his prices are justified despite an unfavorable initial decision, he probably will appeal to the commission. Final decision of the commission may be appealed to the courts.

The alternative procedures may be better visualized by reference to Figure 1. Of the thirteen steps shown, six represent terminal action. The timing aspect of cost presentation will be designed to terminate at one of these positions.

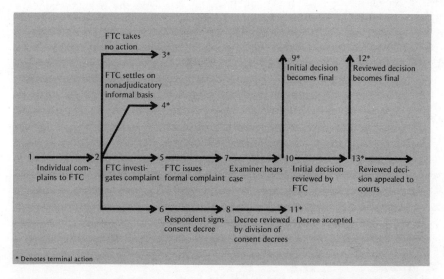

FIGURE 1.   Procedural steps for processing Robinson-Patman action.

DATA PRESENTATION: Previous writers recognized advantages in collecting and presenting cost data before the commission issues a formal complaint. Prior cost determinations may establish the good faith of the respondent and, more concretely, may allow management to determine the limits of price concessions that can legally be granted. In addition, nonadjudicatory settlements may have an absolute advantage:

> Apparently it is frequently possible to convince the Commission's accountants at the investigation stage that some price differences are justified by differences in cost; however, once the Commission's preliminary investigation—in the judgment of the Commission's accountants—suggests the lack of satisfactory proof of cost justification and the Commission proceeds to issue a complaint, successful defense on the basis of cost justification is well-nigh impossible because the Commission's accountants have already reached adverse judgment. Probably this is the reason for the notorious failures of many expensive and elaborate attempts to justify differences in costs.[5]

The actual extent of informal settlement activity is greater than is commonly believed. The FTC dismissed without issuing a formal complaint 74% of all Robinson-Patman legal investigations and 57% of all accounting investigations. In terms of magnitudes, the nonadjudicated cost investigations dropped are more than thirteen times as large as cost defenses attempted in adjudicated proceedings.[6] Thus, the majority of past cost defenses terminated with early settlements.

Financial   The preparation of any Robinson-Patman defense requires both
Considerations   human effort and money. At the same time, there are benefits
                     to be gained. Both the cost and the benefits can be measured:
they are the financial considerations of a cost defense.

Once management decides to use a particular methodology and timing in its defense, a program or programs for gathering and presenting data can be prepared. These programs will list the alternative steps and procedures and will approximate the physical input required, much like feasibility studies for budgeting capital acquisitions. Reasonable prices may be assigned to each input in order to determine the total cost of each defense. Alternative defense programs may then be compared and evaluated by capital budgeting techniques.

In making expense estimates, opportunity costs must be considered. Once a given course of action is undertaken to the exclusion of others, opportunities may be forgone—for example, contribution margins lost as a result of speedy signing of a consent decree. These opportunity costs can have significant magnitudes and therefore may be a determining factor in any decision regarding the cost defense.

The total cost is a function of the objective of the defense, the timing and method of data collection, and the timing of data presentation. However, the functional relationship between total expense and these variables is not direct. Expenses can be increasing, decreasing, or constant functions of the variables; for example, the longer a hopeless case is fought, the greater is the legal expense but the smaller are lost contribution margins.

The total size of financial considerations is partly within the control of management, which decides the magnitude and nature of the data collection effort, and has the option of settling the administrative procedure at most of the terminal points. However, the functional relationship between defense cost and critical variables is so diverse that by minimizing one type of expense the firm may be maximizing another type.

A chief advantage of cost justification over other defenses is that, if a portion of the total price differential is legally justified, a subsequent order to cease and desist issued by the commission will exclude the legal portion. Since partial justification of a price differential is often easier to prove than total justification, a firm may seek less than total justification.

The financial considerations may be used as a guide for evaluating alternative decisions. In each case, the benefits may be matched with the cor-

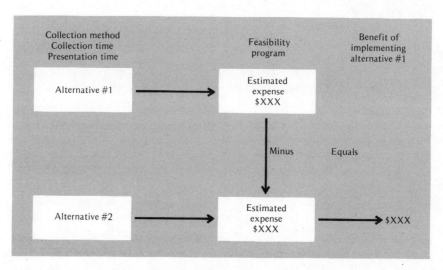

FIGURE 2.   Financial considerations of alternative strategies.

responding expenses, as shown in Figure 2. This is nothing more than conventional capital budgeting logic.

The size of the defense may be either large or small. While some defenses have cost as much as half a million dollars,[7] others may be minimal, as, for example, when the firm makes no prior cost study and accepts a consent decree.

Strategy of a Workable Cost Defense
In the past, writers defined a successful cost defense as one that totally justified the price differential,[8] but this view is unrealistic. Is a successful defense successful at any price? Ordinarily not; it would be true only if a firm were in business to vanquish the government in Robinson-Patman litigation. Since most firms are financially motivated, management must consider the implications of the action on earnings. Victory at any price is obviously not feasible in light of major corporate goals.

Since the legal portion of price differential may be continued, not all cost justifications ending with cease-and-desist orders were failures or were unworkable. Even if a cost justification effort terminates by entering a consent decree agreement, it still may be successful if the remaining hoped-for but unachieved benefits are smaller than the efforts required to achieve total success. On the other hand, success in the U.S. Supreme Court may actually be failure if the benefits derived are smaller than the effort expended.

Therefore, strategy for a workable cost defense should be based upon all of the financial considerations, which in turn are based upon the method of data collection, the timing of data collection and presentation, and the alternative considered. Each strategy involves a unique set of variables. Limits of the expected benefits are determined by comparing, on one hand, the expenses involved in a defense with, on the other hand, the saving of not defending at all. This sets the maximum expense to be considered. In many cases, it may become obvious at this point that any cost justification effort would entail an excessive expenditure. In this situation, the best course is no defense.

Cost justifications have been successfully employed to defend charges of price discrimination under Section 2 (a) of the Robinson-Patman Act more often than is commonly believed. However, a workable cost defense must be economically feasible as well as successful. Workable defenses only result from proper integration of objectives, data gathering methodology, effort timing, and financing. Preconceived plans of action or strategies should define the variables critical to any cost defense decision and provide a method for comparing different combinations of variables. Known capital budgeting techniques could then be used to evaluate alternative defense programs, thus helping businessmen make rational cost defense decisions.

NOTES

1. H. F. Taggart, *Cost Justification* (Ann Arbor: University of Michigan, 1959), p. 549.
2. Robert A. Lynn, "Is the Cost Defense Workable?" *Journal of Marketing*, XXIX (January, 1965), pp. 37–42.
3. For other lists containing these and other practices, see *Cost Justification*, pp. 538–42; J. B. Heckert and R. B. Miner, *Distribution Costs* (New York: Ronald Press Co., 1953), pp. 356–57, 366; Ronald M. Copeland, "Accounting Strategies for Defense of Discriminatory Pricing under the Robinson-Patman Act," unpublished doctoral dissertation, Michigan State University, 1966.
4. Federal Trade Commission, *Organization, Procedures, Rules of Practice, and Statutes* (Washington: U.S. Government Printing Office, 1963), pp. 9–55.
5. J. Parkany, "Federal Trade Commission Enforcement of the Robinson-Patman Act," unpublished doctoral dissertation, Columbia University, 1955.
6. "Accounting Strategies for Defense for Discriminatory Pricing . . . ," p. 13.
7. "Is the Cost Defense Workable?" p. 39.
8. This idea is implied by Lynn in "Is the Cost Defense Workable?" p. 37. Also see *Report of the Attorney General's National Committee to Study the Antitrust Laws* (Washington: U.S. Government Printing Office, 1955), p. 171.

QUESTIONS FOR DISCUSSION

1. To what extent do the antitrust laws improve or restrict the ability of the businessman to market his products?
2. Based upon the history and present status of antitrust legislation, what new laws or interpretations of existing laws do you foresee in the next decade?

3. Do you feel that the present antitrust laws can effectively protect the "small" marketer from the "big" marketer? Is such protection needed?
4. The Borden case demonstrated that the Supreme Court will not attribute a difference in grade or in quality to a difference in a label. What significance is this ruling to the advertising industry?
5. How should the nation establish its budget for the enforcement of the antitrust laws?
6. Do you believe business today is competitive? Explain.
7. If you were asked to make business more competitive, how would you proceed to do so?
8. What causes the enforcement of antitrust laws "to run hot and cold," as indicated by Moore?
9. What arguments have been offered in opposition to the present antitrust laws?
10. Why was the Robinson-Patman Act necessary, since antitrust laws already existed when it was passed?

SUGGESTED READINGS

Collins, Norman R., and Lee E. Preston, *Concentration and Price Cost Margins in Manufacturing Industries* (Berkeley, California: University of California Press, 1968).

Kaysen, Carl, and Donald F. Turner, *Antitrust Policy* (Cambridge, Massachusetts: Harvard University Press, 1959).

Merkel, Edward W., "The Other Anti of Antitrust", *Harvard Business Review* (March–April, 1968), Vol. 46, pp. 54, 58, 59.

Narver, John C., *Conglomerate Mergers and Market Competition* (Berkeley, California: University of California Press, 1967).

———, "Some Observations on the Impact of Antitrust Merger Policy on Marketing", *Journal of Marketing* (January, 1969), Vol. 33, pp. 28–31.

Robbins, W. David, "A Marketing Appraisal of the Robinson-Patman Act", *Journal of Marketing* (July, 1959), Vol. 24, p. 15.

section 12 marketing and the issue of privacy

Marketing research is an accepted marketing function—both by sellers and buyers—and is also a major activity; in 1972 perhaps $800 million will be spent on it. Unfortunately, not all marketing researchers respect the rights of privacy of those they interview or study in the course of their investigations, nor do they always behave ethically.

One of the most common ethical abuses is the use of a "market research interview" to make a sale. In such cases, the purported researcher is really a salesman, and his entry into the consumer's home and confidence is due to deliberate misrepresentation.

There is also a significant ethical question concerning the rights of a survey respondent to refuse an interview or to answer questions that are asked of him. Sophisticated, experienced, and educated people know that the interviewer is totally subject to their whims regarding any responses they may make. On the other hand, the interviewer is too often perceived as an authority figure by respondents who do not have much education or sophistication and who, by virtue of their status in our society, fear authority. Such fears are played upon by the occasional flashing of official-looking cards by interviewers, by an intimidating manner, and by other actions. The result is significant abuse of the survey respondent.

Questions also arise concerning questionnaires that are too long, interviews that are scheduled at inconvenient times, too-frequent call-backs, and the surreptitious use of cameras and microphones. In response to such actions, a number of communities across the nation have devised various regulations to prevent harassment, abuse, and invasion of an individual's privacy.

These regulations include a complete ban on market surveys, a licensing fee to conduct interviews, a limitation of the days and hours when interviews can be conducted, and so on. It is quite likely that additional abuses will bring more restrictive legislation.

The articles in Section 12 point out the scope and nature of the abuses of privacy and ethics in marketing research.

41 The Issue of Privacy in Public Opinion Research

Robert O. Carlson

One of the basic approaches to the development of marketing information is the "interview." The general public has, up to the present time, been remarkably tolerant of interviewing practices with which it has come into contact. Although market and public opinion researchers certainly have a right to seek answers to vital questions, respondents also have rights. In fact, the questioners have *only* those rights given to them by the respondents (with the exception of those cases in which the government asks the questions). The interviewing procedure can and should include respect for respondents' rights.

The following article sets forth some of the areas of respondent abuse and indicates what can be done to assure interviewing procedures on an honest basis.

In this paper I shall view with some alarm the short-term prospects of public opinion research as it relates to the issue of privacy. I believe it is a real issue and that, by the very nature of public opinion work, we must invade the privacy of our respondents in some measure. I feel this invasion can be justified, but unfortunately we have done a poor job up to now of explaining ourselves and our work to our publics.

Things have been going along rather too well for us as a profession, except for an occasional effort to legislate against door-to-door interviewing on a municipal or state level, as well as some scattered instances of pseudo-surveys being used for selling merchandise. This experience compares favorably with the harassment and the investigations which those in the field of psychological testing have undergone. I am concerned that we in the survey research field underestimate the likelihood of our activities facing similar scrutiny and public controversy. As a thriving new profession, exercising considerable power in government, academic, and business circles, it is unrealistic to expect that we can escape the searching eye of critics and the general public with respect to the issue of privacy and the work we do.

Reprinted from Robert O. Carlson, "The Issue of Privacy in Public Opinion Research", *Public Opinion Quarterly* (Spring, 1967), Vol. 31, pp. 1–8, by permission of the author and the publisher.

Some of us seem to operate on the bland assumption that the issue of privacy has little or no relevance for the field of public opinion research. In its most extreme form, this view is reflected in the philosophy that we as researchers have the right to ask people their opinions on a broad range of questions and they, in turn, have the right to answer or to refuse to answer our questions. Let us pause at this juncture and give a little more thought to this beguiling and comforting proposition. However, let us view it from the point of view of a potential critic who turns the tables on us and begins to ask us some questions about the basic tool of our trade—the interview.

For example, what is our answer to the critic who may say, "The people you interview in your surveys are not all alike. Some are well educated, have a high socioeconomic status, are intellectually and psychologically secure and sophisticated, and these, of course, can be expected to know that they do not have to answer the questions your interviewers bring to their homes. But," continues our critic, "what of the others in the population who are old, poor, badly educated members of ethnic groups who harbor fear of authority figures from the outside world and a host of similar categories—are these people equally aware of their right not to answer your questions and are they equally prepared psychologically to exercise this right?" I do not think we have adequate answers to this question, and yet answers would be of considerable interest to us from a purely research standpoint, quite apart from the light such data might shed on the privacy question itself. Why should not the appendix of each opinion survey give the available characteristics of the people who refused to be interviewed as well as those who participated in a survey?

Clearly, the interview situation in a typical public opinion survey is the point at which the privacy issue takes on its greatest meaning. It dramatizes the dilemma of where the rights of the individual leave off and the needs of our society for better scientific information on human behavior take over. It would be naïve and even amusing for me to suggest that interviewers should preface their questions with a reminder to a potential respondent that he has a right not to be interviewed. However amusing and ingenuous this idea may seem, I remind you that our psychological colleagues are very much concerned about it. Many of their leading spokesmen have stated that every individual should be informed that he is free to participate or not in any particular psychological test before it is administered to him.

But there are still other aspects of the interview situation that our critics might insist represent an invasion of the privacy of respondents, and we do well to consider these matters. For example, an interviewer may gain access to a home by indicating in vague terms the nature of the survey he is conducting. Once having been admitted and having established rapport with his informant, the interviewer is free to move from his relatively innocuous initial questions into subject areas of a highly personal nature—posing questions having to do with the political, religious, economic, and moral beliefs and practices of the respondent. Such questions no doubt are essential for many of the surveys we conduct, but they also are capable of generating resistance and resentment. In such instances, does the average respondent realize that he has the right to break off the questioning any time he may wish, even though he has given his earlier agreement to participate in the survey? This rhetorical question merely illustrates one of the many aspects about the interview situation on which we have far too little data. True, there are countless articles on how to win rapport, how to phrase questions, how to probe for more complete answers, how to assess interviewer bias, and so forth—but we have uncommonly few descriptions of the interview as a real life power situation in which both the respondent and the interviewer play out their separate and often conflicting roles. Central to any such discussion of the interview as a social phenomenon would be a consideration of how much the respondent knows about his rights vis-à-vis the interviewer. Such a study would be a splendid addition to the standard textbook, *Interviewing in Social Research*, by Hyman and his associates at NORC.*

Still another related aspect of the privacy issue in survey research work arises when the respondent is asked to report on the actions, attitudes, beliefs, and behavior of his family, his neighbors, his fellow workers, and others who are in close association with him. To what extent do we in the research fraternity run the risk of being seen as professional snoopers and private CIA agents when we employ such questions? Once again, one can see the potential conflict between our valid need for this kind of information in understanding aspects of human behavior and the equally salient concern which the public has that the research process may be abused or misused.

On another score we face a similar moral dilemma. Today there is widespread concern over the extensive use of electronic devices to spy on the most private aspects of our lives. Whether the gadgets are hidden cameras or microphones or tape recorders, they have in common the aim of causing people to reveal things about their lives that they would be most reluctant to reveal of their own free will. With this widespread concern being expressed in the press and in legislative halls, is it possible that we will be criticized for planting projective questions in our interview schedules and thereby psychologically bugging the minds of our respondents and causing them to reveal information about themselves that they otherwise would not? Far-fetched and ludicrous, you say? Perhaps, but it can be argued that when we use projective questions in a general opinion survey, we are employing the tools of the clinical psychologist without always ensuring that the same controls are imposed on the use and analysis of these projective questions that the psychologist imposes with his clients.

---

* National Opinion Research Center (at the University of Chicago).

Of course, one of the most common means of gaining electronic entry to a home is the telephone. Because it is a relatively quick, inexpensive, and convenient research tool (particularly when we are trying to locate certain kinds of respondents from a much larger universe), we all have a stake in encouraging a responsible use of the telephone in survey research. The several telephone companies, interestingly enough, do not feel that this is part of their responsibility. At any rate, it is safe to assume the average telephone subscriber does not see himself as just another potential sampling point in one of our surveys. He pays a monthly rental for his phone and usually has a proprietary feeling about it. The day may come when he reacts to increasing sales solicitations and public opinion surveys by asking why he should help subsidize the research and sales activities of others. There is agitation in some sectors of our country to have phone books indicate by a symbol whether or not the subscriber is willing to cooperate in surveys and sales pitches, and this movement could profoundly affect us.

Still another aspect of the privacy issue is raised when we find it necessary to ask respondents questions about topics that may induce considerable stress and anxiety in their minds—questions having to do with their health or their level of information on diseases such as cancer, or questions on the likelihood of an atomic war or the possibility of a depression. Once these issues have been raised to the surface of a respondent's mind, they may cause him worry and upset long after the interviewer has said goodbye. In most test situations set up by psychologists, provisions are made for some form of psychic support and therapeutic reassurance to be given to respondents after they have been exposed to anxiety-producing questions. Is it totally unrealistic to have our interviewers give some written or oral reassurance to a respondent at the end of an interview when the subject matter of the survey has dealt with an anxiety-provoking issue?

Finally, on the matter of privacy, there are those standard questions one finds at the end of most surveys dealing with the age, sex, socioeconomic status, education, race, and often the political and religious affiliation of the respondent. It is ironic that we have come to refer to these as census-type questions, inasmuch as the Bureau of the Census has the greatest difficulty in getting approval for collecting data on some of these attributes, even when it can prove that it has an elaborate mechanism for protecting the confidential nature of its data.

The issue in this case is not only our right as researchers to collect such data but, more important, our discretion and maturity of judgment in using them in reporting on the attitudes and the behavior of subgroups in our samples which might be identified and damaged by such revelations. Frankly, I am surprised that we have not felt greater pressure from the various action groups organized to protect the rights of minority groups, regarding our practice of categorizing and reporting on subgroups in our samples. In theory, it can be argued that any subgroup that can be identified by data in a survey report has had its privacy invaded. While I personally would be inclined to reject such reasoning as specious and misguided, I feel we cannot dismiss the possibility of this developing into an important issue at some future date.

In summary, then, the first part of this paper has belabored the proposition that the issue of privacy in public opinion research is a very real one, and that it manifests itself in a wide variety of ways, but most particularly in the interview situation. It may also obtain when we use sloppy procedures in screening, hiring, and supervising coders, typists, clerical personnel, and all other employees who have access to personal data collected in our opinion surveys.

If you grant that we do indeed invade the privacy of our respondents in some measure in the work we do, then I think you might also agree that it becomes important for us to ensure that the public understands why we need this kind of information and why we can be trusted with it. Stated bluntly, the issue of privacy then is linked to the question: What does the public get for permitting us to enter their homes, use up their leisure time, and often explore very private nooks and crannies of their lives? The psychological tester in industry or government can point to a number of direct benefits to the individual, his family, and his society from the various psychological tests he administers. What gratifications and rewards do we offer respondents who take part in our public opinion surveys?

The first and most obvious is that we provide a sympathetic ear to them and offer them a way of getting problems and opinions off their chests. Moreover, respondents probably have their self-esteem enhanced when they are asked opinions on important problems of the day. But, alas, there are also many instances in which the subject matter of a survey is pretty dull and trivial and of interest only to the sponsoring client. What do the respondent and his society get from cooperating with such data-gathering efforts?

Analogies may be misleading and misplaced, and yet I feel it is appropriate to use one in discussing this question and its broader implications. Let's face it, we are able to collect our research data only because the general public continues to be willing to submit to our interviews. This acceptance of us by the public is the basic natural resource on which our industry is built. Without it, we would be out of business tomorrow. Other industries also have been built on the exploitation of other kinds of natural resources—our forests, farmlands, and mines—and it is instructive to remember that during the nineteenth century in this country many of these industries made two errors that in time caused public outcry and pressure on government to regulate them. First, they assumed that the public was not interested in what they were doing and so made no serious effort to explain the contributions they were making to society. Second, they failed to find a mechanism to police a certain few of their members who did not serve the public well.

To date, we in the opinion research business have done a poor job of informing the public about the work we do and the benefits it brings to them. On the other hand, we have formulated a sound code of ethics. Unfortunately, we have only informal means by which to enforce these standards and it may be unrealistic to expect that we will ever be able to do more. Those in our business who most frequently do violence to our standards usually do not belong to professional associations and do not respond readily to informal pressures.

What is the story we should be telling about public opinion research and the benefits the public derives from it? The substance of this message will obviously vary, depending on the type of organization that sponsors public opinion research. Broadly speaking, there are three kinds of clients who commission most public opinion research studies. They are (1) the government, (2) academic and quasiacademic research institutes, usually operating on a nonprofit basis, and (3) commercial research firms, usually trying to operate on a profit basis and fortunately succeeding.

I suspect that each of these three groups has a different degree of acceptance from the public. In the case of government-sponsored research, a certain amount is actually required by law, the best example being the census. But even when not required by law, studies sponsored by government agencies, both Federal and state, seem to have general acceptance—particularly those dealing with problems in the field of agriculture, health, education, and public welfare. The research work done by these government bureaus has earned high recognition from scholars as well as the general public. In speculating on the degree of acceptance by the public of government-sponsored research, it should be noted that the public ultimately exercises control over these studies through their elected officials, who can authorize greater or less government research effort. Yet, ironically enough, it is in government today that the use of psychological tests is most widely being called into question by congressional critics and others. Is our turn next? Perhaps now is the time for an educational effort to be undertaken with key members of Congress to explain the role public opinion surveys can play in ensuring better planning by government agencies.

It is difficult to speculate on how much the public is aware of the research being carried out by academic and nonprofit research institutes. I suspect there may be times when the recondite nature of their studies may puzzle the public, but I find no evidence that any appreciable number of people question either the motives or the integrity of these research organizations. I assume most of you would agree that a persuasive case can be made for the benefits that the general public derives from these studies. Once more, however, I find myself generally unimpressed by the quality of the reporting these groups do in telling their story to the non-research-oriented world. Their annual reports, when they elect to publish them, are often pedestrian and dull, apparently assigned to a staff writer, and failing altogether to catch the excitement and significance of the problems on which these institutes are working.

Finally, there is the vast field of commercial research, which is designed to help a client improve his market position or his corporate acceptance. These projects are sometimes treated in a pejorative and patronizing way by those who do not know the rigorous technical standards and the imaginative research designs employed in many of these studies. One frequent justification for the social utility of commercial research is that it permits the public to communicate its likes and dislikes to the companies that manufacture our consumer products; produce our newspapers, television programs, and magazines; and provide a host of other consumer services. We in the research business generally assume this function is perfectly obvious to the general public, but I doubt this.

But telling the story of the contributions public opinion research makes to improving the consumer's products must be done with skill. It would be unwise, for example, to use the old cliché that the public is the real boss of the marketplace and that by asking for its opinion about various consumer products we bring democracy to the councils of the business world. One example of where this theme could come back to haunt us is the automotive industry, which has carried out countless consumer surveys. These surveys may or may not have been a factor in causing manufacturers to put chrome and tailfins on their cars instead of building greater safety into them. But the auto industry, and every other industrial consumer of opinion research data, should make it clear that they employ survey research data merely as one among several sources of information that influence their decisions on product design and changes. Thus, opinion surveys provide the consumer with a forum from which he may speak to management, but they do not guarantee him a seat in the board of directors' room.

Candor requires that we also admit that not all commercial surveys have direct social value to our society. Putting aside the question of whether or not cigarette smoking is harmful to health, it just is plain difficult to see how the public benefits when a client commissions a survey designed to learn why the public prefers Brand X to Brand Y. In such cases, the argument I would offer on behalf of the social value of commercial research is that it frequently helps perfect research techniques that can be applied to problems of greater social importance, provided these new research techniques are made available to the world of research scholars. The Roper Public Opinion Research Center at Williams College represented a pioneer effort in the direction of making such data available, and the newly created Council of Social Science Data Archives consolidates the resources of the Roper Center with those of seven other libraries of public opinion research data. Even so, only a small fraction of the research carried out for private industry ever finds its way into those archives or the public domain.

The time has come, in my opinion, for those of us who earn a livelihood from public opinion research to consider how we might make a more concrete contribution to our society. As a very tentative and inadequate first step in this direction, I suggest that the individual firms (or a consortium of some of our larger commercial and academic research groups) donate several public service surveys each year on subjects of importance to the people of the United States. There are endless topics crying out for such study, and some do not have sponsors with money enough to commission such research.

I have discussed at some length our less than excellent public relations position because I think our profession has the resources and reasons to improve it. This job should be undertaken at once, not alone to forestall government interference and regulation of our work, and not alone to protect the dollar investment and the professional commitment that we have in the field of public opinion surveys, but also because a better understanding of our work could very conceivably improve the quality of the data we get from the public. Once we accept the fact that the question of "privacy" is relevant for us in the public opinion research field, I am convinced we can justify our activities and demonstrate their social worth.

42 The Harassed Respondent: I. Sales Solicitation in the Guise of Consumer Research

Richard Baxter

One of the most flagrant abuses of respondents occurs when salesmen solicit sales while ostensibly conducting a market research interview. This is not just an occasional act of misrepresentation but, as Richard Baxter shows in the following article, has happened to about one-fourth of the adults in the United States. Baxter outlines the nature and dimensions of this marketing problem and suggests some remedies. If future market researchers are not to be increasingly denied interviews with respondents, the abuses he describes must obviously be ended.

The telephone rings, and you answer. A voice says, "Hello, this is _____ calling, of (an ambiguously descriptive firm name). I am conducting a study dealing with the _____ market. I would like to ask you just a few questions which will only take a minute or two." A series of questions are then asked which obtain specific data on certain big ticket items currently owned in the household. If certain models are owned, the interviewer then asks whether the item was purchased *new* or *used* and what the family's buying intentions are for a new model. (If the last item purchased was *used*, the interview is terminated.)

So far so good. To this point, the respondent is being surveyed in a buying-intention study.

But then what happens? On the back of the questionnaires are instructions to the interviewers, including a sample form which the interviewer is given to fill out for each respondent contacted. The interviewer is given a batch of these forms. In addition to pre-codes for circling by the interviewer, indicating the time of the respondent's intended purchase of the product, are the following items: "Salesman's Name," "Date of Sale," "Name of Retail Outlet." The next item reads, "When the sale and delivery

Reprinted from Richard Baxter, *The Harassed Respondent: I. Sales Solicitation in the Guise of Consumer Research*, Report to the Market Research Council (September 17, 1965), pp. 23–29, by permission of the author.

of _____ has been made to the prospect listed above, complete the required information and submit this report of sale to your dealer for approval and forwarding to the (manufacturer's District Office)."

A watch company sends out sale promotional material and a questionnaire. One side of the post-card size questionnaire has a few rudimentary questions on media preferences and preferred retail outlet for watch purchasing. The other side is an order form which the respondent can fill out after having read through a color brochure illustrating and describing various watch models.

A gasoline company uses the name "Research Center" as the return address for a credit-card solicitation.

A mailing house sends questionnaires by mail to develop mailing lists, with the promise that people who fill out the questionnaires will have the opportunity to win "fabulous gifts." When queried about the purpose of the questionnaire, a form letter came back from the firm indicating that the purpose was to "enable us to do a better job of selecting names from our overall list for particular mailings." This form letter also was sent to recipients of the questionnaire who wrote the mailing house to learn more about the project.

Millions of American households have been approached—by mail, by telephone, and in person—by usurpers of legitimate research techniques, for the purpose of making sales.

Once, while I was associated with an advertising agency, a subsidiary of a well-known market research firm asked for an appointment with one of the agency's marketing executives. At a subsequent hour and a half meeting, three were present: the agency marketing man, the sales representative from the outside firm, and I. (I was *not* identified as a researcher). The essence of this firm's offer was to obtain and provide to us the names and addresses of prospects for residential air conditioners. It was made clear that these prospects would be approached as in a market research survey and that they would not know that their names were to be turned over as sales leads.

Marketing and sales executives of manufacturing companies, of advertising agencies, and of other kinds of business institutions are being solicited increasingly—either in person or by mail—by firms that offer their services to obtain the names of customer prospects for products and services. These names are then made available to the client organization. This, of course, is a legitimate activity, provided there is no implication to the prospective customer that he has been interviewed in an opinion or market survey.

The researcher's complaint is that the survey approach frequently is misused to obtain sales leads for later use or to attempt to sell something to the respondent during the course of the interview. Such unethical practices are not easy to control. Cases have been noted, for example, in which the sales solicitor interviewing to identify prospects *departs* from a script that would have been acceptable to the researcher because it did not camouflage the true purpose of the sales call. There is no assurance that an ethically clean sales-canvass script will not be converted into a deceptive survey-approach in actual field use.

It has long been a practice in industrial market research, particularly in studies of market potentials for new products in the big ticket industrial product field, for the names of respondents to be turned over to sales staffs of the client company. This very point, in fact, was about the only bone of contention within the American Marketing Association Ethics Committee when we developed a Code of Ethics three or four years ago. This Code was approved overwhelmingly by the members of the AMA, but there was a vociferous minority which felt we were being unrealistic by insisting on the anonymity of respondents in market research surveys. I know that some experienced, industrial market researchers felt that our committee members were "nice nellies." But we do have reason to be concerned about an apparently increasing misuse of the survey technique by sales canvassers. There are two reasons for this concern.

The first is that public confusion, annoyance, and distrust of field interviewers over a few years, resulting from unfortunate experiences with deceptive "survey" practices, can seriously impede legitimate survey activity. We have a reservoir of public good will to protect. That good will really keeps us in business. It is the *essential* raw material from which opinion and market research is made. We shouldn't jeopardize the public's willingness to submit to interviews.

The second reason we are concerned is that more and more states and local governments are attempting to regulate or restrict bona-fide market and opinion survey interviewing, and there are signs that interviewers are being classified—in the minds of many public authorities—along with peddlers.

Let's look at each of these points. Elmo Roper and Associates included a question series in a nationwide survey that was conducted in May, 1963 (using an area probability sample of 3,919 cases). The first question was: "Has anyone ever said he wanted to interview you on a survey—either in person or by telephone, and then tried to sell you something?"

The percentages who answered "Yes" were:

	Total	Men	Women
	27%	25%	30%
100% =	(3,919)	(1,957)	(1,962)

Note that about one-fourth of adults in the United States believe that they have been approached on a "survey" whose real purpose was to sell the respondent something—with somewhat more women than men reporting such an experience.

The table on page 342 presents some figures on the kinds of products and services which were the subjects of these "deceptive surveys."

The following is a press release from the Opinion Research Corporation, dated October 21, 1964:

PRINCETON, N.J.—Almost as many persons are being asked for interviews by salesmen posing as "interviewers" as by legitimate interviewers for survey organizations, a study by Opinion Research Corporation has found.

A nationwide probability sample of 2,035 adults participated in the research.

Almost one person in four (24%) said he had been approached at some time by someone who claimed to be an interviewer and turned out to be a salesman using a survey as a device to get one foot in the door.

Subject of "Deceptive Surveys"	Per Cent
Magazines	28
Books, encyclopedias	26
Screens, storm windows	10
Electrical appliances (other than vacuum cleaners)	9
Vacuum cleaners	7
Insurance	7
Photographs, pictures	6
Lessons—dance, piano, etc.	3
Sidings	3
Household sundries	2
Cosmetics, toiletries	1
Cars	1
All other	12
Don't know or no answer	10
	100% = (1,061)

On the other hand, some 29% of participants in the ORC study, a slightly larger proportion, reported they had been interviewed previously by legitimate research firms.

Joseph C. Bevis, ORC Chairman, said the findings reflected a serious problem for research organizations and the clients they serve. "The public's willingness to participate in research is based largely on good will and appreciation of the importance of such efforts," he said. "When surveys are misrepresented and the public is misled, obtaining the cooperation essential to effective research becomes increasingly difficult."

Of participants who said they had been approached by phony interviewers, 30% reported the salesman's product was a magazine and 25% said the product was an encyclopedia.

Eighteen different magazines and eleven different encyclopedias were cited.

Some 52 other products and services also were cited including brassieres, dancing lessons, TV sets, freezers, and cemetery lots.

There is, then, convincing evidence of the abuse of public good will by sales canvassers using the survey technique to gain entry or information at the respondent's doorstep or telephone mouthpiece.

What has been the measurable effect of all this deception on getting interviews? The survey evidence we have does *not* show an increase in the interview refusal rate in legitimate market and opinion surveys. At least, we had not found an increase up to 1963. In that year, the Public Relations Committee of the American Association for Public Opinion Research sent letters to certain individual members of AAPOR who also are principals of research organizations. Twenty-six persons replied. Fifteen of the 26 organizations represented have field interviewing activity. This was not a representative sample of U.S. research organizations, but I think the results can be used to illustrate the opinions held by many professional researchers concerning this problem.

By a ratio of about two to one, more survey practitioners expressed the opinion that refusal rates are *not* a problem, or are not increasing, than expressed the opinion that refusals *are* a problem or are increasing. Those who did see a refusal problem were asked what was causing it, in their opinion. Undoubtedly cued to some extent by the content of the inquiry we sent them, more of the researchers mentioned mistrust of market researchers by people refusing to be interviewed than by any other reason. It is evident that there is some concern in our professional fraternity concerning this problem. Many of those replying to the AAPOR Committee gave examples of how fraudulent use of the survey approach has impaired legitimate survey research activity. The tenor of this problem is much easier to understand through exposure to actual field cases than by reading statistics on the incidence of deception involving the survey technique.

1. In 1963, in a Texas town, a telephone interview survey on coffee was conducted, involving a sample of 440 women. Only 380 of these interviews could be completed—a 13.6% refusal rate. This rate is sharply above that found in 16 other cities in which the identical interview approach was used. The normal rate of refusal was under 2%, which also had been the rate for two previous studies in the same town, using the very same interview questions.

   Because of this discrepancy in refusal rates, refusals were analyzed. It was found that a telephone canvass had been conducted in that area about three weeks before this survey. The earlier canvass actually was for sales purposes, and involved the use of a market research telephone survey approach to obtain names of customer prospects for use by local dealers of the company that authorized the canvass. Suspicion of all market studies was cited by respondents who refused to be interviewed in the later bona-fide market and opinion research survey.

2. Another survey operator we contacted referred to a survey conducted in the spring of 1963 in which four out of five eligible respondents interviewed by telephone refused a personal interview that was to follow, largely because of their fear of a later sales effort.

Boston, Providence, and "probably other markets" caused trouble to another of our responding research firms, which was attributed to an earlier automotive study.

Still another survey practitioner said: "The types of studies which seem to run into more closed doors usually involve magazine readership—also—a degree of difficulty on studies (of) baby care products, and with frozen food surveys. The reason is easily traceable to the fact that magazine and book salesmen, diaper services and freezer plan salesmen make a great deal of use out of the public opinion interview as a means of obtaining leads for further sales."

What about the second reason for our fear concerning the abuse of legitimate survey research? The latest statistics I have show that about 250 communities in 34 states have some kind of restrictions on field interviewing for surveys. This is not necessarily bad. Legitimate interviewers can be protected, in effect, by ordinances attempting to screen and control various kinds of approaches made to the public. But the nature of a large share of this local regulation is undoubtedly restrictive, causing additional field problems and expense. The following are some examples.

According to information received from operating research organizations whom we contacted, no interviewing whatever is allowed in the California cities of Arcadia, Beverly Hills, San Marino, and Huntington Beach, and in other scattered communities, for example, one or two well-to-do suburbs of Miami. Licenses are required in Burbank, Pico Rivera, South Pasadena, Chula Vista, and La Mesa, in California. Burbank charges $50, South Pasadena $20. In some of the Chicago areas $5 or $10 is charged, and in some cases every time—that is, each day—that the locale is used. In some communities no evening or weekend interviewing is allowed. The research organizations we corresponded with tell us that there are increasing restrictions and intervention by suburban township authorities and questioning by police.

What does all this mean? Many of us believe that the evidence is clear that respondents are being abused by deceptive market and opinion "surveyers." We believe that continued activity of this kind is endangering the reservoir of public good will, and also will have an effect on regulatory and legislative officials in states and local communities.

What can we do about it?

1. If you or a member of your family is approached as a respondent in a deceptive "survey," get details, such as the name and address of the interviewing or sales canvassing organization, the name of the "interviewer," the time and date of the interview, the nature of the survey, product, or service categories being studied, a copy of the questionnaire. Send this information to the Standards Committee of organizations like the American Association for Public Opinion Research or the American Marketing Association which have Codes of proper practice and which should be prepared to look into the matter.

2. If you are a research professional in the field, you, your firm, or other professionals you might know might be approached by a prospective client who wants a "sales lead" job done, using the survey research method. Such approaches should also be brought to the attention of one of the professional organizations. The American Association for Public Opinion Research recently changed from a loosely organized association of individuals to a corporation—with the express purpose of taking action to stop misuse of the survey technique. Prior to this incorporation, there were legal barriers to effective action. The organization already has moved to stop some deceptive practices.

3. For added pressure from an important agency in the area of deceptive business practices, notify the National Better Business Bureau in New York, if the offending "survey" sponsor is a national or regional firm that you suspect is operating in more than one community. The Bureau has taken effective action on past abuses.

4. Encourage the use by interviewers of the National Better Business Bureau's "Memo to the Public"—or whatever similar form is most effective in a given community (it may be a form by a local Chamber of Commerce or municipal bureau). Such instruments *cannot* be used by the phony interviewer without the danger of a "boomerang effect" on his company's sales effort, because these memos *assure,* in print, that no sales effort will be made.

5. Every research organization should consider the development of a public information program. It need not be expensive, nor complicated. Try to get interviewing supervisors employed by your firm on programs of service and civic clubs, women's organizations, and the like, to explain the value of true market and opinion research in their communities. Your staff people could write up a sample script for such a speech.

The Opinion Research Corporation, for example, made up a kit of materials about two and a half years ago which was distributed to newspapers in some 400 communities for use in feature stories about interviewing, about particular interviewers, and about bona-fide survey research. A very satisfactory proportion of papers did use the materials. ORC also determined which of its interviewers would be willing to be interviewed on local radio and television stations and in newspapers, and then ORC notified the local media of the availability of these interviewers. There are hundreds, probably thousands, of "interview programs" on local stations across the country which are continually looking for interesting program material and personalities.

Our profession needs authoritative action to stop unethical and damaging pseudo-research activity. But this action can be taken only if individuals call infractions to the attention of appropriate professional organizations. The time has already gone by when we can sit by and "let George do it."

43 The Harassed Respondent:
II. Interviewing Practices   Paul B. Sheatsley

Survey techniques can be misused in many ways to the detriment of the respondent. Asking questions that are too personal, holding excessively long interviews, and conducting surveys at unsuitable hours are just some of the abuses with which respondents are faced. Paul B. Sheatsley, author of the following article, sketches the nature of some of these abuses, suggests some ways to correct them, and concludes that they are not *yet* a critical problem but can become one.

The term "respondent harassment" or "respondent abuse" is, of course, a loaded one. Nobody, I surmise, wants to harass respondents. Everybody would agree that they should not be abused. But what constitutes respondent abuse? How do we define it? And assuming we can define it, how prevalent is the practice? What effects, if any, does it have? What can we do about it? I address myself to the subject rather gingerly because factual information on the matter is conspicuously absent.

We all have general ideas about what constitutes respondent abuse. The editor of this book has previously referred to some of them: excessively long interviews, for example; omnibus type questionnaires which skip erratically from one unrelated subject to another; so-called depth interviews on subjects of no interest or concern to the respondent; excessive use of the telephone for survey purposes; excessive reinterviewing of panel populations; interviewer calls at unsuitable hours of the day or night; and so on.

Well, let me confess. The two-hour interview, while not exactly routine, is still not uncommon at the National Opinion Research Center. (I was engaged in one study in which the interview averaged three hours. That, I might mention, is too long.) NORC has an omnibus questionnaire service, in which we have no hesitation at all in mixing up batteries of questions about such diverse issues as the war in Viet Nam, personal drinking habits, the Negro protest movement, and attitudes toward water fluoridation or premarital sex. Gallup, Opinion Research Corporation, Alfred Politz, and a host of state and local polls regularly issue similar omnibus surveys. I confess more. NORC is presently engaged right here in New

Reprinted from Paul B. Sheatsley, *The Harassed Respondent: II. Interviewing Practices*, Report to the Market Research Council (October 15, 1965), pp. 39–43, by permission of the author.

York in making callbacks, either by telephone or in person, every month for 12 months to the mothers of infants in their first year of life. This is, incidentally, after an original interview which lasted one hour and three-quarters. We are now in our tenth month of these callbacks and 89% of the cases are still with us. On the last callback, only 2% of them were rated by interviewers as less than cooperative. Indeed, we have successfully administered a one-hour interview schedule to a widely dispersed population of doctors entirely by long-distance telephone.

I think it is clear that one cannot devise any objective definition of respondent harassment or abuse. A 30-minute interview is not necessarily a pleasant experience. A 60-minute interview is not necessarily harassment. What defines respondent abuse is the respondent's own reaction to the task imposed on him. If he feels abused by the interviewer's demands, we have to assume that he *is* abused, no matter how interesting and simple we thought our questionnaire was. If he enjoys the experience, however lengthy or complicated or uninteresting the questionnaire may seem to someone else, it is difficult to charge any abuse. The role of the interviewer, therefore, becomes an important factor in the equation. A personable and sensitive interviewer can often turn a difficult interview into an enjoyable and challenging experience for the respondent. An aggressive or uncertain interviewer can make the respondent feel uncomfortable and annoyed even though the survey itself is well designed. Two things, then, are required if the respondent is to accept his task cheerfully, without feelings of harassment and abuse. He must, first, accept the goals of the survey and feel that he is participating in something useful; and he must, second, react in a positive way to the interviewer.

In a study conducted recently for the National Health Survey by the Survey Research Center at the University of Michigan,* a team of researchers studying the factors which make for valid reporting in the interviewing situation identified—on the basis of personal observations of interviews and informal talks with respondents later—five major reasons for the feelings which respondents had about the interview. Three of these five represented areas of respondent concern. First, there was concern about the time the interview would take, that it would interfere with other activities or require an inappropriate amount of time. Second, there was concern about the questions to be asked: Will they be too personal, too demanding, repetitious, or otherwise unpleasant? Third, there was concern about the purpose or uses of the survey: Why is the information required; who will use it; for what purpose; and will the respondent have any later cause to regret his participation?

Against these three concerns, two positive factors were noted. First

---

* "The Influence of Interviewer and Respondent Psychological and Behavioral Variables on the Reporting in Household Interviews", National Center for Health Statistics, Series 2, No.26, U.S. Dept. of Health, Education and Welfare, Public Health Service.

was an interest in the chance to be of public service or to help a worthy cause. Most people *wanted* to help. Second was an interest in the chance to interact with the interviewer. Many respondents were lonely or flattered to be asked or just plain friendly, and they were glad to converse with someone who was interested in them.

Now, if this analysis is correct, it is clear that the interviewer, as she makes her first approach to the respondent and as she begins and proceeds with the interview, has two things going for her: the ordinary person's interest in helping with something worthwhile and in interacting with another human being. However, there are also the three concerns of the respondent which threaten the interviewer's success: concern about the time the interview will take, about the kinds of questions to be asked, and about the purpose or use of the study. It is the interviewer's task to maintain and support the two favorable predispositions and to reassure the respondent, by both word and deed, about his three areas of concern.

I submit that respondent abuse occurs when the respondent's anxieties are *not* relieved and when the progress of the interview may even serve to reinforce them. He is concerned about the time required, but the interview goes on and on. He is concerned about the kinds of questions he will be asked, and he is confronted with one after another which strike him as silly, repetitious, overly personal, or entirely too demanding. He is concerned about the purpose and use of the survey, but he has received no straight answer, and the content of the survey seems trivial or threatening.

It is a tribute to the strength of the two favorable factors I have mentioned and to the immense good will of the American people that respondents so willingly put up with all that we demand of them. I suppose there are surveys in which one-third or more of the respondents at some point say to the interviewer: "Enough of this. I won't answer any more." But I don't know of any such surveys. On the contrary, I think most of us find that only 1 or 2 or 3% at most ever break off an interview once they have started it. Once committed, people tend to see it through, no matter how much they may suffer.

It would be better for all if they did not, for observe what happens in such circumstances. The two essentials of a useful interview have not been met: the respondent has not been persuaded to accept the goals of the survey, and he is unable to react in a positive way to the interviewer as long as that individual is making him uncomfortable. First, then, the quality of the data suffers. The respondent becomes surly, suggests skipping certain questions, keeps repeating :"I don't know," or answers unthinkingly or at random. If this happens in any considerable proportion of the cases, the effects are obvious.

Second, what does the interviewer do when faced with such a situation? Her task has become impossible. If she continues to follow her instructions in order to please her employer, her already bad rapport will continue to deteriorate, and she knows already that she is not getting good answers. On the other hand, if she wants to remotivate the respondent to accept the survey, she can do so only by skipping questions, rewording them, or otherwise disobeying instructions. Some interviewers will doggedly carry on. Some will withdraw and simply fake the missing data. Most will compromise somehow, asking enough questions to get a kind of feel for the respondent's views and then filling in the rest themselves on the basis of what they feel pretty sure the respondent would have said.

What the interviewer ought to do, of course, is to apologize to the respondent, break off the interview (or if time is the annoying factor, suggest completing it at a more convenient time), and report what happened to her supervisor. But this would be contrary to everything she has been taught. To complete the quota, to get the interview, is really "the name of the game." If she can't do it, it reflects on her. Her supervisor will tell her that all the other interviewers produced completed interviews; what's wrong with her? (Or the agency will tell the supervisor that all the other supervisors produced completed interviews; what's wrong with her staff?)

The second effect, then, of respondent abuse, besides insufficient or incorrect data, is a demoralization of the interviewer which will reflect itself either in what we call cheating behavior or in a high interviewer turnover. (I might say, incidentally, that I do not believe interviewers can be divided into good guys and bad guys or honest ones vs. cheaters. If properly selected and trained, I have found that 95% of all interviewers will try their level best, sometimes beyond the call of duty, to perform as instructed. However, if asked to do what clearly turns out to be impossible, or impossibly frustrating, 95% of those who don't quit will be forced into some kind of cheating or corner-cutting.)

There is, of course, yet one more effect, and that is the public relations problem about which I know some of us feel very strongly. Consider what happens when the hypothetical abused respondent we have been talking about finally gets rid of that badgering interviewer. What does he tell his family and friends about survey research? And what is likely to be his reaction, and his family's reaction, and his friends' reactions, when the next interviewer comes around with another survey?

How much respondent abuse exists? It is difficult to estimate the magnitude. We badly need a periodic sample survey of all market and survey research interviewers and we badly need continuing measurements of the public's experiences with and attitudes toward interviewers and surveys. We can all cite horrible examples, but we have no real means of assessing their impact.

My own feeling is that the problem has not yet become critical. At least, we at NORC have noticed no long-term trend toward lower completion rates or a higher proportion of refusals and breakoffs. I must admit, of course, that a small proportion of our respondents on any given survey do not enjoy the interview and that a particular question item or procedure is sometimes criticized by many interviewers. But by and large our respondents do not seem to feel abused, judging from their repeated cooperation on panel studies, the time and effort they have been willing to give us, and their own statements as to how interesting or enjoyable the interview was. But I know and you know, of course, that there is an awful lot of shoddy work in this field being done by the other guy.

Eighteen years ago I published an article in the *Public Opinion Quarterly* called "Some Uses of Interviewer Report Forms." Interviewers are asked on such forms, at the conclusion of each assignment, for their general reactions to the survey, its comparative ease or difficulty, particular questions or series of questions which respondents enjoyed, or which were found to be difficult, frequently misunderstood, embarrassing, or poorly worded. I pointed out in the article that such data from interviewers had important uses in three major respects: first, in the supervision and maintenance of the field staff by providing a regular means whereby interviewers can communicate with their supervisors; second, in the analysis and evaluation of the survey findings through the warning they provide of likely misunderstandings, biases, or inaccuracies in the data; and third, in the design and wording of future questionnaires through the advice they provide about what works and what does not.

I would plead that we all solicit the reactions and experience of our interviewers and that we pay heed to what they tell us. We can do this in pretest through meeting with the pretesters, going through the questionnaire item by item, and asking them just what problems occurred. We can do this by means of written reports after each survey, so that we can be alerted to possible kinds of respondent abuse which might not otherwise come to our attention.

It is, of course, true that our main objective is not merely to provide the interviewer and the respondent with a pleasant experience. We have research problems to solve and data that we urgently require. Sometimes the problem *demands* a two-hour interview; sometimes we simply *must* devise questions about personal or threatening subjects; sometimes it is crucial that we lead the respondent through what may seem to him repetitious questioning.

However, there *are* ways—some simple and some necessarily very ingenious—by which a competent researcher can usually manage to do these things. Essentially, they involve meeting the respondent's three major concerns about time, about the questions he's asked, and about the purpose of the questions. Often, it is simply a matter of leveling with him. If it is a one-hour interview and he was assured it would only take 20 minutes or so, he will darn well feel abused. If he wants to know what good the survey will do and your interviewer has not been provided with an acceptable answer, he is likely to feel harassed as the questioning goes on.

Besides leveling with the respondent, let's level with our interviewers. Let's abandon the myth that a good interviewer can make a respondent sit through anything without feeling harassed. If interviewers could be depended upon to tell us frankly when something doesn't work, we, and our data, and our interviewers, and our respondents would all be better off.

Let us remember that abuse is defined by the respondent. If we can get him to accept the goals of our survey and provide him with a reasonably good interviewer, he can be asked to do all sorts of things, and he will not feel abused. If he cannot be persuaded to accept our goals, the fault lies with us, and we had better do something about it.

44 The Law of Privacy and Marketing Research

Charles S. Mayer
Charles H. White, Jr.

The psychological intrusion on an individual's privacy through a disguised questionnaire is a commonplace action in the field of marketing research. Unfortunately, however, such an invasion may leave the interviewer open to a lawsuit. The following article tells why, and at the same time shows how, the law of privacy and the perceived right of privacy are different.

Much has been written about the right of privacy forming a vague outside boundary for marketing research legitimacy. At best the right of privacy is an amorphous thing. Even the courts are struggling with its definition. The commonly felt "right of privacy" and the present state of the "law of privacy" are not necessarily congruent. This paper focuses on the developing *law* of privacy, and attempts to sharpen the boundary for legitimate marketing research.

In his article concerning privacy and public opinion research, Carlson voiced fear that the survey research profession is a possible candidate for "the harassment and the investigations" arising out of governmental scrutiny.[1] He pragmatically states that ". . . we are able to collect our research data only because the general public continues to be willing to submit to our interviews. This acceptance of us by the public is the basic natural resource on which our industry is built. Without it we would be out of business tomorrow." This natural resource is not unlimited, nor can it safely be assumed that it will remain continuously available. It is subject to the environmental constraints of privacy.

The Law of Privacy   That the law of privacy is volatile and complex, while the layman's feel for his right of privacy remains simple if inarticulate, can be partially explained by its genesis. Privacy is not a constitutionally guaranteed right, nor did it come into American jurisprudence through the Common Law. As a viable element of American jurisprudence,

Reprinted from Charles S. Mayer and Charles H. White, Jr., "The Law of Privacy and Marketing Research", *Journal of Marketing* (April, 1969), Vol. 33, pp. 1–4, by permission of the authors. Published by the American Marketing Association.

the law of privacy can trace its lineage to a momentous article by Warren and Brandeis.[2]

In arguing for legal recognition of a right of privacy as a separate and independent entity, the authors analyzed previous cases where other causes of action formally supported the decision, but in which privacy-related issues provided the social rationale. Their article, however, was concerned primarily with policy arguments favoring the judicial recognition of a privacy right. Other legal scholars were stimulated by the Warren and Brandeis article, and the topic received much attention from academic lawyers. Judges began to refer to these academicians' writings in gradually articulating a legally recognized right of privacy.

As is predictable in our federal system, the law of privacy did not develop uniformly among the different jurisdictions. Some state jurisdictions have subsumed the academicians' writings to support a strongly protected right. Others have been slower to recognize such a right. And still others have yet to be called upon to hear a case based on privacy issues. The legal concept of privacy is a growing and changing thing.

It is not the purpose of this paper to restate the history of the concept of privacy. Rather the concern is with developing its present status as a constraint for the marketing research profession. Although the law is complex, an attempt will be made to generalize trends briefly and to look at the whole body of privacy law.

Breach of Privacy   As a start, consider the present kinds of legal action that can be initiated for breach of privacy. Privacy can be categorized under *tort* law. A tort is a civil wrong which will support an action for damages. If the law of privacy is viewed as a whole, four different kinds of tort action arising out of a breach of privacy can be discerned. These four torts represent breaches of four different types of privacy rights. Without any attempt at precise definition the four constituent torts can be thus described:

1. *Intrusion*: the act of intruding upon an individual's private affairs, his solitude, or his seclusion.
2. *Disclosure*: the act of making public embarrassing private facts about an individual.
3. *False Light*: the act of placing an individual in a false light in the public eye—of publicizing misrepresentative statements concerning him.
4. *Appropriation*: the act of appropriating an individual's name or likeness for the appropriator's advantage.[3]

After recognizing the characteristics of the four tort actions arising out of the breach of privacy one can better understand the effectiveness of the law of privacy as an environmental constraint upon the survey research profession.

The four torts—intrusion, disclosure, false light, and appropriation—

are alike only in that they arise under the generic head of privacy. Intrusion and disclosure require the invasion of something personal, secret, or private; false light and appropriation do not. Disclosure, false light, and appropriation require publicity. Intrusion alone is not concerned with publicity. The wrongdoing consists in intrusion per se.

Since publication is an essential element of the torts of disclosure and false light and is an important element of appropriation, the marketing research profession's possible defense based on the fact that public disclosure of *individual* data is not made (that the guarantee of individual anonymity is given) would probably be effective. The rights of privacy, where they are judicially recognized, are strictly individual. A *collective* suit brought on behalf of a body of respondents seeking damages arising out of the publication of collectively embarrassing facts would probably not stand. Collective rights of privacy have not yet been recognized. Since individual data are not disclosed, false light and disclosure actions against the profession would not stand.

A defense based upon the guarantee of anonymity arising out of the nonpublication of individual data, however, is an irrelevant defense against a tort action based on intrusion. Publication is not an element of intrusion. The simple act of intrusion in itself gives rise to the action. It is the tort of intrusion that will pose the gravest future threat for the unhampered execution of marketing research.

Intrusion   The tort of intrusion on an individual's solitude currently encompasses physical intrusion into his presence, visual intrusion, and auditory intrusion as exemplified by the eavesdropping cases. A logical case can be mounted to predict the extension of the tort of intrusion from the physical to the psychological level. If the courts are willing to recognize intrusion on the physical level, they should be even more disposed to entertain intrusion actions at the psychological level where the right to solitude appears to be more fundamental.

In Hamberger v. Eastman,[4] one jurisdiction examined the law of privacy for the first time. Since a privacy issue had not been previously raised in the state, the judge examined the most recent authorities and case law from other jurisdictions. In phrasing the issue of law, the judge asked whether New Hampshire recognizes that "intrusion on one's physical *and mental* solitude or seclusion is a tort." (italics added) His finding for the plaintiff implicitly indicated that mental intrusion would constitute an actionable tort. As one reads the latest intrusion cases from the different jurisdictions, a potential shift toward recognition of the psychological level may be discerned.

If the tort of intrusion continues to be extended to the psychological level, there are obvious implications for the marketing research profession. The disguised-projective questioning technique is designed specifically to gain access to the respondent's psychological level.[5] It is difficult to distinguish logically between physical and psychological intrusion; the individual's "right to be let alone" is being violated in each case. If "Peeping Tom" statutes are written to protect individuals from visual intrusion, is it not reasonable to expect similar protection from psychological intrusion? That professional motives are on a higher plane than prurient ones is insufficient and beside the point. A higher individual right to solitude is being violated.

Consent   The right of privacy in general, and the right to be free from tortious intrusion in particular, can be waived by either an explicit or an implied consent. But whether the simple act of consenting to be interviewed amounts to an implied waiver of the right to be free from psychological intrusion raises an inescapable question for the marketing research profession. The whole philosophy of disguised questioning is built on the assumption that the respondent's psychological field can be tapped by asking carefully designed surface questions. The respondent's consent is to answer these surface level questions; it is unlikely that he would willingly consent to have his psyche plumbed by an interviewer. A defensive argument based on the theory of implied consent would be difficult to sustain. The respondent and the interviewer/agency are by definition on different communication levels when disguised questioning techniques are used. It is unlikely that there has been a sufficient meeting of the minds to support an implied consent argument.

In summary then, the efficacy of the law of privacy as an environmental constraint on the marketing research profession is best understood by delineating privacy into its four corresponding torts. The actions of false light, disclosure, and appropriation are likely to remain inapplicable as long as the profession continues to refuse to disclose individual data and the right of privacy remains strictly an individual right. Legal action for intrusion, however, may provide a serious threat to the researcher if the extension toward the development of a tort of psychological intrusion continues. But it cannot be stated with certainty that such a tort exists today.

If a tort of psychological intrusion does evolve through the workings of case law, the corresponding right to be free from psychological intrusion can be waived by either explicit or implied consent. Under the present methods of disguised or projective questioning, however, it would be difficult for the courts to see such implied consent.

If the respondent is not aware that the measurement is at a deeper level than the superficial questions, then another type of legal action may also be possible, that of *misrepresentation*. It is beyond the scope of this paper to examine fully the law of misrepresentation. Suffice it to say, it is more firmly grounded than the currently evolving law of privacy. A combination of the two causes may also be possible—the invasion of privacy through misrepresentation.

Legislation: A Different Threat   The law of torts is neither self-assertive nor self-initiating. The injured party must set the corrective action in motion by suing for damages. Even if the tort of psychological intrusion becomes established, thereby forming a measurable boundary of legitimacy for marketing research, it would take a highly contentious respondent to mount an action based on the kind of intrusion effected by projective questioning techniques. But a more obvious constraint can be foreseen if the tort of psychological intrusion evolves in our case law.

If this tort becomes established, it is not unlikely that the legal scholars will cast their attention to the practice of projective questioning. The claim of research men that they can ". . . diagnose consumer motives, attitudes and intentions without the consumer being aware that this is being done" [6] would probably strike a dedicated civil libertarian as being socially abhorrent. If the trend toward extending intrusion to the psychological level continues, legal scrutiny of the profession seems a safe prediction.

Environmental Forces   Two present social undercurrents strengthen this prediction. The first might be called "consumer protection." The advent of "people's advocates" and the President's political reaction in appointing a protector of consumer interests underscore a growing collective awareness of the need for protection of the individual.

A vaguer but potentially more dangerous social undercurrent lies in the generalized fear of computer manipulation of confidential data. Business and government (notably the Internal Revenue Service) maintain data files which contain information that individuals regard as confidential. If marketing researchers and businessmen start combining their data files, and if individuals begin to perceive a danger of their private information being compromised, further pressure for legislative action is likely.

It would probably presuppose too much of the man in the street if he were credited with being aware of the specific nature of commercial data files or of the aggregated data maintained by marketing researchers. The vague or shapeless fear of computer intrusion, however, is in itself a fertile field into which the seed of psychological intrusion by the marketing research profession can be dropped. If the respondent believes that his psychological profile can be maintained in a computer file (whether or not this is true), we can foresee a powerful constituency for a legal reformer. He could capitalize on both the innate fear of computer "big brotherism" and the mounting consumer protection pressures to suggest legislation based on the same kind of legal argument that would support the development of the tort of psychological intrusion.

Government
Interest
That high government interest in the issue of invasion of privacy exists is no idle speculation. Several bills are currently before both Houses of Congress to limit the mandatory reply requirements to questioning by the Bureau of the Census.[7] While these limits concern mandatory replies, not limits to the topics of questioning, the arguments used are concerned with the invasion of privacy.

To reiterate, Carlson said "Let's face it, we are able to collect our research data only because the general public continues to be willing to submit to our interviews. This acceptance of us by the public is the basic natural resource on which our industry is built. Without it we would be out of business tomorrow."[8] In using "public acceptance" to describe the profession's natural resource he might be overstating his case. Perhaps "public tolerance" is closer to the point. It is doubtful whether "public tolerance" could withstand an emotional appeal based on the concomitant issues of psychological intrusion and computer omniscience. The risk of unleashing such an emotional issue is the real cost of continued use of disguised questioning if the tort of psychological intrusion materializes in our jurisprudence.

Conclusion
In this article the law of privacy—as opposed to the commonly understood right of privacy—has been examined. It has been found:

1. That as it presently stands in the process of development, the law of privacy does not constrain the marketing research profession as long as the profession refuses to make individual data public.
2. A trend may be discerned in the law of torts toward the evolution of a tort of psychological intrusion. Such a new tort would probably have two implications for the marketing research profession.
   a. Psychological intrusion would provide a clear outside boundary of legitimacy for marketing research in that disguised or projective questioning would be illegal. The initiation of the judicial process, however, would be left to the intruded-upon respondent. Such a lawsuit might be a long time coming.
   b. Psychological intrusion might, however, prove to be an invitation to legal scrutiny if disguised or projective questioning is continued despite the evolution of the new tort.

This article has examined the present state of the law of privacy as it applies to marketing research. The views expressed are not intended to raise alarms, but rather to sharpen the profession's understanding of privacy. The central thesis bears repeating: the law of privacy and the commonly understood "right of privacy" are not synonymous. The law of privacy provides only the most general environment in which the marketing research profession must operate. The profession's own view of the right of privacy properly constitutes the more proximate boundary of legitimacy.

NOTES

1. Robert O. Carlson, "The Issue of Privacy in Public Opinion Research," *Public Opinion Quarterly*, Vol. 31 (Spring, 1967), pp. 1–8.
2. Samuel D. Warren and Louis D. Brandeis, "The Right To Privacy," *Harvard Law Review*, Vol. 4 (December, 1890), pp. 193–220.
3. William L. Prosser, "Privacy," *California Law Review*, Vol. 48 (August, 1960), pp. 383–424.
4. Hamberger v. Eastman, 206 A2d 239 (1965).
5. The degree to which projective techniques in the hands of marketing research personnel penetrate the psychological privacy of individuals is still controversial. See Lawrence C. Lockley, *Use of Motivational Research in Marketing*, Studies in Business Policy No. 97, National Industrial Conference Board, 1960.
6. Ralph L. Westfall, Harper W. Boyd, Jr., and Donald T. Campbell, "The Use of Structured Techniques in Motivation Research," *Journal of Marketing*, Vol. 22 (October, 1957), p. 134.
7. "Census Programs Attacked as Invasion of Privacy," *The American Statistician*, Vol. 22 (April, 1968), pp. 12–13.
8. Same reference as footnote 1.

45 Attitudes of Marketing Executives Toward Ethics in Marketing Research

C. Merle Crawford

Most descriptions of marketing research tend to avoid, or to pass lightly over, the ethical aspects of this field. The reason in large part is the fact that very few data exist that *can* shed light on the ethical attitudes of marketing executives. Fortu-nately, the following article provides an excellent perspective on the attitudes of marketing executives toward some commonplace marketing research actions that many people consider unethical.

Are some marketing research practices unethical? Do marketing researchers have an obligation within the firm to "guard the facts"? Are there, in other words, some practices which society might not approve, were they fully disclosed?

Such were the questions that prompted a study in November, 1968, the results of which can now be reported. This study, conducted through co-operation of the Bureau of Business Research in The University of Michigan Graduate School of Business, consisted of posing a series of "action" situations to a national sample of marketing research directors and vice-presidents or directors of marketing.

Each respondent was presented with 20 instances where the marketing research director of Company X had taken some specific action; the essential question was "Do you approve or disapprove of the action taken?" . . . Six situations concerned actions by the director which are of general business applicability, and thus are not reported here. Space was provided for explanatory comments.

The response was somewhat surprising. Of the total sample of 700 individuals, response came from 401, or 57.3%. The 412 research directors responded at a 62.9% rate, and the 288 marketing line executives at a 49.3% rate. This response on a six-page mail questionnaire, coupled with the extensive array of comments, would seem to indicate more than just a passing interest in ethics.

Reprinted from C. Merle Crawford, "Attitudes of Marketing Executives Toward Ethics in Marketing Research", *Journal of Marketing* (April, 1970), Vol. 34, pp. 46–52, by permission of the author and the American Marketing Association.

One note of caution, however. There is no way of being certain that what respondents *said* is what they truly *believe*. Ethics questions tend to produce conditioned responses or "acceptable" behavior patterns, and the results of this study must be interpreted accordingly.

Findings   The situations covered in this report span several categories of action. Six situations covered potentially disputable research techniques, ranging from ultraviolet ink to a price exchange program. Three situations concentrated on the role of the marketing research director as a keeper of the facts, and possibly as a marketing conscience. Five situations concerned social matters of some importance today.

Selected
Research
Techniques

1. ULTRAVIOLET INK:

A project director recently came in to request permission to use ultraviolet ink in pre-coding questionnaires on a mail survey. He pointed out that the letter referred to an anonymous survey, but he said he needed respondent identification to permit adequate cross tabulation of the data. The M. R. Director gave his approval.

	Approve	Disapprove
Research Directors	29%	70%
Line Marketers	22	77

The feeling generally was that the appraisal turns on two issues. (1) How does one define "anonymous" as used in the letter? Some held that the ink technique violates nothing; others said it means what it says, and the ink constitutes obvious deception. (2) At a more generalized level, the issue seemed to be whether this was intended deception or not, and respondents generally assumed it was: For example, "Obviously this is deception, and I want none of it."

Note that research directors were more lenient than were line executives; although the difference was small, it is meaningful on this and the following situation.

2. HIDDEN TAPE RECORDERS:

In a study intended to probe rather deeply into the buying motivations of a group of wholesale customers by use of a semi-structured personal interview form, the M. R. Director authorized the use of the department's special attache cases equipped with hidden tape recorders.

	Approve	Disapprove
Research Directors	33%	67%
Line Marketers	26	71

Reaction here was slightly more favorable than with the use of ultra-violet ink. Still the survey forms were liberally sprinkled with phrases like "Similar to wire tapping." "Isn't this a federal offense?" "This is patently dishonest." In general, respondents felt this constituted a deliberate attempt to deceive, which they could not condone even if the tapes were used solely within the research department as intended.

Many respondents waved the ethical question aside saying that such deception isn't necessary—recorders need not be hidden. Others approved on the premise that research is better this way, and no one gets hurt. As with the ultraviolet ink, however, cautions were frequent that absolutely no sales use of the information should be allowed.

This is pertinent advice. The legality of this action is open to question, partly because no cases exist covering this particular type of situation, and partly because of the chaotic state of affairs right now in the entire area of personal privacy, at both federal and state levels. It is most likely that the recording would not be actionable, but extra-research use of the tapes would probably reverse this.[1]

3. ONE-WAY MIRRORS:

One product of the X Company is brassieres, and the firm has recently been having difficulty making some decisions on a new line. Information was critically needed concerning the manner in which women put on their brassieres. So the M. R. Director designed a study in which two local stores co-operated in putting one-way mirrors in their foundations dressing rooms. Observers behind these mirrors successfully gathered the necessary information.

	Approve	Disapprove
Research Directors	20%	78%
Line Marketers	18	82

Three ideas ran through the comments section on this question. First, many persons, especially research directors, said the technique was entirely unnecessary—that female observers in the dressing rooms could have gathered the same information.

But, far more overwhelmingly, respondents pointed out "Invasion of Privacy." In fact, one respondent put it quite bluntly: "What if your wife was one of the customers in the store that day?" Some even suggested that the responses would be far more negative if the company were one making men's underwear, and a similar technique were used. The legality of such an approach was also questioned, since there is ample case law to indicate that courts would not condone this type of *research*. A comparable case does not seem to exist, but other use of one-way mirrors in retail dressing rooms has been judged a tort and has resulted in fines and damages.

On the other hand, some respondents assumed that the observers were female, in which case they felt that the moral question was insignificant relative to the need for the information. Another said, "The women don't know they've been observed, and thus can suffer no mental anguish."

4. FAKE LONG DISTANCE CALLS:

Some of X Company's customers are busy executives, hard to reach by normal interviewing methods. Accordingly, the market research department recently conducted a study in which interviewers called "long distance" from near-by cities. They were successful in getting through to busy executives in almost every instance.

	Approve	Disapprove
Research Directors	84%	10%
Line Marketers	84	16

Note the complete reversal from the three earlier situations. Why? Partly because the situation was not completely deceptive—the calls were actually long distance. But more commonly, if executives want to interrupt their busy day to receive long distance calls, that is their decision.

The small number of disapprovers felt that this technique is deceptive, and should not be used. They would counsel that actions should be judged by their character in the absolute sense, not on a scale of "badness" against a scale of gain.

5. FAKE RESEARCH FIRM:

In another study, this one concerning magazine reading habits, the M. R. Director decided to contact a sample of consumers under the name of Media Research Institute. This fictitious company name successfully camouflaged the identity of the sponsor of the study.

	Approve	Disapprove
Research Directors	84%	13%
Line Marketers	83	16

The basis for approval on this time-honored practice can perhaps best be summed by the following typical response:

Most marketing research studies hide the identity of the sponsor. Why should a corporation have to purchase outside services for this privilege? Respondents generally know that research has a commercial purpose and is intended for a sponsor.

Most of the disapprovals involved complaints about the nature of the deception, rather than the deception itself: "Use your agency name instead"; "Better be sure to notify the BBB or Chambers of Commerce"; "Dangerous unless you check carefully to see that some local research firm somewhere doesn't already have this name in use"; and so on. Hiding the name of the sponsor was virtually never criticized.

6. EXCHANGE OF PRICE DATA:

X Company belongs to a trade association which includes an active marketing research sub-group. At the meetings of this sub-group, the M. R. Director regularly exchanges confidential price information. In turn, he gives the competitive information to the X Company sales department, but is careful not to let the marketing vice-president know about it. Profits are substantially enhanced, and top management is protected from charges of collusion.

	Approve	Disapprove
Research Directors	8%	89%
Line Marketers	14	82

Why did respondents so quickly and completely disapprove of this technique? Simple, it is against the law. Most price collusion is illegal, most price exchanges are suspect, the trade association is no place to *informally* exchange information on price, and keeping top management in the dark is no longer an excuse.

Interestingly, very few respondents said they saw this as an ethical question: "This is a legal matter, and should not have been put on a questionnaire purportedly studying ethics in marketing research." This thinking suggests that illegality removes an act from ethical consideration, and that law and ethics are as unrelated as some critics of marketing claim. Critics say that marketers will readily charge through the gray area of ethics right up to the black wall of illegality. The results here would tend to support this criticism, since (1) respondents apparently made their decisions on legal, not ethical, grounds, and (2) the act was rather commonly condemned as unintelligent.

The Role of the Marketing Research Director   A research director is responsible for seeing that his management gets hard facts where possible, knowing when they are not, preventing mistaken interpretations of research data, and in general seeing that the research function is conducted in a competent and professional manner. The next three situations presented instances where such responsibility was at issue.

1. ADVERTISING AND PRODUCT MISUSE:

Some recent research showed that many customers of X Company are mis-
using Product B. There's no danger; they are simply wasting their money by
using too much of it at a time. But yesterday the M. R. Director saw final
comps on Product B's new ad campaign, and the ads not only ignore the
problem of misuse, but actually seem to encourage it. He quietly referred the
advertising manager to the research results, well known to all people on B's
advertising, and let it go at that."

	Approve	Disapprove
Research Directors	41%	58%
Line Marketers	33	66

Those respondents approving the action generally claimed that whether
the misuse should be attacked, supported, or ignored in the advertising, is
irrelevant here. . . . The research man discharged his responsibilities, and
that is the end of it.

The majority would not let it stop at that, for two different reasons. First,
many said the researcher was negligent and that he should have brought
the matter to the attention of the head of marketing. Others said such
advertising is simply not profitable; that product misuse opens the door to
competition; the researcher should have protested along this line.

When those who approved the action are added to those who objected
on grounds of strategy, one finds only a minority who actually claimed to
condemn the action on ethical grounds. For example, here are several
typical disapprovals:

He should pursue the matter. Ultimately, a competitive product will undercut Product B on cost of usage.

The decision is the advertising manager's to make. One would hope, however, that the M. R. Director would point out that the decision to encourage
misuse is not an ethical decision but a pragmatic profit-and-loss decision.

Maybe customer prefers to use it that way. Maybe the company has an
inaccurate view of value perceived by customer. Would advocate accurate
instructions for use—not unusually strong measures to change customer and
reduce revenue.

There were, of course, a number of respondents who echoed one man's
comment: "Disapprove—and I would be *loud*."

Line marketing executives were more concerned than were researchers.
Some accused the marketing research director of being a "gutless wonder."
But, in general, if a marketing head disapproved the action and explained
his thinking, he said something like this: "He should have passed the word
up the line, just to be sure the advertising man's boss knew the facts. But
that's the end of it for him."

2. DISTORTIONS BY MARKETING VICE-PRESIDENT:

In the trial run of a major presentation to the Board of Directors, the marketing vice-president deliberately distorted some recent research findings. After some thought, the M. R. Director decided to ignore the matter, since the marketing head obviously knew what he was doing.

	Approve	Disapprove
Research Directors	12%	87%
Line Marketers	12	86

Those who approved the action said either: (1) "What else could he do?" Or (2) "The boss might have had some good reason or information which the M. R. Director didn't know about."

Disapprovals, however, took a much more complex form. The first, and probably the largest, group felt that some action was called for . . . a private talk, a memo, and in a few cases, an end run. The action should not be dramatic, and if it produced no results, the matter should be dropped.

A smaller, though much more vocal, group demanded strong action. They stood on principle, and stated that if an appeal were lost, the director should either resign on the spot, or move quickly to find a company with a different class of executives.

Perhaps a few quotes will indicate the spread in opinion on this issue:

It's not the M. R. Director's moral obligation to force his superior to be honest.

Decision depends on the reasons for the distortion.

I would drop a written memo to the VP, pointing to distortions. Suggest presentation be changed.

I would resign my position.

•   •   •

3. POSSIBLE CONFLICT OF INTEREST:

A market testing firm, to which X Company gives most of its business, recently went public. The M. R. Director had been looking for a good investment and proceeded to buy some $20,000 of their stock. The firm continues as X Company's leading supplier for testing.

	Approve	Disapprove
Research Directors	40%	57%
Line Marketers	58	38

This situation is difficult to interpret. As one respondent put it, "There's some danger here that he might try to protect his investment!" Yet, almost half of the total respondents approved. It should not be inferred that they were unaware of the potential conflict of interest. Even those approving the action often added that the director must obtain the approval of his supervisor, or that he must be careful to remain objective.

The answer seems to lie in the amount of the investment. If the testing firm in question were A. C. Nielsen, a $20,000 investment would not be the determining factor. In smaller firms, however, a director would realize the direct relationship between his purchase of testing service and the profits of the firm performing the work.

Beyond those who passed the matter on to higher management, it would seem that respondents' answers were a function of their evaluation of the importance of $20,000.

Line marketers as a group actually approved the action. Unfortunately, there was nothing in the comments to explain this difference. It could be the result of confidence that management has acquired for the integrity of researchers, or it is possible that $20,000 has much less significance in their customary dollar frame of reference.

Today's Social Concerns   In the area of social concerns, action situations were to probe the matter of possible conflicts between a firm's self-interest and the natural desire of its marketing people to help their fellow men. Question areas were approached carefully since the strong differences of opinion were known. After some pretesting, it became apparent that most respondents were willing to accept all of the proposed areas of interest as having at least some ethical overtones. Not all did, however, and a few comments came back to the effect, "Don't know why you put this situation in a study of ethics—it has nothing to do with ethics."

1. GENERAL TRADE DATA TO GHETTO GROUP:

The marketing research department of X Company frequently makes extensive studies of their retail customers. A federally supported Negro group, working to get a shopping center in their ghetto area, wanted to know if they could have access to this trade information. But since the M. R. Director had always refused to share this information with trade organizations, he declined the request.

	Approve	Disapprove
Research Directors	64%	34%
Line Marketers	74	25

Votes of two-to-one and three-to-one are rather overwhelming and many respondents voiced strong opinions. "What's good for one is good for all." "Everyone must play by the same rules." "Federal or ghetto has nothing to do with it." The consensus was that out of respect to retailers cooperating in past studies or in terms of company profits, the decision was correct, consistency demands that the data not be shared.

Dissenters were divided into two groups. The first group cited the opinion that this is really a top management decision; the research director should not have attempted to make a judgment on his own. But the second group was more direct: "Assuming that the shopping center could improve the situation in the ghetto area, the director has an obligation to the group that transcends the normally ethical business position." "No—this is silly secrecy." "I strongly disapprove—we need to do everything in our power to assist Negroes in their attempt at economic self-improvement." Whether correct or not, those favoring the release of such information constituted a minority.

2. NMAC REQUEST FOR RECENT PRICE STUDY:

The National Marketing Advisory Council (formed of top marketing executives and marketing educators to advise the Commerce Department) has a task force studying ghetto prices. The head of this study recently called to ask if they could have a copy of a recent X Company study which he understood showed that ghetto appliance prices are significantly higher than in suburban areas. Since X Company sells appliances to these ghetto merchants, the M. R. Director felt compelled to refuse the request.

	Approve	Disapprove
Research Directors	56%	39%
Line Marketers	46	51

Compared to the previous question, the approval rate declined, and line marketing executives actually moved to a point of disapproval. Respondents who felt that ghetto prices should not be higher, or at least not that much higher, were quick to say that social good overrides a loyalty to customers. As one respondent put it: "What's best for the public should have much greater weight than protecting their customers, especially when such customers are engaged in wrong practices." Another respondent went a bit further: "Protecting good and fair customers is one thing—protecting carpetbaggers is another."

These are ethical reasons for disapproval, but many were simply pragmatic: The study could be replicated—NMAC could obtain their own data—so what would be gained by refusing to cooperate?

Those approving the action did so usually on the basis that the company's first obligation is to its customers and to its profits. On the assumption that NMAC would stimulate some action contrary to the best interest of the ghetto merchants, the company would be neither economically wise nor ethically fair to its customers by revealing the data.

3. ASSIGNING MAN TO A GHETTO PLANNING GROUP:

A local Office of Economic Opportunity group recently called to ask that the M. R. Director assign one of his men to the planning group working on the ghetto shopping center mentioned earlier. Since one result of such a center would be to force a good number of ghetto retailers out of business, and since some of these retailers were presently customers of X Company, the M. R. Director refused the request.

	Approve	Disapprove
Research Directors	41%	51%
Line Marketers	39	57

Similar reasoning supported approval here. Why should the research director be expected to act contrary to short-term profits and to the interests of present customers? These respondents saw no overriding ethical consideration and felt simply that the director should be a businessman, not a social worker.

Some dissenters stressed the social angle: "Assuming that the shopping center has been thoroughly considered and felt to be good for the community as a whole, Company X should help it." Others were pragmatic, saying that Company X would be of greatest service to these ghetto customers if it had a man involved in the planning—a man who could bring back progress reports and perhaps try to protect the ghetto merchants' interests in the shopping center planning.

4. NEGRO ACCOUNT EXECUTIVE:

The President of an interviewing firm which had been doing most of the field work for X Company wrote to say that a new account executive had been assigned to X. The new man was capable, personable, and black. The M. R. Director wrote back to say that there were no Negroes in the department at the moment, and that he felt it would be better all round if a different account man were assigned to X Company.

	Approve	Disapprove
Research Directors	5%	94%
Line Marketers	7	92

Little explanation is needed here. Comments ranged from "This has got to stop—God help us if it doesn't," to "This is total bigotry." Respondents were adamant, underlining words, adding exclamation points, and in many cases berating the author for including this situation as an issue.

In fairness to reportorial accuracy, however, there were some approvals, the thought being that the research director knows his location and his people. If he is in a part of the country where feelings tend to run against this action, perhaps department morale demands a refusal on his part.

That the situation is not entirely unrealistic was underscored by one comment: "Give it a chance—it worked for us."

5. HIRING JEWISH MARKETING ANALYST:

When interviewing applicants for a newly created analyst position, the M. R. Director was impressed with one man in particular. But he didn't offer him the job, since the applicant referred to himself as Jewish, and it was well known that X Company wanted no Jewish marketing people.

	Approve	Disapprove
Research Directors	26%	71%
Line Marketers	20	77

This situation was included in the study partly to test the times, and partly to compare with the preceding one on the Negro. Respondents were sometimes quite indignant and disapproval was still quite overwhelming, but a significant minority approved, for two reasons. The first reason was the matter of company policy, and the second was the question of practicality. Is it wise to encourage a man of the Jewish faith to enter an environment where he would face personal abuse, and would find it difficult to work to his capacity?

Those disapproving the action cited the obvious reasons, and with frequent vehemence.

Other Ethical Problems in Marketing Research   A final section of the questionnaire invited respondents to list any other situations found in the field of marketing research which might be questioned from an ethical point of view. Of the many situations given, here are the ones thought to be of greatest interest, though none had more than a scattering of mentions:

1. Performing "research" work, either internally or as a consultant, which is specifically geared to gain conclusions sought by higher management.
2. The solicitation of research proposals from several firms, and then combining the best features of each into the one actually performed by the low bidder.
3. Long technical appendices in a study, or use of technical jargon in written or oral presentations, the intent being to delude the reader or listener regarding the thoroughness of the job or the competence of the researcher.
4. The pretense of survey research by firms selling products door to door or over the telephone.
5. Obtaining information by falsely implying that a respondent's superior has given his approval for disclosure.

6. Continuing a study to completion, after finding out late in the game that major errors have been made, the intention being to hide from management or client that costly backtracking should be undertaken.
7. Raising the payment to a research vendor for an upcoming job to make up for loss on last job, when costs were actually higher than expected.
8. A firm that is in the business of compiling cross-classified mailing lists using a fake survey form to obtain the necessary information.
9. The promising of a report of completed results, in order to gain respondent cooperation, but with intention not to follow through.
10. The failure to use techniques purported to be used—particularly in the case of probability sampling.
11. The use of purported new techniques as a selling technique by marketing research firms and workers.

Conclusions   This study was not designed to yield definitive statements covering the ethics of marketers, or even marketing researchers, and any such conclusions at this point are entirely unwarranted. The study was designed to answer the question: Are there ethical matters within the field of marketing research which might be further investigated and discussed? The answer must be affirmative, since there are substantial areas of disagreement and disapproval.

Specifically, respondents disapproved of the use of ultraviolet ink, hidden tape recorders, and one-way mirrors (in a given situation), a particular price exchange program, an action relating to product misuse, the ignoring of executive distortions, conflicts of interest, the refusal of assigning a man to a ghetto business project, and personnel situations involving racial and religious discrimination. Yet very few veteran marketing researchers would claim they have not encountered such or similar situations.

Except in areas involving at best questionable law, nothing but one's conscience operates to inhibit these practices. There is no broadly applicable code, no board of investigation, no licensing authority, and no federal statement of research practice guidelines.

Thus, a situation seems to prevail where objectionable practices occur at least occasionally, if not frequently, without formal resistance. Under stimulation from the vehemence of attack displayed by respondents in this survey and to forestall investigative action by a marketing researcher like Ralph Nader, the following future actions would seem to be in order (current activities in areas of credit investigations, data banks, and census questionnaires suggest there might not be much time):

1. Organize formal discussions of debatable practices, at the national level, via AMA task force.
2. Seriously investigate again the American Marketing Association Code of Ethics and appropriate enforcement procedures.
3. Develop, from these investigations, whatever program of activities appears necessary to markedly reduce the incidence of unethical research practices

within the field of marketing. At a minimum, honest researchers deserve a public statement of their beliefs and convictions.

The survey also brought out clearly the evidence that top marketing managers have a set of ethical standards very close to that of researchers. The responses were amazingly similar, with management being only slightly less critical and differing significantly only on the matters of possible conflict of interest and the supplying of data to the National Marketing Advisory Council. It would appear that management would support efforts to reduce the incidence of questionable practices.

One might ask whether persons at the other end of the responsibility spectrum (business students) feel the same. Preliminary research here at The University of Michigan would indicate that they do, but this will not be known for certain until further research, currently under way and using the same forms, is concluded.

NOTE

1. See Alan F. Weston, *Privacy and Freedom* (New York: Atheneum, Publishers, 1967), for a complete discussion of this matter.

QUESTIONS FOR DISCUSSION

1. What is a survey respondent's obligation to answer questions?
2. Many psychologists feel that every individual should be informed that he is free to participate or not in a psychological test before it is administered to him. Do you think that such a view is appropriate to market research questioning?
3. What assurances should a survey respondent be given regarding public disclosure of personal information—such as statistics on age, income, expenditures—provided during an interview.
4. Do you think assurances against public disclosure of personal information are given at the present time, and if so, are honestly carried out?
5. What would be the impact upon marketers and society if the area of privacy in market research surveys were regulated by the federal government?
6. To what extent do existing laws of privacy affect the marketing profession?
7. Sales solicitation in the guise of consumer research is a fairly common action. What would your reaction be if you were marketing manager of a firm and found out that some of your salesmen were using this trick to generate sales?
8. Although respondents hesitate to discontinue long interviews, they sometimes become surly and resentful. How do you think this affects their responses? If you were marketing manager, what would your reaction be to an interviewer who told you that "It's all right. I compensate for their resentment as I write down their answers."

9. If you were to draft a model "Marketing Research Code of Ethics," what primary provisions would it have?

SUGGESTED READINGS

Allen, Irving L., and J. David Colfax, "Respondents' Attitudes Towards Legitimate Surveys in Four Cities", *Journal of Marketing Research* (November, 1968), Vol. 5, pp. 431–433.

"The Assault on Privacy", *Newsweek* (July 27, 1970), pp. 15–20.

"Census Programs Attacked as Invasion of Privacy", *The American Statistician* (April, 1968), Vol. 22, pp. 12–13.

Holzman, Robert S., "Banks and Customer Privacy", *Finance* (November, 1967), pp. 27–29.

Kalven, Harry, Jr., "The Problems of Privacy in the Year 2000", *Daedulus* (Summer, 1969), Vol. 96, pp. 876–882.

"Projects. The Computerization of Government Files: What Impact on the Individual?" *UCLA Law Review* (September, 1968), Vol. 15, No. 5, pp. 1371–1498.

Prosser, William L., "Privacy", *California Law Review* (August, 1960), Vol. 48, pp. 383–424.

The Respondent's Right to Privacy (New York: Adopted by the Marketing Research Council, July, 1968).

Shepo, Marshall S., "Media Injuries to Personality: An Essay on Legal Regulation of Public Communication", *Texas Law Review* (April, 1968), Vols. 46–47, Part I, pp. 650–667.

Smith, Donald L., "Privacy: The Right That Failed", *Columbia Journalism Review* (Spring, 1969), Vol. 8, pp. 18–22.

Thompson, Roger H., "Unwanted Telephone Calls: A Legal Remedy?" *Utah Law Review* (July, 1967), Vol. 1967, No. 3, pp. 379–407.

U.S., Congress, Committee on Government Operations, *Privacy and the National Data Bank Concept*, 35th rept., August 2, 1968.

U.S., Congress, House, Hearing Before the Subcommittee on Postal Operations, *Privacy in the Mail*, 90th Cong., 2d. sess., July 23–24, 1968, serial no. 90–42.

U.S., Executive Office of the President, Office of Science and Technology, *Privacy and Behavioral Research* (Washington, D.C.: Government Printing Office, 1967).

Warren, Samuel D., and Louis O. Brandeis, "The Right to Privacy", *Harvard Law Review* (December, 1890), Vol. 4, pp. 193–220.

the
future
of part
marketing four

The contents of the preceding parts of this volume illustrate the close connection between the social values of our time and business functioning. Obviously, marketing practice can no more be divorced from the total societal environment than a plant can be studied without reference to its ecology. The relation is a reciprocal one. What happens in the environment affects marketing practice. And marketing practice affects the broader society.

Thus, when there is an increasing emphasis on youth, goods and entertainment reflect that development. "Psychedelic" stores appear, fashions change, and businessmen adapt rather quickly to the new slogans and phrases that come into use. If scientists and engineers invent new products and techniques, business and marketing innovators help to diffuse them within the entire community. Conversely, advertising slogans and notions move into the general language, and the products offered by marketing help to change our everyday living style. Thus, business continually touches almost all phases of life.

The reciprocal effects of social values and business have probably always existed, but they are especially evident today. It is commonplace to say that one of the watchwords of our time is change. There is every reason to believe that rapid change will continue into the future and that marketing practice will continue to be closely tied to social changes. Some of these changes already seem visible.

In this final section we shall look at the expected changes in marketing and speculate as to their possible influence on society. We shall also visualize prospective social changes and question the effects they are likely to have on the future of marketing. Some of these conjectures will be right, and others wrong. In our view, however, an orientation toward the future is of paramount importance not only to the businessman for whom it may be a matter of survival, but also to all citizens. Imagining the future serves to help us prepare for it intelligently and hopefully, rather than floundering into and through the days and years ahead.

46 Some Changes in Information Technology Affecting Marketing in the Year 2000

Paul Baran

Earlier in this book we saw how distribution systems varied between primitive economies and more developed economic systems. Obviously, significant technological change occurring in any stage of economic development will have a great effect upon a nation's distribution system. With respect to anticipated changes in our own economy, the following selection shows how some of the changes in information technology might affect future marketing.

Our concept of market segmentation is highly dependent upon information flow structures. Change the information flow mechanism by providing instantaneous feedback to the manufacturer and the entire market segmentation process must change.

In this paper, we consider: (1) how far the year 2000 is from today; (2) some of the changes in the information technology we might expect; and, (3) how these changes might affect marketing and its segmentation.

In 32 years we enter the year 2000. This may seem like a long time away. But only 32 years ago, in 1936, George Murphy was playing in "Woman Trap." One year later Ronald Reagan appeared in "Love in the Air."

Both actors were creating a subliminal image base for later acceptance in public office: a senator and a governor of the nation's largest state. This good packaging and 20/20 foresight provided a headstart for elections in the TV era.

The choice of the media suggests unusual foresight. Motion picture film was at that time primarily a media for "one shot" ephemeral exposure. It

Reprinted from Paul Baran, "Some Changes in Information Technology Affecting Marketing in the Year 2000", in Reed Moyer (ed.), *Changing Marketing Systems . . . Consumer, Corporate and Government Interfaces* (Washington, D.C.: American Marketing Association, 1967), Series No. 26, Winter Conference Series, pp. 76–87, by permission of the author and the American Marketing Association.

took the arrival of mass audience TV to resurrect the dusty cans of yellow and embrittled celluloid images of the previous three decades. It was the new mass TV that provided the constant exposure of the pleasant image in the living room, from dawn till the late, late show, so useful to modern political success. (In 1936, TV existed as an under-funded laboratory research project. Few technicians and even fewer wild-eyed businessmen took it seriously.)

Let us flip our 32-year reference period forward to the year 2000. We have a rough idea of our wealth and population (see Figure 1). Figure 2 shows our probability of being around in the future. Three curves are shown for a male 20, 40, and 60 years old today. For example, if you are about 40, your chance of being alive in the year 2000 is better than 50/50. For those who won't, the probability is high that their progeny will. The obituaries of our friends may erode our innate belief in our own immortality, but let us not undercut our responsibility to our future.

This morbid topic is raised only to pinpoint the year 2000, and to describe the nature of long-range technological prediction. It is, of course, impossible to predict precisely who will be around, but we are free to talk with reasonable certainty about the gross framework. The fine-grained structure remains to the gods, uncertain and indefinable.

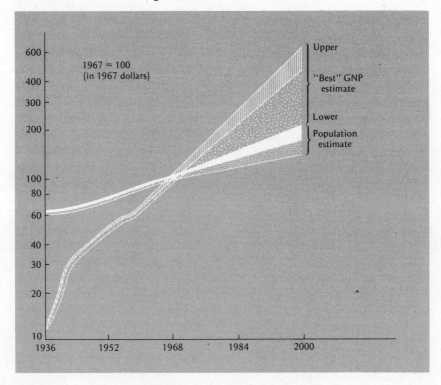

FIGURE 1.   Change of GNP and population in the U.S.

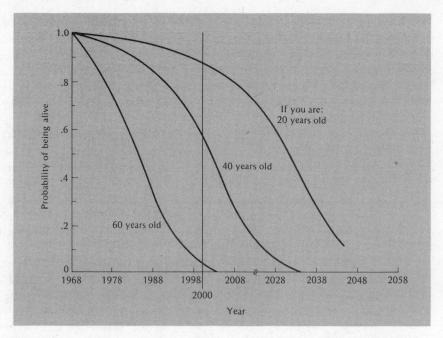

FIGURE 2.   Your probability of being around (and alive) in the future.

Technological advances are proposed in the scenario to follow. What is said will only define the ballpark, the specifics are solely for illustration. It's the game, not the players, that is important.

Early prototypes of the basic hardware components needed for the illustration exist to some degree in the laboratory today. We should not forget that things tend to be in laboratories and not "off the shelf" because they are either not yet practical or economical. However, we are much further along developing the equipment I shall describe than we were toward the economically feasible development of TV in 1936. Further, these proposed developments are today more generously funded, and more actively pursued in 1967 than TV was in 1936. The evolving electronic technology is moving along as rapidly as ever. Many orders of magnitude improvement are clearly visible before exploitation of today's technology. Accomplishing our goal requires neither the revision of the laws of physics nor the circumvention of market place economics. Hopes cannot be based on unforeseen technical breakthroughs. While useful and convenient they occur with regularity only in new laxative advertisements.

Well before the year 2000 we can realistically expect widespread large-screen, color, person-to-person TV communications over cables using a switching network similar to the telephone system. . . . This development will attempt to create the illusion that those in TV communications with one another are in effect within the same room. They must, and will, contain mechanisms to assure privacy. Much of the nation's business will be transacted through these screens. Images may be "conferenced." Any size group will be able to get together. Conferences in which people are transported across a continent to sit in the same room to hear a speaker will have gone the way of the town crier and the Western Union delivery boy.

The TV screen may be the primary means of communication—even partially supplanting face-to-face communications. Our access to the world at large will be *through* the screen to a huge automated information storage and processing base. Push buttons will provide painless individual interaction with a powerful, remote computer capability. To be precise, we should choose a more appropriate term; the word "computer" is too narrow. It derives from the earlier use of digital processing equipment. We are considering something more fundamental. Specifically, an interactive, automated, information processing system which allows rapid and friendly coupling between an individual and a huge information base. Development of improved interaction between the human and the computer is already underway. We seek to obtain the maximum benefits of each; to achieve a whole greater than its parts. Some even call this development "augumented intelligence." The screen will probably become the primary channel of education, partially or wholly displacing those educational institutions based on the brick-and-mortar technology called schoolhouses. Entertainment, even for the smallest select audience, will come via the screen. We no longer will be constrained by the paucity of channels which restricts present television to sponsors fighting for the largest slice of the audience, and in the process catering to the tastes of the lowest common denominator. But, possibly of most interest to us today is that the screen and the computer promise an entire restructuring of today's merchandising concepts.

Before getting into specifics, keep in mind that we are discussing a one-slice projection of a single sector of a multi-dimensional world. Mass TV, new contraceptives, and atomic energy (more familiarly known as the tube, the pill, and the bang) are irreversibly changing our social attitudes and our institutions. The mixed blessing of reduced infant mortality is creating a population explosion in those portions of the world least able to feed their population. This limits these comments to the richer nations of the world. Too many things are happening simultaneously to paint a complete picture. The transitional role of the city, the new role of government, and a potential loss of privacy; the modification of the traditional standards of sexual morality and the value of work for work's sake—the sacred things we take for granted are in a state of flux. The following words are only one frame of a changing picture—nothing more.

For the last several decades, distributive costs were almost as high as the cost of manufacturing. For example, in 1964, the cumulative income in salaries in the distributive industries was about 75% of that in manufacturing industries. Continuing technological innovation in manufacturing is well documented. These innovations make continuing reductions in the cost of manufacturing possible. Not nearly as well appreciated is the automation

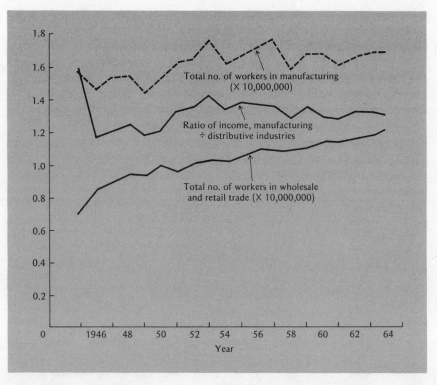

FIGURE 3.   Number of workers and the ratio of personal income from the manufacturing industry relative to the distributing industry.

of the distributive industries also taking place. For example, during the period 1945 to 1964, the salary income from the distributive industry tripled; yet the *ratio* of income in manufacturing to distributive industries remained remarkably constant (see Figure 3). However, during the same period the total *number* of workers in manufacturing increased by only 10%, while the number of workers in wholesale and retail trades increased by 57%.

What does this mean? It seems to suggest that we have already experienced much innovation in the distributive process. But, the increase in efficiency or the ability to enforce salary increases for the workers in the distributive industries is not nearly as high as in the manufacturing industries. This is of prime interest to the computer system designer as one of the characteristics of the distributive industry in that it is primarily an information processing activity.

The advent of computer based technology, including communications, suggests that the next 32 years may produce major technological innovations in distribution even greater than conventional automation has produced in manufacturing. It may not be unreasonable to look forward to a reduction in the *relative* cost of distribution to manufacturing in the future.

In absolute terms, manufacturing itself will, of course, continue to undergo innovation, but a huge untapped domain exists for development in distribution. Here is where the real action may occur.

To give some insight into the changes that this may imply to marketing, let us consider a "limiting case example." That is, where the cost of the goods has dropped near zero and the overriding cost is distribution.

As an example, consider distributing technical information. This is a commodity that is for the most part given away almost free by the manufacturer—the author. The printing and distribution cost of technical articles in technical journals is generally subsidized by professional societies' dues. Technical books can be sold for profit only because most authors are satisfied with a non-compensatory token honorarium. The rest of the *quid pro quo* is derived in the implied form of intangible prestige. The cost of distribution of technical articles published in trade throwaways is covered only by the advertising sold.

To appreciate the negative worth of a technical manuscript in the market place, think of those technical journals that charge the author a page charge even to give his article away. Technical articles, therefore, must be something like today's affluent society's trash—you have to pay to have it hauled away.

Let's examine this case where the cost of manufacturing (writing) is sufficiently low so that the distribution cost is overriding. Within bounds, this strained example could be indicative of the marketing situation in which we might find ourselves in the far future. Consider this process and the messages it might hold for us.

In viewing the burgeoning and chaotic profusion of technical literature, Walter M. Carlson[1] expounds a novel concept. Carlson describes our present publication distribution procedure as "pushing." He defines pushing as the process in which a written product is widely disseminated in the hope that someone will stumble across it and pay to read it. Carlson calls most professional publications which bundle up masses of partially related topics prime examples of the "push" mechanism at work. He suggests that, as the volume of the material being pushed becomes overwhelming, and our methods of access to it more difficult, we would be well advised to convert to a distribution system *where the individual requests specifically what he wants from the primary source.* This process is defined by Carlson as having the user *"pull"* the information of value *to* him. Carlson takes the interesting view that:

. . . the greatest single contribution our engineering and scientific societies can make to technical communication would be to suspend the issuance of technical journals altogether.

This piling of push mechanisms, one on the other, has nearly brought the abstracting and indexing services of our country into a state of chaos that seems merely a prelude to collapse. As these abstracting and indexing organizations try to keep up with the flood of primary literature being pushed their way, they initiate new and clever schemes for pushing out more and more packages for alerting their subscribers to the appearance of new materials. Only a very few of these services pay their own way from subscription fees willingly paid by recipients of the service. The deficits are made up with large amounts of the taxpayer's money through government subsidy. The prospect at the moment is for even greater subsidy as a matter of national policy.

This idea of information overload in our increasingly complex society is not completely new. For example, a different but perceptive statement of the coming problem of information saturation is described by R. L. Meier.[2]

The consumer in tomorrow's marketplace will probably be overwhelmed by the variety of choice, similar to that facing the researcher in the library of today. The development of "pull" mechanisms to cope with this flood of consumer options will be just as necessary as those to handle the uncontrollable profusion of technical papers.

To be more specific, let us consider the "hardware" needed to support a "pulling" concept for the distribution of both goods and paper.

The customer has never faced such a diversity of product choice as in America today—and this trend is on the upswing. There's the old saying about Henry Ford's immovable restriction on marketing his Model T: you could order it in any color, provided it was black. Our early mass production lines did not encourage diversity. Exceptions were a pain in the neck. "Everything the same," was the name of the game. One of the characteristics of automating information flow in the factory is the reduction of the optimum size production run. Watch a trail of different color cars, each with totally different "custom" accessories, roll off today's production line. The computer-tape controlled, general purpose machine tool is coming into rapid use in manufacturing which will reduce the size of the minimum economic production run even further.

To the consumer this promises a large increase in the possibilities of product choice; to the warehouseman, a nuisance; to the seller, a curse. But now the consumer will find rational choice of products a near impossibility. We can choke in a profusion of alternative choices. So much for the problem. How do we harness the new technology to get us out of the dilemma?

U.S. consumer advertising is regarded by much of the world as one of American society's worst features. It is expensive to the producer; wasteful and often discourteous to the audience. It is designed for mass media, selling a few mass produced products. The profusion of products is so great that usually only the selling of brand names is attempted. Advertising often ceases being a public information service and becomes a boorish nuisance. It is basically the "push mechanism" that is at fault. The "push" mechanism floods the recipient with a sea of mostly unwanted distractions. Yet, it is so expensive that it often does not allow conveying specific information useful to those actually interested in buying a product.

Now, let's think in terms of our infinite channel TV set allowing a very large number of separate audiences. To reach all by "pushing" would be even more wasteful than today's procedure. Consider a large number of separate programs that will be transmitted concurrently with the continued explosive growth in the number of products offered for sale. Conventional "push" advertising will subject the audience to interminable commercials of which very few will be of any interest. Stocking the huge variety of products possible is expensive; selecting the objects to be purchased is time consuming and wasteful.

Returning to the problem of distributing technical material, let's examine the proposed use of "pull," in lieu of "push" mechanisms. At the same time, avoiding the social disutility present in much of today's advertising based upon the emotional and irrational behavior of man; and developing "pull" mechanisms that avoid the uncouth pandering to the irrational, character-istic of today's advertising.

Imagine consumers in the year 2000. Much of the shopping will be done from home via TV display. Think of this screen as a general purpose genie. Pressing a few buttons on a keyboard allows interaction with a powerful information processing network. The information network sends back a modified image to the TV display in response to selections. In the following example, it will help to imagine ourselves being electronically conveyed through a huge general purpose store carrying almost every imaginable product. All information relating to each item in the store will be kept in a huge memory. Anything we may wish to know about a product can be displayed on our TV screen.

Consider one way we might have access to this almost infinite data bank, rapidly and painlessly.

When you turn on the screen a list of questions is displayed. . . . We are rapidly carried down the branches of a tree until we come to the specific product or information about the product we desire. For example, suppose we want to buy a saber saw. . . . We push button 7 which says, "We wish to buy a new product." Immediately, the image on the screen changes and a set of boxes or selection categories . . . is displayed. We press button 5, "Hardware." This takes us to ["Hardware"] and we would depress the button "Power Tools." This takes us to ["Power Tools."] We press button 2 corresponding to "Saber Saws." Further lower levels permit consideration of individual brands and specific information relating to price, performance, delivery, etc.

This may seem like a complex process. But, where repetitive selections are to be made within a single category, one would record the indexing number, just as we do for telephone numbers today. If we wanted the latest price of each of three different saber saws, we might quickly punch in: 7542, 32, 52, 72. This would tell us that we wanted the price ( ) ( ) ( ) ( ) ( ) 2 of brands 3, 5, and 7. It's not necessary to back out of the tree all the way; we could stay and shop in one department for many separate items.

The consumer in the year 2000 could make a more rational selection from many more items than available today. It is unfortunate that today's marketing forces the development of "push" mechanisms. But, it is the innate nature of present mass media which causes this blanket approach. "Pushing mechanisms" must by their nature seek to exploit the irrational weaknesses of the population if any message is to be heard in the background of cacophony. Hopefully, one day the consumer will be able to select goods as some researchers are today able to extract a technical paper using experimental retrieval systems of the type previously discussed. If the variety of choice necessary appears difficult to achieve with a few branching decisions, consider the game "Twenty Questions." Here, with a little practice, it is possible to describe almost everything in the universe by "yes" or "no" answers to a sequential set of questions selected as a function of answers to previous questions.

When the consumer reaches the lower end of the selection tree and has narrowed his choice to a small number of contending products, it becomes plausible and appropriate to call up specific advertising for each. *Here is the socially beneficial use of advertising. Here, the recipient wants to read, to see, and to hear advertising.* Now he is attuned to respond to advertising which contains claims of superior features or performance. The consumer can be encouraged to use valid comparative testing information to help decide which product is "best." The sale of information from competing testing bureaus could be allowed and encouraged. Since the sale of information is on a product-by-product basis, entry to the field is cheap. Advertisers can be assured that their advertising will be seen almost simultaneously with all other advertising. Sheer boasting could give way to more rational comparison type advertising.

Consumers can be provided more factual information for more rational decisions in a world of almost infinite options. One of the most wonderful mechanisms in the free enterprise system is the process of survival of the fittest product where the consumer's vote by purchase drives out inferior merchandise. This concept was workable when the number of competing products was few and the markets small. But in a world of too many different, rapidly changing products, its effectiveness needs bolstering. Even more dangerously, it is capable of falling apart by overloading the information channel with too many alternative products. We wish to see a better product sold in preference to a shabby one wrapped in a fatuous sales campaign. The arena of competition should be shifted from repetitious, boastful claims by a large manufacturer to one where products are individually compared.

We have antitrust laws to cope with the problem of the restraint of trade by collusion. But we lack mechanisms to handle the equally destructive threat of irrationality when flooded with too many products.

The customer wants to know prices and delivery before reaching a final decision. The information storage system can tell him whether the pink shirts with tab collars are available, from whom, and when, and at what price. Price comparisons are instantaneous and again reinforce the free enterprise price mechanism.

The introduction of a fast-acting two-way information flow channel has further profound effects on the concept of retailing. Add a more effective transportation system and a distributed warehousing scheme and the role of the conventional retailer will diminish markedly. Direct dealing with the manufacturer will increase, as the goods will be dispensed from the most economic storage point. The function of the retail clerk will have been subsumed by the question and answer machine. It may be a minor loss. Today, too few retail store clerks are capable of providing an intelligent and honest answer to an information request needed to make a wise shopping decision. It is not entirely the clerk's fault; he has too many rapidly changing products to keep track of. Thus, bid this profession goodbye.

Consider another class of goods whose purchase is a total repetitive nuisance to the consumer—shopping for staple groceries. Once finding a brand of pickled string beans that suits your fancy, you wish to reorder the exact product without having to play Sherlock Holmes. You would like to be able to reorder many such items painlessly. Again, the computer can come to our aid by providing us with a stored list for rapid recall ordering. The better information available about alternative prices for the same goods will eliminate the undignified loss-leader game to trick the consumer into the store.

Richard L. Meier in 1962,[3] and Simon Ramo in greater detail in 1965 [4] suggest that a feedback system be connected to TV sets to allow "instant" market research for proposed new products. The suggestion is made that a product trial be described with a special discount one-time only offer if the person agrees to place an order by a certain date. No obligation is assumed by the manufacturer to go ahead with production unless, and until, enough orders were on hand to justify its manufacture. This instant, hard-market-survey could speed new product development by eliminating the large risk investment as the manufacturer faces a guaranteed sale.

As the information feedback loop is continuously shortened with these proposed techniques, manufacturers' inventory declines. The inventory buildup and depletion oscillation, a destabilizing factor to the economy, can be reduced. Even today, smaller inventories are possible using linear programming for decision of production-line runs and warehousing. Even today, some automobile salesrooms send their orders into headquarters by teletypewriter in computer coded form to order custom automobiles. This was infeasible in the earlier day of low information-system-effectiveness mass-production lines. Tomorrow's manufacturer will have to respond to the infinite "custom" demands of each individual consumer or else he may go the way of the dinosaur.

Only one aspect of the improved information flow possible in the year 2000, and how it might affect one narrow sector of life, has been described.

Its influence on the design and location of cities, educational institutions, and government are profound. Although limited, this discussion indicated what the year 2000 might hold for us. All that has been said is applicable to a lesser degree within the next two decades. To wait passively and to restrict thinking to terms of a static technology in a static world will be to invite economic disaster well before the year 2000.

Conversely, the opportunities for the innovator in marketing have never been greater than in the new world coming.

NOTES

1. Walter M. Carlson, "Information: A Status Report," *Engineer,* (September–October, 1967), Engineers Joint Council, 345 East 47th Street, New York, New York, p. 8.
2. Richard L. Meier, *A Communications Theory of Urban Growth* (Cambridge, Mass.: MIT Press, 1962), pp. 132–136.
3. Meier, *ibid.,* p. 129.
4. Simon Ramo, "The Computer and Our Changing Society," *AFIPS Conference Proceedings: Computers: Their Changing Impact on Society,* Volume 27, Part 2, 1965 Fall Joint Computer Conference, p. 10.

47 Dealing with the Future— What Do We Want to Know? And How Do We Start?

The Research Institute of America

To stay in business requires that the executive have a good sense of time. Success involves knowledge of the past, control of the present, and prediction of the future.

We have looked at the past and the present of marketing throughout this book. It is now time to get some perspective as to where marketing may be heading. Today's students should have some idea of the future—the "place where all of us hope to live."

Man's need to know the future is more urgent today than at any time in human history, for we are living in an era of extraordinary change. In the more traditional societies of the past, the general expectation was that the future would not, and could not, be much different from the past; and indeed, it generally was not. But today, thanks to the advanced state of technological development, the computer, and most particularly the information explosion, the rate of change has accelerated to a point beyond the projections of even a decade ago.

It is no longer rational to define stability in human affairs as "a condition of similarity between yesterday and tomorrow." On the contrary, change is the essence of the future, and even the most perceptive insights will likely turn out to be an understatement.

The current dynamism of change is perhaps best illustrated by the rate at which we are now making additions to the store of human knowledge. From the beginning of Man's tenure on Earth until the start of this century, human knowledge—our understanding of the forces around us and our ability to affect these forces—this knowledge doubled roughly *every 2,000 years*. The most conservative calculation we have today is that human knowledge is now doubling *every ten or fifteen years*.

Thus, any effort to peer into the palpable future amounts to an urgent and necessary quest for ways to deal with change and even to profit from change. And, in 1970, the human resources for making projections are con-

The U.S. Business Climate—A Three Decade Look Ahead (New York: The Research Institute of America, Inc., 1969), pp. 7–59. Reprinted with permission of The Research Institute of America.

siderable. The use of advanced mathematics in the construction of econometric models, enormously aided by computers with a prodigious capacity for storing, retrieving, and evaluating data, has turned the business of projecting the economic future into something akin to an exact science. . . .

The real surprises, however, have come from the as yet nonquantifiable aspects of human activity. People, social institutions, the global interplay of war and peace, to name just a few, continue to evade precise measurement; these forces can often knock askew the best laid and most rational projections.

.   .   .

In the absence of absolute certainty about the future, the businessman has to take the next best option: to look at the future, sort out what is known from what is unknown, what can become known from what is unknowable, and then make his decision.

That is what this Report seeks to do. It tries to place the best that economic forecasting can provide into a framework of political and sociological probabilities and uncertainties—an effort, in simpler terms, not to eliminate the risks of the future, but possibly to make them more definable, or at least more obvious.

.   .   .

A Case in Point   Take the example of an owner-manager of a wholesale leather and shoe findings enterprise. Curious about the future of his business, he wants to know how much volume he'll be handling five years from now, and fifteen years from now. This is certainly a legitimate question. Unfortunately, it is also a question that only the crystal ball can answer. A more scientific projection would have to be built on a variety of interrelated data relative to all aspects of the leather and shoe findings business.

Had this businessman been told that the U.S. faced a major depression in five years, he wouldn't have bothered asking his question at all; he'd know his business wouldn't have a future. Thus, it's not that the businessman's first question was the wrong one to ask. It was simply not put in the right sequence of several questions that should have preceded it.

Now suppose this businessman does ask the right question first: What is the long-run economic outlook? He gets encouraging news. He learns that by 1975 the American economy's real growth will push GNP into the neighborhood of $1.2 trillion (measured in 1970 dollars). What's more, he's told the size of the economy will almost double between 1970 and 1985, with a similar growth rate anticipated for the next fifteen-year period. So he sees clear sailing through at least the year 2000, after which he couldn't care less since he fully expects to be comfortably retired by then, no doubt a rich man because of the capital appreciation of his business.

But he still doesn't know much about the future of *his* business. For he can't be sure that the success of the economy means sure success for him. He has to ask more of the right questions. Right now his total volume is derived from sales to neighborhood shoe repair shops. What is happening to these neighborhoods? Are personal incomes going up or down among the people who live there? What proportion of the population will be between 15 and 49 years old, the age grouping with the greatest incidence of shoe repairs? Is the volume handled by the neighborhood cobblers rising or falling in relation to the total number of shoes being repaired? What about the ability of these shops to handle the new man-made "leathers"? What about the spread of the chain repair shops with their labor-saving equipment and capacity to handle great volume? Where do these chains buy their leather and shoe findings? Perhaps most important, will there still be cobbler shops around fifteen years from now? Will we be throwing away "used" shoes the way we dispose of facial tissues today?

These are the right questions. The answers will tell our businessman what his five-year and fifteen-year potiential is, if any. And if the indicated potential is attractive, the answer will tell our businessman what he has to do to realize his expectations.

.   .   .

GNP and   In the year 2000 the GNP of the United States will have soared
National Wealth to the astronomical total of $3.43 *trillion* annually—three thou-
                     sand four hundred and thirty billion dollars, a sum so large it
overwhelms the credibility threshold of most of us.

It took well over 100 years, from the founding of the nation to the year 1900, for the American economy to cross the one-hundred-billion-dollar mark (in 1970 prices).

It took only seventy years after that to cross the trillion-dollar line.

Yet it will take only thirty years more to triple that total and move well beyond the three-trillion-dollar mark!

(Note that all figures in the accompanying charts are in 1970 dollars, which means that the indicated growth is *real* growth and not *apparent* growth derived from inflated price levels.)

.   .   .

. . . the accompanying chart provides a breakdown of the components of GNP demand for the years 1955, 1970, 1985, and 2000. RIA submits this as a *conventional projection* that anticipates no big shifts in the percentage of GNP represented by consumer expenditures, private investment, and government expenditures—except for a slight decrease for government.

There's more to this chart than meets the eye: By 1985, and even more so by the year 2000, the dividing line between private and public expenditures will become too blurred to draw neat comparative distinctions, a good

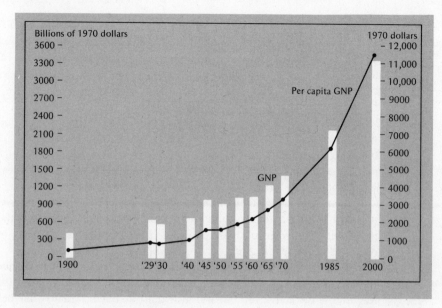

FIGURE 1.   Gross and per capita national product of the United States:
1900–2000.

SOURCE: Dept. of Commerce; Research Institute.

example of how statistics alone cannot provide a sufficient reading of the
nation's future, not even its economic future.

However, even though we can't tell now precisely what the shape of
demand on GNP will be, we do know that personal consumption will go on
claiming the lion's share, even with the transfer of such costs as medical
care.

**The Changing
Population
"Mix"**
The basic ingredient in all human activity and organization is
people, for the economy as well as all forms of commercial
enterprise exist to serve the needs of people. Therefore, anyone
who wants to know what the future of the American economy
is—and what the future marketplace will look like—must begin with a
study of population trends. How many more people will we have? And in
what age brackets will the changing population fall?

•   •   •

*The Recent Past
1955–1970*
In brief summary, the following are some of the highlights of
the changed population mix over the past fifteen years:

The fastest growing age group, by far: the 15–25-year-old bracket, the products of the post-World War II baby boom.

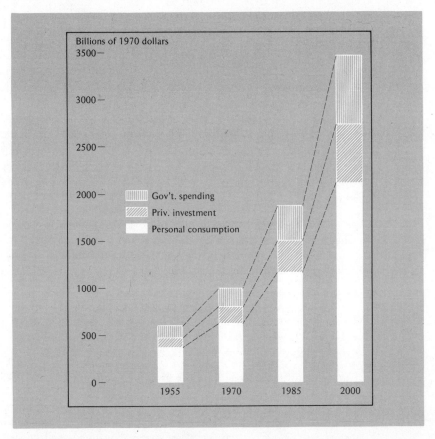

FIGURE 2.   GNP by source of demand.

SOURCE: Dept. of Commerce; Research Institute.

The slowest growing group: the important 35–44 age bracket, the "hollow generation." And the next youngest group, the 25–34-year-olds, has grown almost as slowly.

The next slowest growing group: those under five years of age. Despite the larger population base, there are proportionately fewer young children in the population today than there were fifteen years ago.

The most rapidly increasing adult group: those over 65 years of age.

Each of these changes in the U.S. population mix has brought with it new marketing opportunities, as well as new social and economic problems. Just about every institution—from school systems through the business world to hospitals and nursing homes—has undergone drastic stresses and emerged greatly changed. One need only consider the many facets of the "youth rebellion" among the rapidly growing 15–24 age bracket to realize the possible threat to the status quo. Each reader will best recognize those changes that have most affected his own business.

The Near Future: 1970–1985   The 1970 Census is expected to reveal a U.S. population of 206 million. In the mid-Eighties, conservative estimates put the total at 253 million. That means 47 million more Americans to be clothed, fed, housed, educated, provided for and serviced in a great variety of ways. This 23% growth in total population will, as it has in the past, account for the lion's share of total economic change during the next fifteen years, including steady growth in all consumer markets.

Major shifts in population mix and some of their implications in the 1970–1985 period include these: (Note that increase or decrease in various groups refers to the rate of growth only: in absolute numbers every age bracket, except the 45–54 group, will show an increase.)

A growth lag in the 5–24-year-old group. This is the first of many warning lights flashing on the youth cult market and means a damper on the teen-age boom that emerged in the late 1950's and continued strong through most of the Sixties.

An increase in the 55–64 age group, and an even bigger increase in the over-65 bracket. A larger population of older people will also deemphasize the youth cult. Older people have different needs and interests which influence the way they spend their money. Moreover, they will have more to spend and will thus have more effect on overall market conditions.

The impact of the shift in these two groups could be widespread. TV ads, for example, may be less youth-directed and aim harder at the influential oldsters market. Changes could come in whole businesses with a shift in the next few years away from teens-only records, electronic gear for youngsters, and so on. At the very least, population trends will challenge some of the assumptions underlying the near-dominant youth cult of today.

·   ·   ·

A decline in the number of persons between 45 and 54. Those not born in the mid-Thirties will be sorely missed as potential managers and in other leadership positions in the mid-Eighties. Demands of this group, too, will change. Since there will be fewer of them, they will be in greater demand, able to insist on improved pension plans and other social fringe benefits, particularly in the health care field.

Very rapid growth of the 25–34-year-old bracket. This is a fact of great significance for the home-oriented market: housing, furniture, appliances, garden equipment, do-it-yourself tools. The reason is simply that family formation is largest in this group.

A sharp increase in children under five years of age, despite an expected continued trend toward smaller families.

Clearly, executives who set their long-range goals for 1985 in terms of today's population mix are in for some rude shocks, just as were those businessmen who expected the population trends of the Fifties to continue indefinitely.

The Distant
Future:
1985–2000

Population mix changes in the last fifteen years of the century will be harder to predict since any forecast must take into account the roller-coaster birth patterns of the last quarter-century. This uncertainty is highest for the under-30 half of the 2000 population, much less so for the over-30 group which has already been born. Generally speaking, the years between 1985 and 2000 will see a large shuffle among the various age groups.

The growth rate of our oldest citizens will finally be slower than that of the rest of the population as the "hollow generation" of the Thirties moves into the 65-plus bracket. This will mark the end of the thirty-year boom in the oldster market, at least for this century.

Most rapid growth will be in the 45–54 age group as the postwar baby boom crop becomes middle-aged. This is likely to solidify the economic gains won by the previous tenants of this group, the "hollow generation" men, who could charge a higher price for their services because there were so few of them. The new mob of 45–54-year-olds will certainly attempt to hold these gains and expand them by the sheer weight of numbers. Indeed, this age group will be the fastest growing of any in this fifteen-year period.

Growth in the critical 25–34 age bracket will slow markedly as the second "hollow generation" of the Sixties enters the family-forming stage. This could force contraction of the home-oriented market right after a decade or so of strong expansion to meet the needs of the previous 25–34 age group.

The birthrate is expected to be stable and relatively low in the last fifteen years of the century. Here, however, the analyst encounters one of the paradoxes of statistics: despite a lower birthrate, *there will be nearly 50%*

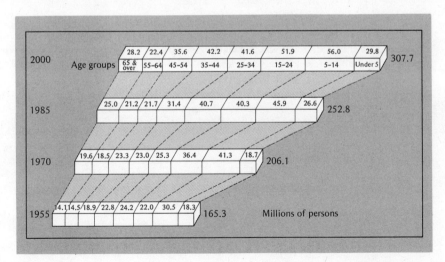

FIGURE 3.   Population of the United States by age group: 1955–2000.
SOURCE: Bureau of the Census; Research Institute.

PROSPECTS FOR BUSINESS There will be a growing market between now and the year 2000 for everything that people buy according to age classification. But there will be significant differences in the rates of growth of the various age brackets. Here's how it all lines up.

Age Brackets	Business Opportunities	1970–1985	1985–2000
65 and over	Health and medical care, dietary supplements, travel aids, special community housing and maintenance services, equipment for handicapped, books, at-home shopping.	Medium increase	Slow increase
55–64	Retirement preparation market, legal and financial advice, equipment for easier living, self-improvement aids, travel, entertainment in and out of home.	Medium increase	Very slow increase
45–54	Same as 35–44, but more expensive and luxurious, professional services.	Slight decline	Very rapid increase
35–44	Personal and investment services, travel, entertainment, pension plans, leisure equipment, objets d'art, vacation homes, boats.	Rapid increase	Rapid increase
25–34	Young homemakers' market, furniture and equipment, insurance, banking services, mutual funds, sporting equipment, transportation.	Very rapid increase	Very slow increase
15–24	The "youth" market, specialty clothing and accessories, personal transportation, electronic equipment, educational aids and supplies, sports equipment, escorted tours, books and magazines.	Medium increase	Rapid increase
5–14	Clothing, books, summer camps, monograms, entertainment, equipment, art and dancing schools, pets.	Medium increase	Medium increase
Under 5	Toys, clothing, food, furniture, pre-school learning aids, day camps and equipment.	Very rapid increase	Slow increase

more children in the year 2000 than now. Remember that only the growth rate, not absolute numbers, is slowing down. The opportunities for the baby and toddler market inherent in these figures are obvious.

Thus, business must watch population trends with extra care in the next decades to prepare for any substantial change that may occur in them. As we have seen, such changes have been taking place with unusual rapidity; and it will take an unusual amount of attention to cope with them.

. . .

Defining "a Family"

There will be roughly 31% more *households* in the United States in 1970 than there were in 1955, and about 23% more *families*. In the official figures, a "household" is simply one or more persons occupying a dwelling unit. This means that many so-called households are actually single persons, either living alone or sharing an apartment with other unattached individuals. A family, on the other hand, is specifically defined as two or more persons, related by blood, marriage, or adoption, who share a dwelling unit. There are always many more households than there are families, and the two sets of figures may—and do—follow very different growth patterns.

However, the number of families and the pattern of family incomes are much more important to business than are the comparable figures for nonfamily households. In this Report, therefore, all projections presented relate to families rather than to households. Families earn more, spend more, and buy differently than do individuals, and make up a much larger segment of the total market. For just one example, the huge home-furnishings industry depends almost entirely on family units for its retail sales volume.

Family Income   There are two aspects of family life that are of interest to this economic outlook: how many family units will there be (essentially a function of the population statistics already surveyed); and what standard of living will these families attain during the indicated time spans?

. . .

It can . . . safely be assumed that most of the economic calamities that continue to plague many low and middle income families today will be well on the way out by 1985 and completely eliminated by the year 2000. Such antediluvian disabilities as poverty and hunger will have passed into history. Individual families will no longer have to bear the crushing burden of hospital and medical costs. The same will be true of the costs of providing a college education.

The Recent Past: 1955–1970   The total number of American families has increased slowly, and there has been little change in age distribution among them since 1955. Age shifts that did occur have had little impact on business.

Per-family incomes have climbed along with the growth of the economy as a whole. The median family income has shown a real increase (in constant-dollar amount) of nearly 40%. In current, or inflated, dollars, the increase has been even larger.

Nearly one-third of all U.S. families have an income of $10,000 or better in 1970 compared with less than one-fifth in 1955 (in terms of 1970 dollars). Some of this increase was due to rising earnings in general, but some was due also to the increasing number of working wives.

This steady rise in family incomes has eliminated the old "pyramid" pattern of incomes, which was characterized by a great many relatively poor families, and has given rise to a "pear-shaped" income distribution, with the bulk of all families in the middle-income range.

While this shift has had very obvious positive effects on the markets for all consumer goods and services, it has also created problems. Those families that have fallen far behind the general uptrend may be fewer in number, but they are more isolated from the mainstream—and more frustrated.

This frustration surfaced massively in the Sixties as the discrepancy between general affluence and the deep pockets of poverty among blacks and whites became more glaring. Most of these contradictions have not been resolved; the war against poverty and hunger has not been won. But some progress has been made. Despite the 1968–1970 inflation, several million people did manage an effective crossing of the income poverty line in the last six or seven years.

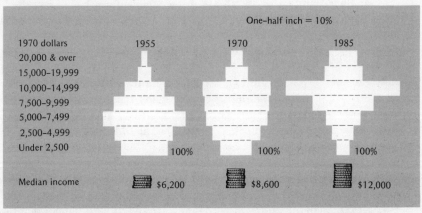

FIGURE 4.   Changes in U.S. family income distribution: 1955–1985.
SOURCE: Dept. of Commerce; Federal Reserve Board; Research Institute.

The Near Future: 1970–1985   The postwar baby boom will have the greatest influence in shaping family patterns in America during the next fifteen years. Not only will the total number of families in the U.S. grow more rapidly than in the recent past, but *young families headed by men between 25 and 34 will grow a spectacular 70%*. And the increase will continue through all the years immediately ahead.

As in the general population figures, this coming bulge in the young-adult age brackets will be accomplished by a much slower growth in the number of families headed by those born in the pre-World War II years. In fact, families headed by men in the 45–54 age group will number the same in 1985 as they do today. The number of families in the next higher age brackets will also grow at slower-than-average rates. *The total number of families headed by someone over 45 will be less than 10% greater in 1985, though there will be about 30% more families than in 1970.*

The market effects of these sharp changes in family age patterns will be as substantial as they are predictable. Older families, in what is known as the "empty nest" stage, spend their incomes in very different ways than do younger families. They buy much less in the furniture, appliance, and other home furnishing fields, and naturally spend less on such things as children's clothing, education, and other child-related goods and services. On the other hand, they tend to purchase better grades of goods and services, and they spend more on "luxury" items. Perhaps most important, older families spend much more on services of all kinds, including entertainment, travel, health care, and so on. And, the older they get, the less such families save of their income, either directly or in the form of insurance and other investments. With incomes generally rising, the propensity to spend of older families is a factor to keep in mind.

Spending patterns of the growing number of younger families will have very different effects in the years ahead. There will be an increasing demand for new housing, and for all of the things that go into new homes. Even assuming that tomorrow's families will have fewer children, there will be rich markets for all of the goods and services that are bought for children, since the total number of children is bound to rise. (Recent statistics, in fact, indicate that the low point in the annual number of births has already been passed.) Such intangibles as insurance are bought heavily by relatively new families, indicating sharp growth in the markets for this industry, among others.

The combination of a number of factors—including economic growth, more working wives, and more families in the high-earnings age ranges—will combine to increase family incomes.

By 1985, the median family income, in constant 1970 dollars, will be $12,000 a year. Nearly 60% of all families will be in the $10,000-and-over income class, while only about one family in nine will have an income below $5,000 yearly.

If the combined patterns of family age groups and family earnings develop as expected, there will be an increasing concentration of families in what will then be the middle-income brackets. About 37% of all families will be earning between $10,000 and $15,000 yearly. This means more disposable income for household equipment and gadgets—for example, automatic garage openers or electric martini stirrers—for coffee table books, prints, and other home beautification items. Spending habits will be heavily influenced, as will the marketing techniques that forward-looking businessmen will have developed.

The Distant
Future:
1985–2000

As the second "hollow generation" of the Sixties reaches the marriageable age, the number of family formations will have traveled full circle, returning to the pattern of the Fifties. The number of new family formations will once again slow down, while those established families with a family head in the 35-plus age bracket will increase in proportion to the total number. . . . It is a reasonable assumption that another 20% increase in median real family income will occur during the 1985–2000 period, with perhaps 70% of all families in the $12,000-and-over income class (in constant 1970 dollars).

Perhaps the most significant development of this period, however, will not be the large number of families falling into the middle-income bracket, but rather *the emerging desire of people to consume according to individual rather than group tastes.* With insecurity over income largely removed (due not only to the substantial growth in income, but also to the widespread pension, social insurance, and income maintenance plans), consumers will be freer to express their individual tastes. Businesses with markets centered on individual consumers will have to cater to this increased emphasis on product and service differentiation.

The trend toward individual taste in consumer goods has already started, most noticeably in the men's fashion industry. In the future, computer-automated assembly lines may well be able to turn out any number of variations of a single product to meet individual tastes—and do it in series large enough to assure high profitability. This is a function of the size of the American market and the versatility of U.S. technology.

The great challenge to businesses of the distant future will be to show special ingenuity in the production, packaging, marketing and servicing of basically standardized goods and services.

Nor does one have to think in terms of complex equipment as the only means of producing a personalized good or service. For example, a young couple looking for furniture that conveys a certain mood in a certain room would welcome the aid of a *visiting* decorator. This "expert" is really in the furniture business, and he offers "custom-made" pieces at reasonable cost (so long as the bulk of assembly can be made from pre-cut parts). In this case, the personalized service is at least as important as the customized product.

To those executives brought up on economies of scale, standardization, and assembly-line processes, this prospect will seem catastrophic. Such consumer attitudes may call to mind the story about a matron who announced that she had taken a 'round-the-world trip last year, and this year looked forward to going somewhere else. But even this idea is not as preposterous today as it was only a few years ago. By the year 2000 people will be going "somewhere else," as well as mass-consuming thousands of nonstandardized goods and services that we can hardly visualize today, much less implement.

.   .   .

Tomorrow's Consumer Spending

The Recent Past: 1955–1970

Businessmen will recollect that the mid-Fifties saw a boom in hard-goods spending. There were several reasons for this, including the aftereffects of the Korean war, relative prosperity, and a number of new technological developments. Much of the increase was in automobile sales, but all sorts of consumer durables—furniture, appliances, sporting goods, etc.—were also being bought in volume. It was the post-World War II boom all over again, or a continuation of it after a brief pause.

Nondurable goods, however, were in a very different position. Year after year, consumers were spending a smaller percentage of their rising disposable incomes on food, clothing, cleaning preparations, and a host of other soft goods.

Among the consumer services, outlays on housing—rent, mortgage interest payments, property taxes, etc.—climbed steadily; but spending for most other services remained fairly stable as a proportion of total expenditures.

At the close of the Sixties, this picture started to change in a number of important ways. The most striking change, and the most highly publicized, was the rapid growth of spending for services. Total consumer outlays on services is already on a par with spending on nondurables.

Some of this shift in relative importance is due to the lag in soft-goods outlays, and some is due to the sharp rise in the prices of many services. Much of the increase, however, must be ascribed simply to the growing consumer dependence on these services.

One of the fastest growing categories, for example, is that of "personal business and financial services." This is the money spent for the services of insurance agents, stock brokers and investment advisers, credit sources, lawyers, accountants, and others. As more American families reach relative affluence and require these services, the total amounts spent on them will continue to rise.

As already mentioned, the proportion of disposable income spent on nondurable goods has steadily fallen over the past fifteen years, and more. This, too, is largely a result of growing affluence. There is just so much that a family can eat or wear; as its income level rises, a family buys more and better food and clothing, but not so much more that the percentage of its disposable income spent on these items rises significantly. Note, however, that the amounts spent on feeding the family car, and on many nondurable items not in the category of "necessities," have risen faster than total spending over the period.

Hard-goods outlays, in total, have changed very little in relative importance over the years. In each business cycle, durables spending rises more than proportionately during prosperity and falls more during recession; but over the long run there hasn't been much of a trend.

Automobile spending, the most volatile segment, has gone both up and down during the years since 1955, but it has been relatively steady recently. There are several theories about what consumers do with the money not spent on automobiles in years of low auto outlays, and there is some truth in all of them. Part of the money, certainly, is not spent at all but goes into savings. Some of it, too, goes into the purchase of home entertainment items like television and hi-fi sets, and other "non-essential" durable goods. And some, finally, is spread over everything else the family buys. The point is that in the future a good or bad auto year will not be the bellwether factor in consumer outlays that it has often been assumed to be. In fact, economic diversification will be such that there will no longer be any "bellwether" industries.

HOW CONSUMERS SPEND THEIR MONEY
PERCENTAGE DISTRIBUTION OF CURRENT-DOLLAR TOTALS

	1955	1970	1985	2000
Durable Goods	15.6	15.0	14.8	14.5
Automobiles and Parts	7.2	6.4	6.0	4.5
Furniture and Equipment	5.4	4.7	4.5	4.0
Radio, TV, Sporting Goods, etc.	3.0	3.9	4.3	6.0
Nondurable Goods	48.5	42.4	38.2	30.0
Food, Beverages, Tobacco	28.4	23.0	19.5	16.0
Clothing, shoes, etc.	9.1	8.3	8.0	7.0
Gasoline and Oil	3.5	3.7	3.8	2.0
Household Supplies	3.8	3.4	3.1	2.0
All Other Nondurables	3.7	4.0	3.8	3.0
Consumer Services	35.9	42.6	47.0	55.5
Housing	13.3	14.7	15.6	16.0
Utilities and Communication	5.5	5.9	6.0	8.0
Medical and Health Services	3.9	5.8	6.9	5.0
Personal Business Services	3.9	5.8	7.3	7.0
Transportation	3.2	3.1	3.5	5.0
Education, Welfare and Religion	2.2	3.1	3.6	8.0
Recreation and Leisure	1.7	1.6	1.6	4.0
All Other Services	2.2	2.6	2.5	2.5
Total	100.0	100.0	100.0	100.0

The Near
Future:
1970–1985

At present, about one-third of all consumer spending on services is in the special category of housing services. This will continue to be true in the future, but the content of this spending will be different.

Many more families will be paying rent or mortgage charges on second homes—either vacation cottages or homes bought with future retirement in mind. A growing proportion of housing outlays, also, will go for installment payments on modular or prefabricated housing units—the descendants of today's "mobile homes"—rather than for conventional mortgage payments on completed homes.

Spending for many other types of consumer services will also be climbing rapidly. *More will be spent on medical and health services,* for example, partly because costs will continue to rise, and partly because new and improved services will be available—but largely because there will be more older persons able to afford better health care. A program of national health insurance is sure to be enacted by then, pushing up health care demands nationwide. Similarly, *education outlays will rise faster than total spending*, because many more young people will be enrolled in colleges, and because many more adults will be engaged in retraining activities to keep up with the pace of technical change and information flow.

With the coming of the jumbo jets, and eventually the supersonic transocean air transports, *outlays on nonbusiness travel should rise sharply*. The actual amount of air travel will undoubtedly be increasing even faster, but high-volume traffic will bring rates down.

Recreation outlays are not expected to increase as a percentage of total spending. This category of services includes theaters, movies, spectator sports and other forms of entertainment, as well as hotels, motels, and other accommodations. Though every executive probably believes that his family spends much more of the family income on these services than formerly, the actual figures show no relative increase—and none is likely in the foreseeable future, in view of the growth of home entertainment, boating, golf, vacation-home ownership, and other leisure developments in which the purchases of equipment, as distinct from services, figure prominently.

The gradual decrease in the proportion of income spent on nondurables is expected to continue, but at a somewhat slower rate. One factor here will be the changing population mix. With slightly smaller families, and a higher proportion of childless adults in the population, per capita spending on nondurables—even on staple items such as food, soap, and reading materials—will rise for many.

Durable goods outlays will claim a steady percentage of total income, but the relative importance of the major groups of durables will change. As income climbs, for instance, the share going for automobiles should shrink a bit. There is a limit to how much families can spend on major items like automobiles, even with more and more families graduating into the two-car class.

Outlays for home entertainment and recreation items should soar. This spending will cover not only electronic equipment for the home (including advanced models of a computer for home use that now sells for $8,000) but snowmobiles, small boats, go-carts, and still other "leisure" products not yet available.

Home furnishings in general will hold about even, with a trend toward less expensive and even "disposable" furniture offset by a growing number of new households. The desire to remain mobile, the ability to shift the locale of residence, will be a major factor here.

The Distant Future: 1985–2000   The farther into the future that projections of consumer spending are carried, the less meaningful become the traditional break-downs between goods and services, and between durables and nondurables. This will become evident to some extent by 1985, if not sooner.

For example, the automobile and appliance leasing industries are already growing rapidly. Manufacturers of such items as home freezers may some-day be leasing more of their output than selling them. When major items of consumer equipment are leased or rented, should the payments be figured as installment outlays for durable goods, or as charges for services?

In another direction, what we now call "pay TV" may eventually make nearly all theatrical and sporting events available to viewers in their homes. That trend could mean the end of the movie house as we have known it, leaving only the specialty cinemas located in a central area of town. This will result in a heavier investment in home equipment; but it isn't clear today whether such outlays will be counted as a business investment of the system operators, or a durables expenditure by the consumer. The one thing that is certain is that there will be much smaller outlays for entertainment "tickets."

Still another example: When more food items are prepackaged for serving, and disposable plastic utensils and "china" have replaced much of the real thing, will the government statisticians classify the spending for such items as outlays for "kitchenware" or for "nondurables"?

Finally, as more families rise substantially above subsistence income levels, *the proportion of total spending for traditional nondurable staples will continue to decline gradually*. Among traditional hard goods, too, those classified as necessities will show slower growth. The affluent consumer of the future will spend more and more of his rising income on what today are considered luxury items.

The Emerging Service Economy   Long before the close of this century, services will account for more of total outlays than hard goods and soft goods combined. Already the U.S. stands alone in the prominence of the service sector of the economy.

Since 1960, the nongoods-producing sectors have been accounting for just a shade less than 50% of the total gross national product. Already in 1960, blue-collar employment in manufacturing, mining, construction, and agriculture accounted for only 40% of total employment. This means 60% of all those employed were busy with nongoods-producing jobs, mostly engaged in trade, finance, transportation, white-collar endeavors in manufacturing, and thousands of other service positions that gain prominence in a highly productive, developed economy.

In the process, services proliferated until today there are many categories of specialized services scattered throughout the economy. There are, first of all, personal services that have always been rendered: barbering, hair dressing, shoe shine and repair, dental care, dry-cleaning, laundry, and legal services. Business services include advertising, management consulting, market research, and public relations. Finally, there is the brand new category of "services for other services." Among these are tax services for accountants, lab testing centers for doctors, and, still in its infancy, computerized information centers for doctors, lawyers, and other professionals, including a wide range of researchers and experts who themselves service our public and private institutions.

The big increase will come not so much in the type of service offered as in the clients to whom it is offered. Services for other services, therefore, will see the greatest expansion as the United States enters a fully developed service economy.

Precisely what new consumer services will emerge can be only dimly surmised: whatever makes life easier, more comfortable, more fashionable, more interesting, more changeable, more like one's neighbors, but always just a little different. Convenience, culture, entertainment, leisure, education, growth and health are the cornerstones of the $300 billion worth of consumer services that business will be providing in the next few years. And if these are to be properly understood, they must be taken not as separate entities, but as much as possible as overlapping services: education which is entertaining and easy; leisure which is easy, entertaining and convenient; food which is healthful, interesting, convenient and educational; health which is effortless, entertaining and fashionable.

·   ·   ·

The Near Future: 1970–1985   In the service economy, which will surely be emerging by 1985, only a minority of all workers will be required to produce goods in highly mechanized and automated factories, to erect buildings that will benefit from a high degree of prefabrication, and to engage in similar work. The majority will be engaged in a bewildering variety of service occupations, including selling, teaching, programming, maintenance (of factories, commercial buildings, and homes), government, and other "nonproduction" occupations not yet in existence.

The fact that productivity in manufacturing and construction is growing and will continue to grow much faster than in the service fields will tend to shift the balance of employment even faster to the service areas.

Along with this shift there will be a major increase in spending on capital investments of all sorts. New housing, and even the construction of entire new towns, will be a big part of this total, to meet the needs of the growing and changing population. And much of the new investment will be going into the creation of the capital equipment that will make the service economy itself a reality. This will include automated equipment for the production of goods with a minimum of workers, and "housing factories" for the prefabrication of construction modules, not only for homes but for hotels, schools, hospitals, and commercial buildings, as well.

A great deal of money will be spent, also, on the computer-based total information systems that will increasingly be at the heart of giant enterprises serving the financial, "knowledge," and other industries.

Government, as well as private industry, will be taking a part in the emergence of the service economy. The present trend toward government-financed provision of services will undoubtedly continue. Education, health,

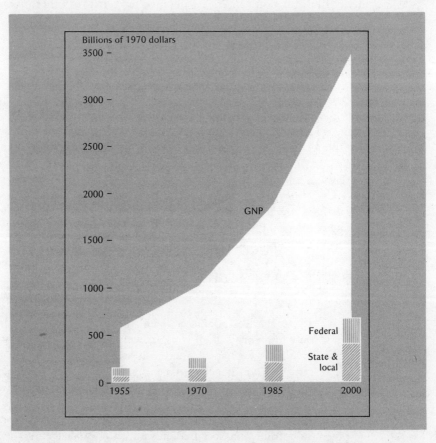

FIGURE 5. Gross national product and government spending.
SOURCE: Dept. of Commerce; Research Institute.

care of the elderly, communications and transportation, and other tradition-ally public services will be accounting for an increasing proportion of all governmental outlays.

There is little doubt that an increasing share of this larger government spending will be coming from local and state governments rather than from the federal government. The conviction is growing, among legislators and experts in government planning, that local, state, and regional authorities can do a much better job of administering the provision of services than can a central authority in Washington. Much of the basic financing, how-ever, will still be federal, with funds reaching the spending bodies through such mechanisms as tax-sharing, block grants, and other devices.

Finally, there is a strong likelihood that much of the provision of services in the years ahead will be by joint government-business organizations, mod-eled roughly along the same lines as COMSAT, the Communications Sat-ellite Corporation. They would tackle a large list of environmental problems such as air and water pollution, housing, construction of new cities, and so on. These public corporations are expected to be one of the major organiza-tional developments that will mark the emergence of the service economy. There will be a blurring of the present lines between government and business spending in the national output statistics. However, due to the sheer size of the total economy, government spending of all sorts is expected to account for a smaller part of the 1985 gross national output than is the case today.

· · ·

The Distant
Future:
1985–2000

Most long-range economic projections usually turn out, in retro-spect, to be woefully conservative. The Research Institute Staff has assumed, in looking toward the economy of the year 2000, that an average annual growth rate of over 4% is a reasonable goal for the total output of goods and services in the United States. In our projection, therefore, the total gross national output is expected to grow as fast, in relative terms, from 1985 to 2000, as it probably will from 1970 to 1985. Though the numbers involved tend to become so great as to be almost meaningless in comparison with today's, the fact remains that the total economy of the year 2000 can be expected to be more than three times as great as today's nearly trillion-dollar economy.

There is not much point in attempting to state, even tentatively, how particular industries will fare in the year 2000, just as there would have been little point, in 1940, to speculation about how much money would be spent in 1970 on computers, jet aircraft, or freeze-dried foods. In fact, even the general category of "personal consumption" may have a consider-ably different meaning in the future economy. For one thing, consumers may be receiving from government or government-backed public corpora-tions, as tax-supported services, many things they now buy on their own, such as medical care. For another, the expected increase of leasing of many major consumer products will predictably alter the patterns of consumer goods purchasing.

. . .

Looking Beyond   . . . Despite problems and change, however, it appears abun-
the Statistics   dantly clear that the American economy will yield more goods
                       and services than ever. Americans, therefore, will enjoy greater
wealth than ever, in both per-capita and per-family terms.

But what does this promise of greater wealth mean? Are we, as individuals and as a nation, going to feel happier, healthier, and more satisfied in 1985 or in the year 2000 than we are today? The criteria of success and progress vary, of course. Many attach great importance to higher wages, lower taxes, bigger net profits, good health, a balanced investment portfolio, a paid-up mortgage, time and money to travel, children settled away from home (but not too far away), a healthy savings account. Others may use still other criteria.

The overriding question for the future is simply whether we will have more of the things that give meaning to our lives. Will you, for example, be able to manage success out of the potential of the economic future RIA has projected?

. . . Anyone who has lived through the last thirty years, or even a decade of it, knows that a bigger and better economy does not guarantee personal or business growth.

The only thing economic progress guarantees is change. And change can mean instability in the fortunes of those who learn too late to adapt to new opportunities.

For example, within a generation coal became secondary as an energy source; the movies and radio became the pawns of a new siren called television; steel, once king among industrial giants, slipped farther down in the rankings; the railroads that once moved a nation now move pity better than anything else. For many, these changes were not happy ones.

The next thirty years will be far more dynamic and revolutionary than any previous three-decade period in our history. The economy is sure to be bigger and more productive. But will our life goals and business targets, as envisioned today, share this expansion? Indeed, will they have any meaning in tomorrow's world? In what kind of world will be be living by the year 2000? What will it look like? What kind of lives will we lead amid the new physical and psychological surroundings? Even a brief glimpse into the startling world of tomorrow may provide some clues and help us decide between the important and the irrelevant:

Most people will be able to work at home, and the work force of many business organizations will be drawn from a worldwide talent pool.
The manufacturing process will be almost totally independent of human

labor; electronic sensors and feedback systems will provide the data and mechanical controls of all enterprises; and by far the greater part of human effort will be turned to providing services for business, government, and individuals.

Currency and checks will have been displaced by automatic computer-controlled credit and debit systems, with bank balances transmitted to homes and offices instantly, upon request.

Consumer and business purchases will be conducted from home or office; choice will be exercised on the basis of three-dimensional color displays transmitted to the buyer's location; and custom requirements will be negotiated between buyer and manufacturer via computer-controlled, multimedia communication.

Medical diagnoses and treatment will be taking place in computer-monitored "treatment capsules," in many cases right in the home.

Ground transportation will be provided via underground air tubes, aboveground high-speed monorails, and hook-on conveyor systems for private vehicles.

Long-distance air transportation will be handled by rocket propulsion, and shorter trips by magnet-controlled flying-saucer-type vehicles.

Communication by sight, sound, or written message with anyone anywhere will be instantaneous—and reproducible for the record.

Information and entertainment centers in home, school, office, and factory will make available a wide range of the performing arts, as well as facsimile newspapers from all parts of the world, the contents of libraries, medical diagnostic services, business information, market analyses, and much more.

Students will get their education from computer-stored knowledge fed to individual points of contact, without benefit of centrally located schools and with greatly accelerated comprehension levels.

Unwanted genes will be eliminated from the reproductive process, and heredity, like the physical environment, will be under Man's control.

Climatic conditions will no longer be an "act of nature," but within the means of man to modify, over large areas, according to his needs.

Earth satellites will have become stepping-stones to the Moon and jumping-off points to farther reaches of the universe.

If any of this sounds too much like Buck Rogers, remember that a good deal of his paraphernalia is already old hat and that, after Apollo 11, Man should cease to be amazed at anything.

It is possible, then, to conceive of a world vastly changed physically by the year 2000. Is it likely that nothing else will really change between now and then except the look of how we live, work, learn, and play?

Will the things that seem important today still be important thirty years from now? Will there be scarcities of anything? And if so, of what?

What about the real function of business in a society so rich it takes for granted the availability of goods and services?

What kind of labor-management relations will prevail when the work week is only 25 hours, and work stoppages of any kind cannot be tolerated because each part of the commercial world is hooked electronically to the whole system?

How much control will the manager have over his own "shop"?

These are questions that force us to go beyond the statistical projections of the future economy, the *quantitative* dimensions. Inevitably, we must consider the *qualitative* needs of a society that lists economic demands as only one of many made on the future.

. . .

What methods will most accurately gauge the needs and demands of a changing market for goods and services? This is a more familiar problem: but it will be an increasingly difficult one because the demands of the future will be based less on national economic needs (the 1930's and 1940's) and "being like everyone else" (the 1950's), more on self-esteem and status-in-society factors (the 1960's), and increasingly more, during the 1970's and beyond, on individual whims and tastes, desires for self-fulfillment, and responses to intuition and the physical senses.

The expected upward shift in incomes and levels of educational achievement will undoubtedly suggest a more sophisticated market, one that will be less affected by claims (testimonials in advertising) and more receptive to better quality, service, and information (truth-in-lending, for example).

Product differentiation will help boost sales, provided manufacturers avoid *over*differentiation in the wrong direction. For example, consumers can buy any kind of large automobile today, but the large car market proved to have built-in limits when it came to purchase of second cars. Most families preferred smaller vehicles and thus opened the way for the invasion of Volkswagens and other small imports that filled that need more conveniently. Nor is there a direct link between big cars and high incomes. Indeed, wealthier, better educated consumers often buy small, inexpensive cars simply because personal transportation does not rank that high on their list of values. They want a practical, efficient vehicle, not a showpiece even though they could easily afford the Lincolns, Cadillacs, and Imperials.

This is an important fact to keep in mind as yesterday's luxuries become tomorrow's basic needs. For no one can project yet how many people will follow the traditional step-by-step approach up the economic ladder and how many will leapfrog in their demands and desires, bypassing the intermediate steps on the way. The expectations of the poor in ghetto areas and elsewhere illustrate the problem: many of these people who don't have enough to eat want new cars and color television *now*, without moving up through second-hand sets and second-hand cars first. Equally, people who can afford high-quality luxury items may not want them, but instead spend their money on other needs or on those not yet discovered.

It is by no means certain, for example, that as incomes rise, more and more families will seek to own their own homes in the suburbs. How many people of family-forming age will there be, relative to the middle-aged and the retired? What will be their prevailing attitudes toward raising children?

What, indeed, will be their aspirations for their children? What will be the alternative to living in the suburbs? What will be the desired life-style for the young parents themselves?

Tomorrow's executive, therefore, will have to be master of a great many more different fields than he need be today. Management expert, marketer, psychologist, sociologist, political scientist, economist, packager, efficiency expert, salesman to his work force as well as to the consuming public, strategist *cum* computer-based information, realist, maestro in the use of intuition—these are only some of the things he will have to control and know. Obviously, no man can be all these things. The executive will simply have to learn to evaluate the contributions of hired experts.

With so many possible shifts in demand, diversification may be in order as a hedge against dynamic change. Perhaps attaining and holding a desired percentage of a particular market is not the way to achieve and maintain a steady growth rate.

On the other hand, if the market in question promises to be an expanding one, concentration on one product that saves research and development costs for others could be the correct strategy.

Or perhaps the best move of all for a smaller business will be specialization in rendering individualized, personalized, value-added features to the products of a giant firm, such as fine art designs on toasters, or customized installations in the home to match the decor of mass-produced furniture, or gold-leafing the outer page edge of a large special edition of a book, or supplying fittings of distinctive design to the manufacturer of bathroom sinks and tubs.

The correct decision will depend on how accurately the business executive has gauged the demand curve of the future. And that will involve skill in projecting the changes taking place within society—a skill that will be at least as important as, and probably more important than, the traditional skill of reading correctly the economic statistics of the marketplace.

In Summary   The institutional dimension of business will expand from one of supplying the goods and services for which an effective demand exists, or can be made to exist, to one of accepting responsibility for activities that attempt to fulfill the market's demand for qualitative improvements in life-styles.

This will entail substantial change in the prevailing concepts of what makes a business profitable, and of what factors enter into the definition of profit. New costs of doing business will arise, and these will be offset by decreases in taxes on business income. But this development will substantially alter the purpose and mode of operation of business enterprise in the United States.

The business executive of the future will have to be a man of diversified talents and interests, sensitive to the social, political, and cultural temper of his times, as well as to the economic realities at his disposal—and capable of translating the indicated nuances of an increasingly complex market to a profit opportunity for his company.

The executive of tomorrow will be as different from his counterpart of yesterday as the captain of a supersonic jet liner is from the pilot of a propeller-driven plane.

QUESTIONS FOR DISCUSSION

1. Paul Baran discusses one relatively small section of improved information flow in the year 2000. Discuss what other areas of marketing might be improved by new information technology.
2. Is it feasible to believe that manufacturers, as suggested in Baran's article, would let their products be placed in such close proximity to their competitors' for the purpose of "instant" comparison by the consumer?
3. The author predicts the eventual disappearance of the retail store in business because of the improved flow of information about products. Do you agree or disagree? What implications might this have for marketing?
4. The system proposed by Baran implies a large, centralized information storage center. Discuss the economic, social, and ethical implications of such a center and its effect on the marketing concept.
5. Advertising is an integral part of the marketing process. Discuss some of the effects on advertising that new information technology would bring about.
6. Assume you are a businessman trying to assess your future markets 10 to 20 years ahead. What types of information would you be most interested in? Why?
7. Explain the relationships between "population mix" and "marketing strategy."
8. Discuss the "emerging service economy" and its implication for the future.
9. Discuss the impact of steadily rising family incomes on the marketing strategy of tomorrow's businesses.
10. Looking ahead 20 to 30 years, what changes do you see in American consumption patterns?

SUGGESTED READINGS

Cook, Donald C., H. Bruce Palmer, and Lynn Townsend, *The Future of American Enterprise* (Michigan Business Papers No. 46; Ann Arbor, Michigan: Bureau of Business Research, Graduate School of Business Administration, University of Michigan, 1967), pp. 15–26.

Crawford, C. Merle, *The Future Environment for Marketing*, Michigan Business Studies (Ann Arbor, Michigan: Bureau of Business Research, Graduate School of Business Administration, University of Michigan, 1969), Vol. 18, No. 2.

Drucker, Peter F., *The Age of Discontinuity: Guidelines to Our Changing Society* (New York: Harper & Row, 1969).

Gabler, Nancy B., "The Art of Making a Politician Sexy", *Marketing Communications* (November, 1970), Vol. 298, pp. 26–30.

Galbraith, John Kenneth, *The New Industrial State* (Boston: Houghton Mifflin Co., 1967).

Johnson, Arno, Gilbert E. Jones, and Darrell B. Lucas, *The American Market of the Future* (New York: School of Commerce, New York University, 1966), p. 122.

Kahn, Herman, and Anthony Weiner, *The Year 2000* (New York: The Macmillan Co., 1967).

Pensyl, William E., "Will Population Changes Make You or Break You"? *Pittsburgh Business Review* (April, 1967), Vol. 38.

Servan-Schreiber, J. J., *The American Challenge* (New York: Atheneum Publishers, Inc., 1968).

South, John D., "The Changing Face of Marketing", *Duns Review and Modern Industry* (April, 1966), Vol. 87, pp. 46–47.

U.S., Department of Commerce, *Current Population Reports* (Washington, D.C.: U. S. Government Printing Office).